MANAGING RESOURCEFUL PEOPLE
Human Resource Policy and Practice

MANAGING RESOURCEFUL PEOPLE
Human Resource Policy and Practice

FRANK M. HORWITZ
Graduate School of Business
University of Cape Town

1991
JUTA & CO, LTD

First published in 1991

PO Box 14373, Kenwyn 7790

ISBN 0 7021 2705 1

Printed and bound by
The Rustica Press, Old Mill Road, Ndabeni, Cape.

D873

'Where there is no vision, the people perish'

Proverbs 28: 18

ACKNOWLEDGEMENTS

The process of researching, writing and editing is invariably an interactive one. Several people and organisations gave much of their time. I am deeply grateful for this.

I would like to thank the many companies who participated in the research projects referred to in the book. In particular, my colleagues in AECI, SASOL and Sentrachem deserve special thanks.

Professor Charles Cogill of the Department of Industrial and Organisational Psychology at the University of Cape Town provided valuable, critical comments in reviewing the manuscript. He gave of his time, for which I am indebted.

I would also like to thank Debbie Stubbs for her typing of the manuscript, and Gavin Stanford and Adele Levitan of the publisher, Juta and Company, for their help and patience.

My wife Dianne, and children Justine, Michele and Gavin, have given me space and constant support. To them I remain deeply grateful.

The opinions expressed and the conclusions reached are my own and do not necessarily reflect the policies and views of the organisations and individuals mentioned above. Many people have been an inspiration to me over the years. None more so than my parents and family, colleagues at the University of Cape Town, and the many people who have been part of my teaching, research and organisational experiences over the years.

FRANK HORWITZ 1991

PREFACE

Managing people in an environment of uncertainty and complexity creates unique and challenging demands for innovative managerial thinking and workable policies. Needless to say, these demands also create much stress and anxiety. Well-worn phrases such as 'the management of change', 'managing the future', 'management in the 21st century', reflect an almost desperate cry for management wherewithal to reduce uncertainty and increase control. The constant managerial search for stability and equilibrium is contrasted with the idea of perhaps beginning to raise managerial effectiveness and capability to a level where dealing with a highly turbulent and volatile environment becomes a given, an almost taken-for-granted state.

The anxiety of managing in this environment is exacerbated by what can be called the 'quick-fix adhocracy' syndrome — knee-jerk responses to crises. South African society has become highly politicised, yet many are politically illiterate. Analytical frameworks containing sound, workable principles are vital for understanding the big picture issues rather than the 'cocktail party' levels of understanding so often apparent. It is presumptuous to offer definitive solutions or prescriptive advice on such complex issues. The idea of this book is based on a belief that the starting point for enhancing an organisation's effectiveness in coping with change, or indeed influencing it, is the formation of policies and strategies which clearly articulate core values and principles — a corporate framework of beliefs for which strategies are developed to internalise them into the behaviour of the organisation. Considered industrial relations and human resource policies can help organisations to understand and cope with change and the inherent conflicts in the South African business environment. This can go a long way to reducing uncertainty and enhancing organisational effectiveness.

Policies reflecting universally accepted values such as fair employment and labour practices, equity in payment systems, and basic employee rights begin to address the problem of 'adhocracy'. A principled approach to management is vital in this exciting age. The focus of this book is on principles for sound industrial relations and human resource policies, and basic imperatives for operationalising these espoused principles. This is not a 'how-to-do-it' book on the practice of industrial relations and human resource work. It is a book which I hope raises important questions and offers some 'practical principles', which must precede good managerial practice. It has been said that there is nothing as practical as a good theory. It is hoped that the theoretical propositions raised in this book will firstly, illustrate the link between sound industrial relations and human resource policy and the strategic goals of an organisation, and secondly, will help to address the practical challenge of bridging the gap between espoused corporate principles and managerial practice. Policy formation is not difficult. The process and prerequisites for effectively internalising policies pervasively throughout an organisation represent one of the more complex and important tasks of management.

CONTENTS

1

MANAGING PEOPLE: POLICY, IDEOLOGY AND PRACTICE

> 'To gloss over contradictory interests, incompatible ideologies and opposing cultures as sources of conflict is more than antipolitical. It is dangerous. Those who have long held a mirror to the world and seen only themselves are apt to be shocked and panicked when the mirror is removed, as inevitably it must be. On the other hand, to accept the reality of otherness is not to be condemned to a war of all against all. We are not then compelled to see in each other the focus of evil in the work. We are still enjoined to love our neighbour as ourselves; only it no longer becomes an exercise in narcissism.'[1]

INTRODUCTION

The prominence of contemporary industrial relations (IR) in South Africa and its dynamic and complex nature highlight the need for understanding underlying social processes, and their relationship with managerial policy. Practice can be more thoroughly understood by a knowledge of theory and critical analysis. This helps to avoid a simplistic 'cocktail party' conception of labour and management issues. Conflict and power in organisations and the creation of rights are fundamental in understanding employment relations. Theoretical perspectives on managing people vary, given the multi-disciplinary nature of the subject and its complex interrelationships. There is no general or consistently broad theory of people management. Rather, conceptual frameworks exist which facilitate understanding. Conceptual frameworks provide plausible and meaningful interpretations of events and trends and fa-

1 Krauthammer, C. (1983)

cilitate the formulation of questions which have a predictive focus[2].

HUMAN RESOURCE POLICY

A distinction is often made between human resource (HR) and industrial relations policies. HR policy focuses mainly on the individual within the organisation. An industrial relations policy is intended to regulate the relationship between management and employees, between management and organised labour, and between management and external agencies that play a part in labour relations. This distinction is useful, as it can reflect differing assumptions about employees and management–employee relations. Yet the reality of these relationships often reflects the interdependence of individual HR policies and procedures and collective issues, for example matters such as job grading, wage setting, and termination of employment policies. In most parts of this book the two terms will be used together. Where basic assumptions, differing values, ideological questions, and policy choices are raised, the intrinsic differences in meaning of these terms is explored.

THE PROBLEM OF DEFINITION

Flanders's (1970) notion that relations in enterprises are primarily concerned with the institutions of job regulation has been criticised as placing little emphasis on social relations and informal interaction between individuals and parties/actors.[3]

Dunlop (1958) adopts a systems approach, which includes the interaction of actors within a framework of constraints, namely market, economic, technological, and prevailing power realities. These emphasise the employment relationship as mainly a process of forming rules and the content of

2 Douwes Dekker, L. (1986)
3 Flanders, A. (1970)

these rules.[4] Hyman (1981) lays strong emphasis on the inherent nature of conflict, power, change, and competing interests which pursue the distribution of scarce resources, namely wealth. Hyman's radical perspective views the work-place as a struggle for control and therefore as a dynamic, changeable environment.[5]

The theme of job regulation has been expanded to include the process which incorporates varying degrees of conflict, consensus, and structured and unstructured relationships.[6] The extension of Flanders's concentration on institutions, systems, and rule-making allows more variables to be examined when attempting to explain the reasons for particular norms having been established.[7] These variables include factors in the wider environment as a social system, such as political, economic, legal and socio-cultural trends which influence the organisation as a sub-system. An open systems framework of analysis considers the interactions between these environmental factors, various interest groups or actors, and the structures and procedures for regulating or institutionalising conflict.[8]

Oram's (op cit. pp. 22–24) critique of the normative orientation of the job regulation, institutional and systems approaches is their two-dimensionality, focusing mainly on employers and employees, with insufficient attention to the role of state regulation. This suggests an ideological basis where state direction or even control of relations in organisations occurs. The latter perspective implies that political philosophies may vary in the extent of corporatist forms of state regulation. The notion of corporatism is based on the principle

4 Dunlop, J. (1958)
5 Hyman, R. (1981)
6 Clegg, H..A. (1978)
7 Oram, S. (1984)
8 Craig, A. (1981)

of an integration of political, social and economic aspects of life. It is characterised by the incorporation of employer leadership and labour organisations within state institutions to represent interests.[9] Ideologically, the focus of corporatism is on centralised, collective rather than individual interests, dealing with macro-economic and social policy.[10] The degree of state influence on the organisation or the degree of voluntarism reflects values systems and ideologies. The latter may have correlations with managerial assumptions about employers; for example, the appeal by the state to employers and unions to behave in the interests of the nation, legislative or executive erosion of trade union rights and imposed incomes policies such as a wage freeze. These may reflect unitarist and neo-conservative forms of state control.

The essential mechanism in Western market economies to improve wages and working conditions is through collective bargaining, with the right to industrial action ie the strike or lockout. The state (and its agencies), labour (through unions and union federations), and capital (through employers' associations or directly), seek to exercise influence and control over respective policies and actions which may influence their constituent's interests. Where state control is dominant, limiting the autonomy of trade unions and their ability to strike and protect their interests, state corporatism is said to exist.[11] This has occurred in the post-independence period of certain African countries, and Eastern Europe, where trade unions became an administrative arm of the state, thus losing their independence.

9 Salamon, M. (1987)
10 Poole, M. (1986)
11 Douwes Dekker, L. (1987a)

UNDERSTANDING INDUSTRIAL RELATIONS POLICY

The subject of industrial relations has become an accepted area of academic study.[12] Yet, as implied above, definitions are often limited in scope. Dunlop's analytical focus on a network of rules governing the work-place and work community is limited in its explicative value. Although the focus on IR as a range of rule-making processes providing for the governance of social relations in the work-place over time was expanded on by Flanders (1981), who concluded that 'the study of IR may be described as a study of the institutions of job regulation', both these important contributions have been strongly criticised. Hyman (1983, op. cit. pp. 12–17), rejects these approaches as focusing exclusively on organisations and institutions, and devaluing the part played by human actors and the processes of social relations. The institutional approaches of Dunlop and Flanders can be criticised for their normative orientation which has a limited explicative value for central questions in IR such as the nature cf conflict, its inherency in social and economic relations, the notion of power, and countervailing pressures of influence.

Hyman (1983 op. cit p.. 26) argues that the following themes are important to understanding relationships at work:

- the ongoing process of power relations as a central feature,
- conflict and change as inherent at all levels in organisational relations,
- conflicts of interest in organisations are linked with structural conflicts within an economic system, and
- employment relations occur within and are part of a political economy.

It cannot be limited therefore by an understanding of the institutions of job regulation alone.

12 Hyman, R. (1983)

Webster (1984) concurs with Hyman in focusing on the relative and varying degree of control over work relations between the main actors. Periodic crises in the control of work relations may develop following an organised worker challenge from below and associated human resource reforms from above. Emerging shop steward structures in South Africa tend to be rooted in the theory of worker control, according to Webster (p. 225).[13]

There are fundamental underlying differences in both the social and industrial agendas of those who represent the interests of management and labour. The absence of inherent conflicts of interest and disputes of rights would be associated with one or other of these institutions ceasing to exist as a party to a pluralist system of IR, and could give rise to a form of state corporatism.

THE EMPLOYMENT RELATIONSHIP

Poole (1986) defines IR as a discipline concerned with the systematic study of all aspects of the employment relationship. The three main actors have both common and divergent interests. Poole acknowledges that conflict between interacting groups is inevitable, but that there are generally mechanisms to institutionalise conflict in various ways in different societies. This occurs mainly through collective bargaining and IR procedures. The notion of IR as dealing with the employment relationship establishes a focus on HR policies associated with patterns and styles of interaction beyond the basic inequality of the contractual relationship between an individual and an employer. The employment relationship covers both individual HR and collective relations. The development of regulatory mechanisms in South Africa for the creation and institutionalisation of rights, for example through the legislature in the form of the Industrial Court, has begun

13 Webster, E. (1985)

APPROACHES TO CONFLICT		CREATION OF RIGHTS
UNITARISM		Legislature (statute, use of courts)
PLURALISM	Voluntary, independent, private, self-regulation by employers and unions	Private agreements (recognition agreements)
RADICALISM		Bilateralism at sector or industry levels, and union federations
		Trilateral framework of social consensus (societal corporatism) between three major actors: the state, employer federations, and union federations

Figure 1.1
Industrial relations frameworks

to formalise the primacy of the employment relationship over the contractual relationship. The emergent unfair labour practice jurisprudence in South Africa in the 1980s, is an important feature of this process. Social regulation of the employment relationship also has rights-creation processes in the extra-statutory processes of negotiating private agreements such as trade union recognition and collective bargaining agreements (Figure 1.1). The processes of negotiating rights and procedures for institutionalising conflict has important elements of power, collectively mobilised through the principles of freedom of labour association, rights to organise, bargain and industrial action. A relative or 'near' balance of power is more feasible if we see relationships in an organisation in terms of a fair employment relationship rather than a contractual relationship. Power is, however, not a fixed sum. It is variable, expandable, and retractable over time. Factors associated with the variable nature of power between the parties may also determine the extent to which conflict is institutionalised and the quality of the employment relationship. These variables include the prevailing ideologies of the main IR actors and associated HR, economic and political state policies, their variability over time, together with socio-economic and technological change.

EMPLOYEE RIGHTS AND HUMAN RESOURCE POLICY

When the value of freedom of association is adopted by a society it needs to be translated into structures, procedures and processes for its realisation in practice.[14] Procedures are an index of the 'near' power balance between the parties. The parties accept the constraints of procedural steps to provide a degree of certainty and power focus through channelling its expression. Douwes Dekker argues that the right to strike is a part of collective bargaining procedure and affects the power relations of the employment situation. This mode of intervention by collective labour action seeks to move management, through concerted action, towards some acceptable reconciliation by concession and compromise. Fundamental to the legitimation of procedures is the degree of trust between the parties. Procedures per se may *not* be sufficient to institutionalise conflict. Similarly, unrealistic perceptions of potential gains through use of power, can result in a breakdown of procedural adherence, especially in circumstances of heightened mistrust and polarisation of attitudes.

In most market or mixed-market societies in addition to the right to strike, a second important principle associated with the collective bargaining process is the peace obligation. This limits uncertainty regarding labour costs during the duration

14 Douwes Dekker, L. (1985)

of an agreement. It implies that strike action becomes a last-resort weapon to be considered only if negotiation and dispute-settling processes break down. In South Africa the peace obligation has been institutionalised at the industrial council level and increasingly in plant-level substantive agreements on wages and conditions of employment. Its significance does however, require further exploration by the parties as it may often be taken for granted.

The institutional structures and procedural mechanisms through which the power and trust dynamics of industrial relations occur differ for each society. Industrial relations deals with the values arising in the minds, intuitions, and emotions of individuals and the groups to which they belong.[15] These variables arise from the historical traditions and processes of a society. The value considerations lead to ethical issues regarding the nature of rights and use of power.

At all levels, South Africa is undergoing a fundamental reassessment of individual and collective rights, with changes under way giving rise, in the industrial relations arena, to a restructuring of the social reality in the work-place. Powers derived from rights concomitant with freedom of association are being institutionalised. Procedures of the recognition agreement require for example, that (1) the principles of fairness, industrial justice and due process direct the behaviour of managers and trade union representatives, and (2) define the rights and responsibilities of the union and the company in collective bargaining and industrial relations. Trials of strength in the industrial relationship tend to focus on power-conflict problems and have not begun to address the challenging area of wealth generation that benefits both parties.

15 Douwes Dekker, L. (1987a)

Variables which influence the nature of a country's industrial relations practice include:[16]

- The extent to which the three rights of freedom of association, collective bargaining and use of industrial action are endorsed and respected by the parties in their interaction. The condition necessary to facilitate the emergence of these rights is the policy level endorsement of civil liberties required to promote engagement in the democratic process of these rights. If the state does not protect or indeed erodes these rights, employers and trade unions might seek to provide compensating institutions and agreements where considered necessary.
- The propensity for federations of unions and employers' associations to enter into basic labour–management agreements to set the parameters for their interaction at various levels of the industrial relations system.
- The extent to which tripartism in the form of societal corporatism is utilised by the labour market parties.
- The perceived importance of political ideologies, such as socialism, and party political alternatives as offering primacy in respect of the achievement of working-class objectives.
- The extent to which the peace obligation has been incorporated into the procedural cycle of the relationship.
- The extent to which managers and union leaders understand the reciprocal considerations which guide their interaction, for example, the paradox of acknowledging the independence between organised capital and labour and HR policies which seek to develop *co-operative relationships* deriving from the economically interdependent nature of the parties.

16 Douwes Dekker, L. (1987a)

HUMAN RESOURCE MANAGEMENT, IDEOLOGY AND POLICY

A useful framework for evaluating the development of managerial policies is through the analytical prism of ideology. HR policy and initiatives, including Human Resource Management (HRM), seek to facilitate the achievement of organisational goals through the effective procurement, development, motivation, integration, and involvement of employees. While these processes reflect humanistic intentions the preferred focus on the individual rather than collective relations has led to the criticism of a sophisticated or neo-unitarist motivation.

Ideology may be described as an action-related system of ideas concerning a given reality. Defined in this way, ideology provides a cognitive framework involving value and policy choices, given that elements of uncertainty and equivocality remain.

The functional purposes of ideology have been discussed by several writers.[17, 18, 19, 20] Ideologies help to define and advance core interests of a group, mobilising and uniting members to protect and defend their interests against opposing groups. Ideologies can also serve to underwrite or reinforce dominant value systems of those in control or those challenging such control. They may also serve as an instrument of persuasion. Managerial approaches may reflect the following characteristics:

- an image of the organisation as an organic whole;
- strong prevalence of the notion of a dominance of congruent interests and values between management and employees;
- attribution of conflict to external sources, denial of conflict inherency; and

17 Allan, V. (1971)
18 Bendix, R. (1954)
19 Fox, A. (1981)
20 Nichols, T. (1969)

- rejection of challenge to or questioning of managerial control and authority.

Seen from a radical perspective, such a unitarist ideology seeks to confer legitimacy on and perpetuate managerial control. It may therefore help to maintain prevailing power realities regarding relationships with and control over employees. The regulation of conflict by institutional means, such as collective bargaining, reflects a preference for a pluralist ideology. This latter model acknowledges organisational conflict and differing interests as inherent. Certain recent developments suggest a reassertion of a neo-unitarist ideology in certain Western countries. Before discussing these developments in more depth it is considered appropriate briefly to elaborate on the nature of ideological frameworks.

IDEOLOGY AND VALUES

The values issues in policy choices are considerably more complex than those of a knowledge or skills nature. Here questions centre less around what people know or are able to do than around what belief system underlies behaviour, its interpretation, how values change over time and the implications thereof. An understanding and organisational definition of core organisational values is at the heart of policy formation in IR and HRM.

In order to attempt to deal with values issues, coherence to particular sets of beliefs can be provided by an understanding of frames of reference in IR and individual behaviour. Three broad frames of reference have been identified — the unitarist, pluralist and radical change approaches. These are briefly outlined below, before proceeding to a discussion of their relevance for policy formation in the South African context.

The unitarist approach

From a unitarist perspective the 'organisation logic of the enterprise is seen as pointing towards a unified authority and loyalty structure, with managerial prerogatives being legitimised by all members of the organisation'.[21] Employee behaviour is only 'rational' to the extent that it follows the 'rational' goals and policies of management. Characteristic of the early human relations school, this approach presumes a state of 'unity' to be normal in an organisation. Conflict is perceived as an aberration, and the existence of trade unions the product of poor management, sectional greed, poor understanding of economics or the 'national interest', or the existence of 'subversive elements' and 'agitators'. Consequent policy approaches to dealing with conflict tend to be collaborative in the sense that efforts are made to 'educate' labour into the norms of the management process. Efforts are made to communicate more effectively with employees, and 'negotiate' through problem solving processes. Alternatively, or where such efforts fail, the tactics employed may be coercive, characterised by management practice which seeks to provide a justification for the strict maintenance of managerial prerogatives, control and unilateral decision making. Typically, a 'we can manage without the union' sentiment prevails, reflecting a conception that trade unions are the 'cause' of conflict.

The pluralist approach

From the pluralist perspective, the unitary approach is inadequate in that 'the enterprise is not a unitary structure but a coalition of individuals and groups with their own aspirations and their own perceptions of the structure which they naturally see as valid'.[22] In essence an organisation may be seen as comprising groups with varying degrees of dependence and

21 Fox, A. (1981 op.cit. p. 302)
22 Fox, A. (1981, op. cit. p. 304)

independence. Despite considerable variance in goals they collaborate within a structure to achieve their respective goals. Conflict is seen as being inherent in this relationship, and accepted as a normal, if uncomfortable phenomenon. The manner in which this conflict is handled to enable a continuation of the relationship so each can achieve their goals is through the process of collective bargaining. Fox states: 'Trade unions are . . . accepted by pluralists as legitimate challenges to managerial rule' and even welcomed as a manifestation of a healthy democratic society.[23]

'Such an approach would hardly make sense without an accompanying assumption that the normative divergencies between the parties are not so fundamental or so wide as to be unbridgeable by compromises or new syntheses which enable collaboration to continue.' In other words all participants in the system must adhere to a philosophy of mutual survival, conflict must be amenable to compromise or creative problem solving, and be 'able to operate procedures of negotiation and dispute settlement characterised by a consensual code of ethics and conduct'.[24]

Clack (1964) sees the employment relationship as comprising human (individual) and labour (collective) relations components. (Figure 1.2) The former is evident in the direct one-to-one and small-group relationships of employers with workers in each factory, usually through HR and attendant policies and techniques for improving the work environment and increasing output. The latter emerges when employers are also able to negotiate and bargain with workers (and vice-versa) on an equal basis through independent representation and negotiation with a trade union.[25] The labour relations approach stresses the inherent nature of conflict between management and labour. It postulates the need negotiated rules

23 Fox, A. (1981, op. cit. p. 305)
24 Fox, A. (1981, op. cit. p. 306)
25 Clack, G. (1964)

LABOUR RELATIONS	HUMAN RELATIONS
Conflict abnormal	Conflict inherent
Company - happy family/team	Groups - common and conflicting interests
Unitary approach	Pluralist approach
Conflict caused by: outsiders, agitators, poor communication, management and interpersonal skills and personality clashes	Conflict caused by: - group interaction - reactions to external pressure
Mechanistic human resource management systems and procedures	Established structures to regulate conflict
	Collective bargaining between parties

Figure 1.2
Comparison of human and labour relations approaches

and procedures to regulate conflict. The labour relations approach also tends to suggest that effective conflict management is more likely when there is a relatively equitable (or near) distribution of power between the parties. In addition there is an implicit belief that power is not so inequitably distributed between the parties that duress is regularly introduced into the process.

A distinction has been made between autocratic unitarism and attendant strategies aimed at union suppression through coercive and legal action, and sophisticated, paternalistic, unitarism which seek union avoidance through human resource management initiatives such as direct employee involvement and financial participation.[26] A further distinction is also made between two forms of pluralism: constitutional pluralism, which seeks union accommodation through collective bargaining, and consultative pluralism which seeks union collaboration through worker (representative) participation. These IR strategies reflect a variation in management styles and value system. In South Africa, there is evidence of use of all of these approaches in various companies. Legal constraints in the form of unfair labour practice provisions of the Labour Relations Act (1989) and trade union vigilance limit policy options such as autocratic unitarism and possibly sophisticated paternalistic unitarism, if such policies and associated strategies contravene the provisions of labour legislation (for example discriminatory selection procedures which limit freedom of association). None of these approaches should be seen as absolutes. It is possible for the coexistence of enlightened HR policies and innovative human resource practices, and the institutionalisation of workers' rights through constitutional pluralism.

The radical change approach

This approach focuses on the *political economy* and the interrelationships between political and economic variables. It is based in the critical analysis of class divisions in capitalist society by the neo-Marxist or radical school. From this perspective all types of unitarist (HR) and pluralist (IR) policies are perceived as status quo-oriented. From the radical stance, efforts to institutionalise conflict through collective bargaining tend to reveal a normative orientation rather than seeking, or resulting in, a meaningful redistribution of power, wealth and opportunity. Marginal, incremental wage gains and improvements in conditions of service occur within definite

26 Clack, G. (1964)

parameters, the limits of which are defined by those in power at a given point in time.

Fox suggests that 'pluralists do not envisage as the outcome of joint regulation by management and labour any major change in the organisation of industry, or in the fundamental distribution of power and control (op cit, p. 314). There is an implicit acceptance of the status quo or incremental improvements within existing structures, as being desirable. Pluralism, from a radical perspective, despite its 'realism' about conflict and its stated faith in the collective bargaining process, reflects an ideological preference for preserving social institutions and class structures, or the promotion of reformist, marginal change to these institutions and structures.

For those seeking to overthrow or change radically the existing system, pluralism represents, then, an obstacle rather than a vehicle for change. 'Collective bargaining' wrote Harbison (1954) 'provides one of the most important bulwarks for the preservation of the private enterprise system.' Similarly, institutionalised mechanisms for identifying and regulating conflict could, given certain conditions, be defined not as a threat to, but as a prerequisite for social stability and integration in its deepest sense.[27] Flanders (1970, p. 172) writes that 'the paradox, whose truth managements have found it so difficult to accept, is that they can regain control by sharing it'.

Thus, both the unitarists' efforts to suppress or control conflict, and the pluralists' to regulate it are perceived by radical change theorists as efforts to stabilise an unjust system, and to enlist worker's subservience to capitalism.

HUMAN RESOURCE POLICY CHOICES

The human relations school and associated HR policies were often associated with benevolent paternalistic forms of management and bureacratic organisational structures. However,

27 Silverman, D. (1970)

these issues are more complex if one recognises certain patterns of organisational development (ranging from autocratic, Taylorian scientific management oriented organisations to decentralised, participative, and 'flat' matrix structures). Other variables which are important in this regard, include the historical evolution of the 'personnel management' field from the paternalistic, unitary approach of the human relations school to the current *human resource approach* which tends to lay greater emphasis on employee development, integration and participative management, and a flatter organisational structure. Yet within the South African employment context with its unique contradictions of both race and class divisions, its inequality of wealth, opportunity and power, the task of defining the most meaningful and relevant contribution of the HR function, is complex but immensely challenging.

Both the HR specialist and the trade union official are constrained by their respective organisational goals. Trade unionists are usually required by the union's constitution to observe democratic procedures and processes. HR managers are mandated by senior management, and are not therefore required to report back to the entire organisation. If the the HR manager's perception of his role is primarily orientated towards organisational goals and objectives, the difficulty of establishing a value system or philosophy which is clearly articulated and legitimised in terms of workers' perceptions, is considerable. If one considers the tenets of the labour relations approach, (as compared to the human relations approach) as postulated by Clack (1964) in this context, the inherency of conflict between management and labour, strongly suggests that although there are common goals and interests between management and labour, there are also conflicts of goals and interests between these parties.

Purcell (1983) has indicated that while many industrial relations and HR specialists may be pluralist in their views, the vast majority of managers are more likely to incline to individualist and often unitary views, whose values have been strongly inculcated into their training, and which are uncomplicated and self-assuming in nature. Industrial relations is not just an added dimension to the traditional role of the IR or HR practitioner. It includes broader perspectives, new alignments, role definitions and new value(s) dilemmas.

The employment relationship comprises a complex network of relationships, fluctuating power shifts and conflicting interests between the three independent, yet interdependent actors. With its internal focus, the HR function is perceived from a neo-radical perspective as an instrument for maintaining managerial control. At a broader level, the state, while espousing a pluralist approach in industrial relations since 1924 when it established the machinery for labour and management to govern their own affairs through the Industrial Conciliation Act, at the same time took steps to see that this process of collective bargaining excluded a major section of the workforce, viz black workers. This latter group was dealt with by essentially unitarist state approaches prohibiting de jure trade union rights. Only in 1979 and 1981, with the Labour Relations Act coming into effect, was the pluralist ideology reflected more cogently in South African industrial relations legislation. Nonetheless, the deracialisation of labour legislation can be viewed as an unsuccessful attempt at co-option and control of non-racial unions.

The continuation of pluralism as a basis underlying both the legislature and practice is, however, a fragile notion. Its erosion by executive state action against trade unions and legislative amendment during the latter part of the 1980s raised doubts as to its permanency.

It could be argued then that IR during the 1980s shifted towards a more constitutional pluralist phase of industrial relations practice. It is, however, possible to view industrial relations in South Africa eclectically, with ingredients of all three approaches, prevalent. In view of the country's racial and class divisions, contending political ideologies, reactive radical change groups and the processes of change, this is not particularly surprising. The espoused philosophy of some groups is frequently incongruent with their behaviour. Some examples are illustrated below:

- The ideology and populist rhetoric of some trade unions is of a radical change nature, yet their policy approaches often reflect a preference for institutionalised conflict regulation, i.e. recognition and procedural agreements, bargaining at company and industry levels and the use of the courts.
- The espoused philosophy of the state in the 1980s tended towards pluralist non-intervention, yet detentions without trial and restrictions on trade unions and union federations reflect a strong, emotive unitarist emphasis.
- Some employers espousing a pluralist policy have taken active steps to exclude unions or to marginalise their presence, evading negotiation and removing 'agitators' in retrenchment programmes — essentially unitarist tactics.
- Certain trade unions as vehement opponents of registration and industry-level bargaining, registered and joined industrial councils in the mid-1980s. Several employers have reversed previous commitments to centralised bargaining by withdrawing from industrial councils.

These shifting patterns of behaviour often reflect policy and strategic approaches adapting to evolving economic circumstances, managerial practice, organisational growth of unions, the extension of their power base and the development of unfair labour practice jurisprudence.

What is important in this argument is that a salient frame of reference is hard to define in a South African context. The taking of snapshot analytical pictures at a particular moment in time, ignores the importance of socio-historical factors, the impact of internal and external pressures for change and shifting values and strategies as being important for understanding IR and HR policy formation as a process. Normative behaviour in the field, from the point of view of all parties involved, appears to be undergoing a process of ongoing change. As a result the usual 'safe' means of assessing the acceptability of certain behaviour against norms, guidelines, conventions and laws, is not tenable.

If the policy frames of reference discussed are subjected to a more in-depth examination it can be concluded that essentially they centre around one central concept — power. Those in possession of power tend to dominate in order to seek its preservation. Agents for radical change may seek to remove power from those in possession and to replace the system with an alternative one. Pluralists, while tending to be more collaborative, are viewed by the neo-radical school as entrenching existing distributions of power, albeit in an overtly 'civilised' regulatory manner.

Changes in the flows of power between parties vitally affect social institutions and laws, and criteria for assessing what is acceptable in any given situation. 'Laws in modern society are ideological formations given legal form and sanction by the state . . . ideologies enforced by social power are laws . . . regardless of the ways in which they are enforced and in whose name . . . ideology is converted into law by those with the power to do so.'[28]

Power and change, therefore, would appear to be central elements in the policy formation and practice of IR and HR. They reflect its complexity, and how its meaning may change in a given political context. Questions of interest and standards of right and wrong all depend on who is judging, under what conditions, by what criteria and for what purposes. This underlines the importance of analytical frameworks and ethical approaches to policy formation.

28 Marsden, R. (1982)

ETHICS AND POLICY FORMATION

If it is concepts of power and change that are involved, then discussion must centre around processes, rather than existing states.[29] Further, if judgements are to be made about the values and behaviour of those involved in these processes then some basis is required on which to do so.

Frames of reference have been referred to as the starting point for such an exercise, and a code of ethics may reflect a framework of desired *values* underpinning any policy. However, the values, tactics and ethics of a particular grouping may reflect the position in the existing system of that grouping as defined by their power base and aspirations. These could change in line with changing socio-political circumstances. If this is accepted to be the case, questions arise as to the place of ethics in what appears to be a process wherein parties are engaged in tactics designed to entrench or change existing states.

According to Lewicki (1982) two approaches to ethics may be discerned — absolutist and relativist. 'Relativists argue that we cannot determine what are good ethics without understanding the situation or culture in which they apply; in contrast ethical absolutists believe that some standards of right and wrong are common, regardless of culture.' (p. 426)

This raises the broader policy issue of employer social responsibility to both its own workers and in relation to decisions which may affect people in a wider social context. This would include, for example, the decision of a company as to whether or not it should take up representation in the case of a worker, or a full-time trade union official with whom the company has established a relationship, who has been detained without trial. A decision either way is unavoidably a political statement of either support for the status quo or

29 Horwitz, F.M. and Anstey, M. (1984.)

conversely of opposition to practices which are perceived by business as not being not morally defensible.

Therefore such practices by agencies or institutions considered to be 'outside' the realm of the individual company may have a profound effect on intra-organisational worker–management relations, and relations between the company and other independent bodies such as a trade union. The important issue of business ethics is a crucial part of the debate on the human resources and industrial relations interface. Leatt (1983) refers to business ethics as the manner in which organisations make significant decisions which affect the lives of their own employees and other people, and the criteria used in this decision-making process. This process therefore concerns the impact of business policies and decisions on a company's own workers and society in general.

Lewicki argues that in the business context, those ethical dimensions and concerns that have the most direct relevance for conflict and competitive behaviour need to be identified. He contends that the concept of ethical relativism questions whether ethical principles apply universally or whether they can be judged only within particular social and cultural contexts. In the employment relationship in particular, it may be asked what strategies and tactics could be regarded as ethical or unethical and by whom — in the context of the concept of relativism. Lewicki appears to imply that the process of interaction between individuals and groups, tends to evolve normative frameworks of acceptable and unacceptable behaviour. He suggests, for example, that in collective bargaining, tactics such as bluffing and concealment are often used and that the use of such tactics, given a positive trust relationship between the parties, may not be unethical, or construed as a failure to bargain in good faith.

It is important, especially in the South African context, to acknowledge that *the range of relationships is considerably wider than the collective bargaining process alone,* and that there is a variety of interactions between individuals (the HR focus) and groups (the IR focus) which do not occur only on the basis of distributive bargaining. In addition, the application of the concept of ethical relativism, as a policy question, to situations where either management or labour is unwilling to bargain or even interact, such as the refusal of management to recognise or meet with a union representing its workers, as in the now classic case of *Fodens* v *United African Motor and Allied Workers' Union* (1983), needs to be examined. Put simply, the question is posed as to whether a refusal to interact may be unethical. The *Fodens* industrial court case, which involved a refusal by the company to engage in a specific type of interaction process, namely negotiating with a representative trade union, seems to have facilitated the development of an evolving jurisprudence on the duty to bargain. This tends to confirm Lewicki's point that the development of norms within a social context helps to clarify acceptable and unacceptable behaviour and is a fundamental pre-cursor for policy formation. Ultimately, however a 'responsible value system' should be nurtured intra-organisationally, not only to avoid the threat of internal dissent (e.g. a strike) and external sanctions (such as legal action) but as a conscious effort towards achieving a higher level of decision-making through the evolution of policies that reflect a corporate conscience and social responsibility. It would seem that some broad normative frameworks are developing regarding acceptable principles of fairness in management–employee relations.

SHIFTING COMPARATIVE DEVELOPMENTS

Given that the employment relationship may be considered as a sub-system of a wider socio-political system, developments in work-place representation reflect a decline in private sector trade union membership during the 1980s and early 1990s in several Western countries, for example, in the United States,

Great Britain and in European countries such as Italy, France and Spain.[30] This decline can be attributed to the following:

1. structural changes in the economy — for example, technological change and a growing white collar work force in most Western countries;
2. changes in worker attitudes and needs — trade unions may be seen as less instrumental as in the past for improving working conditions in some advanced industrial societies;
3. new employer initiatives and strategies denoting a stronger focus on HRM and union marginalisation or even exclusion;
4. broader transformations of IR institutions; and
5. shifting socio-political trends.

Rather than one single factor being predominant, a combination of these factors may be associated with changing patterns of IR.

In developing African countries, for example, the organisational development of trade unions has been stunted by the state Corporatism eroding trade union independence by executive intervention and central wage fixing and control over dismissal decisions, as for example, in Zimbabwe and Mozambique. In contrast to developed industrial societies, trade union density in some developing countries is increasing, however, (for example in Namibia and South Africa), with industrial relations policy choices reflecting a strong ideological content. The assertion of unitarist ideologies in the latter context can be associated with employer responses to political conflict and the extent of polarisation in the society, with organisational manifestations in lower commitment, the strong prevalence of instrumental attitudes to work, and poor labour productivity.[31] However, HR approaches in both developed and developing countries, are perhaps for different

30 Kochan, T. (1987)
31 Blunt, P. (1985)

reasons, sometimes associated with practices and strategies which seek to achieve the following:

- persuading employees away from collective forms of indirect or representative participation, towards individual, consensual forms of direct involvement, such as financial participation and quality circles;
- provision of a personal, economic stakeholding in the organisation through financial participation, for example, employee share-ownership plans, profit sharing and performance-related incentive schemes; and
- de-emphasis away from interest-based models of collective bargaining towards decentralised joint consultation and problem solving, strike-free agreements (for example in the United Kingdom and United States), and single-unionism.

The somewhat dominant and persuasive emphasis on achieving organisational and particularly managerial objectives, belies the pluralist concept of organisations. The latter approach views organisations as comprising groups with common and competing interests with various coalitions of power, given that pluralism itself, represents an ideological form.

HUMAN RESOURCE MANAGEMENT (HRM) AS UNITARIST IDEOLOGY

- Seeking strategies and practices to attract employees away from collective forms of participation
- Focusing on common interests only
- De-emphasising or undermining collective bargaining especially at centralised levels, in favour of decentralised structures and a fragmentation of organised power
- Re-assertion of the ethic of individualism

TRADE UNION RESPONSES TO HUMAN RESOURCE INITIATIVES

In Western European countries such as West Germany, and in the social democracies of Scandinavia, unionism tends to be acknowledged as a societal rule, and as part of the democratic process. Through support of legislation or basic agreements, effective joint consultation in the period between annual collective bargaining occurs. Worker representatives are thus empowered. An important underlying assumption in the social democracies of Western Europe is the societal (corporatist) institutionalisation of the basic rights of freedom of association, the right to organise and to collectively bargain. The extent to which pluralist principles and policies are internalised as a pervasive societal value may limit the expression of unitarist HR policies and strategies.

This raises important questions regarding trade union responses to unitarist strategies. Unions tend to consider HR practices of employee involvement as undermining the independent nature of collective representation and the power base derived from collective obilisation.[32] Attendent responses include:

- direct rejection and vetoing the introduction of management initiatives;
- active subversion once introduced;
- malicious compliance and subtle forms of protest;
- grudging, passive cknowledge;
- exerting union influence beyond collective bargaining by a reconsideration of participation in other forms and levels of both direct (for example, the TUC's position on employee share ownership in Britain) and indirect participation; and
- influencing corporate strategic decision making centrally.

32 Bird, A. (1988)

The limitations of traditional institutional analysis are underlined by changing patterns of industrial relations. Consideration of a neo-institutionalist approach to IR has been suggested,[33] in which both management and unions are regarded as *strategic actors*. This approach holds that both actors need to be sufficiently unrestricted so as to entertain strategic opinions independently of traditional institutions of job regulation.

Trade unions could therefore endeavour to act innovatively in order to influence industrial relations and HR policy and indeed corporate business policy of employers. The radical view of the 'trade union as a vehicle for the struggle of the working class against capital is however, limited by the fact that (independent) trade unions which are products of the capitalist system, are tied to the system. They can bargain with society but not transform it'. The neo-institutional approach rests on the assumption that environmental change affecting IR actors, their workplace policies and their power position, may be relatively permanent and on-going. These changes require leadership to develop long-term policies to cope with change and minimise exclusive reliance on short-term defensive tactics. However, the extent to which freedom of independent action or social agency is possible varies temporarily within particular societies. Limitations in social agency can be imposed curbing the independent assertion of power and narrowing strategic options.

COMMON VALUES

HR policies which seek the attainment of homogeneity or *mutuality* of organisation culture and values may be unrealistic if viewing organisations as a diverse, pluralist society. While a shift in the direction of commonality and convergence of values and objectives is desirable to optimise organisational

33 Reshev, Y. and Murray, A. (1988)

performance, and reduce attitudinal polarisation, it raises important ethical and ideological questions such as the following:

1. whether it is appropriate for the values of the managed to be decided by people other than themselves, or at least formulated jointly;
2. the extent to which these values are desired by other employees — and whether they are likely to be relatively congruent or consistent; and
3. the role of sound industrial relations principles, policies and processes which seek to create and maintain basic worker rights, and the democratic value base of pluralism as underpinning these rights.

This raises sensitive issues regarding the methodology of formulating and implementing specific values reflecting a policy desired by a particular interest group. The organisational expression of particular value systems requires perceived and institutionalised legitimacy. The imposition of a value system considered alien and possibly hostile to prevailing values poses significant problems in respect of legitimacy and the defensive protection of interests. The 'values issue' in policy formation cannot be over-simplified. Prevailing and often competing value systems, multi-cultural environments, sub-cultures and even counter-cultures within organisations reflect the diversity and complexity of modern organisations. Change processes therefore require careful consideration, planning and contextual sensitivity.

Whilst there are overlapping and common interests between different groups within organisations, the pursuit of complete identification by employees with the company and its values reflects a more sophisticated and paternalistic unitary ideology, or a dominant human relations orientation. The notion of a plurality of common and competing interests, values diversity and sub-cultures, suggests that the organisational promotion of overlapping values and goals, accommodation of diversity and the regulation of conflict may enrich organisational experience and effectiveness. The notion of freedom of organisational association and the attendant employee rights in respect of trade union affiliation would be regarded as an anathema to the somewhat utopian goal of the complete identification of employees with the company's values and ethos. Organisational accommodation of multiple loyalties can however, be problematic. The 'sophisticated' unitary perspective views company and trade union loyalty as mutually exclusive. However, many organisations do formulate policies and practical strategies to adjust to complex environmental demands. This requires appropriate policies which are accommodative and perhaps synergistic of multiple value systems, cultural diversity and differing interests.

MANAGERIAL INITIATIVES

Modern HR themes positively seek employee *involvement*.[34] The scope and level of involvement tends to focus primarily on enhancing productivity at individual and small-group level. The participative goals often tend to be managerially defined in efficiency terms, for example, quality circles. Collective or representational participation in the governance of organisations beyond the level of individual jobs is not adequately addressed in HR literature.

The increasing popularity of direct employee communication and involvement, while having important advantages for management and employees, can mask a deeper underlying distaste for unionism. Attendant managerial strategies seek to formulate more 'effective' techniques for humanising the work environment, gaining co-operation and competing with the union for employee support. It is in this ideological context that formal employer union recognition and practices may not

34 Horwitz, F.M. (1990)

always successfully regulate conflict. The ideological externalisation of conflict sources is often reflected by the labelling of employees as 'the union' when contesting the legitimacy of managerial decisions, but when supporting managerial initiatives and organisational goals, they are referred to as 'our employees' or as 'loyal members of the team.' Management constantly seeks to enhance its ability to exercise policy and operational choices. While the effectiveness of HR strategies seeking to optimise co-operation and organisational loyalty varies comparatively, being most successful in the United States, the question of HR as a method of control in the unitarist sense implies that a strong ideological orientation is required. Taking the initiative, the exercise of managerial choice may, however, occur either on an ad hoc or policy basis, and the degree of informality in IR may facilitate incremental changes rather than sharp shifts such as union de-recognition in the United States.

Although union membership has declined in the United Kingdom and European countries, many IR structures and institutions have endured. The latter are indeed developing in certain African countries in the absence of broadly acceptable political structures and, on occasion, either in spite of, or in conjunction with HRM practices and strategies.

Similarly stated, there is in several Western market economies, a threat of erosion of interest-based or pluralist models by HRM philosophies, trying ideologically to 'win the hearts and minds' of workers. This is evidenced by a focus away from interest-based centralised relations to flexible and decentralised HR practice and employee involvement. This has been a factor in the erosion of unions as public parties in most advanced Western countries and, with corporatism as a form of regulation declining, a neo-conservative and micro-level regulatory model has begun to develop.[35] In developing Afri-

35 Muller-Jentsch, W. (1987)

can countries however, the opportunities for developing centralised corporatist regulation have not been adequately explored. Employers are mainly concerned with facilitating decentralised, organisation-level improvements in economic/productivity objectives by defusing employee polarisation and enhancing commitment to organisational objectives. Employee involvement schemes have therefore assumed greater managerial prominence. This shift of managerial strategies to the decentralised-level seeks to reduce the adversarial relationship patterns of collective bargaining and enhance co-operation and trust by direct communication with employees and union-avoidance policies. In this sense, trends in developed and developing countries show similar patterns.

A fundamental question in this regard concerns the feasibility of the *coexistence of both interest-based and co-operation (wealth generation, HR) models*. It is perhaps unrealistic in both developed and free-enterprise-orientated developing countries to expect trade unions to accept an exclusively co-operative role at organisational levels for an indefinite length of time. The potential for coexistence and de-emphasis of the ideological role of HR initiatives is to a large extent a function of variables affecting prevailing power realities, including economic factors, changing values, technological advancement, and labour market patterns. The notion of political pluralism acknowledges the economic sector as a potentially democratised zone of real interdependence between capital and labour, given an acknowledgement of the independence of interest groups as inherent to a pluralist society.

COEXISTENCE OF INTEREST AND CO-OPERATIVE MODELS

1. Acceptance of freedom of association by management at all levels

2. Acceptance of the paradox of both inter-dependence of goals and independence of employee representation
   - Common and differing interests
3. Relative or near balance in power distribution
4. Legitimation of managerial authority and participative leadership styles
5. Formalisation of conflict regulation mechanisms
6. Mutual trust and respect for the individual
7. Employment security

Both economic and political crises have led organisations to consider greater *flexibility* in the management of financial, material and human resources. This has been associated with shifts towards decentralisation of organisational structures, and decision processes, enhanced individual relations and employee involvement schemes, as for example, in France and Great Britain.

In Britain and Europe, but to a lesser degree in some African countries, there seems to be an increasing focus away from collective towards individual HR relations. Where this shift occurs, it is often associated with managerial initiatives such as innovative and 'sophisticated' HR practices which may reflect unitarist preferences for challenging union legitimacy, or the marginalisation or even exclusion of trade unions, in order to optimise individual commitment and identity with the organisation.

CONCLUSIONS

The critique that managerial developments in the 1980s and early 1990s, reflect a determination to impose new forms of managerial control, facilitated by power imbalances created by political, economic and technological change could indeed carry some credence with pluralists too, with the latter's support for interest-based models of institutionalising conflict through social regulation. This ideological viewpoint is however, an open question given the voluntary nature of direct forms of participation or employee involvement and the belief that various types of participation can evolve pragmatically at all levels of an organisation. However, the intent, intensity and zeal of contemporary managerial initiatives may reflect strong ideological overtones. Yet shifting power relations, and variations in trade union density comparatively, cannot be explained solely by reference to HR developments and ideological motives. New forms of individual, consensual participation are, however, different from participation by negotiation.[36] Strongest resistance to HR initiatives and participative practices which seek greater loyalty, commitment and motivation is more likely where unions are still developing and workers have strongly positive views about the instrumental benefits of union membership. A strong, powerful and established trade union movement is less likely to see these managerial approaches as potentially undermining their traditional role. Unions in these circumstances may indeed be willing to consider alternative forms of participation in a more favourable light, given the durability of existing institutions and structures.

Co-operative HR policy activities seek a reduction of coercive forms of control, although from a radical perspective they introduce a different form of control. Greater participation of employees in decisions affecting their interests may complement the competitive processes of collective bargaining and procedural resolution of labour relations disputes. The co-presence of both interest-based structures and processes, and co-operative, participative HR policies and practices within the same organisation, is possible. The extent to which either becomes predominant and a potential threat to the other, rather than keeping a functional and strategic balance, poses significant policy dilemmas for management and labour.

36 Dror, A. (1987)

The processes of mobilisation of power, through mechanisms such as collective bargaining, or the sharing of power through co-operative HR interventions, are not necessarily mutually exclusive. Co-operative HR activities are difficult, though not impossible to achieve alongside collective bargaining relations. An integrative focus on the employer need for better productivity and employee concerns about fairness and security is a vital challenge in the 1990s.

2

POLICY FORMATION: THE EXTERNAL ENVIRONMENT

INTRODUCTION

Amidst the divisions and polarisation in contemporary South Africa fair employment practices and the notion of democratic participation have become more prominent.[1, 2, 3, 4, 5, 6, 7, 8, 9, 10] However, little reference has been made to policy functions of employee participation, the equity process and the extent to which these are mutually exclusive or potentially accommodative. There is, therefore, a need to consider the socio-political *context* of IR and HR management, the extent to which the creation and institutionalisation of rights and enlightened practice is facilitated or impeded, and the factors associated therewith. This chapter explores some policy issues arising from the relationship between employee and employer influence, and the broader political process in South Africa. An attempt is made to broaden the debate on factors relating to the development of HR and IR policies and attendant rights creating processes, by briefly examining socio-political questions for IR, and HR policy.

1 Anstey, M. (1986)
2 Douwes Dekker, L. (1987)
3 Godsell, R. M. (1982)
4 Horwitz, F. M. (1983)
5 Horwitz, F. M. (1988)
6 Human, P. (1986)
7 Krause, G. and Nel, C. (1986)
8 Lamprecht, A. (1987)
9 Project Free Enterprise (1986)
10 Viljoen, J. (1986)

HISTORICAL DEVELOPMENT

The extension of the principle of freedom of association to black workers by Statute in 1979 followed the legislative exclusion and restrictions on black trade union organising and bargaining rights dating back to the Industrial Conciliation Act of 1924. Over this period, black trade unions though never illegal, led a marginal existence with an absence of de jure and actual recognition by employers, occurring within a context of restrictions and harassment by the state. Large trade unions such as the Industrial and Commercial Workers Union (ICU) which mobilised over 100 000 workers in the 1920s foundered as a result of leadership and organisational difficulties, pressure by the state and the absence of a legal compulsion to bargain with black trade unions. The 1973 Durban strikes and subsequent worker protests highlighted the inadequacies of the dualistic IR system which provided for collective bargaining rights through industrial councils for white, coloured and Asian employees only. Black workers were excluded form the definition of 'employee' in the Industrial Conciliation Act and as a result were denied access to industrial council bargaining and dispute resolution machinery. They could form works and liaison committees aimed at facilitating better communication with management in terms of the Bantu Labour Relations Act of 1973. The latter did not offer the rights of freedom of association, labour organisation and collective bargaining through representative and independent trade unions. A gross power imbalance prevailed until these rights were granted by the Industrial Conciliation Act of 1979, following acceptance of the recommendations of the Wiehahn Commission of Inquiry into labour legislation. The new Act removed this legislative dualism, although a 'new' dualism emerged in respect of the paradox of the industrial enfranchisement and political disenfranchisement of black workers in the 1980s and early 1990s.

This paradox, together with attempts at state control and restrictions on black political mobilisation through the state of emergency imposed in June 1986, resulted in an intense politicisation of industrial relations in the 1980s, with the non-racial trade union movement as one of the few institutions able to reflect the inseparability of political and economic aspirations at the time.

THE COMPARATIVE CONTEXT

The creation of rights and fair employment policies and practices cannot be inherently reflective of purely economic interests and productivity goals. 'While the Japanese system with its accent on labour-management co-operation, is based on the cultural value of belonging to a group or family, and on the economic value of productivity, the West German system has its roots in ideas about a different power structure in the society at large, and these roots must be sought in political history.'[11]

However, the policies underlying the systems of both countries are fundamentally different, according to Schregle. These differences are economic, cultural and socio-political. HR policy in Japan 'aims at mobilising workers at shop-floor level and enhancing productivity (micro-economic) goals. The creation of worker rights in Germany is expected to reach *equal distribution of power* and influence in the whole society (macro-economic goals).'[12]

IR and HR policy in the West German context may therefore be considered as constituting a *pervasiveness of social relations,* extending considerably wider than job-oriented direct forms of employee involvement.[13] These forms of involvement cannot be regarded as having as a major objective, the creation

11 Schregle, J. (1986)
12 Park, S. J. (1986)
13 Guest, D. (1986)

of worker rights through the distribution of power within the organisational and the societal contexts by means of the processes of collective bargaining and legal determination. The introduction of co-determination in West Germany in the 1920s, was associated with the idea of democratisation of the economy or the *extension of democracy* beyond the confines of individual organisations. A primary rationale for the introduction of co-determination in West Germany was a political one, rather than a productivity objective, according to Schregle. The political objectives were the introduction and extension of democracy, and seeking an accommodation of the market system and the formerly centralised and planned economies of Eastern Europe.

PARTICIPATION AND EQUITY: FUNCTIONS AND OBJECTIVES

Terms such as industrial democracy, rights creation, fair employment practices, participation and equity are not merely different nomenclatures to describe the same phenomena. There may also be problems in ensuring a measure of concept-equivalence, across societies, since what are nominally identical structures or institutions, e.g. works councils, may perform varying functions, or have different significance.[14] IR 'models' and HR policies are more readily understandable within the context of their unique socio-historical, cultural, functional development and defined purpose within the society concerned. Essentially, their meaningfulness is more appropriately established by an understanding of the self-definitions of the key actors or institutions within that specific social context.

At issue in European employment structures is the *balance of power between social partners* within a liberal or social demo-

14 Bean, R. (1986)

cratic economic and social order.[15] Job-orientated worker involvement refers to direct rather than indirect or representational forms of workers' participation. The main objective of these HR schemes is the economic and largely managerially defined goals of improved productivity and wealth creation. Unitarist preferences may provide the underlying premises for direct forms of IR. This often appears to be the management position in the South African context. Krause and Nel (1986) for example, argue that 'participative systems should not be viewed as being participation by workers at the highest managerial levels. It should rather be seen as the process whereby managers utilise and involve workers in the everyday running of the business.' The focus on the productivity goals of participation in South Africa has been referred to by other writers.[16, 17, 18, 19] Direct forms of involvement as distinct from democracy in industry, are associated more strongly with HR policy and practice. Democracy in industry relates more specifically to processes involved in the creation and regulation of worker rights and the associated distribution of power between IR actors. The institutionalisation of inherent conflict is therefore associated with the establishment of democratic rights of the actors.

IR structures and HR procedures in South Africa have historically, reflected a dualism along racial lines with the creation of separate structures, until the definition of employee in the Industrial Conciliation Act was amended to include workers of all races in 1979. Until then black workers were denied access to the central collective bargaining structures of industrial councils. Black trade unions were not illegal

15 Thusing, R. (1986)
16 Daniel, R. (1984)
17 Douwes Dekker, L. (1986)
18 Viljoen, J. Ibid.
19 Horwitz, F. M. (1988a)

but a legalised exclusion process and restrictions on their leadership limited their organisational effectiveness.

The post-Wiehahn era has seen a more fundamental re-ordering of relationships between management, workers and shareholders. The emerging focus on various types of employee financial involvement in organisations in several Western countries and South Africa reflects managerially defined advantages of economic and ethical involvement goals. Notwithstanding the economic arguments, the *social partnership model* proposes an employee stakeholding in the business which extends to more pervasive goals than productivity achievement alone. These include the distribution of power, and the identification of employees individually and collectively with the organisation and its performance, ie a synergy between HR management goals and worker rights. Clearly, from the above arguments, direct forms of employee involvement cannot be regarded as constituting industrial democracy.

The relationship between the policy and *goals* of democracy, e.g. fairness or equity, and the *means* of achieving and legitimising them is complex and often confusing. What constitutes goals and means is not always clear. The achievement of qualitative goals such as fair labour practices, equity, non-discrimination, social justice and dignity may be seen as arising from means such as democratic structures. Some might argue conversely that democratic structures are in themselves moral and ethical goals worth pursuing. While a superficial analysis might suggest that this is a 'chicken and egg' situation, it is important to define both the means and the goals clearly, if the values of fairness and equity are to become enduring processes in organisational policy and governance.

Further key questions in this context relate to *who defines* policy, its context, content and goals or functions, within what framework of values and through what types of institutional processes. In West Germany, for example, there seems to be a relatively broad association between rights created by Statute (e.g consultation and information disclosure,) and social peace. The interrelationship between key parties and institutions such as trade unions and employer associations, IR procedures, and processes such as collective bargaining and environmental variables such as the labour legislation of a country, may be critically assessed. Conceptual frameworks for such analysis would require inclusion of variables such as power relations, ideologies, and the values context within and between these interrelated factors. This suggests that the effects of IR structures and processes could be evaluated only in relation to certain defined and desired policies, aims, and that explanations in terms of a single course, could be misleading.[20]

THE POLITICAL ECONOMY AND HUMAN RESOURCE POLICY

The complex array of external and internal pressures affecting policy choices for the business sector, organised labour and the state in South Africa, raises the question of the extent to which pro-active and strategic thinking rather than knee-jerk reactions are becoming more important for decision-makers.

A study of the survival strategies of multinational companies operating in a South American revolutionary climate found that a conscious managerial effort is required to develop adaptive thinking, the ability to redefine strategies and to carve out new relationships with key interest groups.[21] In order to secure long-term goals, visionary leadership for developing resources and forging relationships with interest groups such as trade unions, community and political organisations, becomes fundamentally important. Leadership choices would also reflect a shift from autocratic and coercive modes, to negotiation and participation options.

20 Weiss, M. (1986)
21 Austin, J. and Ickis, J. (1986)

The extension of the industrial franchise to black workers has not assuaged black political aspirations. If anything, the reform process has increased expectations and highlighted perceptions of relative deprivation, with the erosion of apartheid structures. It is no understatement that the policy implications of an environment characterised by heightened uncertainty, economic and political isolation and intensified external and internal pressures for change, created profound challenges, especially as some of these elements are removed.

A resurgence of right-wing militancy has had a deleterious effect on the process of positive change. A legacy of discrimination however, left a residue of mistrust and suspicion, manifested, for example, in boycott politics and an associated resistance to participation in (imposed) government structures at local government level.

Economically, it is vitally important to enhance international competitiveness by maintaining access to modern technology and the latest trends in management practice. In addition, the internal fluidity of funds for local investment without significant foreign investment is a limiting factor for the long-term growth needed to address poverty, create jobs and train and develop a budgeoning population, even with a more favourable international political climate. The geographical isolation of South Africa is in any case a barrier to a highly successful export oriented strategy, notwithstanding the negative effects of isolation from ideas, 'enlightened or progressive values', technology and foreign investment. Whilst it is argued that South Africa was able to get new technology at a price 'through the back door', the additional costs involved sapped the fluidity of the economy given the lack of foreign investment, difficulty in obtaining foreign loans and low productivity. Short-term prosperity created by an inward industrialisation policy may therefore be illusory. (Le Roux, op cit. pp 210–216).

This policy can be referred to as a 'redistribution for political stability strategy' aimed at buying political stability by economic benefits — the idea of creating a pervasive middle class. The difficulty of economic determinism as a viable policy option is that it has distinct limitations in securing the legitimation of the political and economic systems. The latter requires not only economic empowerment but also political rights in order to provide a tangible voice in the formulation of co-ordinated national policy choices, especially to address inequality of income and poverty (over 5,5 million unemployed in 1991).

SANCTIONS AND HUMAN RESOURCE POLICY

The precise impact of economic sanctions on employment levels and job creation is difficult to estimate. According to one study, an estimated one million jobs would have been lost if total sanctions were imposed on South Africa by 1990.[22] If 600 000 black workers were retrenched, compounding current levels of unemployment, 31,9 % of all economically active blacks would then be out of work. Current estimates of unemployment in several parts of South Africa such as the Eastern Cape are of the order of 40 %, although it is difficult to attribute what proportion of unemployment is a consequence of sanctions, aside from specific industries known to have been affected.

Another quite rigorous attempt at quantifying the economic effect of comprehensive sanctions (were they to work), estimates that nearly 40 % of South Africa's exports were vulnerable, with coal being the biggest.[23] The rest, led by precious metals, are either fungible or essential. Loss of half the vulnerable category in 1986, would have amounted to approximately R8,4 billion which, on crude calculations, could

22 Nel, C. (1986a)
23 Lipton, M. (1988)

have reduced GNP by 9 %. Admittedly, however, import savings and adjustment strategies are not taken into account.

Another estimate similarly puts the potential jobless toll at nearly 9,8 million by the end of the next decade, if sanctions had been pervasively effective and economic growth was brought to a halt.[24] This would have dramatic, if not explosive, socio-political effects. Even if South Africa averages 3,1 % a year real economic growth over 1980–2000, there will be over 7,9 million people without full-time employment in the formal sector by 2000. Coal mining has been one of the more seriously affected industries by economic bans on the importation of South African coal in Europe and Scandinavia. Retrenchments in the coal-mining industry threatened to increase the number of jobs to be made redundant from 3 000 in 1987 to almost 13 000 in 1989, because of a dramatic decline in exports. Sanctions by the United States (US), Denmark and France have alone resulted in about 9 million tons a year in losses since 1986. Between 1989 and 1991 over 150 000 jobs were lost in the mining industry due to price decline and recessionary conditions.

South African exports to the United States crashed by 45 % from R2,6 billion in the first half of 1986 to Rl,4 billion in 1987. Exports of uranium products, iron, steel and coal fell from R351 million in the first six months of 1986 to almost zero in the first half of 1987. Imports were unchanged, but South Africa's trade surplus with the United States fell from Rl,4 billion to R200 million.[25]

With economic growth rates averaging at less than 1 % over the past 6 years, the scenario becomes more dramatic with over 400 000 new employees entering the labour market each year. The threat of mass unemployment to societal stability is exacerbated by the inadequate social security system

24 Bethlehem, R. (1988)
25 Leach, I. (1987)

in South Africa. It also underlines the imperative for fair labour practices in respect of dealing with redundancies and considering policies aimed at enhancing job and employment security. There is also a desperate need for employer organisations, trade unions and government to review jointly their macro-policies on unemployment insurance and medical schemes. Unlike other Western countries there is virtually no effective economic cushion in South Africa to alleviate the emotional and material trauma of prolonged periods of unemployment. There is a great danger that in a developing economy, the immediate challenge of merely maintaining employment levels may assume a higher priority than employment creation and the training and development of human resources.

CHANGING INTERNATIONAL PERCEPTIONS

The isolation of South Africa, although on the wane, at economic and other levels has been associated with a moral repugnance of apartheid, frustration at its resilience, and changing international perceptions of South Africa's strategic importance.

This economic isolation is further underlined by the reduction of the number of Sullivan Employment Code signatories from 183 at the end of June 1986 to 92 in 1987.[26] Fifty-two signatory companies withdrew during 1987. In total over 160 US organisations have disinvested from South Africa. Some 520 foreign companies had left South Africa by 1988 (Table 2.1).

Notwithstanding the economic and symbolic impact of these withdrawals, the tendency towards a siege economy in the 1980s could, however, have been said to reflect a diminution of Western influence on IR and HR policy imperatives in

26 Russel, S. (1988)

Table 2.1
Number of foreign companies to leave South Africa by 1988

COUNTRY OF ORIGIN	NUMBER OF COMPANIES
Australia	17
Belgium	1
Canada	21
Finland	2
France	6
FDR Germany	10
Italy	4
Netherlands	3
New Zealand	3
Norway	3
Sweden	6
Switzerland	2
United Kingdom	92
United States	35
TOTAL	520

Note: The list of Companies to have left South Africa was identified by the United Nations Social and Economic Unit.
Source: *Independent Trade Union Guide* 1989, p 121.

organisations. Sanctions nevertheless have been a dramatic symbol of opposition to apartheid, and have played a role in eroding it.

Their social and economic impact has, however, been incremental and attritional. It is arguable whether sanctions per se, were capable of displacing the government. External pressure was, however, an important factor in facilitating the isolationist features of an economy in siege, but as argued by Harry Oppenheimer, the former Chairman of Anglo American, the largest corporation in South Africa, 'the ultimate reason for sanctions lies in the totally unacceptable policies of the South African government'.[27] Ultimately apartheid or institutionalised racial inequality is the major cause of conflict and polarisation in South Africa.[28] This underlines the need for organisational policy to address issues such as upward occupational mobility, management development and fair employment practices.

STATE POLICY AND EMPLOYEE EXPECTATIONS

The extension of the industrial franchise in 1979 to black workers has resulted in an evolving process of democratisation in the workplace. Over 3 000 recognition agreements between employers and trade unions have been negotiated since freedom of labour association was extended legally to black workers in 1979. More than 25 % of the economically active population have joined trade unions. This represents a dramatic increase since 1979, when less than 10 % of the workforce was unionised. The processes of collective bargaining and procedural conciliation have also given black and white people meaningful negotiation experience in industry and commerce, and have contributed significantly to the economic empowerment of black people.

The siege society of the 1980s was a consequence largely of the failure to enter into similar negotiations towards an acceptable political franchise. The resultant crisis and conflict of expectations among black employees rapidly politicised labour relations, with stayaways or demonstration strikes and racial polarisation becoming serious issues. The detention of trade union leaders during the state of emergency erodes prospects for co-operative, democratic processes in the workplace. The government's espoused economic liberalisation policy of moving towards more free enterprise, privatisation,

27 Oppenheimer, H. (1988)
28 Welsh, D. (1988)

less intervention in the economy and negotiated political solutions has not reduced black resentment. For trade unions, job protection and survival policies have become even more vital in this uncertain environment. Ill-conceived privatisation moves would also exacerbate job losses already occurring as a result of sanctions and disinvestment.

STATE POLICY AND HUMAN RESOURCE PRACTICE

Following the intensified politicisation of industrial relations and the trade union movement, in particular, a feature of the move towards a siege state in the 1980s was the restrictive actions taken against the trade union movement. Certain aspects of legislation — the Labour Relations Amendment Act of 1988, introduced measures which were seen by the unions as an attempt to curb their power and erode a limited right to strike.

Restrictions on the activities of the Congress of South African Trade Unions (COSATU) in terms of the Public Safety Act 1953, were imposed in February 1988. Such state action is potentially more dangerous politically to the fabric of South African society, than to developed Western economies. The historical absence of a political franchise, the state of emergency in the latter 1980s and attendant restrictions on political organisations have had the 'functional' effect of socially channelling political aspirations through one of the few remaining viable collective institutions in the black community — the trade unions. State action against the union movement can subvert a significant area for resolving conflict. This tends to lead to greater unorganised conflict and strife with statutory industrial relations dispute conciliation processes and institutions, becoming less effective in regulating conflict.

The implications of state policy on deregulation and privatisation affect the socio-economic position of employees. These have to be carefully considered, particularly the cases of minimum wages and conditions of employment and the possible retention of state ownership of certain corporations in spite of economic deregulation. There therefore seems to be a contradiction between privatisation and deregulation. State control of what it sees as essential industries such as the transport sector could continue even with limited or extensive deregulation.

If the free enterprise system, however, is associated by employees with large-scale retrenchments and poverty, it is not surprising that many black people perceive it to be collaborating with apartheid. A number of surveys on black employee attitudes indicate a strong association between free enterprise and apartheid.[29, 30]

Basic wage rates and conditions of employment are negotiated at industry level in many parts of the South African economy, including sectors with the largest employers of labour — such as iron, steel and mining. Research findings have shown that in the 1980s wage rates were, in over 80 % of the industries concerned, below the minimum living level calculated by the University of South Africa.[31] While many companies do negotiate further improvements at company or plant level, there is no legal obligation to bargain twice on the same item, and most companies do not. Jay Naidoo, the General Secretary of the largest union federation in South Africa, the Congress of South African Trade Unions (COSATU), asks: 'How can we get into a debate on profit sharing when there is no evidence that employers are prepared to concede to our most fundamental demand — a living wage?'[32]

Recently, there has been debate on the removal or reduction of minimum wage increases and exemptions from these

29 Nel, C. (1986a)
30 Beaty, D and Harari, O. (1987)
31 See South African Labour and Development Research Unit Report on Industrial Council Wage Rates, 1987.
32 Naidoo, J. (1986)

rates, on the basis that they may affect the viability of businesses.

Steps have also been taken to relax regulations for small businesses, by exempting businesses which employ fewer than 15 people from minimum wage agreements. The policy implications and consequences of this issue have not been carefully considered. Employee confidence in the market system will, however, also be further eroded if it is associated with a lack of job security.

The political economy: the franchise paradox as a new form of dualism

HR and industrial relations management face the difficult policy issue of seeking a strategic accommodation and relative balance between the efficiency goals of the enterprise's management and workers' goals of institutionalising fair labour practices, basic human rights and structures and processes enabling an equitable power distribution. It has been argued that several factors would influence the form in which workers will in future participate in the South African labour relations system. (Lamprecht op. cit. p 25). The rationale for extending workers' rights encompasses both justice and greater economic effectiveness. A major focus of the 'new'[33] trade unions has been the establishment of a shop-floor worker power base through the union recognition process and the pursuit of a living wage through multi-level collective bargaining.

Although the trade union recognition barrier appears in the main to have been overcome, the goal of a comprehensive living wage has not. While the latter, together with the development of an independent power base, and the protection of job security, remain major objectives of non-racial unions, in the absence of political democracy for their members, the

33 Bendix, D. W. F and Verster, E. (1986)

achievement of a pervasive institutionalisation of industrial rights remains elusive. A key policy question in this regard, is whether defined qualitative values, norms and structures of industrial rights and justice are attainable without the *support of similar values, processes and structures* in the wider society. Some prominent trade union leaders suggest that it would be inopportune to pursue this question at the present time in South Africa. In 1986, Jay Naidoo, the General Secretary of the Congress of South African Trade unions (COSATU), asked: 'How can we get into a debate on profit sharing when there is no evidence that employers are prepared to concede to our most fundamental demand — a living wage?' This view is reinforced by the National Union of Mineworkers' (NUM) call for a living wage at its annual congress in February 1987. The living wage issue is compounded by (and some may consider it substantively associated with) the absence of the political franchise for most South African workers. Camay (1986), of the then Council of Unions of South Africa (CUSA) and the Azanian Confederation of Trade Unions (AZACTU), argued that 'one cannot talk about participation in the economic sector when there is still discrimination on a political level'. He voiced suspicion at the notion of workers accepting a joint stakeholding. There appear, therefore, to be reservations regarding the intentions and objectives of the proponents of some form of social partnership between management and labour based on co-operative relationships, and extending the area of common interests. Although generalisation is difficult, for several reasons, including a fear of undermining trade union independence and eroding their power base and worker rights, trade unions in South Africa would seem to prefer to advance their interests through the interest-based processes of collective bargaining. A widely successful and institutionalised pursuit of the economic/productivity goals of HR management is seemingly inhibited in the absence of a legitimated political democracy, a pervasive living wage, and coercive action by the state against trade unions.

This paradox highlights the dualism and juxtaposition of economic enfranchisement and political disenfranchisement. The 1988 amendments to the Labour Relations Act elicited renewed suspicions of collusion between the state and business. Security restrictions on trade unions and their leaders undermine the prospects for institutionalising conflict and developing bilateral employer and union consensus models at industry and national levels, with the exception of the recent accord on labour legislation between COSATU, NACTU, SACCOLA and the Department of Manpower.

The validity of the notion of interposing business between labour and the state is, however, arguable. If there is a hardening of attitudes and polarised positions. (There is some evidence, though, of a greater tolerance in racial attitudes, especially in the work-place.) Socio-political variables, such as the question of power distribution referred to previously, a high degree of political fluidity, fundamental structural inequalities in South African society, the apparent fluidity of some contemporary trade union alliances, unresolved philosophical and strategic questions in the trade union movement and disunity amongst employer organisations, are limiting variables regarding the development of relatively enduring pervasive democratic institutions in South Africa. This process is more likely to occur effectively in the context of a restructuring of the socio-economic and political fabric of South African society.

THE LEGITIMACY ISSUE

In his classic work nearly four decades ago, Barnard (1948) argued that 'it is impossible to get to the root of HR relations or understand labour troubles or successes on the unrealistic assumption that economic motives exclusively govern'. The achievement of socio-political goals and worker rights of equity and fair labour practices within a democratic framework are related by necessity to behaviour which is also of a co-operative mode. There 'is no question of democracy in an aggregate of hostile, opposed, isolated or non-co-operative societies'.[34] Democracy in the business context is essentially associated with a *system of governance relating to power sharing*, decisions and formal processes. It is arguable whether fair labour practices are achievable by the legislature or distributive collective bargaining relations alone, or whether other factors including formal structures and the quality of informal, direct relations between managers and workers, are not also requirements in the effective democratisation of the daily social relations of industrial and commercial activity.

In their penetrating analysis, Adam and Moodley (1986) assert that the notion of legitimacy may, however, be overrated as a determinant for stability or strife. They suggest that even with the absence or loss of legitimacy, stability and compliance may occur through coercion or co-optation. It is however, problematic whether business organisations could sustain long-term viability without the relative consent of employees, their intrinsic commitment to the policies and goals of an organisation and the legitimation of managerial authority. In contemporary South Africa, the erosion of unilateral and arbitrary managerial authority appears to be occurring in the context of the influence of increasing unionisation, industrial court rulings and progressive IR and HR policies. Yet, there remains a very delicate and fragile relationship between the degree of state control and its influence on the regulation of industrial conflict.

A vital prerequisite for the institutionalisation of industrial rights in a pervasive economic and social context, is the process of securing formal consent and legitimacy of both man-

34 Barnard, C. (1948)

agement and labour. State intervention and attempts at controlling actors in the industrial arena, is an important factor in the current divisiveness and polarisation of the South African body politic. This makes the long-term legitimation of negotiated and legally created industrial rights paradoxically both more necessary and yet illusive. A degree of formal bilateral democratisation seems to be evolving given the creation of certain rights though unfair labour practice jurisprudence and the extension of collective bargaining since the granting of the industrial franchise to black employees. Sound principles of fairness have begun to evolve in the policy and practice of disciplinary action, grievance resolution, union recognition and redundancy procedures. Yet South Africa has the paradox of adopting most aspects of a sophisticated labour code without the political climate needed to make it work smoothly. One cause of South Africa's 'legitimation crisis' is however, the proclamation of industrial democracy without having first established political democracy — which has preceded economic conflict regulation in Western states.[35]

In most industrial societies there is a relative harmony between the political and industrial sectors. The economic system also reflects the ethics of the political system in which it operates. In South Africa, the disunity between the political and industrial relations systems is taking an inevitable toll on industrial peace(Lamprecht, op. cit. p. 24).

The failure to provide a concomitant political and civic franchise and attendant rights of freedom of political association, 'organisational membership, free and open political activity, constituency-building and mandate-seeking processes, has been associated with conflicts of expectations, heightened philosophical differences in the labour movement, and a deeper alienation of the black community. This raises a policy dilemma for organisations in seeking an extension of

35 Adam, H. and Moodley, K. (1986)

democratic ideals within the economic arena, and beyond this sector, to the broader social milieu. Given the suspicions and highly critical perspectives of the black work force in respect of the dissonance between management's espoused policies and objectives, and actual behaviour, the consequences of a failure of business to seek both co-operative opportunities and social partnership and a distancing of itself from the apartheid system in the eyes of black labour and prominent political organisations, can exacerbate polarisation. This risks weakening managerial legitimacy and opportunities for establishing acceptable policies. The political disenfranchisement of the majority of South African workers and the attendant absence of a widely legitimised political democracy, has been an important interactive variable. It paradoxically inhibited the potential for successful synergy of both democratic structures and processes in the work environment, and HR policies seeking economic, productivity-focussed participation, and yet created a more insistent need for their co-development in a 'post-apartheid' society.

Political legitimation: role of the state

The state has an important impact on the policy and organisational cohesiveness of employers, employer organisations and the labour movement. Employers and their organisations are weaker in relation to the state, and their cohesiveness lower in countries in which democratic government is absent. Similarly, the curtailment and attempts at control of trade unions by the state can reduce the prospects for institutionalising conflict, effective bilateralism and joint employer/trade union policies and initiatives for change.

South Africa's ongoing socio-political crisis is partially a function of the natural conflict between groups with competing interests and ideologies; but more profound is the absence of legitimately perceived political structures. While policies acknowledging recognition of trade unions and the mutual interdependence of industrial relations parties, this recognition of interdependence has not occurred between actors in the political arena.[36] An industrial relations model based on the pluralist tenets of freedoms of association, and expression, and workers' rights to organise and negotiate, is necessary for a democratic society. In the absence of the latter, industrial relations policies and processes such as collective bargaining offer a political safety-valve for frustration and anger. However, the prospects of extending the principles and practices of an industrial relations policy model into the wider society are muted by the circumstances under which many trade unions struggle. A corporatist policy of social partnership between employers and labour, while reflecting a mutuality of goals and acknowledgement of a near balance of power between these parties, cannot however, detract from the strong desire to retain the independent agency of the non-racial labour movement in spite of potential state action attempting to weaken labour organisations. The somewhat utopian idea that industrial relations could be an island of peace in a sea of political turmoil, is therefore unrealistic, given the political and economic fluidity in South Africa.

Institutionalised racial discrimination and structural inequalities which remain endemic in the social fabric of South African society cannot be divorced and externalised from the policies, attitudes, values and ideologies prevalent in enterprises. The search for fairness in labour practices, equal opportunity, and social justice at work, is interdependently and substantively associated with the institutionalisation of these precepts in the extra-organisational social milieu. The historical absence of political democracy and the contingencies of a state of emergency and a siege economy, reinforced the notion

36 Jowell, K. (1988)

of the inseparability of politics, and economics. The state of emergency in the 1980s 'amplified the state's involvement in industrial relations'[37] for example, by the actions against the Congress of South African Trade Unions (COSATU) during 1987 and 1988. Direct interventionist and coercive action against parties in the industrial arena (e.g the idea of requiring employers to perform the state's function of rent collection) and institutions, obfuscates perceptions of independence between he parties. This tends (1) to undermine worker perceptions of collusion between the state and employers, and (2) to reinforce trade union concerns about co-optative HR policies and initiatives. An associated climate of mistrust and suspicion is inhibitive of the requisite conditions for creating a democratic IR context, and requisite fair employment policies and practices.

SOME CONCLUSIONS

Serious policy options cannot view political change and economic change as mutually exclusive or of different priority. The political will necessary for the state to press further change should not be constrained by the populist and party political gains made by the ultra-right and its embracement of a siege strategy.

This could further a clearer prioritisation of national agenda items with security, economic and socio-political change considerations occurring in that respective order, rather than the parallel strategy of reform and security of the early 1980s.

A still most promising arena for democratic and co-operative HR policies, and fostering of the values of fairness and equity is that between management and labour. This suggests that extra-parliamentary inter-racial negotiation at leadership level occurs in the industrial context. It is here where the new

37 Cunningham, P. (1987)

balance in power relations between business and labour reduces the prospects of co-optive politics and a fundamental erosion of created rights.

However, popular references to the 'business community' imply the existence of a co-ordinated group capable of acting together. In reality components of that community are often in vigorous market competition. This may constrain companies from co-operating in employers organisations under certain circumstances. Thus employers and their organisations are generally not united in their overall business perspectives and industrial relations policies.[38] Employer fragmentation also reflects differing perceived interests in terms of ideology, and ethnicity.

The policy option of evolving a pervasive process of creating rights and a culture of fair employment practices 'from below' presupposes the following:

- greater unity of purpose amongst employer organisations (which is currently lacking) with such unity obtaining clear change mandates from members;
- that the organised business sector proactively endeavours to address the impediment of reactionary attitudes prevalent amongst many members; and
- further impetus towards unity within the trade union movement and a willingness even tentatively, to develop a bilateral forum with organised business. Such a social partnership would need to consider developing joint tactical, if not strategic policies, beyond specific ad hoc issues; (given the unlikelihood of consensus in the short-term between business and labour on a preferred socio-economic system.)

The 'democracy-from-below thesis' holds that the values and norms of democracy — a 'democratic culture' could evolve

38 Finnemore, M. and Van der Merwe, R. (1989)

organically within and between key societal actors, such as the non-racial labour movement and business actors and that the presence of democratic structures at the political constitutional level, while strongly desirable, need not be a prerequisite for the development of democratic values and structures from below.

In the context of debate on political economic scenarios, bilateral negotiations between organised business and labour could begin to negotiate some degree of *social consensus* on and a strategy for influencing the state on the following issues:

- a means for providing a more rational and fair reallocation of economic resources and, therefore, the issue of access to and distribution of power;
- providing basic rights and tangible benefits such as an improved quality of life and socio-economic development, including employment, greater job and employment security, a living wage framework, upgraded and comfortable accommodation, equal non-racial education and training, social and occupational mobility, and medical and retirement care;
- dealing with the question of a fair distribution of created wealth.
- providing a new political and social order which is free of racial discrimination and oppression;
- developing a greater commonality of societal values and symbols; but also creatively managing the independence and diversity of interest groups in the work-place; and
- creating a labour law framework acceptable to both employers and labour.

The expectations and demands of the majority of South Africans will continue to present a vital challenge and opportunity for the union movement and HR and IR specialists, business and the state to formulate innovative policy directions and strategies. The political solutions reached through negotiation should acknowledge sound economic policies for:

- advancing work-place rights through fostering collective bargaining;
- achieving enlightened HR practices, fairness and equity within and perhaps even beyond the workplace;
- striving for a framework of mutual values and symbols; and
- increasing economic growth through joint industry analysis and co-determination of priorities, for example, the recent mining industry initiative.

Free and independent collective bargaining is an index of the extent of societal corporatism and political pluralism. Collective bargaining is more a feature of market and social market economies than of the planned political economies now in crisis in Eastern Europe. It is therefore in employers' interests to foster collective bargaining and negotiate a *modus vivendi* in appropriate bargaining levels.

3

ESPOUSED AND OPERATIONAL POLICY: A QUESTION OF FIT

INTRODUCTION

The formulation of strategic approaches to IR and HR management has assumed greater importance, particularly in business environments characterised by rapid change and uncertainty.[1] Strategic approaches to IR and HR management also tend to become more prominent as these imperatives gain legitimacy as a general management concept. Strategic operationalisation of IR and HR policy as organisationally generic, requires an identification of variables associated with policy legitimation.

This raises complex questions regarding:

1. the effective matching of IR and HR policies and organisational culture;
2. the nature of the relationship between culture and policy;
3. the extent to which these are reflective of common, congruent; or
4. the operational effectiveness of policy implementation in terms of appropriate patterns and processes of leadership, motivation and reward.

A methodology for approaching these issues requires consideration of the extent to which IR and HR strategies are considered a consequence of business decisions, or a necessary input into the formulation of corporate values and business strategies. This chapter focuses on the nature of the relation-

1 Thurley, K. and Wood, S. (1983a)

ship between IR and HR policies and business strategies, and particularly the question of implementation. Certain issues associated with formulating a strategic approach to IR and HR management are also considered, given that particular paradigms may be subject to different contextual factors and therefore different processes of operationalisation. In this context, a review of research findings on variables associated with reducing the distance between espoused and operational policies, is presented.

CONCEPTUAL DEFINITION

A policy may be described as a set or system of principles by appeal to which we can answer the question, as to what should be done in a certain set of circumstances (Figure 3). It reflects a system of principles which guide managerial interaction with employees, and which communicate the following to employees at all levels:

1. the organisation's philosophy or core values about its employees,
2. 'acceptable' and unacceptable behavioural standards, and
3. reference points for establishing the organisation's approach to employees (for example, the principle of freedom of association).

Difficulties faced by most companies are less with the formulation of an industrial relations policy, than its integration with business strategy, effective implementation, and legitimation by employees.

POLICY

Broad statement of organisation's espoused philosophy and principles regarding employees.

STRATEGY

An action plan to operationalise espoused values and principles linked to business objectives.

OBJECTIVES

Enhancing the organisation's effectiveness through sound management of people.

Resolving conflicts in a manner acceptable to both parties

Developing a sense of cooperation between both parties

STRUCTURES

Formal systems, procedures, or institutions within which interaction between the parties takes place. Personnel systems include selection and recruitment, job grading and evaluation, and performance appraisal procedures.

PROCESSES

The type and quality of interaction between the parties

CONTENT

The issues that arise in the relationship between the parties

Figure 3.1

Industrial relations and human resource policy framework

ESPOUSED POLICY

Brewster and Richbell[2] distinguish between espoused and operational policies. They posit that the espoused policy is the way top-level management would like the organisation to treat employees. It therefore reflects the stated corporate philosophy regarding employees. Methods of expressing this philosophy include a comprehensive formal policy statement or code of conduct, mission statements and policy handbooks.

When policies are formalised it is the espoused policy or senior managerial intent which is committed to paper. It is argued that espoused policies frequently fail to be internalised and implemented by managers and supervisors who are responsible for managing people in the organisation.

OPERATIONAL POLICY

The action or behaviour of managers and supervisors according to a set of defined principles is referred to as an operational policy.

The operational policy may be defined as the way that senior management orders various and sometimes conflicting policy objectives, monitors outcomes and rewards or takes corrective and sometimes punitive action against line management for meeting or failing to meet the priorities determined.

Espoused and operational policies may, however, conflict with each other, or with other priorities. It is vital, therefore, for industrial relations policies not only to be integrated into the strategic objectives of the organisation, but for these objectives to consider industrial relations variables in order to achieve optimum congruence between organisational, individual, and collective objectives, and the development of employees and their capabilities.

2 Brewster, C. and Richbell, S. (1982)

- The organisation culture and business strategies may be in juxtaposition to the values contained in the policy, thereby thwarting its implementation.
- The de facto organisational reward and authority structures are not congruent with espoused corporate values, and hence policy performance is frustrated.
- Job performance objectives and criteria of success are inappropriate to espoused corporate values.
- Other work priorities are rewarded by the individual's superior or manager and IR and HR policy performance is compromised.
- Anxiety leading to avoidance behaviour, and a preference for dealing with technical rather than industrial relations and attendant conceptually ambiguous issues.
- Inadequate monitoring and evaluation of the policy's effectiveness, for example by audits, analysis of employees' grievances and other indicators of disruptive conflict and dissatisfaction such as excessive absenteeism, labour turnover and unresolved disputes.
- Inappropriate managerial behaviour e.g. authoritarianism

Figure 3.2
Barriers to operationalising policy

A strategy which seeks to develop and articulate desired organisation values should however, consider (1) the notion of conflict inherency in IR and (2) that strategies aimed at co-opting employees into a managerial ethos tend to ignore the fact that organisations are:

1. not a harmony of interests reflecting common values;
2. not inherently democratic bodies which institutionalise human rights and fairness.

In the context of policy implementation, conflicts of interest may occur when objectives regarding production and profit targets generate pressure on costs, and hence the job security of employees. This may tend to result in heightened uncertainty and reduced commitment to the organisation. Research in South Africa, regarding the formalisation of IR/HR policies suggests that such formalisation may facilitate a reduction in uncertainty, particularly if negotiated with representative employee organisations such as trade unions.[3]

Frequently, the espoused policy reflects the good 'people management intent' while the operational policy reflects a preoccupation with goal achievement, such as optimisation of production output. The operational policy may therefore, more accurately signal the de facto organisational climate and practices.

Definitions of policy give weight to top-level strategic decision-making which is intended to give consistency to the actions taken toward particular goals. Thus Brewster and Richbell (1982) refer to IR policy as assisting management to establish and maintain a coherent and consistent framework for the conduct of IR. Even where such a policy is not manifested as a written document, there could exist a shared set of principles and expectations on the part of management about IR and HR practices which guide managerial behaviour.[4] As

3 Hall, R. (1983a)
4 Horwitz, F. M. (1986: 87–92)

with business strategy in general, IR and HR policy is not always as coherent as definitions would suggest. Thurley and Wood (1983) suggest that there exists a continuum in organizations, from the continuous policy development and strategic planning which is acted on in an orderly way, to the minute-by-minute decisions taken by managers in response to pressures and with the sole objective of personal survival. To the extent that managers 'evolve a consistent approach to medium- and long-term goals out of their reactions to the issues selected and thrust upon them', even 'muddling through' could be said to constitute some form of strategy.

VARIABLES ASSOCIATED WITH POLICY PERFORMANCE

The extent of effective operationalisation of espoused policies may be associated with several variables. These may include the choice whether to centralise or decentralise decision-making which, in turn, tends to be influenced by organisational structures, internal control mechanism and corporate structure.[5] Organisational size also appears to be a variable relating to the proximity or separation of strategic and operational decision-making. In large organisations, such decision-making processes may be more clearly separated between corporate and divisional operations.

The extent of congruence between operational decisions and long-term strategy may also be a function of the strength or dominance of a value system in an organisation, and particularly the degree to which a shared or common superordinate value system prevails without creating dysfunctional incongruence with personal values of employees. Values homogenisation, as an organisational strategy, may raise important ethical and moral questions regarding the legitimacy of

5 Marginson, P. and Purcell, J. (1986a)

both espoused values and the process of implementing them. The accommodation of a diversity of values in the context of seeking an overriding commonality of specific superordinate values is a fundamental characteristic of democratic institutions.

While there may ultimately not be a complete alignment between espoused and operational policies, it is the extent of incongruence, between them which could be considered as dysfunctional. For this dysfunctional incongruence to be minimised, it is contended that a shift is required for a closer alignment and a more harmonious relationship between IR and HR policies, procedures and the value system of the organisation.[6]

Successful policy implementation may be retarded by inadequate attention given to the question of definition (Brewster and Richbell 1983). Some authors argue that 'policy and strategy' may have common elements (Davie et al, 1987). Thurley and Wood[7] state that HR strategies refer to long-term policies which are developed by the management of the organisation in order to preserve or change the procedures, practice or results of people-management activities. The definition and actualisation of core organisational values and mission is fundamental to the formulation of business strategy and the strategic direction of the organisation. This raises the question whether policies are underpinned and driven by desired values, and to what extent these values, the

culture of the organisation, and its reward systems are philosophically harmonious or incongruent. Effective operationalisation and legitimation of policies may therefore be a function of these variables.

IR and HR policies reflect a framework of principles and standards. Strategic decision choices of objective setting and

6 Davie, B., Mitchell, L., and Scott, D. (1987a: 11–12)
7 Thurley, K. and Wood, S. (1983a)

behaviour in organisations may be determined by both the defined organisational values considered desirable and strategic decisions taken within the context of a framework of IR and sound people-management principles. The integration of IR and HR policy and business strategy, therefore, requires a mutuality of values and goals. The second requirement is that of legitimation by employees in an organisation. Such legitimation will be a function of the absence of coercive of manipulative forms of policy performance, imposed processes of implementation, and the extent to which policy principles and espoused organisational values are shared by employees. Important fundamental issues in this regard include the following:

1. Relative congruence between the principles contained in a policy and business objectives. Alternatively stated, does business strategy formulation actively seek the incorporation of industrial relations and HR principles?
2. If desired organisational values are a defined fundamental component of business strategy, these values and policy principles need to be relatively harmonious and congruent; for example, a defined value system may reflect a unitarist ideology, focusing predominantly on teamwork and the formulation of strategies for managing without trade unions, whereas an IR and HR policy may embody pluralist values and principles, such as the right of freedom of association and promotion of negotiation.
3. If espoused values and policy are congruent, the extent to which the organisational culture is supportive of performance of these values and is actively developed and changed to facilitate values operationalisation.
4. The degree to which espoused organisational values and IR and HR policies are 'lived' by the leadership behaviour and styles of managers and supervisors and not solely

statements of intent. Is their behaviour and action perceived as giving credence to these policies?

5. Associated with 4 above, is the question regarding the reward system in respect of both psychological and substantive compensation being conducive to facilitating IR policy performance. This would necessitate consideration of HR systems such as selection and recruitment, performance appraisal and development, promotion and potential assessment policies and procedures and human resource development, to be 'values-driven' and therefore strategically and not merely functionally orientated. These conventional HR policies and systems become, in this context, more effectively integrated with specific objectives and desired behaviours which are rooted in a framework for reflecting, inculcating and reinforcing the core values and strategies of the organisation.
6. Common values may be more attainable under circumstances of a power balance or near power balance, than in a context of a gross power imbalance. The effective operationalisation of espoused policies cannot therefore be considered in a vacuum. The internal organisational context and external environmental demands and strategic issues arising therefrom, suggest a holistic, generalist, and less functionally orientated conception of IR and HR policy.[8]

INDUSTRIAL RELATIONS AND HUMAN RESOURCE POLICY RESEARCH IN SOUTH AFRICA

Policy formulation

A relative paucity of research exists in the area of human resources and industrial relations policy in South Africa.

8 Evan, p. (1984)

Research findings in the United Kingdom reveal that 84 % of respondents claim that their organisations had a policy regarding the management of employees. Just over half indicated that these were formally documented.[9] Bluen, Godsell and Malherbe[10] conducted a survey of the extent of in-company IR policies, structures and practices in mining, manufacturing and construction companies in South Africa. Eighty-two per cent of the respondent companies had formal IR/HR policies. A similar study, but wider in scope was conducted by Nel.[11] This survey found that 87 % of the organisations had some sort of IR policy, either written or unwritten.

However, only 50,5 % had a formal written policy. These results suggest a lower degree of formalised policies than those of Bluen et al. This could be due to methodological differences, as the surveys were conducted in different organisations, and the scope of the studies varied. Nel warns that an enterprise that has no formal policy could be 'subject to a large measure of potential conflict arising from a lack of guidelines for executing such a policy effectively'. (op. cit. p. 28). He concludes that a well designed and workable IR policy is associated with the establishment of sound IR structures. Poorly developed policies could lead to acrimonious labour and management relations and could place a severe strain on in-house labour relations.

Hall[12] also examined company policy in a variety of South African organisations. He found that in 1983, 73 % of the companies studied had formal written policy statements, whereas in 1980, only 51 % had such formal policy statements. It is also likely that the number of companies with formal IR policies will have increased since the studies were conducted.

9 Marginson, P. (1986a)
10 Bluen, S., Godsell, G. and Malherbe, J. (1982).
11 Nel, P. (1984)
12 Hall, R. (1983a)

These results suggest that there is a growing awareness of the importance of formal IR/HR policies.

THE IMPLEMENTATION OF POLICY

In the context of rapid unionisation since the principle of freedom of labour association was granted to Black workers by the Industrial Conciliation Amendment Act in 1979, the establishment of an Industrial Court, its increased use by labour, and a turbulent and uncertain socio-political environment, companies in South Africa have become increasingly aware of the need to formulate and espouse human resource and IR policies. Two interrelated issues have become more relevant:First, consideration of the extent to which these policies are operationally effective and secondly, how such effectiveness can be evaluated. The implementation of a policy is not carried out by senior management, but rather by line management and supervisors in their daily interaction with employees. Bluen et al., found that operational line management plays the most important role in decision performance of human resource and IR matters. Industrial relations and HR managers play the role of facilitator and advisor by giving advice and assistance to those responsible for managing employees.

One of the reasons why line managers may not practice sound IR and human resource management is the inadequate support and guidance of top management. As previously argued, other reasons for the ineffective implementation of policies by managers include insufficient training in managing people, conflicting priorities, time demands, organisational constraints such as an organisational climate which is unsupportive of progressive policies, and a lack of appraisal and reward of IR and management skills. Another reason cited by Napier and Peterson (1984) is the delegation of IR management responsibility to the HR department. This statement is supported by the research findings of Hall and Nel who found that in most cases the IR function is performed by the HR department.

ATTITUDES TO POLICIES

Will[13] studied the attitudes of workers, supervisors and management to HR policy statements. He hypothesised that the propensity to believe in the sincerity of policy statements would tend to decline as one descended the organisational hierarchy. He focused on a single component of HR policy, namely safety policy, in order to test this hypothesis. The results of the survey supported the hypothesis that statistically significant differences in attitude towards safety policy statements are related to differences in organisational level. Will concluded that HR policy statements are often not perceived as wholly sincere. This findings adds further support to Brewster and Richbell's (1982) postulate that espoused policies do not always become effectively operational.

In an exploratory research project conducted in a large multi-national manufacturing organisation, employing 1 400 people in the South African chemical industry, it was proposed that perceived incongruence between espoused and operational policies will increase progressively down the organisational hierarchy, from senior management to blue collar factory employees (Horwitz and Knipscheer 1987). The espoused policy was ascertained by a documentation analysis of company policy statements relating to two areas of policy, namely: employee advancement and redundancy. Ten policy statements relating to these two areas were isolated. Questions were formulated on the basis of these statements in order to determine perceptions of the practised operational policy. These questions were posed during eight semi-structured in-depth group interviews. The eight groups included: Senior

13 Will, M. (1981)

managers; foremen/supervisors, artisans, two groups of trade union representatives, and three groups of blue collar factory employees. Each group consisted of eight participants.

In this research, with its relatively small sample, particularly in respect of blue collar employees, and the varied nature of the sample organisationally, convenience sampling, a non-random method of sampling, was preferred. In convenience sampling, data is collected from available population elements at the time of sampling. Dense sampling (over 50 % of the population) was applied in respect of senior managers.[14]

Not surprisingly, the results derived from an analysis of the group interviews indicated that a larger disparity between espoused and operational company policy is perceived at blue collar factory employee level than at senior management and supervisory levels. The findings seem to support those of Watts[15] and other researchers who have studied the implementation of codes of conduct.

Will (1981) suggests that the credibility gap between management and workers is widened as a result of insufficient communication between the two groups. This communication problem is influenced by the infrequency of personal contact, and the social distance between management and workers. This may be associated with a feeling of alienation among workers. As a result of this, workers are less likely to trust the intentions of management. This may result in certain misconceptions of both espoused operational policy intent and rationality by workers. It may be possible that espoused policy is indeed being practised, but this is not always perceived to be so by workers. However, poor communication may be only one pertinent variable impeding policy implementation. These difficulties are exacerbated in hierarchical organisations with a multiplicity of job grades and status levels.

14 See Denzin, N. (1973), for an evaluation of these sampling methods.
15 Watts, J. (1985)

Flatter organisational structures facilitate greater ease of communication and a diminution of social distance between groups. Another result of the social distance between management and workers is that an alienated employee is aware of his/her lack of ability to influence company policies affecting the work situation. Hence, certain policies may be espoused, but these are not necessarily fully implemented. As a result, workers may experience a form of cognitive dissonance which can lead to increased dissatisfaction.[16]

These conclusions appear to concur with those of Will (1981) and Brewster and Richbell (1982) in the United Kingdom, who found that policies were frequently not implemented in spite of their formal endorsement by the organisation. This was found to be associated with employee dissatisfaction and insecurity, since the sincerity of the policy was perceived wanting. The dysfunctional disparity between espoused and operational policies may reflect employees' perceptions that a different value system prevails in parts of the organisation which appears inconsistent with espoused policies and values. It is in this sense that the operationalisation of strategically orientated policies becomes problematic and the legitimacy of both the policy and the process of implementation may be questioned, either overtly or subtly by partial withdrawals of labour, such as a go-slow or work-to-rule.

ORGANISATIONAL VARIABLES

While organizational size and the degree of centralisation or decentralisation of IR, HR and business decision-making may be variables associated with inadequate policy operationalisation, this incongruence may also be associated with enduring attitudinal prejudices and discriminatory practices, which particularly in the South African context, are associated with

16 Festinger, L. (1957a)

the maintenance of prevailing positions of power. This is often reflected in a plethora of job grades and levels in organizations with access to advancement/upward occupational mobility from semi-skilled and unskilled jobs to higher level positions being difficult and slow for the predominantly Black occupants of these positions. This variable was indeed found by Horwitz and Knipscheer to be substantively associated with negative perceptions of the effective and fair operationalisation of employee advancement. The fact that the majority of workers were unionised seems to reveal little significance in respect of attitudes to espoused and operational policies, since non-union employees held similar attitudes.

Davie et al.[17] argue that the identification of policy with strategy enables one to comment on an issue which Ansoff regards as one of the 'key characteristics' of what he terms 'administrative decisions'. These decisions are concerned with structuring the resources of the firm in such a way that creates the maximum performance potential and their key characteristics are the 'conflict between strategy and operations' and the 'conflict between individual and institutional objectives.'

Thus, before even considering the specific problems of IR and HR policy implementation in South Africa, it is clear that the implementation of any long-term strategy involves considerable difficulty, since personal/value and organizational/output variables place a real constraint on line managers in enacting strategic objectives. 'Considering the very real constraints facing line management, in terms of maximizing outputs, it is not surprising that they sometimes 'undermine longterm goals.'[18] It may further be argued that, in the absence of effective integration of an IR and HR policy and strategy with the overall business strategy, these strategies could contradict one another, making their legitim-

17 Davie, B. et al. (1987)
18 Purcell, J. (1983)

ation particularly difficult. Another reason for the divergence between operational and espoused policies is that 'many managers are also unclear as to what the espoused policies are' (Brewster and Richbell, 1983).

Though there are naturally implications as regards training and communication, this may also be due to an espoused policy which is too wide to admit rational interpretation, and too vague to be meaningfully implemented.

According to research conducted by Davie et. al.,[19] the intra-organisational political dimension is also a determinant of whether any strategy will be implemented. Political opposition to a strategy in an organisation could result in its modification, or even abandonment. Conflict between functional and line staff may add a problematic dimension to sectional conflicts of interest.

Policies cannot, however, cover all eventualities; they can either be too narrow, i.e. specific to certain circumstances, or too broad, ie 'general statements of intent'. While the operational policy may be less clear, it is certainly apt to be more dynamic. Nevertheless, if an effort is to be made to

prevent short-term decisions taken in the 'heat of battle' from cancelling each other out (Thurley and Wood, 1983), it is necessary to have an understanding of potential points of divergence.

An important component of effective strategy implementation is the will, pervasively throughout the organisation, that it should be implemented. However, such a 'will' may be a necessary but not sufficient condition. Implementation of strategy will always be problematic. Some of the problems are 'rooted in organization of production and the processes of recruitment to management, its lack of training, the conflict between functional and line staff and the way top management makes decisions'. (Thurley and Wood, 1983). Thus,

19 Davie, B. et al (1987 a)

changes in organisational structure, culture, recruitment, reward and appraisal systems, employee development and broad political changes are necessary if top management sees the need to draw espoused and operational policies closer. The 'degree of divergence depends on the extent to which changes in espoused policy are accompanied by complementary changes in the organization's value system' (Brewster and Richbell, 1983).

Implementation determinents

Davie et.al. (op.cit. pp. 20–50), sought to identify in three disparate groups of companies, the relative importance of determinants which impact on the extent to which espoused policies are effectively operationalised and become part of the organisational value system. It is argued that determinants which comprise the value system may be reformulated, and may change over time, and thus provide the superordinate basis for the espoused IR policy. Their findings lend support to the importance of establishing a framework of values which are reflected in specific determinants and are reinforced by procedures. The determinants identified included: selection and recruitment processes, job descriptions, training techniques and communication systems which impact on the value system as interaction between key actors in the organisation occurs. A second category of determinants which were substantively associated with the aforementioned include performance evaluation, sanctions/rewards and feedback on performance, which accentuates the espoused values of the organisation by rewarding appropriate behaviour and sanctioning that which is considered inappropriate. This information, together with feedback channels on IR practices provides opportunities to centrally reformulate policy if and when necessary.

The values of the espoused policy will according to Davie et al., either reinforce the operational actions, or allow digressions from the policy. Although a divergence may occur, the closer espoused policy and values of the company are, the closer will the espoused and operational policy be. Realistically however, even when a conscious attempt is made to bring espoused and operational policies into line, it is unlikely that those responsible for them would be able in practice to assess their effects so minutely that there would be no disparity between them' (Brewster and Richbell, 1983).

Factors associated with policy legitimation

- Effective matching of IR/HR policies and organisational culture;
- nature of the relationship between culture and policy;
- extent to which these are reflective of common, congruent or divergent values; and
- operational effectiveness of policy implementation in terms of appropriate processes of leadership, motivation, reward and the achievement of both relational and organisational outcomes.

BUSINESS AND INDUSTRIAL RELATIONS/HUMAN RESOURCE POLICY CONSIDERATIONS

An evaluation of the studies discussed in the previous section seems to suggest that the following factors, inter alia, require consideration, when seeking to develop a values based industrial relations policy and strategy:

- The nature of conflict, as well as superordinate, common goals within organisations.
- Organisation culture and structure including the locus and extent of centralisation or decentralisation of business decision-making, authority and responsibility.

- ❑ Power as a variable relating to intergroup (collective) and inter-personal relations.
- ❑ Types of authority within organisations (such as sapiential, traditional, coercive and referent authority). Where management authority is not perceived as legitimate by employees and supervisors, the internalisation of the philosophy and content of policies will be undermined.
- ❑ Variations in managerial style which may be situationally appropriate or inappropriate.
- ❑ Plurality of interest groups with common and differing values, interests and ideologies.

The main strategic objective regarding IR and HR policy is for espoused policies to become operationally legitimated in order to achieve organisational effectiveness, competitive advantage and sound employment relations. Such policies, if they are to be effective, must be integrated with the following:

- ❑ Extrinsic and intrinsic reward systems which reinforce the organisation's philosophy and the values and principles contained in the policies.
- ❑ Job descriptions, performance and potential appraisal systems which incorporate key industrial relations management responsibilities, together with conceptual ability, technical and financial responsibilities.
- ❑ Recruitment and selection procedures which establish selection criteria compatible with desired people values, such as equal opportunity, merit and fairness.
- ❑ A pluralist philosophy which acknowledges freedom of association, and procedures which institutionalise conflict and the principles of freedom of association, equity and fairness, merit and participation of employee representatives such as shop stewards, in the monitoring of the application of company policies.

It is submitted that line managers seek not only a descriptive knowledge of company policies but also their essential meaning relative to the substantive and procedural performance of their jobs. Given the inherency of conflicts of interest within the organisational context, the imperative of industrial relations policy implementation nevertheless necessitates a broader understanding and internalisation of the organisation's philosophy and objectives, facilitating a congruence or sharing of corporate, collective means and interpretations, and those of the individual within the organisation. Prerequisites for the effective introduction of industrial relations/HR policy include:

- relating the policy to and integrating it with strategic organisational policies and objectives.-securing senior- and middle-management commitment by involving them in policy and strategy formulation. (They must see the need and benefits of the policy);
- allaying fears that these policies may undermine the authority of supervisors (supervisors' possible concerns should be addressed prior to designing training programmes);
- a needs analysis based on the principles of the policy should ideally be done within the context of consultancy-based organisational development initiatives (training is not, however, a panacea for all organisational problems); and
- a relationship with employees and trade unions where trust has been earned within the context of an organisation culture and an industrial relations climate which is compatible with the espoused policies and the institutionalisation of employee rights.

Strategic IR and HR management entails the deliberate alignment of IR/HR plans and actions to the business/ organisational strategy of the firm in order to ensure appropriate human behaviours as required by this strategy. The concern is therefore with both the organisational context and the detailed content of procedures and systems.

ACHIEVING CONGRUENCE BETWEEN ESPOUSED AND OPERATIONAL POLICY

1. Policy and implementation strategies are formulated *participatively* and initiated at the highest levels with will and sensitivity to methodological process.
2. Its initiators accept responsibility and tolerance for a degree of divergence, and therefore develop evaluation systems which facilitate legitimated cooperation, rather than reluctant compliance or active dissent.
3. The organisational culture and values are supportive of policy performance.
4. Business strategy is acceptable and the policy is in congruence with its objectives.This alignment occurs within an organisational framework of interactive and countervailing influences on strategic decision-making. Industrial relations and HR policies and influences should form an integral part of business or organisational strategy, rather than being a consequence of such strategies.

The centralisation/decentralisation question

The above-mentioned approach poses a significant challenge for reviewing current perspectives on industrial relations and HR policy formulation, implementation and training.

Decentralisation of industrial relations decision-making has been found to be associated with the extent of business diversification.[20] Enterprises diversified across industrial sectors are more likely to provide local establishments with IR decision autonomy than enterprises whose activities are concentrated in a single business. The decentralisation of collective bargaining also appears to be associated with greater policy discretion. While the findings of Hall's South African survey indicate a transfer of responsibility from line manage-

20 Marginson, P. (1986 a)

ment to the HR department, the centralisation of such decision-making may in the long term risk creating a line management over-dependency on industrial relations and HR specialists.[21] A potentially over-dependent relationship may inhibit the enhancement of line management people-management capability and personal responsibility for decision-making on these matters. The search for a generally acceptable locus of decision-making and appropriate reward structure in industrial relations is a critical organisational variable which is substantively associated with levels of conflict between key interest groups. The organisational clarification of these philosophical and strategic principles is a necessary prerequisite for the effective implementation of policies and strategies.

Industrial Relations and HR policies need not by necessity be centralised, but might be deliberately allowed by the parties to reflect local conditions, issues and practices, given that a high degree of co-ordination and integration of bargaining parameters are established between decentralised operations. To some extent, this practice would, according to Davie et al.,[22] seem to conflict with the need for guidelines to be universal and inviolate, and there is an argument for a fairly high degree of centralization of IR and policy. Marginson and Purcell[23] argue that 'it might be expected that decisions on IR policy would be subjected to a greater degree of central control than decisions of a routine nature', since IR decisions belong in the strategic substratum, and strategy is usually a function of the Centre. They argue three rationales for central involvement:

- the interdependence between divisions;
- the advantage that internal audit (evaluation and feedback) may be utilized as a performance indicator; and
- the fact that IR/HR may be a critical function.

21 Hall, R. (1983 a)
22 Davie, B. et al (1987 a: 16–17)
23 Marginson, P and Purcell, J. (1986a)

The level of centralisation or decentralisation appears to depend on variables relating to business strategies, locus of power, organisational structure, monitoring and control mechanisms, and organisation culture. While most models of strategy formation assume that the initiative and responsibility for such formulation should be centrally determined by top management, operational management participation in the strategy formulation process is a fundamental requirement for its effective operationalisation and legitimacy. It is therefore suggested that a model of policy formation and implementation requires rigorous attention to areas of co-mutuality in respect of the relationship between process and content. This implies that the dimensions of decentralisation/centralisation cannot be considered as disparate in respect of the involvement of operational-level managers in both policy formulation and implementation. The efficiency of policy implementation is frequently eroded by the absence of a pervasive operational commitment philosophically and motivationally, to formulated strategies. This is often a function of a lack of decentralised managerial involvement in policy and strategy formation. An overlap of participation at both centralised and decentralised levels is therefore required methodologically, for the effective formulation, implementation and legitimation of IR and HR policies. Process considerations are therefore crucial.

CONCLUSION

The procedural integration of industrial relations and sound people management objectives in performance management and appraisal, role definition and job descriptions, is fundamental for an organisationally pervasive understanding and commitment to the operationalisation of policies. However, policy formulation and implementation processes cannot be considered in a vacuum. Organisational culture and the rewards and sanctions applied for promoting conformance or managing deviation around the values and norms of the culture, are important variables associated with the potential success or failure of policies and strategies. Consideration of these variables holistically and integratively is paramount if incongruence of reward processes, objectives, and priorities is to be minimised.

However, as previously argued, implementation may never be totally assured. Thus political influence has to be exercised in order to ensure the effective translation of policy, and political coalitions formed to see it through (Thurley and Wood, 1983). In sum, relative congruence between espoused and operational policy is possible, given the extent to which factors such as the following are realised:

1. policy and implementation strategies are formulated participatively and initiated at the highest levels with will and sensitivity to methodological process;
2. its initiators accept responsibility and tolerance for a degree of divergence, and therefore develop evaluation systems which facilitate legitimated cooperation, rather than reluctant compliance or active dissent;
3. the organisational culture and values are supportive of policy performance; and
4. business strategy is acceptable and IR/HR policy is in congruence with its objectives.

Given that it is impossible to legislate labour peace, a situation in which organisational practices are in relative or near congruence with espoused policies can only contribute positively to the quality of management–worker relations.

4

MANAGING PEOPLE EFFECTIVELY

INTRODUCTION

A high degree of complexity and uncertainty characterise the business environment in South Africa. The consequences of decision-making about people have an important bearing on organisational goal achievement in both the short and long term. Similarly, strategic business decision-making has important implications for HR and IR policy and practice. The variables of strategy and behaviour of groups in an organisation have been used to extend the Dunlopian systems model of IR.[1] The problem of defining effective people management according to these authors can be considered from a strategic perspective which seeks to explain choices and decision outcomes by particular constituencies and individuals.

There are, however, differing perspectives on defining and assessing effectiveness in managing people (Robbins, 1987). Robbins identifies four approaches. First, the goal attainment approach; secondly, the systems approach; thirdly, the stakeholder or strategic constituency approach; and fourthly, the competing values approach. These approaches are examined in this article.

Templer and Hofmeyer (1989) also refer to the difficulty in defining effectiveness.[2] They suggest that there is a range of criteria which focus on both efficiency and behavioural factors such as morale and job satisfaction. The distinction is often

1 Kochan, T., Katz, H. and McKersie, R. (1987)
2 Templer, A. and Hofmeyer, K. (1989)

made between efficiency and effectiveness and between internal and external measures of effectiveness.[3] The focus of this chapter is to identify and evaluate determinants of effective people management considering the internal and external organisational environment.

DEFINING EFFECTIVENESS

Various approaches to effectiveness occur.[4] The goal-attainment approach views effectiveness as the degree to which an organisation realises its goals. This tends to be the most widely-used criterion of effectiveness. Its focus is on achieving ends rather than means. The assumptions of this approach consider organisations as rational, goal-seeking entities with both measurable means of monitoring understood and legitimated objectives. An example of this approach is Management by Objectives. Problems with this approach relate to the assumption of the prevalence of common goals and interests. Questions as to who defines the goals, whether they are long-term or short-term and whether they are espoused or actual goals, are raised. Mission statements do not necessarily reflect what the organisation is actually trying to accomplish, or the behaviour of individuals and groups. The goal-attainment approach assumes consensus on goals. Multiple goals and conflicting interests occur in organisations. Espoused goals may tend to provide rationalisations for particular stakeholders, rather than a valid and reliable indication of purpose.

The systems approach implies an organic interrelationship between inputs, throughputs and outputs of organisations. Sub-systems within an organisation interact with each other and with its external environment. The systems approach emphasises criteria that will enhance the long-term survival of the organisation, including its ability to acquire resources,

3 Kilmann, R. and Herden, R. (1976)
4 Robbins, S. P. (1987)

maintain internal social stability, and interact externally with its environment. This approach implies that a clear connection exists between inputs and outputs. It can be criticised as at worst, a static one or as reflecting a bureaucratic orientation achieving change through slow incrementalism.

The strategic constituencies or stakeholder approach suggests that various stakeholders have a powerful and dynamic influence on organisational decision-making, and that the organisation itself may influence its stakeholders. The ability to satisfy or placate the demands of these internal (e.g. employees) and external (e.g. customers) stakeholders—individuals, groups and institutions upon which the organisation is dependent for its success, constitutes effectiveness, in terms of this approach. A 'satisficing' decision may be made in conditions of uncertainty or complexity. This is a 'satisfactory' instead of a rationally optimal decision.[5] The competing values approach is an extension of the stakeholder thesis. It suggests that the main assumption regarding criteria of effectiveness depends on the personal values held by individuals and groups, for example, management, trade unions and specialist staff such as IR and human resource people. An assumption of this approach is that superordinate values — a common overarching belief system, with which most employees can identify, is difficult to attain unless the organisation is very clear about is priorities. Changes in performance criteria and in values of stakeholders over time may detract from the purity of this approach.

The competing values approach approximates the pluralist IR model. The first two models in themselves reflect a particular value orientation, as does the idea of at least minimally satisfying strategic constituencies. Although the competing values approach cannot be considered a conclusive model for understanding effectiveness, it does offer a more

5 Simon, H. (1957)

holistic analytical tool which is helpful in looking into the *means*, that is, both perceptual and behavioural aspects of IR effectiveness. The emphasis, therefore, on systems outputs of IR behaviour, such as reduced labour turnover or strike incidents, limits the qualitative analysis of means. It is this latter emphasis which forms the basis of this study.

Templer and Hofmeyer refer to the work of Steers (1977) who proposed that effectiveness is a function of the interplay between the following variables: organisational characteristics such as structure, environmental characteristics such aseconomic and market conditions, employee characteristics such as job performance, and managerial policies and practices. Arguably, these criteria can be understood in terms of the systems approach, though some elements of the strategic constituency approach are implicit. The values orientation suggested by Robbins is not clearly evident, however. This latter approach is considered relevant for an understanding of HR/IR specialists' perspectives on factors relating to effectiveness.

According to Barnard (1938) the notion of effectiveness refers to the relationship between individual and organisational goals. Effectiveness is therefore associated with individual behaviour which is contextually appropriate within a framework of particular organisational goals.[6] A further analytical framework for effectiveness is that of role dimensions[7] Four role dimensions are posited: role models, role expectations, role conceptions and role action. Scholtz (1989) drawing on the literature, distinguishes between paternalistic, professional and technocratic role models.[8] From the stakeholder perspective, it is argued that various individuals and interest groups define the role of IR/HR practitioners in particular

6 Barnard, C. (1938)
7 Kellerman, A. (1980)
8 Scholtz, G. (1988)

ways. This definition may in turn be related to the values and interests of the stakeholder. The work of Purcell and Sisson (1983) is important in focusing on managerial expectations of the role of IR and HR specialists.[9] They distinguish between, first, *traditional* role expectations which tend to deny the rights of trade union affiliation, secondly, *sophisticated paternalism*, or neo-unitarism, which offers progressive human resource policies and practices which may have the effect or goal of marginalising unions, thirdly, the *standard modern role*, which is pragmatic, pluralistic but reactive, and fourthly, the *sophisticated modern role* which legitimates trade unionism as being conducive to managerial interests of stability and regulation, but also acknowledges the need for individual development. This is a constitutional or corporatist approach which seeks to institutionalise industrial conflict procedurally and through collective bargaining. The role conception of IR/HR specialists can therefore be considered analytically. It may also be viewed in terms of a values dimension.

Some research attempts to quantify human resource (HR) management effectiveness in terms of developing measurable indices.[10] These indices include human resource auditing, attitude surveys and human resource accounting. The justification of this approach is the necessity for objective data showing the contribution of HR and IR to organisational effectiveness. Horwitz (1989a) has identified constructs which IR practitioners consider important in determining effectiveness.[11]

RESEARCH FINDINGS IN SOUTH AFRICA

The notion of IR/HR effectiveness is considered in terms of the variables in the internal environment of the organisation and the external environment. The internal environment is not

9 Purcell, J. and Sissons, K. (1983)
10 Phillips, J. and Seers, A. (1989)
11 Horwitz, F. M. (1989a)

independent of the external socio-political, legal and socio-economic environment. An interactive relationship between these variables occurs. This may have an important relationship with effectiveness. Giles (1987) concludes that effectiveness may be limited by multicausal factors rather than a single determinant.[12] These include role ambiguity, role conflict, work overload, often conflicting organisational pressures, and stress resulting from assuming the role of a change agent in an often unreceptive environment. By internal environment is meant the impact of policies, organisation culture, situational factors in the immediate work environment including managerial styles, 'significant others' such as the immediate manager, shop stewards and peers, and their interpretation of policies, and initiatives.

Effectiveness is not considered in terms of defining outcomes as in the systems and goal attainment models, but in terms of IR and social processes. This is a qualitative and more subjective approach which deals with the assumptions about an organisational reality held by key constituents or stakeholders. IR and HR specialists in three major chemical corporations were the focus of one study. The study was part of a three-phase research programme, the first phase of which has been described (Horwitz, 1989a). In the second and third phases, a semi-structured survey questionnaire was used. This sought to identify organisational and external variables associated with effectiveness constructs identified in Phase 1. Phase three involved a survey feedback of findings whereby Phase 1 respondents were asked to evaluate and offer their understanding of the survey findings. This inductive process facilitated an on-going relationship between the researcher and respondents over a two-year period. This helped to acquire better understanding of the social reality of the HR and IR specialists, and to explore comparative perceptions be-

12 Giles, E. (1987)

tween companies and between different parts of the same company. A questionnaire was sent to 80 IR specialists and general human resource managers in the three companies: A response of 33 (41 %) was obtained.

MANAGERIAL ROLE EXPECTATIONS

The median length of IR and HR experience of the specialists was 5 years. Most of them (70 %) were located in factory HR departments, with the balance at the head offices of the companies concerned. Role definition of specialists can be defined by various constituencies, most directly by expectations of the individual's immediate manager, but also by line managers and trade union representatives. Although most specialists (61 %) felt that there was a common understanding of expectations, nearly 40 % felt that their manager had different expectations regarding what constituted effectiveness. This is a relatively high figure. There are, however, differences in role definition of IR/HR jobs at various levels, and between head office and factory work. Effective conflict handling is a prominent part of factory work, while monitoring adherence to corporate policies is an important head office role. The specialist's manager is usually in a generalist human resource position requiring a more strategic and developmental approach. IR specialists, in particular, may face expectations from their managers for adapting a more proactive role, notwithstanding the immediate short-term pressures which prevail. Individual respondents related the following examples as reasons for different expectations:

> 'My main customers are not necessarily the same as his.'

> 'By definition an IR or HR specialist has sometimes to take a position that may not be entirely business focused.'

> 'My manager does not understand the role of the IR practitioner. He feels that I should relieve the line managers of

> hassles, so that they can get on with their job of producing chemicals.'

These and other responses to open-ended probing questions suggest that whereas the specialist may believe that his identification is a horizontal one with peers, managers at similar level, or with employee representatives, there is a belief that his/her immediate manager's reference group is a vertically orientated, primarily with senior senior management.

Seventy-three per cent of the respondents indicated that they identified with a particular group or constituency. The group most strongly identified with was line management (including heads of department, divisional and section managers (40 %); secondly, with functional area (industrial relations/human resource) management (23 %); and thirdly, with black employees (20 %). Trade union identification as a reference group accounted for 5 %. Reasons given for the strong identification with line management related mainly to sociability, the stronger likelihood of informal relationships being developed with managers and peers and secondly, to specialists' belief that the need for a professional service was greatest with line managers who are responsible for managing people in their plants. It would seem, though, that the reasons for management identification are more diffuse than just that of professional needs or an identification with a set of values, such as fairness. Several respondents (10 %) argued, for example, that they consider themselves automatically as part of management. Some are on executive management committees and they represent employer interests in negotiations with trade unions. Expectations of reward, both formal and informal, play a role in group identification.

Although there appears to be an identification with line management and peers, perceptions regarding level of acceptability and supportiveness rate IR/HR peers highest. Specialists regard middle management as their main 'customers', but find greater support from top managers and colleagues.

Respondents cited the main reason for this as the greater likelihood of a common approach and understanding based on similar values and philosophies occurring amongst fellow specialists, the opportunity for open discussions, a sounding board, and similar job demands and pressures. There was also a greater likelihood of a shared commitment to policy at top management level where the focus of senior executives is on policy and strategic issues rather than operational detail. Research has shown that as one moves down the hierarchy, the attitude of line managers to policy becomes more questioning and the gap between espoused and operational policy increases.[13]

There is, however, according to several respondents interviewed, a possible halo effect, where IR and HR specialists' own views of their acceptability to particular constituencies could reflect an over-optimistic view. The distinction between the need for affiliation and personal acceptance, and professional credibility is not always apparent. A senior IR specialist described this self-rating as 'an indulgent overstatement of our own acceptability. Perhaps IR specialists tend to exaggerate the social importance of their jobs as a sop to their liberal conscience.' Factors which should also be considered, include differences in the nature and emphasis of IR and HR roles between a head office and factory and also job-level differences in respect of strategic and operational orientation.

CAREER DEVELOPMENT

The IR and HR specialists in this study appeared to have a strong internal locus of control. They have a confident view of their ability to influence their career progression and mobility. Although highly marketable, there also seems to be a fairly strong commitment to remaining within the same organisa-

13 Horwitz, F. M. (1989b)

tion and advancing into general human-resources management (45 %) or within the IR function (12,5 %). Some 25 % saw themselves as moving externally into IR or HRM consulting, a small business, or an academic post, and 12,5 % envisaged a general human-resource position in another company in the next five years. Only 5 % wish to move into a line position in the same group. The centrality and prominence of IR as an important management function is underlined by these findings. Specialists are acutely aware of the need for professional IR policy and practice in organisations. A confident and positive self perception of their organisational contribution was found.

A high proportion (76 %) of respondents felt that black IR specialists faced unique demands. Socio-political pressures such as trying to reconcile work and community positions, and particularly contradictory internal demands relating to perceptions of work role and internal credibility problems associated with a perceived lack of managerial support, are amongst the demands faced by black IR specialists. A consequent experience of marginality has been found, whereby black managers may not be sufficiently part of the normative managerial culture of the organisation to be integrated and accepted automatically.[14] This problem occurs where conflicting and ambiguous demands are faced by black people in higher status positions. One black respondent argued that 'maybe in due course the problem will disappear as blacks acquire more economic clout in companies and are seen by the black community to be in control — empowered to be part of real decision-making'. Respondents offered a variety of

reasons for particular demands on black IR specialists. Most of these related to the dissonance of 'living in an oppressed community with a political cause requiring an identification with that oppression in everyday behaviour. In other

14 Human, L. (1987)

words, one has to show support for the liberation struggle, but still risk being accused of selling out because of the personal desire to advance up the corporate ladder.' This corporate ladder remains predominantly white and according to several respondents, still reflects white stereotypical attitudes. An example, is the statement made that suggests black views are homogenous: 'we need a black IR specialist to tell us what blacks think.' Social pressures to conform to particular expectations of different interest groups can place the individual in a marginal position experiencing much stress and cognitive dissonance.[15] A senior IR manager suggested that 'IR colleagues may not be racist but many think in racial terms. There is not always an appropriate fit between the individual and prevailing organisational culture. The latter is not supportive enough even within IR departments.' The same respondent argued that 'among senior managers there is a genuine desire to change, but they want to be guided gradually to overcome their fears. Managers cannot assume that their values are shared down the line. A process of involvement is important in 'negotiating' core values and developing a model of evaluating performance against these values.'

WORK-PLACE DEMANDS

These are categorised under three main headings: time pressures, problems relating to resistance to change and role clarification.

Time pressure demands include balancing short and long-term demands, the difficulty in making time for developmental work and reflection, given both an excessive volume of work and inability to predict pressure. Reactive problems and crises cause constant interruption. These occur together with frequent and urgent demands for information and advice. There are also time constraints imposed by statute and proce-

15 Festinger, L. (1957)

dures regarding grievance and dispute resolution. The drawing up of documents relating to legal action also occurs within strict time limitations. Industrial relations work particularly in a factory context, appears to be reactive and crisis-orientated with short-term problem-solving and dispute resolution demands limiting proactive, strategic and developmental work. There are, however, indications in the sample that line managers are becoming more pre-emptive in anticipating problems and improving communication with employees.

The second main demand in the work environment relates to *resistance to change*, especially the prevalence of racial prejudice and conservatism amongst many white managers, supervisors and operating staff. Incongruent political ideologies and a resistance to operationalising and institutionalising the espoused company IR policies and corporate values remain problematic. Given the polarised nature of South African society, the work place is often a mirror of the diversity of attitudes prevalent in the wider community. Companies such as AECI and Sentrachem have, however, done much work in organisational change seeking to achieve a greater tolerance of attitudes and shared values in the work-place. Structural factors, including the large size of factories in all three companies and complex organisational structures, are seen as additional factors which inhibit change. Fear associated with job insecurity was also mentioned by some respondents as a reason why blue-collar white workers and supervisors resist change.

The third work-place demand is that defined as *role clarification*. This relates to the definition of IR/HR responsibility and accountability. The problem was generally described as a competency issue whereby middle management and supervisors often were unwilling or unable to take responsibility for managing and developing people. Reasons given for this included a lack of knowledge, analytical ability and sensitivity to social issues, with managers and supervisors frequently remaining 'technical operatives' rather than effective managers of resources. Poor commitment and application occur where responsibility for managing people and accountability are not part of the defined job requirements, critical success factors or performance objectives. Reward systems in terms of both financial reward, such as salary increments and promotion prospects, are not generally explicitly linked to people-management responsibilities. This tends to result in an overly dependent reliance on IR specialists.

Additional internal pressures relate to the consultancy and advisory role of specialists requiring extraordinary social skills and constructive relationships with both line managers and trade union representatives. The final work-place demand relates to the process of dealing with conflicting interests and expectations of managers and workers. This requires a constant need and preparedness to influence and challenge management and often trade union representatives too. Giving disparate attention to a variety of issues simultaneously, as well as the substantive content of IR issues, may cause a great deal of dissonance, testing the personal values of the specialists. In some cases, respondents indicated that managers were getting used to the specialists' role of challenging their assumptions. This aspect of the role was becoming more institutionalised. Hall (1988) refers to this as the exercise of socialised power, (rather than personalised power), where power is valued for purposes of serving and influencing an organisation to the benefit of an individual or group(s).[16] Although managers may be made to feel uncomfortable this was 'acceptable' provided that the specialist was seen to be acting 'responsibly'.

The expression of work-place demands occurs in several ways. Most respondents categorised these as relating to time wasting on ad hoc unpredictable problems — 'sweeping up

16 Hall, J. (1988)

the mess after events have been poorly handled', and 'inadequate attention to complex and strategic issues, which results in satisficing not optimising.' Trade-offs are made which result in 'just acceptable' decisions rather than optimal decisions.

DEALING WITH INTERNAL DEMANDS

There was no dominant method of dealing with internal demands. A variety of processes was found. These included delegation to subordinates, planning and setting of priorities, consciously improving time management, enhancing communications structures and interpersonal relationships. Other processes included taking administrative work home, actively seeking to exert influence on significant constituents such as line managers by persuasive argument, internal negotiation, improving informal relationships, education and training. A number of respondents found it important to develop outside interests, such as sporting activities and making time to be with their families. Dealing with work demands also required innovative and resourceful action, setting performance standards, procedural conventions, and keeping up to date with trends and developments, especially industry-related issues.

Many of these processes would normally be a necessary functional part of management work, for example delegation, communication and relationship-building. A relevant question is whether the responses of specialists are necessarily different from those of other managers. Often they are not. However, certain IR conflict-institutionalisation mechanisms are important, though perhaps more as an organisational process than an individual response to pressure. The emphasis on relationship-building with various constituent groupings and the perceived need to influence their thinking is intrinsic to the consultancy and advisory roles of a service function.

EXTERNAL FACTORS

Not surprisingly socio-political factors were most frequently mentioned as having an impact on internal IR and HR effectiveness. Several factors were interrelated both with each other and with internal demands. In practice, socio-political issues and community involvement cannot be divorced from the internal social milieu of an organisation. Domestic circumstances influence, and may be influenced by, internal job demands. It is the whole person who comes to work, bringing with him a complex set of values, perceptions and life experiences. Nonetheless, it could be argued that the prominence of socio-political demands found, is a feature of the extraordinary paradox of political disenfranchisement and industrial relations rights for the majority of South African workers. The role of the trade union movement in advancing socio-economic and equity goals, and pressing for political rights, has a discernible impact on the role of IR and HR specialists in terms of the manner in which they define effectiveness.

The effect of external demands on performance is manifested in a number of ways. A perceived dissonance between personal and organisational/managerial values may occur. This was found in nearly half (48 %) of the respondents, although it often surfaced only in relation to particular issues. However, most respondents identify with management as a reference group. Where dissonance occurs, it is often in the context of simultaneous empathy with workers' aspirations and at times not being able to meet these needs due to business or other organisational constraints, for example on retrenchment issues. Views of specialists frequently run counter to those of line management whose position they may have to defend. The conflicting values and strategic constituencies models of effectiveness are relevant in this regard. This may for some, be associated with unresolved stress affecting motivation, confidence and a sense of self worth, given the finding that most specialists were nevertheless confident and positive about their role. This could affect the soundness of IR judgements and decision-making.

Responses to external demands are similar to those relating to internal demands. This underlines the interactive nature of external and intra-organisational factors associated with effectiveness. Only 10 % of respondents suggested the need for strategic planning as a response to these demands, while 22 % highlighted the need to achieve a balance between individual, organisational and community interests. Most were concerned about the possibility of sometimes being pressed to compromise their own values where these were different from economic business goals. The difficulty, it would seem, is not that specialists have significantly different values from those espoused as corporate purpose or policy, as they may have been party to or indeed have influenced the adoption of these values. Some held a positive view of pressures and demands as reinforcing their reasons for choosing IR/HRM not just as a career but as a 'calling' which offers the opportunity for expressing strong personal values and a commitment to change.

The difficulty lies with the inability of organisations to comprehensively internalise these values at all levels. Behaviour of individuals may, therefore, deviate from the espoused corporate values and such deviation may be positively reinforced by the actual job priorities set by the individual's manager. One senior IR manager argued, however, that effective IR people have a strong internal locus of control. It was suggested that 'less effective' IR and HR specialists tend to externalise or displace problems, often blaming line managers for their lack of commitment to sound IR/HR, rather than acknowledging that if they themselves were professionally competent and strongly committed, they would be able to improve line management's competence in managing people.

STRATEGIC CONSTITUENCIES

As mentioned, line management are the primary reference group with whom IR and HR specialists identify. Even though there may be conflict and disagreement between these managers and specialists, they are seen as the main constituency requiring advice, services, information and development, since ultimately, effective management of people is in their hands. This begs the question as to whether this responsibility has been clarified and defined as an integral part of the manager's job and how corporate values and culture influence the way roles are defined (Purcell and Sissons, 1983). Other constituencies identified by IR and HR specialists as affecting their performance include various levels of local management (24 %), employees (16 %), IR/HR peers (16 %), shop stewards (14 %), senior and top management (mainly divisional (12 %), full-time union officials (6 %), supervisors (5 %), and subordinates (5 %).

The demands of these constituencies vary, but can be condensed into five categories. First, as necessitating a *consultancy role* (38 %), company policy, collective agreement and labour law interpretation. This role entails providing advice, information and support services where the level of professionalism and resourcefulness is most important. Specialist's knowledge and information base also enhances their credibility. Sapiential rather than traditional/hierarchical authority is an underlying factor in the power base of specialists given that theirs is a service function. The power of access to information and the imperative of relationship-building, are underlying factors in a specialists' effectiveness. This supports Hall's (1988) notion of the socialised power need. A disadvantage of this powerful localisation of knowledge and expertise is in the possible creation of a line management over-dependency on specialists. This can result in a failure to raise the IR/HR capability of line managers and the organisation as a whole.

The second category of demand relates to that of requiring *strategic and tactical allegiances* (23 %) whereby groups make particular demands on specialists to address their interests exclusively, ie to 'champion their cause'. Such demands are made by both line managers, who may, for example, wish to dismiss a particularly troublesome worker, or shop stewards, who demand the dismissal or removal of a 'racist' foreman. This finding supports the strategic constituency model of effectiveness.

The third category relates to *adherence to group policies* (20 %) ensuring fair, equitable courses of action, consistency and the maintenance of standards. Where there is strong pressure to work within accepted procedures and rules, the formation of dysfunctional alliances is limited. The fourth category can be described as a *demand for development*, enhancing the people management capability of managers and subordinates (5 %). This is done in several ways in companies, including annual HR conferences, seminars on particular topics such as labour law and dispute resolution, supervisory training programmes and on-the-job training. These are organised by head office or local IR or HR development departments.

Respondents from an one factory referred to problem-solving on people issues as a line management responsibility. Specialists have an educative and consultative role in helping managers and supervisors develop the means for taking ownership of solutions by taking them through a 'thinking process', exploring issues, options and consequences, which enable them to be more willing to make sensible decisions. This is an influencing process which goes beyond merely providing advice or a service. It is an attempt to help managers raise their analytical ability in dealing with complex and ambiguous problems. The notion of a high socialised power motive is again appropriate here.

Finally, organisational demands require efficient HR and IR administration in backing up *support services* to managers (9,5 %). The above-mentioned categories of demands help define a specialist's role. They suggest support for the strategic constituency model, with consequent conflicting interests leading to a paradoxical functional cohesion. Gluckman (1973) argues in this regard that the future need for interaction leads to conflict resolution.[17] He refers to the curious notion of 'peace in the feud'. The interdependence of strategic constituencies draws people together. Rules and customs are created to institutionalise conflict. Interdependence necessitates cohesion.[18] In terms of the pluralist IR framework and the strategic constituency model, the natural existence of interest groups competing for resources in organisations creates both inherent conflicts and the imperative of social cohesion and normative regulation, for example, through use of procedures. Conflict may then prove to be socially functional.[19]

In practice, there is a mix of various functional roles which are situationally dependent and which also characterise particular IR and HR jobs and decision levels, to a varying degree. As one respondent remarked, 'sometimes you advise, sometimes you consult, and sometimes you read the riot act'.

CONCLUSIONS

Although it is feasible to develop constructs of IR and HR effectiveness in terms of individual performance, this performance is a function not only of individual ability and motivation, but also of situational factors within and beyond organisational boundaries. Within the organisation, performance expectations of an individual's manager and significant other constituents such as line managers and shop stewards,

17 Gluckman, M. (1973)
18 Syce, D. (1989)
19 Coser, L. (1956).

contribute interactively to role definition. The strategic stakeholder model defined by Robbins (1987) is helpful analytically in this regard. The conflicting values model suggests that conflicting and incongruent expectations may reflect differing values. This is perceived to be the case according to the respondents. However, the notion of achieving homogeneity of corporate values pervasively, implies a primacy of these values over individual values. This may be problematic. Achieving changes in corporate culture requires an internalisation of corporate values into the consciousness and behaviour of individuals.

Patterns of leadership, performance objectives and reward systems have to reinforce desired behaviour required by corporate values. There is a potential conflict between corporate and individual values, and also between managerial behaviour which is reinforced by other priorities, and good IR/HR practice. This question of fit or alignment is being sought to varying degrees in South African organisations. It is, however, questionable whether a total alignment between desired corporate values and organisational behaviour is achievable or even desirable. Complete fit could lead to a strong but rigid culture which does not adapt quickly enough and which may lack flexibility in coping with change. A tension between different organisational constituencies may well contribute to a dynamic, healthy and open organisation which acknowledges inherent conflicts of interest constructively.

Research reveals differences between organisations in the same industry, and between factories and head offices within individual companies. These differences appear to be rooted both in variations of corporate culture internally and prevailing socio-political climate and attitudes in the local community. Geo-political factors therefore play a role in terms of the external factors relating to effectiveness in managing people. There is support for Templer and Hofmeyer's conclusion that effectiveness is a function of the interplay between internal and external variables. The findings also suggest that there is some support for a varying presence of the sophisticated paternalism and standard modern roles of IR (Purcell and Sisson 1983). Although these require further research, corporate values and managerial styles and expectations are important in defining specialist roles and the nature of people management effectiveness. It is not merely a question of defining or implementing core values but indeed of the *intent* and *nature* of these values. The neo-unitarist or pluralist *content* of corporate values will have a direct bearing on role clarification and practice.

The identification of IR and HR practitioners with management does not imply that they support management on every issue. The contrary does occur. This identification with management as a reference group is intrinsic to the definition of IR and HR work as management is the interest group with the organisational power to determine de facto IR and HR effectiveness in the company and are responsible for allocating rewards. It is therefore understandable that they are the main 'benefactors' or customers for specialists. Yet their values and behaviour may conflict with those of specialists. Respondents revealed a strong sensitivity about how their role was, and should be, defined. Some evidence was found reflecting the technocratic role model, but the paternalistic and professional models seemed more obvious, given variations between and within companies. Dominant corporate values, organisational structure and strategy, together with changing institutional patterns of IR, affect the definition of the practitioner's role. These variables require further research to obtain a more comprehensive understanding of the determinants of effectiveness.

Based on previous research on IR effectiveness (Horwitz, 1989a; 1991 and Sorsa 1991)) and the current findings, a model of factors relating to HR/IR effectiveness is proposed (Figure 4.1). The model indicates factors distributed along the axes of

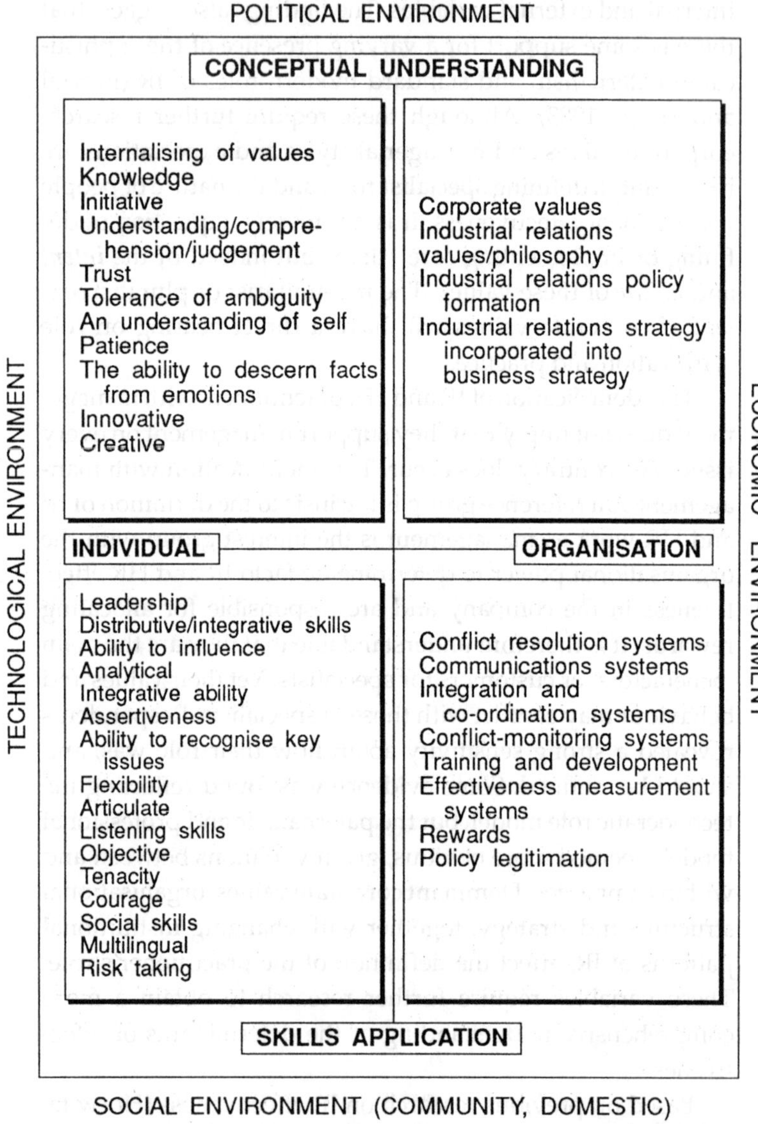

Figure 4.1

Human resource and industrial relations effectiveness

application or practice, the individual and the organisation. The model includes: (1) individual constructs, (2) skills, both social and procedural, and (3) knowledge (conceptual, procedural and environmental). Factors in the external environment interact with internal organisational variables, as previously discussed. It is hoped that this model can form the basis for further research. IR/HR specialists' understanding of their role has been compared with line managers' and shop stewards' understanding of HR/IR effectiveness.[20] Although line managers showed greater concern about operational issues such as output, and shop stewards were more concerned with quality of life issues, there was nevertheless a surprising degree of similarity between the three groups in the sample. Perceptions of other strategic constituencies including line managers and trade unions are therefor vital. A deliberate focus has been placed on constructs, processes and interest groups relating to effectiveness rather than on outcomes, such as better morale or improved employee retention. Further work needs to be done on defining effectiveness more rigorously, given Robbins's view that it may be more appropriate to consider situationally appropriate working definitions, than to try and develop an 'ultimate' definition. Given the theoretical and practical challenges in developing the notion of effectiveness in managing people, it may be apt to conclude with a quotation from a survey respondent: 'In this country, there unfortunately seem to be too many prophets with future visions, but disturbingly, very few saints.'

20 Sorsa, K. (1991)

5

HUMAN RESOURCE PLANNING AND INDUSTRIAL RELATIONS: SOME POLICY ISSUES

INTRODUCTION

Human resource (HR) planning has begun to occupy an increasingly important role in relation to business plans and corporate strategy in South Africa. The manner in which management matches the unique skills at its disposal with the specific opportunities in the environment will be important determinants of the success of an organisation.[1]

There are a number of models for HR planning which have been used with varying degrees of success in South African organisations. These include the use of input/output approaches which attempt to relate the determination of the internal HR needs and demands of an organisation and its projected labour turnover levels to the availability of external labour supply. The process of HR planning includes three inter-related phases: forecasting, programming, evaluation and control.[2] Shown in Figure 5.1.

A somewhat colloquial definition of HR planning is '. . . the integration of *HR policies*, practices and procedures so as to achieve the right numbers of people in the right jobs at the right time' (Lynch op. cit. p. 12). Another definition considers HR planning as '. . . a strategy for the acquisition, utilisation,

1 Lynch J.J. (1972)
2 Henneman H.G., Schwab D.P., Fossum J.A. and Dyer L.D. (1980)

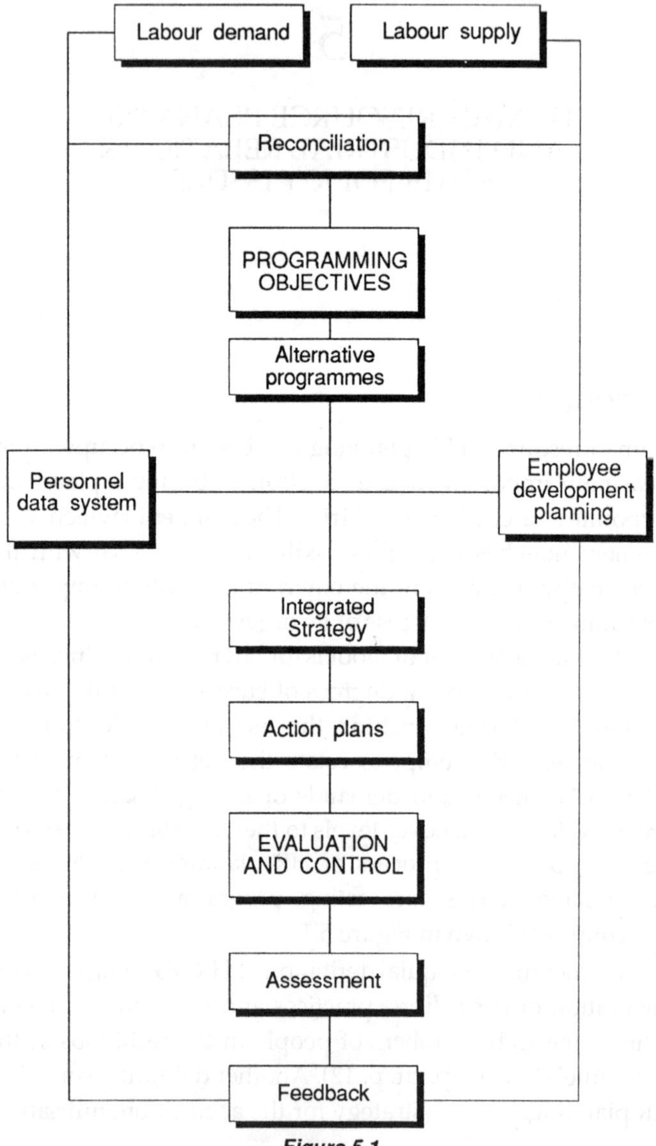

Figure 5.1

Model of the HR planning process and associated activities

(Henneman et al., 1980)

development and retention of an enterprises human resources'.[3]

Most textbooks dealing with HR planning refer to the need for integration of the HR planning process into the corporate planning strategy of an organisation, thus inter- relating a number of disciplines which deal with financial, physical and technical resources and people in an organisation. [4]

BENEFITS OF HUMAN RESOURCE PLANNING

The benefits derived from HR planning include the following:[5]

- ❑ improved understanding of the human and social implications and business strategy;
- ❑ improved and more effective career management;
- ❑ employee development and succession planning;
- ❑ redundancy and retrenchment planning;
- ❑ ability to recruit experienced talent in advance of needs; and
- ❑ facilitating the achievement of corporate objectives.

Effective HR planning can be seen as an effort to find a possible or probable future rather than to attempt definitive forecasts. It facilitates current decision-making in the light of a possible future (scenario). HR planning cannot attempt to eliminate risk, but is rather an attempt to understand risks being faced by an organisation. It is not a blueprint of the future either. Rapid change and uncertainty can render a blueprint inoperative. HR planning should involve a flexible process of systematically and creatively addressing the internal and external alignment or strategic fit of environmental and organisational variables. Optimising individual and organisational goals in the context of strategic alignment is a fundamental part of HR planning.

3 Bramham J. (1978)
4 Cascio W. F. (1978)
5 Owens, J and Nema L. (1988)

It is not the intention here to evaluate in detail the various functions, processes, benefits and difficulties of HR planning. The main focus is on the current practices and problems of HR planning in relation to industrial relations in general, and redundancy and retrenchment in particular.

In this context, one of the main areas in which it is alleged that HR planning has failed to achieve its objectives is to plan effectively for a relatively stable workforce under changing economic and organisational conditions, particularly during economic downturn cycles. Most HR plans also seem to focus on the recruitment, training and development, reward structure, succession and career planning of middle and senior managerial levels, and tend to neglect the blue-collar areas of unskilled and semi-skilled labour. Undoubtedly, it is in the latter job categories where the most significant strides in unionisation have been made by trade unions over the last decade. The question of unfair labour practices has increasingly become the focus of attention between employers and trade unions during recessionary periods and accompanying retrenchments, with recent industrial court rulings resulting in the re-instatement of employees. Trade unions, during an economic downturn, tend to make use of both legal rights and bargaining power to seek redress of grievances relating to job security.

HR objectives and strategies tend frequently to be developed in isolation and do not integrate effectively with long-term production, financial and marketing objectives. As a result, short-term measures of reducing HR costs are frequently introduced during an economic downswing. The danger of such expedient approaches is essentially their damaging impact on morale and productivity within the organisation, and the harmful industrial relations impact which is consequently generated.

The whole spectrum of HR-planning activities has traditionally been considered as a managerial prerogative in the same sense as other strategic planning activities. Yet the question may be asked whether the activities of HR planning in most organisations integrate effectively with industrial relations policies and procedures which in the 'post-Wiehahn' era have begun to focus increasingly on enterprise and plant-level consultation, negotiation and participation in decisions affecting employees. HR planning is certainly a process which in virtually every way affects the interests and aspirations of employees. It is fallacious for employers to assume automatically that short-term reductions in manpower will offer long-term solutions to poor labour productivity. Contrary to what many employers may believe, although overall manpower cost reduction may be achieved and reflected in terms of bottom-line financial results by retrenchments, retrenchments per se tend to reduce the moral, job and organisational satisfaction of remaining employees as a result of the consequently increased level of uncertainty and insecurity.

The idea of involving people in the HR and planning process may appear horrifying to many employers. Objections are likely to be based on the fear of erosion of managerial authority and control and on the view that HR planning requires a high level of numeracy, skill and technical expertise. The participation of employee representatives in this process is thus seen as being likely to reduce the overall efficiency of HR planning and the business itself.

There is, however, a long-standing precedent of trade union participation in HR planning in South Africa by established industrial council trade unions.

Prior to the 1979 amendments to the Industrial Conciliation Act arising from the recommendations of the Commission of Inquiry into Labour Legislation, recruitment, employment levels and access to skilled work were virtually controlled by the established trade unions, to the detriment of efficient planning and utilisation of all human resources regardless of race. The monopolisation of skilled labour by the white trade

1. HUMAN RESOURCES
   - People mix
   - Outflows
   - Surpluses
   - People gaps
2. INFORMATION AND RECORDS
   - Manpower audits
   - Information systems
3. DEMAND FORECASTING
   - Derived demand
   - Industrial engineering
   - Use of statistics e.g. multiple regression
4. SUPPLY FORECASTING
   - Measurement of LTO
   - Survival and wastage curves
   - External labour supply
5. PEOPLE FLOWS
   - Age distributions
   - Service distributions by job category/grade
   - Inputs/throughputs/outputs
6. RECONCILIATION OF DEMAND AND SUPPLY
   - Identify discrepancies
   - Develop action plans to optimise best demand/supply fit
   - Succession planning, high flyer potential identification
7. SCENARIO PLANNING

Figure 5.2
Technical elements of human resource planning

unions effectively denied access to apprenticeship training for black employees. The stranglehold on the planning access and upward mobility to skilled and managerial positions, was reinforced by closed-shop agreements. This in effect, prohibited the effective HR planning for skilled and supervisory levels in South Africa, and has contributed to the shortages of trained manpower in this area. It would seem that management often experiences a strong ambivalence between the perceived need to satisfy demands arising from a spurious power base accorded to skilled (white) people, and which has generated an artificial manpower shortage), with the increasingly insistent demands from black employees.

Non-racial trade unions are increasingly focusing attention on the criteria for decisions on staffing levels, recruitment, training and development, advancement and particularly the employment security of their members in the future. The credibility of the HR planning function is important in this regard. If HR planning is perceived by employees and trade unions as a secretive management technique which supports the perpetuation of white monopoly over the skilled and managerial labour structure, as limiting upward mobility or being either instrumental in or failing to prevent retrenchments, then HR planning may well be perceived, at best, as an academic number crunching exercise and, at worst, as a management tool which heightens, rather than institutionalises conflict in industry. An integrated strategic approach to HR planning which is based on the principle of participation in the decision-making process which affects employee needs, can improve the overall status and credibility of HR planning in an organisation. It may also assist in easing established manning practices based on ideologies of white exclusivity and may indeed reduce uncertainty in industrial relations. The potential benefits of this approach include greater cooperation of workers in introducing flexible work practices and in sensitive measures which avoid retrenchments such as overtime reduction and short-time working. It may not be expected that trade unions would wish to participate in the 'technical' facets of HR planning, such as statistical data analysis and forecasting. However, as discussed above, the formulation stages of decision-making and the processes of implementation and evaluation of HR plans are indeed areas where participation could have benefits for both management and workers.

IMPACT OF ENVIRONMENTAL FACTORS ON HUMAN RESOURCE PLANNING

The previous discussion focused on defining HR planning and its implications in terms of industrial relations, with particular regard to the development of a participative approach to HR planning. The question of the impact of external environmental factors on internal or intra-organisational planning is critical in terms of the practical value of HR planning. Environmental factors such as economic and business cycles have previously been referred to in the context of HR stability or instability. It is felt that the definition of redundancy and retrenchment needs to be elaborated upon at this stage. It is suggested that a distinction between redundancy and retrenchment is made. The former may be said to be the falling away of a particular post as a result of product demand reduction (sales decline), technical innovation or organisational restructuring. In terms of this definition, a post may be declared redundant, but it does not necessarily imply automatic retrenchment or termination of the incumbent's services. Various methods of avoiding retrenchment have been identified.[6] These include cutting recruitment, re-training, transfer and re-deployment, reducing or eliminating overtime, reducing or eliminating the use of sub-contracting (temporary) employees, consideration of short-time, work-sharing

6 Anstey, M. (February 1983)

and lay-offs. Retrenchment refers to the actual process of terminating the services of an individual whose job has been declared redundant.

Recognition of the importance of socio-economic, legal and political variables in the context of HR planning is vital if a balance between organisational objectives and the social responsibility of employers is to be achieved. Much has been said and written about the advisability of furthering the principles of the market economic system in South Africa. What is frequently included in this debate is the question of evolving mechanisms for convincing the majority of the population of the benefits of this socio-economic system. It may be argued that, given the plurality of interests within a heterogenous society such as South Africa, any economic system which does not provide tangible opportunities, equality of treatment, material well-being, and employment stability and security, is likely to be viewed with suspicion by the majority of the population. The fact that the vast majority of retrenchments tend to involve primarily black people reduces the perceived benefits of the market system; this, coupled with the complex network of legal restrictions which governed the movement and employment opportunity and accommodation of black people in particular, put major obstacles in the path of effective HR planning in the South African context.

Anstey stresses the importance of employer awareness of the psychological and social consequences of contributing to already high levels of black unemployment in South Africa, by retrenchment of workers. He states that many unemployed in the homelands are displaced urban-unemployed — they have few chances of obtaining work in these impoverished areas (op. cit. p. 16). Anstey also quotes from Simkins who observes that the economic situation of the homelands is highly vulnerable to any contraction in demand for labour in the white areas (op. cit. p. 16). Rising levels of unemployment and consequent poverty have tended to be related to political instability in many countries. These macro-level considerations tend not to be given the sufficient consideration by HR practitioners and senior managers who are responsible for overall corporate strategy at organisational levels, which they warrant. Yet it is frequently those who are responsible for strategy formation, who argue in favour of the market system. In any society, there is an interdependent relationship between socio-economic, legal and political institutions. It is not the purpose here to analyse the extent to which South Africa operates on the basis of a market or mixed economic system, save to note that there were until recently a host of statutory directed controls on the effective development of people which, coupled with frequent short-term expedient plans, discredited attempts to 'sell' the market system and resulted in the HR planning process being viewed as manipulative.

If the organisation finds that it has excess staff and cannot avoid a reduction in staffing levels, the planning process should avoid the harmful social consequences of sudden retrenchments. Planning should provide every prospect that employees can not only be retained, but developed and re-deployed to other jobs with the organisation. Non-replacement of leavers and other retrenchment prevention methods should be used.[7]

HUMAN RESOURCE PLANNING MODELS

A number of models of HR planning exist. These include conventional HR forecasting approaches using computer simulation techniques with emphasis on HR development career and succession planning. These models reflect a distinction between 'hard', quantitative approaches seeking to optimise the fit between supply and demand for people at various organisational levels, and 'soft' approaches, which aim at

7 Bramham J. op. cit. pp. 124–

developing both the organisation's receptiveness to HR development, preparing the internal environment, and plans for the growth and advancement of individuals. The latter reflects a holistic and integrative model which concentrates on development of human resources as a multi-faceted process rather than on attempting to forecast future statistical possibilities. 'Soft' approaches also include scenario planning. These are hypothetical futures based on current data and interpretive judgements.

This does not detract from the need for well-constructed HR information systems and statistical projections. These processes form an integral part of the means for developing human resources. Rigid quantification must, however, be avoided, as it can become an end in itself. This creates an impression that HR specialists seek to justify their contribution by emulating natural science methods. This can be a sign of insecurity and lack of sophisticated thinking amongst HR specialists. Another question which is raised is the appropriateness of HR planning for all levels in an organisation as an oversupply of unskilled and semi-skilled people and an undersupply of technically skilled, professional and managerial people exists in South Africa. HR planning goals may differ. The emphasis on basic skills training is important at the unskilled and semi-skilled levels, with a broadening emphasis on managerial development and education at higher organisational levels. Similarly recruitment and selection approaches would differ in this regard. Chapter 7 deals with employee development imperatives in greater detail. It would, in sum, appear that the emphasis in HR planning in future will need to be on developing a model which integrates the development of people with strategic organisational goals. The model presented in Figure 5.3, for example, shows the specific relationships between the 'hard' and 'soft' components of HR planning for managers.

PARTICIPATION IN HUMAN RESOURCE PLANNING

Basic mistrust by management and the trade unions of each other's motives could be an initial stumbling block in seeking participation in HR planning. This is not likely to be an easy process, but there should be little dispute about the desirability of involving employees in decisions that affect them. Bramham, in this context comments that '. . . many managers appear to be living through a private virility ritual, with the trade unions cast in the role of the beast' (op. cit. p. 127). Some companies in South Africa have instituted the concept of a social policy audit, and regular discussions with recognised trade unions are held to report on developments/progress of HR plans. This is certainly a positive attempt at involving workers more fully in the monitoring and evaluation of specific plans. Many trade unions have strong links with community-based organisations. Future relations between employers and unions will be likely to be influenced to a large extent by the propensity of employers to demonstrate visibly their social responsibility towards both employees and the environment from which they draw their people. Any organisation which attempts to operate in isolation from the extra-organisational environmental influences affecting its activities is bound to experience the adverse social and economic effects of such an approach.

Following recent agreements in the metal, engineering, iron and steel, and mining industries, it is also argued that the process of collective bargaining at various levels and the agreements reached as a result, are increasingly likely to focus attention on items which form part of the HR planning process, for example manning levels, training and development, advancement and redundancy prevention.

Participation in decision-making appears to be slowly on the increase in South African companies through a number of techniques which focus on improving productivity and job satisfaction, such as quality circles and Nissan green areas.

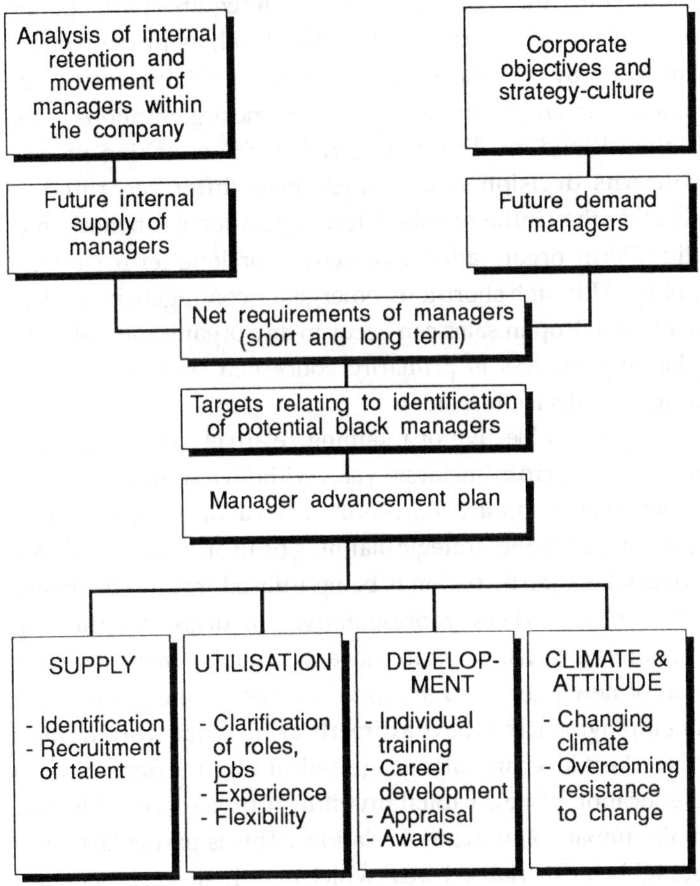

Figure 5.3

Manpower planning model

Source: Adapted from Human, L, and Hofmeyr, K. *Black Managers in South African Organisations.* Juta & Co Ltd, Wetton, 59, 1985.

Participation in European countries is, however, institutionalised either through legislation which requires participation in decisions at factory or enterprise level, as in the Netherlands, or by specific voluntary agreements between trade unions and employers, as occurs in some organisations in the United Kingdom. The managerial decision-making process concerns decision items which may differ according to whether they influence short-term operational functions, medium-term organisational objectives or long-term strategic policy. Although short-term emergency contingencies such as a sudden drop in sales can occur in any organisation, the HR planning process is primarily concerned with medium or long-term decision-making.

A policy objective of retaining relatively stable employment levels across business cycles without a significantly detrimental effect on the short-term survival of the organisation is of concern in the strategic planning of an organisation. Other areas where participation is being utilised include the involvement of workers' representatives in decisions affecting economic expansion, for instance the establishment and location of new plants. As the social and economic problems of unemployment may have a direct bearing on the working lives of workers in a particular geographical area, the decision as to the location of new capital investment projects could have a major impact on industrial relations. This is particularly true of highly industrialised areas which have high levels of unemployment, though the decision-making process to invest in new capital projects in relatively under-developed areas is also obviously of vital strategic importance. Clearly, a number of dilemmas are created in this context, particularly the need for an organisation to optimise the balance between its economic and financial objectives and its social responsibility to the environment in which it operates, and to the development of its employees.

In European countries, such as the Netherlands, works councils are required by law to be consulted by management on financial and economic decisions which affect the interests of workers. In certain industries in Germany, notably coal, steel and printing, works councils may negotiate over manning levels and training and development policy, either on the basis of enhanced bargaining power due to the co-determination system, or as a result of work group sanctions. Despite the increasing degree of participation of workers in HR decision-making areas in European countries, Miller (1982) concludes that the '. . . situation seems to be one of where there is an information deficit in the area of HR planning and a lack of workplace institutions such as joint committees to deal with such issues' (op. cit p. 52). For trade unions '. . . workers' participation in times of recession entailed a drift of emphasis from the traditional concern with bargaining, wage rates and the securing of better conditions of employment, to the attainment of a bigger role in the running of enterprise'.[8]

In the South African context, joint management/shop steward committees have exerted more influence on enterprise level decision-making processes.[9] An area which is relatively well suited to enterprise or plant-level joint problem-solving and co-decision is that of HR planning and particularly HR development policies and strategies. Decentralised structures for consultation, communication and negotiation tend to stress the maintenance of a strong relationship between the trade union as an independent body and shop steward representation on these structures.

Regarding the operation of recognition agreements at plant level, trade unions are increasingly demanding union representation in decisions regarding HR planning, utilisation and development.[10]

8 Cordova E. (March-April 1982)
9 Horwitz F.M. (1984) pp. 26–34
10 Horwitz, F. (1984)

The potential for meaningful participation in decisions affecting the manning of companies and the utilisation of manpower could be channelled through mutually agreed structures. The agenda associated with HR planning may represent an area of increasing conflict between management and labour in South Africa. This conflict has tended to be regulated by the maintenance of white worker and management skills — and an associated high wage monopoly through the exclusion of black employees from access to skilled and managerial positions. The extension of trade union rights to black workers has tended to result in the development of alternative plant-level bargaining structures, and although the current debate on mechanisms for achieving complementarity between the more centralised industrial council bargaining system and plant-level structures is an ongoing one, HR planning tends to be a function associated with the specific corporate policy and planning objectives of a particular organisation.

Its immediacy to the needs and concerns of employees in individual organisations may tend to focus attention on the relationship between the degree of influence of workers in the organisation, and factors such as the organisational philosophy, structure and culture — particularly regarding the need for a pervasive culture and ethos of employee development. Crucial in this regard is the propensity of management for involving employees in decisions affecting their own development.

Participation may assist in channelling potentially disruptive conflict into constitutional power-sharing. Although HR planning can be and has been done, on industry or sectoral levels in some European countries, such planning tends to focus on broad issues, the translation of which tends to occur through more specific decision-making processes at less centralised levels. Clearly, in the South African context, it may be argued that one of the potential benefits of involving workers from particular organisations in the decision-making process at organisational level is the fact that involvement at the workplace level may increase the visibility not only of the results of the HR planning process, but of the involvement of workers in the process of the development. The credibility of the HR planning process and of management could, therefore, be enhanced. This process could, therefore, lead to managerial authority not being perceived as coercive or manipulative. The participation of employees in decisions affecting their development may, indeed, increase managerial influence.[11]

Short-term needs and long-term HR objectives need not necessarily be in conflict. In terms of the model illustrated in Figure 7, the process of involving employees in the developmental processes of HR planning may assist management in counter-balancing short-term needs and long-term objectives. In particular, involvement of employees through their representatives could occur in the following areas:

- evaluating data regarding supply and demand for labour;
- strategies for overcoming resistance to change — conditioning the internal environment;
- discussing alternative programmes (including changes to established racially orientated development and advancement practices);
- developing strategies and action plans; and
- evaluating and control (e.g. use of social policy audits).

EMPLOYMENT SECURITY

The need for HR planning not to be seen as a mechanism for contributing to unemployment has been referred to. Ideally, effective HR planning should identify surpluses in advance so that mechanisms for preventing retrenchments may be introduced. If people are being poorly used, it would hardly be surprising for a surplus to be identified. One of the biggest

11 Mulder M. and Kassen, M. (1976)

criticisms of HR planning is that surplus labour tends to be highlighted only during an economic downturn and action which is frequently arbitrary and of a short-term emergency nature, is taken to reduce the surplus. Rarely is the question of effective employment level control addressed during an economic upswing. Indeed, the reverse appears to be true in South Africa. Major recruitment drives including the importation of skilled labour from abroad aimed at increasing manpower strengths seem to typify economic upswings, while significant reductions occur during the downturn. Although different skill levels may tend to be involved, this trend is hardly indicative of effective HR planning and, indeed, throws the HR planning process into disrepute. The importation of skilled labour from abroad is likely to face increasingly stiff opposition from trade unions in the future, and will be a practice employers may find difficult to defend.

The question of maintaining relatively stable employment levels despite business activity fluctuations is an important factor in sustaining employee morale and commitment to organisational goals. It has nothing to do with the frequent managerial cry of 'we're not a welfare institution'. It has everything to do with the effective long-term HR policy planning and putting these plans into action, taking cognisance of business cycles, but with a commitment to relatively stable employment patterns and people-development irrespective of these cycles. Managers and employee planners may '. . . be given directives to attempt to smooth out peaks and valleys in employment levels. Such attempts, of course, will be affected by the degree of diversification in products by the requirements of customers, and by cash flow realities. Successful efforts by a firm to minimise wide fluctuations in its labour force may be rewarded by such gains as enhanced community relations, reduced recruiting and training and development costs and reduced unemployment (retrenchment) compensation costs'.[12]

EVALUATING THE EFFECTIVENESS OF HUMAN RESOURCE PLANNING — SOME QUALITATIVE FACTORS

The focus has been on analysing the role of HR planning and its importance in terms of industrial relations. The quantifiable benefits of HR planning include the more productive utilisation of people in terms of their development, and reducing costs of, inter alia, recruitment, labour turnover and absenteeism. Not detracting from the importance of quantitative factors, it has been attempted to focus on the importance of qualitative factors which concern the role of HR planning in the context of long-term organisation strategies and the social responsibility of employers, particularly in terms of the involvement of employees in the decision-making processes of developing the organisation's potential. These qualitative aspects may indeed have measurable long-term gains for the organisation in terms of the following criteria:

- stability of employment levels;
- degree of employee security;
- levels of employee morale and organisational commitment;
- quality of management and trade union relations;
- legitimisation of managerial authority;
- extent and quality of community relations; and
- reduction of retrenchment compensation costs.

The HR planning process, if seen to be actively promoting the practice of a broader social responsibility on the part of employers, and the active participation of employees in their own

12 French W. L. (1982)

development, may have much potential for achieving greater organisational effectiveness.

6

MANAGING PEOPLE AND PRODUCTIVITY IMPROVEMENT

INTRODUCTION

The relatively low level of productivity improvement is much written and talked about in South Africa. Yet there remain more questions than answers, as the pop song of a few years ago proclaimed. Productivity as a strategic management imperative is a function of the interplay between internal organisational behaviour and the external environment. It relates to the alignment or fit between the organisation's business goals, its human and other resources and particular factors in the external environment.[1] These influence and are influenced by strategic business decisions. This chapter examines these relationships and considers a people development approach to productivity improvement.

IMPERATIVES OF THE POLITICAL ECONOMY

A number of macro-economic factors, including sanctions and disinvestment, hamper economic growth, with a consequentestimated loss of 7 % of South Africa's traditional exports. However, one should keep in mind the basic reasons for trade boycotts and disinvestment, namely South Africa's unacceptable political policies. The cost of maintaining the apartheid system has been calculated at some R78 billion in lost economic growth (ILO, 1989). Similarly per capita disposal income has dropped some 14 % from its 1984 level. The cost of main-

1 Horwitz, (April 1990)

taining an ideology of political separation and white control stand in contrast to the economic imperatives of integration and common corporate purpose. Per capital gross national product could be considerably higher if apartheid had not existed. The problem of low economic growth and poor productivity also mask very serious unemployment levels of over 5,5 million people.

The National Productivity Institute (NPI)(1989)[2] has stated that the economy is failing abysmally to absorb many more people trying to join the work force. Employment in non-agricultural sectors remained virtually constant between 1981 and 1987, while the population increased annually by an average of 2,5 %. Unemployment and poverty will unfortunately remain one of the greatest social dilemmas in the decade ahead. Manufacturing, which accounts for 25 % of activity shed some 67 000 jobs between 1989 and 1987, while the public sector attracted 304 000 more people over this period.

The high unemployment rate and low economic growth tend to be self-reinforcing, with economic stagflation a major contributor to unemployment, which is in turn kept high partly because of poor productivity. The economy has averaged less than 1 % real growth since 1981. The NPI (1989) has argued that productivity has made a very small contribution to overall economic growth, whereas in many of South Africa's trading competitors, productivity was responsible for almost 60 % of growth. An annual population growth rate of over 2,5 % needs an economic growth rate of at least 4,5 %.

INVESTMENT IN HUMAN RESOURCE DEVELOPMENT

Only 10 % of South Africa's manpower is being trained in a technical field. It has been argued that 75 % should be trained

2 National Productivity Institute Annual Report, (1989)

to meet manpower requirements.[3] However, recessionary conditions and a lack of managerial will have tended to lead to cuts in spending on training by industry. There were nearly 13 000 apprentices in the metal industry in 1982. In 1988 this figure had fallen to around 8 000, with new registrations dropping from 5 500 in 1982 to below 3 000 in 1988. [4] Government figures show that in 1986, 5 % of graduates received degrees in engineering, 11 % in natural sciences, 2 % in mathematics and 82 % in other subjects. There is no reason to believe that these figures have changed significantly since then.

Inefficiency in education investment is an important cause of low productivity in South Africa, as are restrictions on the occupational and residential mobility of black employees[5] In spite of the removal of influx-control legislation, the migrant labour system with its oscillating mobility persists. Certain aspects of migrancy, such as single-sex hostel accommodation with its attendant social problems create a harsh environment which is not conducive to a productivity ethic.

South Africa's per capita output is about a sixth of Switzerland's, a fifth that of the United States, and a quarter of Japan's. There was a 1.7 % decline in GDP per capita between 1981 and 1986, while Taiwan achieved a growth rate of 5,7 % (Figure 6.1). There were some encouraging signs between 1987 and 1988, when capital, labour and multi-factor productivity grew by 2,8 % in the private non-agricultural sector, according to the NPI. Blame is, however, often put on South Africa's educational system or on the fact that as a developing society, we should not compare ourselves to developed countries. The problem is that South Africa's main economic competitors are developed post industrial societies, and economic growth will depend on the extent to which South Africa is able to compete successfully in international markets. There is no denying that

3 Bot, M. (1989)
4 Hutton-Wilson, D. (1989)
5 Rees, D. (1985/86)

Table 6.1

Western Cape industrial relations issues ranked by chief executives in descending order

1	Productivity
2	Unions and politics
3	Wage demands
4	Union assertiveness
5	Communication
6	Middle management inability

South Africa's separate and inadequate educational system hampers a productivity ethic. The historical pursuit of ideological interests based on race and perceptions of black inferiority have developed a managerial mindset which often doubts the ability of black people to perform in a so-called white business environment The consequent marginality of many black people with high potential is less a function of individual abilities than of social closure, whereby in spite of promotion into senior positions, opportunity to perform and social acceptance remain problematic.

In a survey conducted by the Graduate School of Business at the University of Cape Town, 35 chief executives of companies based in the Western Cape ranked productivity as the most important strategic industrial relations issue facing their organisations.[6] Productivity as a concern rated more highly than issues such as unions and politics, union assertiveness, and the need for improving communication (Table 6.1). In probing these factors, links were found between issues such as productivity and perceptions regarding the 'realism' of wage demands.

6 Horwitz, F., Malan, L. and Sakinofsky, I. (1989)

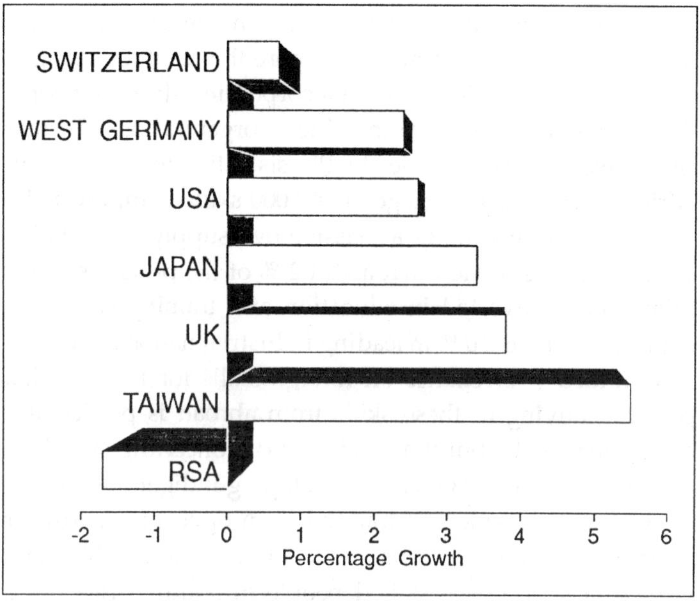

Figure 6.1
Comparative productivity levels:
Average annual growth rate per capita (real terms) 1981–1987
Source: National Productivity Institute

DEVELOPING PEOPLE AS CORPORATE CULTURE

Given the low level of productivity growth compared to its international trading partners, it must be asked who is ultimately responsible for improving productivity in South Africa. If an employer wishes to run a competitive and enduringly successful organisation, productivity improvement must be a managerial initiative, which involves negotiation and problem-solving together with employees. The President's Council investigation of productivity in South Africa, has urged for strategies at all levels aiming at a productivity growth of 3 % per annum. Several companies do in fact exceed this. So there is indeed experience and opportunity for addressing this issue.

Effective productivity improvement 'is, however, not the product of some magic formula, but more the result of changed attitudes' [7] There does not exist a corporate culture of people development in most South African organisations. Former Manpower Minister Pietie du Plessis estimated that South Africa could face a shortage of 200 000 skilled employers by the year 2000 in spite of a massive oversupply of unskilled people.[8] It is estimated that about 2 % of the private sector's salary bill is invested in education and training each year compared with 6–10 % in leading industrial nations.[9] There is a continued overreliance on foreign skills for large capital projects. Buying in these skills from abroad is particularly costly financially, but it also gives a disconcerting signal regarding the priority given to developing indigenous human resources. The neglect of training is an opportunity lost for giving more South Africans a stake in the economy. Not only is there a shortage of skilled people in South Africa but a structural change of the skills profile is necessary. Only 3 % of 85 000 black matriculants in 1988 had mathematics as a subject. In 1990 there were even fewer, yet some 73 % of people in tertiary institutions in South Africa are in universities.[10] Sixty percent of the schoolgoing population in Israel and Taiwan is engaged in vocationally orientated studies, while in South Africa less than 10 % of white and black children are (Hutton Wilson, 1989.) However, inputs for occupational training also tend to overemphasise educational rather than job related technical skills which focus on outputs and actual performance.

Burgess (1989) argues that HR planning is an area which is generally neglected, but which should be the first link in the chain of productivity improvement.' There is indeed a

7 Newall, I. (1989)
8 International Labour Organisation. (1989)
9 Van der Walt, T. (1989)
10 Leatt, J. (16 January 1989)

desperate need for a national human resource development strategy which identifies the skilled, managerial and professional needs for career entry, with co-ordinated national, industry an organisational strategies to give effect to the immediate and longer term needs for developing the country's human potential. These imperatives will endure and perhaps become even more pronounced whatever political dispensation evolves in South Africa. To facilitate this, a dialogue between employer organisations and the trade union movement on human resource development policy should be initiated. Bilateral development approaches need to be explored at national forums as is currently occurring on labour law issues, as well as at industry and organisational levels. Industry level examples include the recent agreement in the tyre industry for the establishment of a union–management training board, and established bodies such as the furniture industry's training board. Ultimately, prosperity and quality of life in South Africa will depend on the extent to which the challenge of human resource development is met. Developing people is, therefore, an organisational and national social policy issue requiring influence by key stakeholders including organised business and labour, in order to establish legitimate goals and agreed priorities.

Productivity and employee rights

Wage increases for unskilled workers since 1988 averaged some 3 % above the inflation rate. Labour productivity increases of a similar level have not been attained. However, it cannot be denied that the demand for a living wage, however difficult it may be to define, is a legitimate demand both morally and economically, in improving the buying power of employees. Wage increases represent a cost factor within organisations and reflect an inherent conflict of interests between employers and employees. This conflict requires mutual acknowledgement of both the independence of trade unions and the co-operative interdependence necessary for productivity improvement. If employers wish to preserve a free market economy this economy has to provide tangible material benefits and opportunities for employees. The answers do not lie in avoidance of bargained wage increases, but rather in seeking a simultaneous acknowledgement of both employees' needs for fair labour practices and equitable wages, and employers' need to enhance wealth creation. Employers must promote a philosophy that moves away from viewing the need for wealth creation and industrial justice as mutually exclusive. A more constructive dialogue with trade unions can form part of an employer initiative on this issue.

Invariably the word 'productivity' is associated with labour productivity and tends to imply rationalisation and cost reduction. This is a limited conception which ignores the question of how effectively other resources such as capital and technology are utilised. Domestic capital investment and utilisation have been poor in the last decade in South Africa, given the instability of the political economy. A domestic 'go slow' of capital expenditure has accompanied foreign disinvestment.

Although trade unions have made gains in terms of wage increases for their members, and a narrowing of the white/black wage gap is gradually occurring,[11, 12] a double-digit inflation level has eroded the real net gains of wage increases. The notion of productivity therefore has negative connotations for trade unions who may tend to feel that productivity initiatives such as employee participation schemes, may undermine the power base considered necessary for achieving negotiated wage increases. Yet co-operation and problem-solving are fundamental in achieving productivity

11 McGrath, M. (1989)
12 McGrory, V. (May 1989)

gains. Conflicting interests need to be acknowledged and the power dynamic of collective labour relations institutionalised in mutually satisfactory procedures based on a relationship built on trust. The ostensibly competing needs of collective bargaining over scarce resources and co-operative relationship-building can find expression in the work-place if the managerial will exists. Prerequisites for a creative coexistence of the wealth-creation and industrial justice imperatives include:

- Acknowledgement of the right of independent trade union representation.
- An internalised culture of employee participation, not ad hoc interventions which may conflict with an unreceptive internal climate and conservative attitudes.
- Strong, established trade unions who are involved in negotiating on staffing and skill levels.
- High levels of trust between employers and unions and visible respect for the dignity of individuals.
- Ongoing communication and sharing of information on company performance and goals, as part of a 'learning culture'.[13] Such a culture reflects values which include growing expertise from within the organisation, encouraging curiosity and self-development while providing both educative and experiential opportunities for personal development. There has to be a strong focus on a reward system which supports a participative learning culture and which meets basic needs for human dignity.
- Co-decision-making on changes contemplated by management, for example, manning practices.[14]

The current reactive emphasis on industrial relations fire-fighting and associated legalistic strategies, inhibits a longer

13 Miller, D. (14 June 1989)
14 Douwes Dekker, L. (July 1989)

term strategic emphasis on developing human resources and consciously planned organisational change.

Productivity bargaining and corporate culture

Productivity bargaining, to be successful, can occur only where there is a mutual recognition of needs, willingness to accommodate the interests of other parties, information sharing and a relationship of trust. As previously mentioned, trade unions, especially in the absence of a living wage, have serious concerns about employer motives for improving productivity. A factor often preventing successful productivity bargaining is a concern of employees that better productivity might result in job losses. Productivity improvement is more likely to occur if the industrial relations climate in the organisation is conducive to it, and direct, open discussions with employees and their representatives occur. Substantive negotiations on productivity normally extend beyond basic wage increases and may involve job design, training and development, job restructuring, flexibility and new technology. These are sensitive issues which could become problematic if they result in job insecurity.

The initiative must be taken by management, since the productivity imperative is an imperative of organisational success. Enduring productivity improvement is more feasible if it is intrinsic to an organisational culture, for example, as in Cape Cabinets, P.G. Bison and Volkswagen. This requires intensive, ongoing organisational renewal, through committed leadership who are willing to 'live' a productivity ethic with appropriate organisational structures and supportive reward systems.

Organisations also require the capability of implementing strategic organisational changes aimed at productivity improvement. It is easier to formulate than implement business strategies. Successful implementation is a function of three factors:

1. a relentless desire for improvement and adaptation, self critique, gathering and sharing information;
2. a focus on both formal reward systems legitimately perceived by employees, and appropriate evaluation and monitoring measures; and
3. agreement of employees and their representatives.

PRODUCTIVITY THROUGH HUMAN RESOURCE PLANNING

Productivity improvement through effective strategic planning, and development of human resources regards people as able to make a difference in the competitive edge of an organisation. But the emphasis on productivity improvement through people has to accept that individual change is more likely to be achieved through conscious, focused changes in organisational behaviour. This means that a strategic thrust is given to productivity improvement by transforming the so-called 'soft' people issues into 'hard' critical success factors.

This can be achieved through a combination of championing by top management leadership and the explicit definition and rewarding of key performance areas of each employee based on the company's articulated values. There is therefore an emphasis on 'living the corporate values', investing time, effort and money in human resource development. This requires evolving a developmental and learning culture, passionately pursued by managers with participative goal setting and performance measurement[15] behaviourally reinforced at all levels. A cautionary word, however: these ideas suggest a need for a strong corporate identification. Commitment of employees to a productivity improvement culture should ac-

15 Nel, C. (July 1989)

knowledge conflicting interests as an organisational given. Part if this developmental culture requires a process of procedural institutionalisation of conflict and a willingness to bargain collectively in good faith. This is a difficult challenge given the polarisation in South African society. It is essential, however, that creativity and innovation also be extended to finding ways of enhancing collective labour relations with trade unions, rather than viewing a developmental culture as a means of marginalising trade unions. If this does not occur, the legitimacy of productivity programmes will be problematic and they are likely to be viewed suspiciously as a sophisticated 'neo-unitarist' ideology. So the emphasis on productivity improvement must be an emphasis not so much on ad hoc substantive interventions, but rather on processes of organisational change which acknowledge *both* conflicting and common interests. This is a more holistic and strategic approach which looks at organisational change as necessary for individual growth and development. It is also a long-term investment of 'intellectual capital' in people rather than an ad hoc quick-fix intervention. Effective performance of human resources is a function of the abilities of individuals, their levels of motivation and the extent to which the organisation allows and encourages the development of the first two factors. The latter is a strategic question which is determined by the nature of leadership, and prevailing values, training and development and reward systems.

CONCLUSIONS

A crucial question for companies is, therefore, whether the legitimate employee imperative of enhancing real earnings, and the tough economic imperatives of improving workplace productivity can co-exist. It is very interesting that South Africa's blue collar wages are ahead of most middle-level countries including Greece, Portugal and Turkey, in fact are around the level of Hong Kong, South Korea and Singapore. These latter countries are 'economic miracles' [16]. Yet actual conditions of employment in these countries are frequently inferior to those in South African industry. While comparative analyses are often problematic, internal factors within a society have an important impact on the general level of productivity. South Africa has, according to Godsell (1989), a political culture of powerlessness which inhibits discussion of realistic options.[17] Such a culture is self-reinforcing and often tends to externalise blame for personal failure fatalistically, eg to the 'system' or 'capitalist exploitation'. Individual self-esteem is often low and locus of control is externalised.

Secondly, the socially and politically fragmented nature of South African society does not offer any unifying symbols of a common national destiny. Different national anthems and flags reflect the fragmentation of a divided society. As Mike Burgess of Anglo Alpha states: 'Up to now all our systems have been designed to keep people apart and more emphasis has been put on our differences rather than those aspects on which we can build a common destiny' (1989). Multi-cultural societies can be, and many are, very dynamic and socially cohesive. The management of diversity can be a great opportunity for realising the creative potential of employees provided that diversity is seen as a strength.[18]

Given the socio-demographic realities and economic squeeze of disinvestment and sanctions, business in South Africa cannot afford to adopt a fatalistic view that productivity improvement is possible only once the crises and contradictions of education and politics have been resolved. The conditions of political and economic siege create an even more insistent imperative for creativity and innovation in economic endeavour.

16 Schlemmer, L. (June 1989)
17 Godsell, R. (June 1989)
18 Horwitz, F.M. (April 1990.) Ibid.

7

DEVELOPING PEOPLE

> '. . . Human resources — not capital or income, nor material resources — constitute the ultimate basis for the wealth of nations . . . Clearly, a country which is unable to develop the skills and knowledge of its people and to utilize them effectively in the national economy will be unable to develop anything else.'[1]

INTRODUCTION

'The emphasis on meritocracy in American culture and in the business organisation has reduced the scope for a more democratic organisation in the immediate future.'[2] Although corporate culture in South African organisations might not be quite as meritocratic as in the United States, this raises the question of the relevance of some techniques which are transplanted into an incompatible organisational structure and culture. While the 'not-invented-here' syndrome should be avoided, the opportunity to formulate an effective and accepted culture and structure in South African organisations would be enhanced with the removal of organisational barriers to upward mobility.

This process will also be enhanced with the industrial franchise being complemented by empowerment in the structures of governance in the wider society. A crisis of expectations arose in the 1980's and early 1990's as a consequence of this paradox. This raises the important oportunity and chal-

1 Harbison, F. (1973)
2 Witte, J. (1980)

lenge for developing strategic approaches to the development of people in organisations (Figure 7.1).

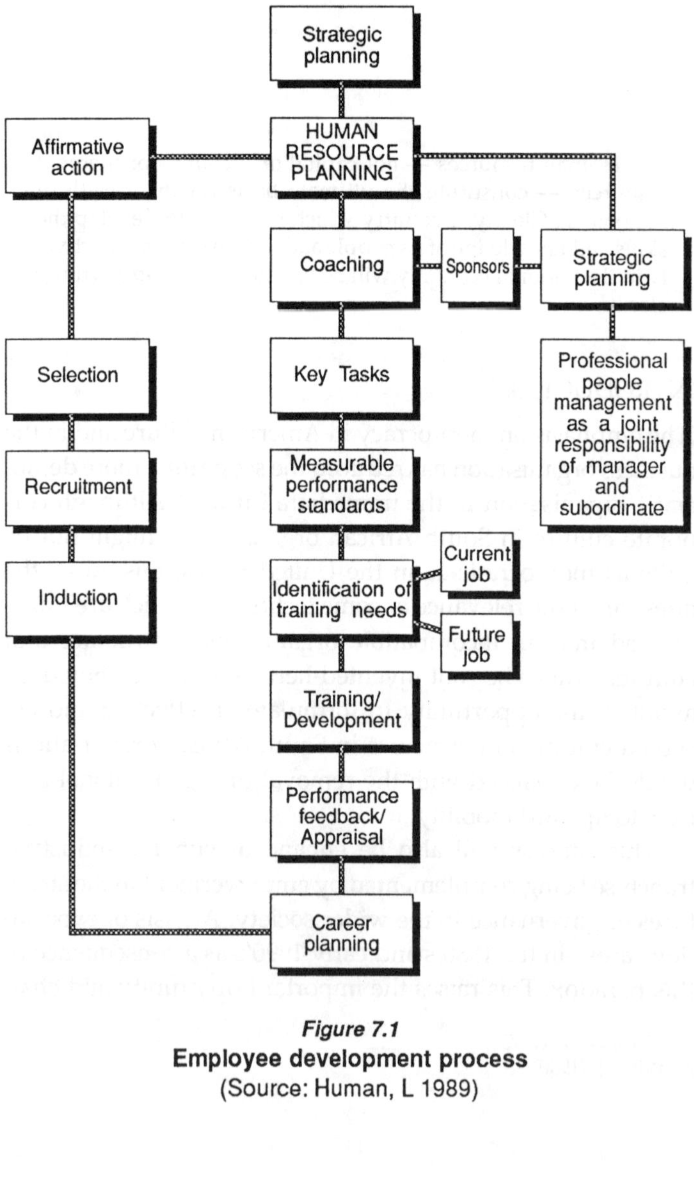

Figure 7.1
Employee development process
(Source: Human, L 1989)

Rigid race and class demarcations between predominantly black unskilled and semi-skilled workers and largely white supervisory and managerial levels reduce prospects for upward mobility of black employees and inhibit the achievement of greater legitimacy of managerial authority. A restructuring of the work force at all organisational levels to reflect a visible non-racial mix of employees is a prerequisite for the legitimisation of managerial authority. This constitutes a *strategic reorientation'*, of organisational structures and power and is not just a human resource management question. It relates to the overall policy, organisational strategy and the collective and individual interests of management and employees.

ASSUMPTIONS ABOUT DEVELOPING PEOPLE

'If we are seriously interested in developing employees it is important to clarify the basic assumptions underlying the paradigms of the main actors, in other words, the values of dominant and powerful groups in organisation and those with less power. Social closure through a process of exclusion limits upward mobility. This closure becomes problematic when perceived as illegitimate by aspirant individuals and groups. There is a need for a paradigm shift amongst managers if employee development is to be taken seriously as integral to the development of an organisation; but this requires a "surfacing and evaluation of current taken-for-granted assumptions".'[3]

Human and Human (op. cit. p. 16) argue that the theory of social closure helps us to understand those social processes by means of which dominant groups, who have interests of their own to protect, exclude the dominated groups from competition, as well as those social processes by means of which the dominated attempt to usurp the advantages of the powerful. It has been argued that collective criteria (such as race, gender and

3 Human, P. and Human, L. (1989a) p. 6, p. 12, p. 14, p. 16

religion) have been made anachronistic by the process of industrialisation. In most modern societies, these criteria have been replaced by the individual criteria of credentials and property. However, a tension often exists between collective and individual criteria in organisations. This tension can be exacerbated by the values of those with power. As exclusion is often based on the values of the powerful, and as it appears that values tend to reflect in the attitudes and behaviour of a dominant group appear, contrary to the espoused public policies of an organisation, it may be neither able nor willing to develop non-racial cultures, nor to provide management development with the impetus required. Research suggests that the paradigms of most white South African managers are such as to place a low priority on management development.[4] Other research also indicates an antipathy to the development of blacks.[5, 6] This research suggests that, while professing to accept equal opportunity and affirmative action in the organisations in which they work, the majority of white South African managers still doubt the inherent capabilities of blacks.

PLANNING EMPLOYEE DEVELOPMENT

Manpower planning, as part of the strategic process, provides an opportunity to determine current and future manpower requirements. This in turn links into the succession planning process which provides an opportunity to develop individuals with potential for future positions. Succession planning is linked to the process of professional people management. Managing people, as the joint responsibility of a manager and subordinate, involves a process whereby key tasks and measurable performance standards are determined, (current and, in terms of the succession plan, future) training needs are

4 Human, P. (1988a)
5 Human, P. (1988a)
6 Human P. and Hofmeyer K. (1987)

identified, training, development and coaching takes place, and performance feedback/appraisal and career planning are undertaken. Professional people management is a critical aspect of the development of people of all races.

This process treats people as individuals and provides a logical structure in terms of which individual training needs can be identified. Coaching, training and development should, moreover, be geared to individual needs and career plans.

'It is, however, with the processes of selection and recruitment that the real move from collective criteria of inclusion to individual criteria of exclusion has to take place in a meaningful way. An organisation may confuse educational qualifications with standards and assume that if the educational requirements attached to specific jobs are lowered, then standards will also drop. This is not necessarily the case, however, as standards may also drop if the educational level is too high and people are bored with what they are doing, or if other job-related criteria are more important than education. Also, if through inadequate definition and understanding of the job at hand, we attach educational criteria which are too high to the job, we unfairly exclude disadvantaged groups from competition.'[7]

Human resource development is a function of both the individual's personal growth, and organisational growth through successfully coping with the internal and external environment.[8] Effective HR planning and policy therefore extend beyond the conventional technology for forecasting future needs on the basis of the amount and quality of manpower supply and demand. Individual and organisational development are symbiotic processes at the core of HR planning (Figure 7.2).

7 Human, P. and Human, L. (1989a)
8 Schein, E. (1982)

ORGANISATIONAL NEEDS	MATCHING PROCESSES	INDIVIDUAL NEEDS
Primarily initiated and managed by the organisation		
Planning for staffing		**Career or job choice**
❑ Strategic business planning Job/role planning ❑ 'Manpower planning and ❑ human resource inventory'	❑ Job analysis ❑ Recruitment and selection ❑ Induction, socialisation, initial training ❑ Job design and job assignment	
Planning for growth and development		
❑ Inventory of development plans ❑ Follow-up and evaluation of development activities	❑ Supervising and coaching ❑ Performance appraisal and judgement of potential ❑ Organization rewards ❑ Promotions and other job changes ❑ Training and development opportunities ❑ Career counselling, joint career planning, and follow-up	**Early career issues:** Locating one's area of contribution; learning how to fit into the organisation; becoming productive; seeing a viable future in the career.

Planning for levelling off and disengagement	❑ Continuing education and retraining ❑ Job design, job enrichment and job rotation ❑ Alternative patterns of work and rewards ❑ Retirement planning and counselling	**Mid-career issues:** Locating one's career anchor and building one's career around it; specialising vs. generalising.
Planning for replacement and restaffing	❑ Updating human resource inventorying ❑ Programs of replacement training Information system for job openings ❑ Reanalysis of jobs and job/role planning ❑ New cycle of recruitment	**Late career issues:** Becoming a mentor; using one's experience and wisdom; letting go and retiring.
		New human resources from outside the organisation

Figure 7.2

Source: Schein, E. (1982). *A Developmental Model of Human Resource Planning*

AN INTEGRATED APPROACH TO EMPLOYEE DEVELOPMENT

The technology of HR and succession planning is beginning to be superseded by a much stronger emphasis on employee development. It has been argued (Schein, op. cit. pp. 3–6) that the nature of HR planning and development is changing due to the following:

- changing nature of managerial work — greater complexity and equivocality;
- changing social values — the importance of a management career is not as central to young people as in the past. Other values such as personal growth and quality of life are becoming more important;
- technological change; and
- changing needs of an individual at different stages of his/her

The policy and process of development requires that employees be developed to their full potential. The key elements of HR planning remain important in order to identify potential and design an integrated development programme for an individual. Such a development programme may be multi-faceted, emphasising not only technical and/or managerial training and education, but providing opportunities for growth which may include:

- job redesign, enrichment and rotation;
- induction, socialisation and initial training;
- special projects and assignments;
- planned job experiences, e.g. short-term stints in another department(s);
- continuing education programmes and retraining;
- deputising in another job at a more senior or even at a similar level; and
- career counselling, planning and review.

Institutionalised racial discrimination endemic to the social fabric of South African society cannot be externalised and divorced from the attitudes, values and ideologies in enterprises. The search for fairness in employment practices, positive equality of opportunity and social justice at work is substantively associated with the institutionalisation of these precepts in the social environment outside the organisation.

Human resources techniques such as HR planning and career development programmes have hitherto been relatively unsuccessful in ensuring relatively stable levels of employment across business cycles. Economic upturns have been characterised by recruitment drives for skilled labour including overseas recruitment, to increase employee strengths, while the highlighting of surplus staff during downturn periods, has occurred, with attendant arbitrary and short-term action taken to reduce such surpluses. An unstable political economy will, however, not prove attractive for potential overseas recruits. More important is the training and development of existing (indigenous) employees with identified potential for advancement.[9]

The effective development of human resources is the core of HR planning and is most effective as an organisational expression of a policy commitment. Human resource development is not merely about sending people on relevant training courses. It concerns a holistic organisational strategy which is led by line managers and supported by reward systems and the culture of the organisation.

TRAINING AND DEVELOPMENT TO FACILITATE POLICY PERFORMANCE

An espoused policy is part of the information and knowledge element of training. Once attempts are made at making policies operational, skills training in the application of

9 Horwitz, F. M. (1987)

policies should be given, for instance, in training supervisors to effectively handle the interpersonal requirements of a grievance procedure, or managers in negotiating skills and chairing a disciplinary enquiry.

Training and development assists not only in 'selling' a policy, but in reducing the anxiety which many managers and supervisors have when asked to carry out their responsibilities as required by a policy. The need for training in order to clarify and increase understanding of policies is perhaps even more important than the communication of policy information and skills training. Line managers seek not only a descriptive knowledge of company policies but also what they mean in terms of their jobs. This is why communication by written brief only is inadequate, if commitment to the implementation of policies is required. Given the inherency of conflicts within an organisation, the imperative of policy implementation necessitates a broader understanding and internalisation of the organisation's philosophy and objectives, facilitating a congruence or sharing of corporate, collective meanings and interpretations, and those of the individuals within the organisation. Prerequisites for the effective introduction of policy education and training include:[10]

- relating the policy to and integrating it with strategic organisational policies an objectives;
- securing senior and middle-management commitment by involving them in policy and strategy formulation. (They must see the end and benefits of the policy);
- allaying fears that such training will undermine the authority of supervisors (supervisors' possible concerns should be addressed prior to designing training programmes);
- a needs analysis based on the principles of the policy should ideally be done within the context of a consultancy-

10 Horwitz, F.M. (1986)

based organisational development initiative (training is not a panacea for all organisational problems); and

- a relationship with employees and trade unions where respect has been earned in an organisation culture and climate which is compatible with the espoused policies.

APPROACHES TO RELATIONS TRAINING IN THE MANAGEMENT OF PEOPLE

The approaches used might vary according to organisational size, structure and differing needs at various levels. There is an inverse relationship between the extent of human relations/interpersonal skills training and the development of conceptual and strategic thinking capability at different organisational levels.

For supervisory and junior level managers, a stronger focus should be made on knowledge and interpersonal skills development, whereas for middle to senior-level managers, the focus should be mainly on the raising of strategic thinking, conceptual capability and socio-political awareness.

Figure 7.3 depicts this mix of conceptual, social and procedural/ technical skills.

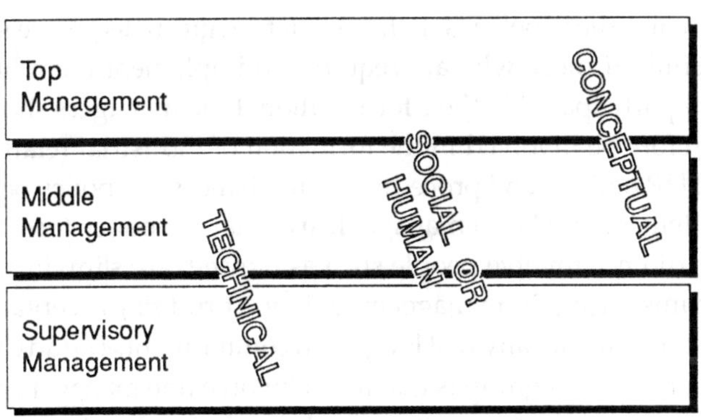

Figure 7.3

Management skills at various levels of an organisation

Source: Hersey, P. and Blanchard, K. (1988)

Training and development programmes should be integrated with overall corporate goals but should also explore the interrelationship between common, superordinate goals and areas of differing independent interests in the management-employee relationship. This would essentially reflect a pluralist conception of employee education and training. In-house seminars should focus on key strategic issues and environmental factors likely to affect the future direction of the organisation, and the responsibilities of managers.

There is a need to develop proactive behaviours and to raise managerial sensitivity to and awareness of the impact of social and political issues on the management of people. Extensive planning, organising and preparation, in the context of a detailed analysis of specific organisational problems and future demands is required for such a learning to be effective. An industrial relations or HR forum/contact group is potentially an effective method of gaining clarification and understanding of and support for policies. It is particularly beneficial at middle-management and supervisory levels. Regular contact group meetings can be held in an environment which is relatively 'safe' or non-threatening.

It also gives line managers and supervisors a chance to influence these policies. Policies can be legitimated more successfully if those who are required to implement them have fully participated in their formulation. Line managers should therefore be involved in the formation of industrial relations and HR policies and procedures. The chances of a policy being implemented when a manager learns that the policy formulation did not involve people such as himself, are slim. In such circumstances, the manager may show a grudging acceptance, but certainly not any real long-term commitment. The advantage of a contact group is that it can involve line managers and supervisors in policy matters in a defined job-related way, and can be designed to generate a sustained level of interest and involvement.

At middle or senior-management level the raising of social and political awareness by addressing key environmental issues is becoming increasingly important, particularly since these issues bring in to focus the need for defining core organisational values and strategies. Learning should aim at heightening sensitivity of the contextual process of influencing and linking decision-making in an interactive manner. The interdependent ramifications of decisions in the financial, technological and social/organisational and specifically the industrial relations spheres as well as in the wider environment, are depicted in Figure 7.4.

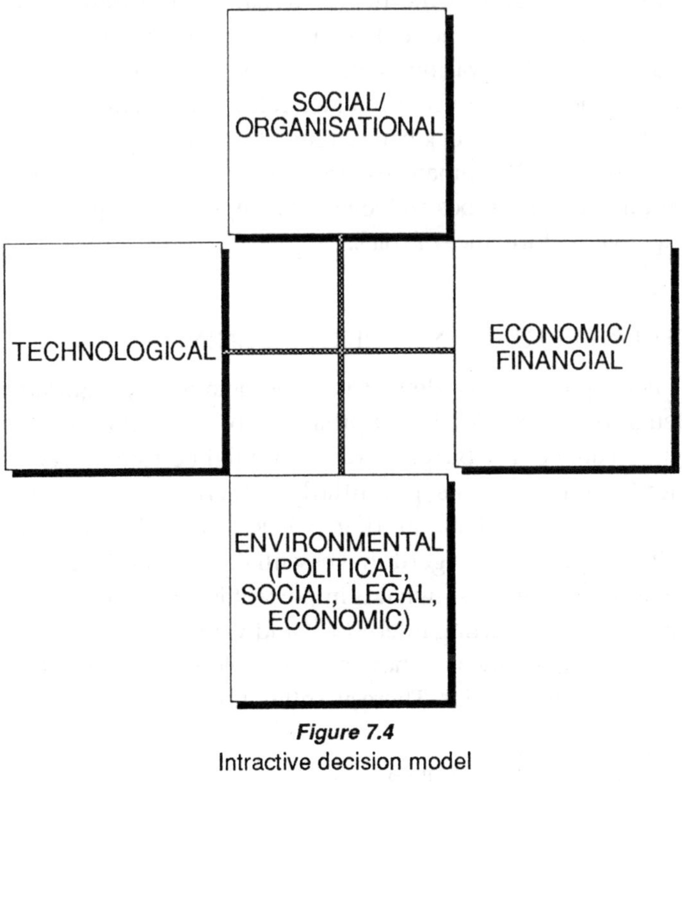

Figure 7.4
Intractive decision model

Creating a *learning culture* particular to an individual organisation's policies usually requires an internal job-orientated development programme which focuses on a number of areas including policy. The difficulty of including policy matters on a general training course tends to relate to the other objectives of the course, which may include knowledge, information and skills training. The question of time allocation for this as a major course element may, therefore, be limited, if it is included in a more 'general' course Preferably a learning programme focusing specifically on policy items should be instituted. Its emphasis should be on maximum participant involvement and job-relatedness with discussion and debate being encouraged to the full. A dynamic approach in this regard is one which moves beyond a focus on knowledge and skills required at various levels, to one which links critical competencies to a future-orientated role model.[11] This requires (1) the identification of job requirements derived from a critical evaluation of IR/human resource scenarios, and (2) identification of various types and levels of competency, required for effective performance of roles.

RECONCEPTUALISING POLICY TRAINING

This chapter has not delved into the details or programme items to be used for the approaches to policy training described above. The purpose was to highlight certain development approaches as potentially effective methods for implementing and monitoring policies. O'Neill and Lynas (1986) argue in this regard that essentially 'the method is not the important issue — what is important is the exploration of mutual and conflicting interests',[12] and values.

Training is only one, though nevertheless vital method for implementing policies. There are other multi-faceted ways of

11 Pieterse, D. (1989)
12 Lynass, O. and Neill, D. (1986)

implementing and monitoring the effectiveness of policies in addition to training, its evaluation and follow-up. Feedback from the participation of trade unions in regular joint meetings with management, use of grievance procedures, policy audits and an analysis of conflict indicators such as excessive absenteeism, are of vital importance in assessing the operational effectiveness of IR and HR policies.

An effective HR function should focus more on a process and consultative role, helping evolve less formal processes that line management can use to better manage people. This means that instead of developing and running a series of costly and time consuming training programmes for managers and supervisors, the HR specialist should help line managers evolve a simple effective process for developing managers and supervisors on the job. The consultation orientation will also require industrial relations and HR managers to help line managers learn and evolve new processes for managing people more effectively. This is essentially a *generalist* conception of people-development which focuses on the development of strategy and the shaping of organisational culture.

IR and HR management entails the deliberate alignment of plans and actions to the business strategy of the firm in order to ensure appropriate human behaviours as required by the business strategy. The concern is with organisational decision-making and behaviour rather than with the detailed content of 'traditional' HR systems. It is submitted, however, that the alignment referred to above should occur within an organisational framework of interactive and countervailing influences on strategic decision-making. Industrial relations and HR policies and influences should therefore form an integral part of business strategies rather than being a consequence of business strategies.

The development of a corporate culture supportive of employee development requires strategies and objectives to prepare and 'condition' the internal organisational environment. Setting specific goals for advancement cannot be successful without the requisite involvement of managers and supervisors in addressing values and attitudes which may impede the communication of corporate values and espoused policies. Downward communication alone usually fails to address employees' concerns, fears and prejudices. Processes for confronting these issues are vital.

HUMAN RESOURCE DEVELOPMENT AS A COMPONENT OF BUSINESS STRATEGY: THE PROBLEM OF TRANSFER

The development of human resources has to be a value intrinsic to the strategy and culture of an organisation. This makes the issue of transfer of learning a matter of strategic importance for the achievement of organisational goals.

As previously discussed, although human resource development is a process considerably broader in scope than training alone the latter is an important and often problematic concept of the complex task of development. Many organisations invest considerable sums of money annually in management and supervisory training programmes. Training is concerned with intentionally produced learning occurring. Off-the-job training is frequently associated with the problem of a lack of visible evidence of the results of training.

Most human resource development specialists agree that the effective transfer of off-job learning is problematic. Yet few organisations seem to have a coherent approach to addressing this issue. The absence of such an approach reflects poorly on the contribution of HRD specialists in identifying and facilitating the implementation of critical success factors for effective HRD. The problem is multi-faceted. It is typically revealed when trainees rate the learning they have received highly but fail to apply (i.e. transfer) the knowledge and skills in the work situation.

Other symptoms of the problem include frequent complaints expressed by HRD specialists about the lack of management support for HRD, a managerial concern of insufficient tangible benefits of training courses in spite of well-designed programmes and a vague understanding by both HRD specialists and managers of the root causes and basis of the transfer problem. In essence, the problem is one of *effectiveness.*

If the learning derived from training is not associated with enhanced job performance or raised capability, then the credibility of this process is at risk. The identification and implementation of factors associated with HRD effectiveness is therefore vital.

CRITICAL SUCCESS FACTORS

Transfer of learning can be simply defined as 'the degree to which an individual applies knowledge and skills learned through training and development programmes'.

If training and development is to be transferred effectively, it requires line-management commitment, management participation in training and most importantly, managerial responsibility for the development of their human resources.[13]

Commitment and involvement of line managers in this process are considered as two vital, but not necessarily identical processes. It is the latter, namely involvement, which is more closely associated with the effective transfer of learning.

HRD specialists are seen, ideally, as playing a facilitative and consulting role in advising and guiding management on how to ensure that what is learned is applied. Central to this role is the recognition that the trainee's manager plays a crucial part in the transfer process, given his/her power and influence.

13 Horwitz, F. M. and Rip, G. (1989)

Various barriers to the transfer of learning have been identified. A useful categorisation of these is in terms of the learner, the manager and the organisation. Two main factors which inhibit the transfer of learning are 'overload of work' and 'crisis work' both of which are inevitably influenced by the individual's manager.

Managerial actions in support of training and development can be grouped into five categories:

- upper management involvement;
- pretraining preparation;
- support during training and development;
- job linkage
- follow up.

Reference can also be made to the interactions between line management, trainees and trainers over a defined time period — before, during and after training.

With regard to preparing managers for transfer of training, it is important that managers:

- have their training and development role defined as a job responsibility and as a critical success factor in their performance objectives;
- are trained in how to facilitate transfer of learning; and
- be held accountable for transfer.

These approaches begin to address the strategic linking of HRD to organisational objectives. A strategic approach to transfer of training and development raises important questions regarding the responsibility, accountability, performance management, and reward systems in respect of training.

The definition and clarification of these four organisational factors is fundamental for developing a strategic approach to HRD and the transfer of learning.

THE ROLE OF HRD SPECIALISTS

The role definition of HRD specialists is an important factor associated with the effective transfer of training and development. Here too, the definition requires a clear specification of the HRD contribution to organisational goals, the responsibilities and accountabilities involved as well as the means towards achieving this contribution, for example, the balance between consulting, and providing training services.

The contribution of HRD specialists is crucially, their ability not only to offer services, knowledge and technical expertise; this is a necessary but not sufficient requirement for an effective contribution.

The ability to influence managerial decisions regarding HRD and to work as a respected partner in a jointly responsible endeavour to raise the capability of employees, is a primary responsibility of the HRD specialist.

Line managers, in turn, need to understand not only the training and development their people receive, but also the factors that may hinder the application of learning and their own attempts to reinforce it.

This understanding is also crucial in providing organisation culture where the knowledge and behaviours required of employees are displayed by their managers — the role-model concept. These requirements are again associated with the prevailing culture, reward systems and strategic goals of the organisation.

Criteria for effective transfer

A high degree of espoused top management commitment and support, while necessary, is not sufficient for the effective transfer of learning. The following factors adversely affect transfer:

- inadequate definition of training and development responsibilities and accountabilities of line management and HRD specialists;
- an absence of managerial reward systems for recognising and encouraging transfer;
- insufficient incorporation of training and development into managerial performance objectives and career planning systems including managerial advancement criteria
- insufficient managerial participation in training needs analysis, programme design, presentation and follow-up;
- an absence of processes for reinforcement and follow-up, and
- a tendency to emphasise quantity of training — numbers of people trained and not qualitative factors such as effectiveness and transfer.

The gap between espoused intentions and actual behaviour is an important concern. Three explanations are offered.

First, managers and supervisors lack the necessary knowledge and skill; secondly, they are not held responsible and accountable for the transfer and effectiveness of training and development; and, thirdly, this responsibility is not integrated into performance objectives and evaluation systems of managers. Only when there is a high probability that transfer of learning will occur is it worthwhile developing a training and development programme.

An emphasis on the quantity of training done may not indicate the extent of effective application or otherwise, of the knowledge and skills gained during training.

If training and development is to provide a satisfactory return on investment, it is not the number of people trained that is important, but the extent to which senior management ensures that appropriate evaluation and reward mechanisms focus the attention of management and HRD specialists on strategies which enhance the effectiveness of such development. This is a qualitative criterion.

In addition to the earlier points, some guidelines are suggested to facilitate the effective transfer:

A comprehensive statement of HRD philosophy and policy should be developed and communicated by top management — not the training and development department.

HRD's broader responsibility for managing a learning process rather than primarily presenting training courses should be clarified and agreed with top management. A strategic approach which is client/customer-need-orientated should be adopted.

INVOLVEMENT OF MANAGERS

This approach should seek the involvement of managers in all phases of HRD including need identification, programme design, presentation and reinforcement, and integration with manpower and career planning.

Each level of management should be held accountable for developing their human resources including the selection and evaluation of training given.

Consideration should be given as to whether the HRD specialist function can fulfil its role effectively without reporting directly at a senior executive level.

The achievement of these guidelines can be facilitated by addressing the question of HRD as a component of business strategy with attendant performance objectives and reward systems.

The development of human resources has to be a value intrinsic to the strategy and culture of an organisation.

This makes the issue of transfer of learning a matter of strategic importance for the achievement of organisational goals.

CONCLUSION: IMPERATIVES FOR DEVELOPMENT

South Africa has the anomaly of a shortage of high-level skilled, managerial and professional manpower, and an oversupply of unskilled labour. Estimates indicate over 40 000 vacancies in high-level manpower positions — a rate of 4,7 %. South Africa could face a shortage of up to 200 000 skilled employees by the year 2000. Yet over six million people could be unemployed,[14] and unemployment could reach nearly 10 million by the end of the century. The Institute for Futures Research at the University of Stellenbosch reports that the labour pool is likely to grow from 12 million in 1985 to 17,9 million at the turn of the century. Yet by that time, if past trends continue, the modern economy is likely to be able to employ not many more than 8,1 million people.[15] The shortage of skilled and managerial staff in construction, building, financial and other sectors is in sharp contrast to a huge surplus of unskilled, mostly black employees. South Africa has experienced a net loss of high-level manpower over the past decade. Not only is there an egress of knowledge and skills, but valuable leadership talent is being lost to the country. Yet over 62 % of the workforce has less than a standard-five level of education. Regarding unemployment according to educational level, more than 60 % of all black unemployed have an educational level of not higher than standard five, and a further 20 % of not higher than standard seven. [16] The skills shortage, on the other hand, is further aggravated by the tendency for many skilled and experienced people to retire before their official retirement age.

There is also a disproportionately high number of people obtaining a university education, with some 73 % of all students in tertiary institutions being at universities. According

14 Du Plessis, P. (1988)
15 Chalmers (1988)
16 Van der Merwe, P. (1989)

to the South African Institute of Race Realtions (1991), countries such as Germany and Japan could boast that 80 % of their people have technical rather than university education. The number of people in technical colleges is dropping in some areas. The value of technical education to society is considerably underemphasised.[17]

South Africa will have a projected 3 times as many black matriculants than whites by the year 2000, even if boycotts of schools are taken into consideration. In 1988 and 1989, over 80 % of apprentices in South Africa were white and 87 % of students in technical education institutions were white.

Clearly these 'demographic' imperatives for developing human resources offer an obvious rationale for achieving higher economic growth and prosperity. They underline the need for greater equity at all levels of development. Historical, socio-political and other factors relating to black exclusion, remain, however. While direct discriminatory legislation regarding the development and training of human resources has largely been removed, indirect and subtle barriers to occupational mobility remain, such as resistance to change and social exclusion within organisations.

The universal difficulty with human resource development lies not only with the lack of equality of opportunity for acquiring technical and managerial skills but also with the need for:

1. obtaining 'life skills', and increased self confidence; and
2. an organisational culture and reward system which encourages opportunities for development and growth.

Effective job performance is a function of:

1. knowledge, skills and experience,

17 Leatt, J. (1989). Address to Seminar on Management Education, Graduate School of Business, University of Cape Town. February 1989

2. ability,
3. motivation and willingness to perform, and
4. opportunity.[18]

Relevance and quality of the education and learning process is more important than 'playing the numbers game'. The latter may not necessarily provide employees or potential recruits with relevant knowledge and skills. This highlights the obvious need for equality of opportunity, integration, and the more effective utilisation of educational institutions at all levels. Even more importantly, it raises the imperative of both a national strategy for human resource development and holistic strategically linked organisational policies for optimising people development. South Africa is a developing society, not a First or Third-World country, nor an amalgam of both. While the daunting task of the politics of the long haul cannot be underestimated, when a more widely acceptable political system is instituted, and when the political intensity and predominance of industrial relations recedes, these demographic imperatives pose a stark and desperately urgent reminder of the need for a co-ordinated national policy and innovative organisational policies for human resource development. This constitutes South Africa's most fundamental challenge. We can hope, but we cannot wait for utopia.

18 Human, L. Lecture to MBA course delegates. Graduate School of Business, University of Cape Town, 2 March 1989

8

HUMAN RESOURCE MANAGEMENT: EUPHEMISM OR NEW PARADIGM?

INTRODUCTION

> 'More and more organisations are thinking globally about their employees. There is a trend towards thinking and planning for the more effective use of human resources. This is reflected in a change in terminology away from 'personnel' to 'human resources.'[1]

The term Human Resource Management (HRM) has become more widely used in South Africa. It is not, however, a very recent formulation.[2] Its roots go back to the 1950s, when Drucker advocated visionary goal-directed leadership and McGregor stressed the strategic importance of integrative management.[3] Some of the literature reflects a rather critical view of this apparent terminological shift.[4] Some critics argue that this shift is cosmetic and trendy. This chapter explores some of the apparent similarities and differences and offers an integration. Differences between functional, professional personnel and IR management on the one hand, and a generalist, organisational conception of managing people are differences in emphasis. These approaches are not mutually exclusive.

1 Harvey, L. (1986)
2 Nord, W. and Durand, D. (1978)
3 Armstrong, M. (1987)
4 Fowler, A. (1987)

This difference in emphasis seems 'real', but could facilitate both more enlightened and equitable management of employees, and the attainment of wealth creation..

It is possible to make a descriptive comparison based on a literature survey, of the HRM approaches.[5, 6, 7, 8, 9] Given that a more pervasive literature on HRM exists, there is little empirical work which seeks to clarify the alleged differences between Personnel Management and HRM. These differences are not always clearly articulated. A summarised, ideal-type comparison is presented here (Figure 8.1). This offers a simple overview of features of the two approaches. Application and practice may be blurred or less distinctive as the comparison in the table might imply. Figure 8.2 compares the HRM model with professional Personnel and the Paternalist Welfare model of the human-relations school.

The idealisation or romanticisation of HRM as a newfound panacea to organisational problems, is misplaced, as is the suggestion that 'traditional' personnel management systems and techniques, such as performance management and job evaluation systems are no longer appropriate. While most of the literature on HRM is not quite as explicit in these criticisms as stated here, some caution is necessary. A holistic approach to the management of people in organisations requires emphasis on *both* strategically-focussed management processes as well as supportive procedures and systems.

A comparison of features of personnel and human resource management approaches

It is instructive to explore briefly some of the more controversial issues associated with HRM.

5 Evans, P. (1984)
6 Fombrun, C. (1984)
7 Fowler, A. Ibid
8 Harvey, L. Ibid
9 Nord, W. and Durand, D. Ibid

PERSONNEL MANAGEMENT	HUMAN RESOURCE MANAGEMENT
Strong policy formulation orientation.	Strategically orientated, focusing strategic integration of HRM with business strategies. Tends to assume that commonality or mutuality of values is possible within and between organisations.
Emphasis on improving employee productivity through appropriate systems, procedures and training.	Emphasis on optimising common interests between management and employees.
Functional, specialist orientation with the value system of 'industrial humanism'.	A holistic approach: reinforcing desired organisational culture and business strategies.
Focus on education and professionalisation of specialists. Personnel manager responsible for personnel management. Personnel systems, procedural development and refinement (e.g. selection, job evaluation) are technique orientated.	Generalist conception of management of people. General line manager's responsibility for HRM shared with HR manager. Focus on performance management in the context of objectives derived from organisational values and strategy.
Performance management and appraisal systems focusing on job objectives and key performance areas.	Emphasis on qualitative decision-making: 'sensible judgements'. Strong focus on 'inspirational' general management leadership.

Figure 8.1
A comparison of features of personnel and human resources management approaches

PERSONNEL MANAGEMENT	HUMAN RESOURCE MANAGEMENT
Tendency towards formality of relations due to emphasis on personnel systems.	Tends to seek less formal relations.
Stresses long-term corporate planning and forecasting.	Stresses formulation of strategic direction and scenario planning. Seeks integration of individual with general business management seeking participation, commitment and initiative.
Employee participation: managerial-goal orientated — efficiency concern; to cope with productivity problems.	Long-term institutionalisation of innovation. Employee participation part of organisational culture. Focus on guiding values and people-orientated philosophy, but criticised as trying to reduce union influence.
Priority of professionalisation and functional competence.	Influence-based, not only on HRM's functional competence, but on relationships with line managers.
Service orientation.	Influence orientation.
Industrial, social psychology orientation.	Integrative and multi-disciplinary.
Focus on productivity sometimes perceived by employees as paternalistic.	Search for balance between equity, social justice, productivity and innovation remains problematic. (This is more strongly evident in industrial relations literature.)

	Paternalist welfare model	Profes-sional personnel model	HRM model
Orientation	Welfare, moral and humanist	Occupa-tional, ser-vice and manpower management	Managerial
Ideology	Paternalist	Collectivist	Individualist
Role	Person man-agement	Systems management	Resource management
Relationship with line management	Administrative	Advisory/ executive	Strategic
Generic activity	Human rela-tions	Industrial re-lations	Employee relations
Status of workforce	Staff	Employees	Professionals
Contract with workers	Social	Legal	Psychological
Role of unions	Marginal	Adversarial	Collaborationist
Change	Slow	Moderate	Continuous
Market position	Protected	Stable	Competitive
Attitude	Cost contain-ment of labour	Cost effectiveness	Human resource mutuality

Figure 8.2
Classification of the personnel function
Source: Farnam, D. Sunridge Park Management Review (Spring 1989)

MANAGING THE INTERNAL ENVIRONMENT: ORGANISATION BEHAVIOUR

The notion of 'managing the organisational context' relates to behaviour in an organisation and decision-making processes rather than personnel management. But it can underline the importance of supportive policies, and professional systems, procedures and practices. Visionary leadership and inspirational management may be necessary but not sufficient for sustained and enduring employee commitment. Effective motivational, reward and performance management systems remain important, and can be integrated with desired organisational values and individual behaviour. The provision of professional expertise in this regard has assumed greater paramountcy in the context of the complexities of contemporary labour relations developments in South Africa.

The attainment of mutuality of organisation culture and values may be unrealistic, in the context of viewing organisations as pluralist societies. While a 'toenadering' in the direction of commonality and convergence of values and objectives is desirable for optimisation of organisational performance, and reduction of attitudinal polarisation, it raises important ethical, ideological and socio-political questions.[9] These include the following:

1. Is it appropriate for the values of the managed to be decided by people other than themselves, or not at least formulated jointly?
2. how does senior management know whether these values are desired by other employees — are they likely to be relatively congruent?

This raises sensitive issues regarding the methodology of formulating and implementing specific values desired by a particular interest group. The organisational expression of

9 Horwitz, F.M. (1990)

particular value systems requires perceived and institutionalised legitimacy. The imposition of a value system considered alien and possibly hostile to prevailing values poses significant problems in respect of legitimacy and the defensive protection of interests. The 'values issue' cannot be over-simplified. Prevailing and often competing value systems within sub-cultures in organisations are not immutable, but change processes require careful consideration and planning.

While there are overlapping and common interests between different groups within organisations, the pursuit of complete identification by employees with the company and its values is reflective of a unitary ideology or an exclusively human-relations orientation. (See Chapter 1). The notion of a plurality of common and competing interests, values diversity and sub-cultures, suggests that the organisational promotion of overlapping values and goals, and the accommodation or institutionalisation diversity and conflict may enrich organisational experience and effectiveness. The tenets of pluralist and stakeholder perspectives view organisations as having a multiplicity of common and conflicting interests. Hence, the notion of freedom of organisational association and the attendant employee rights in respect of trade union affiliation, would be considered anathema to the somewhat utopian goal of the complete identification of employees with the company's values and ethos. Organisational accommodation of multiple loyalties may, however, be problematic. The unitary perspective views company and trade union loyalty as mutually exclusive. However, many organisations formulate strategies to adjust to complex environmental demands. This requires appropriate policies and a philosophy — democratic pluralism, which may be accommodative of multiple value systems, and differing interests.

'As long as the work values of the management class (which is white) and those of the managed (largely black) remain incongruous, human resource management will continue to be conflict-ridden.'[10] Khoza proposes that providing blacks with a real stake in the economy and incorporating them substantively into the corporate management structure, could bring about a convergence of Protestant work ethic and humanistic work value systems. The values accommodation thesis is supported by Adler (1980) [11] who suggests that changes in organisational culture may be brought about so as to facilitate a balanced 'cultural synergy', incorporating the values of different groups in the organisation. The development of workable methodologies for achieving this is an important challenge for HRM specialists.

The notion of power

The notion of power, its locus in terms of group interests, and the infuence of 'dominant coalitions', may indicate temporary variability of power, and the development of multiple relationships in an organisation between key power figures. These may also be groups other than management, such as trade union representatives. Many HRM professionals seem to have forgotten that the group is the most important target for Organisational Development (OD) strategies.[12]

Employee involvement

The HRM theme positively seeks employee involvement.[13] [14] This is an important development in principle. The scope and level of involvement tends to focus primarily on enhancing productivity at individual and small-group level. The participative goals often tend to be managerially defined in efficiency

10 Khoza, R. (1986)
11 Adler, N. (1980)
12 Strümpfer, D. (1986)
13 Beer, M., Spector, B., Lawrence, P., Quinn Mills, D., and Walton, R. (1984)
14 Harvey, L. Ibid

terms, e.g. quality circles. Collective or representational participation (IR model) in the governance of organisations beyond the level of individual jobs is not adequately addressed in HRM literature.

The IR notion of power, and its distribution at various organisational levels, is also not prominent in HRM literature. This might imply a 'blindness to the role of trade unions in providing a degree of balance in the exercise of economic authority.'[16] The much-vaunted idea of a equal partnership between mnagement and employees can only start to become relatively meaningful in the context of a near power-balance between these interest groups at a collective group level.

Hierarchical and bureaucratic organisational models tend to be maligned in contemporary management writings (Fowler 1987, op. cit., p. 3) in favour of decentralised and flat organisations. However, these models may be appropriate for certain circumstances. Mintzburg (1984)[17] proposes that with organisational growth and cyclical change, different power systems tend to develop and become entrenched. This would have potentially important consequences for the type, and overall nature of HRM in the organisation.

General management conception of HRM

A general management conception of HRM and the adoption of strategic approaches,[18, 19, 20] are important developments in a shift in emphasis from functionally orientated personnel management to line management of human resources. There nevertheless remains a crucial need for the specialist provision of professional support and influence to line managers at all

16 Fowler, A, Ibid
17 See Mintzberg, H. (1984) 'Power and Organisation Life Cycles'. *Academy of Management Review*, 9(2. 207–224
18 Fombrun, C. Ibid
19 Horwitz, F.M. (1988)
20 Pansegrouw, G. (1985)

levels within a relevant framework of well planned, 'user friendly', but principled HR and industrial relations systems and procedures.

Contemporary writings on human resource management tend to reflect a shift towards paradigms of organisational culture change.[21, 22, 23]. This more holistic approach to the management of human resources also suggests that the context of human resource management has significant theoretical derivation from organisation theory and may have application integratively, through OD interventions. The practice of HRM and its support by professional personnel practices and procedures is, however, by necessity, a continuous developing and innovative process, which can be linked to business and organisation strategies through OD approaches. In itself, HRM is not necessarily an intervention except when introduced into organisations for the first time, and in the context of an articulated organisational philosophy and strategy.

A proactive consultative orientation by specialists may reflect an on-going interaction and countervailing influence on management decisions and processes. It is not by necessity reactive, but helps in the formulation and learning of new processes for managing human resources effectively. While, a strategic HRM concern with the organisational culture and context is important, the need for professional expertise and innovation in respect of extending and improving personnel and industrial relations policies, procedures and practices, necessitates the continued institutionalisation of personnel and industrial relations functionalist expertise. This is particularly important in assisting the organisation and its internal stakeholders, such as management groups, employees, and their representatives, in dealing with change and uncertainty.

21 Beer, M. et al. Ibid
22 Evans, P. Ibid
23 Fowler, A. Ibid

Locus of decision-making

One of today's major organisational trends is toward decentralisation.[24] As organisations decentralise, however, they may tend to centralise certain HRM and industrial relations and control functions. In general, it would seem that policy development is formulated centrally, but greater freedom is being granted regarding operationalisation of policies, and values, at lower levels (Harvey 1986). Broad policy parameters and monitoring controls may tend to be formulated centrally even in operationally decentralised organisations.

In the South African context, research findings indicate a transfer of responsibility for decision-making responsibility to the HR or industrial relations department.[25] The centralisation of such decision-making in a service function, albeit often an influential one, risks creating a line-management over-dependency on specialists in HRM and industrial relations. A potentially over-dependent relationship of this nature may have the following consequences:

1. There is a shift in the locus of power and decision-making away from line managers to HR and industrial relations departments. Employees may as a consequence find that executive authority rests with people outside of their departmental management. The expectation may be created that grievances and problems can be addressed only by the HR or Industrial Relations department, rather than resolved by general management.
2. It discourages managers from assuming responsibility for the management of human resources, and attendant decision-making.
3. There is a shift in leadership and the emphasis of reward structures for managers away from the imperative of excellence in HRM and IR towards other priorities.

24 Naisbitt, J. (1984)
25 Hall, R. (1985)

4. It reduces the incentive for raising managerial HRM capability.

The attainment of a generally acceptable locus of decision-making and appropriate reward structures for managerial HRM performance are important variables potentially substantively associated with levels of conflict between groups in organisations. The shifts suggested by Hall's findings are not reflective of a generalist conception of human resource management. The organisational clarification of these philosophical and strategic issues is a necessary prerequisite for achieving a productive balance between managerial HRM practices and professional systems and procedures. The two models are not mutually exclusive. HRM is, however, neither a euphemism for Personnel Management, nor a replacement for the continuing need for professional functionalist and specialist expertise. It is none the less reflective of a realisation by managers at various organisational levels of the imperative for the institutionalisation of HRM into the decision-making responsibility, operational practice, and reward systems (formal and informal) of management work. This need becomes more prominent in order to realise organisational values, objectives and strategies and also to manage effectively the power relations involved in contemporary industrial relations.

CONCLUSION

While the shift towards a generalist, line management conception of HRM suggests a greater awareness of the need for strategic operationalisation of HRM principles, the functional specialist contribution of IR and personnel practitioners serves to provide an important influence in several areas (Figure 8.3). The specialists's effectiveness is derived from:

1. his/her expert power/sapiential authority, rather than traditional or hierarchical authority,

Custodial

Policies and personnel systems (e.g. selection, testing, performance appraisal, industrial relations policies and procedures)

Advisory

Interpretation of policies, procedures and agreements' decision consequences:

- ❑ organisational/social and economic
- ❑ labour law
- ❑ environmental

Consultative

Improving managerial processes, leadership capability and organisation climate.

Informative

Micro and intra-organisational developments e.g. legislative changes

- ❑ changes to agreements and procedures
- ❑ briefing systems

Administrative

Personnel systems: recruitment (e.g. advertising)

- ❑ compensation/remuneration
- ❑ people flows: transfers, promotions, leavers

Developmental

Policy and procedure formulation, intra-organisational negotiation, implementation, monitoring and update

Strategy formulation, internal negotiation

implementation, monitoring, and change.

Figure 8.3

Personnel and industrial relations: functional contribution

2. the ability to forge positive, co-operative relationships with line managers and employee representatives, and
3. the ability to influence both strategic and operational decision-making, and cultural change in an organisation.

Figure 8.4 presents a model, depicting the functional role differences between the qualitative emphasis on social processes and organisation change reflected in a strategic HRM approach, as contrasted to the perhaps more quantitative systems orientation of Personnel Management.There is a necessary interdependence between a professional, specialist function, its organisational contribution, and the managerial challenge of implementing strategically effective, and equitable management of people. There are no instant solutions to the complex task of managing in turbulent times. Innovative management approaches are, however, more likely to facili-

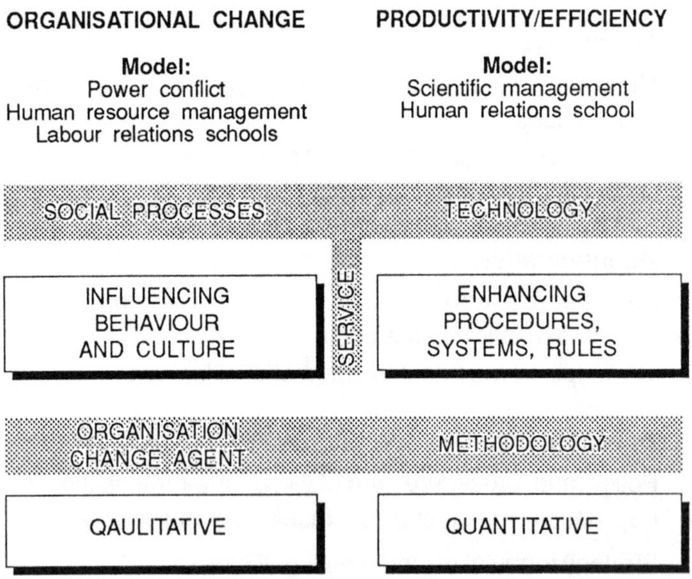

Figure 8.4
Functional HRM definition

tate enduring change, if the propensity for adopting the latest fads were to be avoided. Soundly principled, relevant developments based on building from past experience and current research, may offer both unique opportunities and realistic goals.

9

MANAGING PEOPLE: STRATEGY, FLEXIBILITY AND CHANGE

Intense competitive pressures, changing demands on political leadership, transnational economies and the emergence of knowledge societies have created a new global reality.[1] This reality in all its complexity creates new demands on how organisations manage their people. The notion of strategy in people-management requires definition.

Strategic human resource management can be defined as achieving competitive edge through the effective attraction, motivation, development, rewarding and involvement of people in organisations. But this definition does not tell us enough about how competitive edge is achieved. The key principle in this regard is that of *strategic fit* — how the organisation aligns its priorities, goals and resources to identified external demands. An organisation can achieve this focus by adapting to its environment or influencing and *shaping* its environment. Adaptation is largely reactive. Shaping is proactive where organisations seek to influence and change relevant aspects in the environment in which they operate. Handy (1989) in describing the adaptive organisation uses the metaphor of the frog in boiling water.[2] Its body adapts to the heat by becoming larger and more bloated until it is boiled alive. The frog has not acted on its environment. Adaptation involves responding, the shaping process requires strategic ac-

1 Drucker, P. (1990)
2 Handy, C. (1990)

tion. Yet in practice both may occur in organisations. Figure 9.1 illustrates this process.

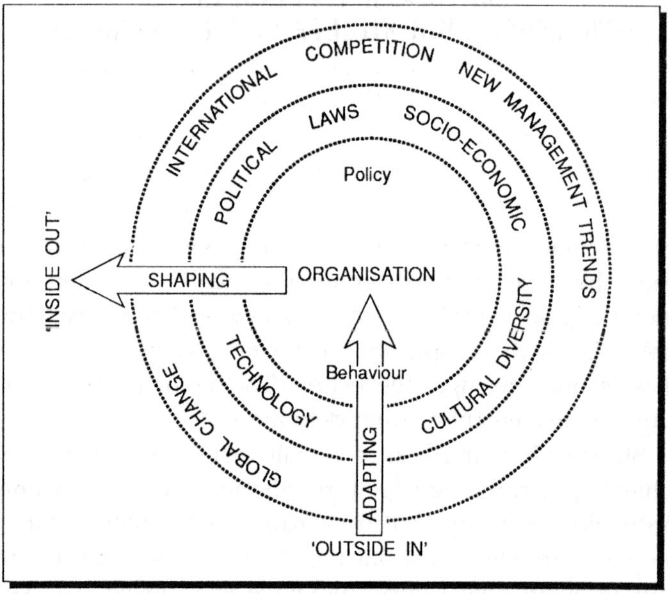

Figure 9.1
Adapting to and shaping change: internal and external fit

The question of strategic fit has two components; the first being the internal/external environment fit. The second 'fit' is the internal fit between espoused values and policies and their practice and actual behaviour in organisations. If internal fit does not occur, external fit is not possible. The alignment of policy, strategy and behaviour in organisations towards achieving defined goals is a key requirement for a strategic approach to managing people. Yet total fit and complete alignment may be problematic.

The problem with complete fit is that an organisation may develop such a strong entrenched culture as to be unable to cope with rapid change in the environment. The environment itself is not static, and just as a fit is attained, a significant new wave of change may occur in the external environment. On the other hand, complete flexibility and adaptiveness may according to Zaleznik (1990), detract from the substance of the business and the organisational cohesion and common purpose needed to achieve goals.[3] The environment of the 1990s will experience continuous change where old assumptions about organisations and managing people will no longer be valid. Handy (1990) rejects the distorted 'accountancy view' of people in organisations. Traditional accounting procedure sees people as costs and not assets. Assets can grow and expand. He notes that countries in Europe pay the highest wages, work the shortest hours, and yet several are amongst the most prosperous in the world. Handy refers to the emergence of 'brain skill jobs' rather than muscle skill jobs. He estimates that nearly 80 % of jobs in Europe and the United States will require technical, occupational or professional qualifications. These post-industrial society developments may seem remote for a developing economy such as South Africa with some 60 % of its work force with a primary school education or none at all and with a severe oversupply of unskilled people. Yet the South African economy is an international competitor and its businesses have to compete effectively in global markets. In spite of frequent arguments of 'uniqueness', South Africa is not an island and shares many similar problems with other developing countries, one of them being the need for economic growth and productivity improvement.

INDIVIDUAL EMPOWERMENT

The HRM notion of individual empowerment is linked to the idea of people as assets which are capable of growing. Chair-

3 Zaleznik, A (1990)

man of Pick and Pay, Raymond Ackerman, refers to the importance of 'people power' in organisations — not only in a collective sense through trade union representation, but particularly through empowerment of individuals through opportunity and support for development and encouraging participation and involvement in decision-making. Individual empowerment includes the following:

Individual empowerment

- ❑ Involve people
- ❑ Listen, recognise, celebrate and reward achievements
- ❑ Upgrade education
- ❑ Train and retrain
- ❑ Problem-solving teams
- ❑ Remove —
  - unnecessary structures
  - bureaucracy
  - divisive thinking

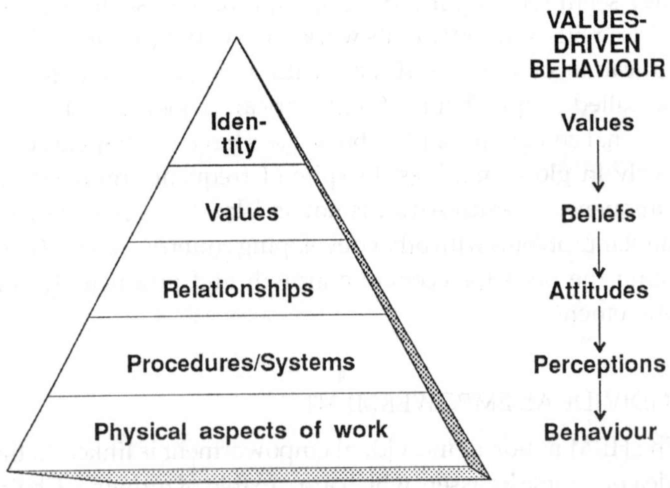

Figure 9.2
Levels of addressing organisation issues

Integration

- Management strategy
- Vertical integration of strategic and operational priorities
- Employee identification, stakeholding

Employee commitment

- Involvement of individuals
- Higher job satisfaction and performance
- Longer tenure/retention
- Acceptance of change

Flexibility

- Organisation structure
- Job content/work design
- Pay systems
- Working time
- Training and skills versatility

Quality

- Competencies
- External image
- HR policies
  (e.g. selection criteria, training, job design)
- Service

Figure 9.3
Policy goals of HRM

POLICY GOALS IN HUMAN RESOURCE MANAGEMENT

Guest (1990) identifies HRM as having four policy goals.[4] These are integration, employee commitment, flexibility and quality.

1. Integration

Integration has four components: management strategy, vertical integration between strategic priorities, management and operational concerns, line management attitudes and behaviour, and the view that all employees should be integrated fully into the business. Underlying these elements is the proposition that if HR management is integrated into strategic planning, if human resource policies are aligned and line management have internalised the responsibility for managing people as reflected in their behaviour and employee identification with corporate goals occurs, the organisation's strategic plans are more likely to be implemented successfully. Change is facilitated and resistance to it reduced.

2. Employee commitment

Employee commitment seeks to develop a sense of involvement by individuals in the organisation. This, according to Farnham and Pimlott (1990) is likely to enhance job satisfaction, productivity and adaptability of employees. The theoretical proposition is the organisational commitment together with job-related behaviour commitment is associated with higher employee satisfaction performance and longer tenure.

3. Flexibility

Flexibility is based on the proposition that flexible organisational structures, work design and job content, reward systems and skills, will result in greater capacity to respond

4 Guest, D. (1990)

swiftly and effectively to change thereby ensuring high utilisation of people.

4. Quality

Quality has a number of elements. These include people and their performance in terms of desired core organisational values, managerial practices, public image and particularly the employer's HR policies. To ensure high quality, attention has to be focused on incorporating core values into the recruitment and selection process and criteria, training and development, performance management, goal setting and job design. Emphasis is on achieving competencies and not just skills. Quality and flexibility are key related HR concepts with the latter emphasising more effective utilisation of people through multi-skilling, knowledge pay and reward systems such as gainsharing. These more recent HR practices focus on a different use of job descriptions. These become results and performance orientated in their wording, rather than focusing on duties, task and hierarchical position. HR systems are therefore forward-looking and performance-orientated. Their prime purpose is to give effect to the organisation's goals and purpose and they seek to achieve a strategic fit between HR and organisational priorities in order to enhance competitive edge of the organisation and its performance. Guest argues, that the origins of HRM are based on the competitive need to improve product and service quality. HRM seeks to optimise the fit between human resources in an organisation and the latter's main stakeholder, namely customers. The attempt to give strategic *focus* to people in organisations who are closest to the customer can be expressed in the form of an inverted pyramid (figure 9.4)

The inverted pyramid suggests that people higher up the hierarchy may be furthest away from being in touch with customer needs. This underlines the importance of reinforcing and rewarding strategic behaviour at *all* levels. The notion that

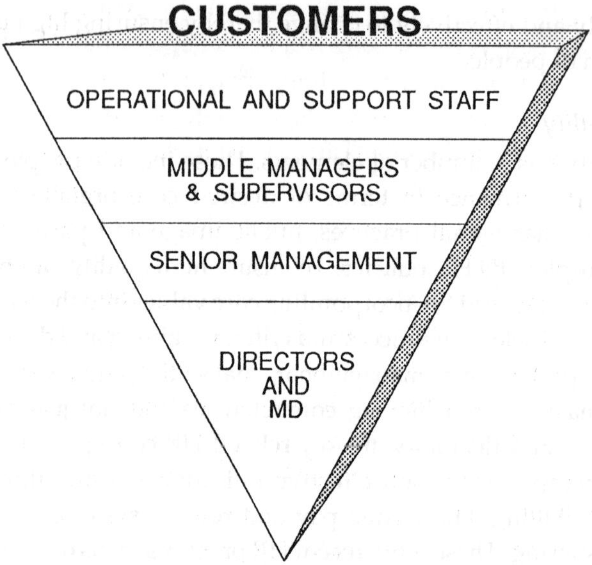

Figure 9.4
Inverted pyramid

strategic thinking and action is possible only at senior management levels is false. It is a denial of the talents and potential of other employees, who usually know their jobs better than their managers and who are more likely to know their immediate customers' expectations.

ORGANISATION STRUCTURE

Handy argues that organisations will concentrate more reserves on activities at the core of the business and achieve greater flexibility through contracting out activities at the periphery or by establishing a cadre of temporary and part-time employees. The core is likely to become more professional in the versatility, range of competencies and knowledge. He suggests that with decentralisation and diversification, federal-type structures which are relatively decen-

semi-autonomous and flexible are likely to become more prevalent. These organisations will be leaner and flatter. Development is more likely to be horizontal and on the job and by job rotation, new assignments, and lateral moves aimed at increasing the individual's array of competencies and knowledge of the organisation. Employees will, more and more, become 'knowledge workers', with a decline in manual work occurring. Handy argues that these changes will require a different leadership style. He refers to the notion of the 'post-heroic' leader managing highly trained, versatile and independent people by consent rather than by decree. Technical, human and conceptual skills are required in this leadership style. The 'post-heroic' leader lives vicariously, getting kicks out of other peoples' successes — as old fashioned leaders have always done (p 132).

Prominent authors[5 6] argue that the centre in decentralised organisations is neither in full control, nor on the other hand, are decentralised business units completely autonomous. Handy (op. cit. p. 100) refers to the term subsidiarity, which means giving away power. The core is a *learning organisation* which provides opportunities for personal growth and development. He argues that effective leadership from the centre is leadership of ideas not of personalities.

Zaleznik (1990), however, argues that decentralisation actually serves control rather than the reverse. He states that 'dividing organisations into profit centres or centres of initiative, became a possibility when managers realised they could exercise control through a process in which people were left alone, relatively speaking, and still conformed to expectations' (p 95). He contends that self-determination and therefore decentralisation is illusory, since ultimately the budget, which is the main determinant of autonomy, is in most organisations

5 Goold, M. and Campbell, A. (1990)
6 Handy, C. Ibid

approved by the centre, even if some 'negotiation' occurs. Autonomy in meeting approved targets is autonomy of operations but not of policy. Internal financial and human resource expenditure controls invariably occur under the guise of co-ordination needed for decentralised units. No organisation is completely decentralised. Autonomous units might share research and development, marketing, financial, legal, HR and information systems procedures (Zaleznik, p 155).

New forms of alliance occur in decentralised organisations. Senior managers form alliances mainly with their staff. This may pit decentralised management against divisional or group executives who may seek to exert influence or control from the centre. This also reduces the possibility of a pervasive corporate culture across various decentralised operations forming part of a large group. Employee and managerial

identification is not with that of the group and its corporate values but is more localised. Decentralisation and the associated vaunted flexibility may, therefore, limit the expansion of a common corporate culture across units, and may indeed limit effective group policy implementation.

Zaleznik argues that if individuals and organisations were totally adaptive and flexible, there would be little room for creativity and leadership (p 194). Social cohesion created by internalised values and a corporate culture provides identity and direction. Norms of behaviour, symbols and cultural rituals then follow. These form the glue which binds people together in co-operative pursuit of organisational goals. Zaleznik refers to this as the 'institutional character', with the danger of a diffusion of identity in flexible organisations, with totally adaptable people. He argues that too much adaptability and flexibility reflects a lack of substance and an overemphasis on process. Good substantive ideas and leadership reflecting strong core values seek common purpose in organisations. Too much flexibility may militate against common purpose. Yet well-known, successful case studies in flexibility, quality and teamwork, such as in Nissan[7] and General Motors' Saturn Project, highlight innovative ways of managing and developing people in modern organisations. Guest (1988) argues, however, that there is some doubt as to the extent of these practices occurring in the United States (US). He criticises the tone of much of the Harvard Business School writing, which emphasises the importance of HRM rather than to claim it is currently practiced to any great extent. A key article in this regard is Walton's (1985) 'From control to commitment', in the *Harvard Business Review*. Guest estimates that not more than 10 % of US companies are practicing HRM effectively as a general management function. Research cited by Guest indicates that in the US, less than 20 % of companies have HRM planning fully integrated into strategic planning. Kochan et al (1988) estimate that no more than 23 per cent of employees are affected by human resource policies.[8] In a critical article, Kantor and Mirvis (1989) argue that the 'marketing of individualism in HRM obscures a form of free market liberalism in which only the toughest survive'.[9] It is an individualism which flourishes on self interest. They conclude that 'the messianic rhetoric of HRM is well ahead of the reality in industry, in all but a handful of companies'. Guest, however, underlines the notion that the creation of a learning culture, and an environment of opportunity may create an organisational microcosm of values desired in the wider society.

Armstrong (1990) refers to shifts in the *assumptions* about how people should be managed.[10] Central to HRM thinking are the following notions:

1. A long-term *coincidence of interest* between all *stakeholders* in an organisation.

7 Wickens, P. (1988)
8 Kochan, T. et al (1988)
9 Kanter, D. and Mirvis, P. (1989)
10 Armstrong, M. (1989)

2. Power equalisation is key to encouraging openness and collaboration.
3. People are capable of *growth* in terms of skills, values and commitment, when the work environment encourages it.
4. *Legitimacy* of organisation objectives is needed to secure motivation.
5. *Participation* in problem definition and solution increases commitment to new directions.
6. A *mutuality* policy aimed at eliciting employee commitment, thereby improving organisational effectiveness and optimising common interests is a core component of HRM.
7. Redefining the *nature of work*, giving the rapid advances in new technology intense competition and changing values. New types of organisational structures, flatter, leaner and more flexible with multi-skilling, autonomous teams and variable pay systems, are becoming more prevalent. Performance-related payment systems focusing on results achieved, using flexible compensation designs, are becoming more widely used at various levels in the US, Britain, Japan and other Pacific rim countries.

CONCLUSIONS

Wickens (1988) in his acclaimed book *The Road to Nissan*, strongly argues a similar theme to that of Walton, namely the perceived need to acquire employee commitment and identification as stakeholders in the business. Much contemporary writing and initiatives in HR seek to reduce the 'us and them' dichotomy between managers and employees — rather creating a so-called 'we' or 'just us' attitude. The emphasis is clearly on enhancing the individual relationship and trying to move away from the adversarial tradition of collective bargaining. The emphasis on individualism in HR positively seeks personal growth and development, together with task-level involvement. Participation is direct rather than indirectly through trade union representatives. Teamwork is seen as an important part of the work process.

The paradigms of individualism and collectivism have been written about extensively by Purcell (1988), who argues that ideally, organisations should enhance effectiveness through individual growth, development and commitment and also build co-operative relationships with trade unions, in order to institutionalise conflict.[11] The creation and internalising of employee rights and relationship building are not mutually exclusive. They can, indeed, reinforce each other. Ultimately, the distinction between rights and employment relationships may become blurred, as indeed might the distinction between individual and collective relationships. Unless co-operative individual relationships are nurtured, the collective relationship will tend towards adversarialism.

Individual relationships and HR initiatives emphasize the creation of wealth through progressive management of people integrated into the organisation so as to achieve focus towards its goals. The collective or indirect relationship paradigm concerns the distribution of wealth through collective bargaining and the protective or defensive goals of trade unionism in ensuring fair labour practices and the advancement of rights. The collective paradigm stresses committee and representative structures and redress, while the individualist paradigm focuses on teams or autonomous work groups. The distinction is further made in respect of the performance and job competency orientation as compared to the emphasis on conditions of employment in the collective relationship. Clearly, the issues dealt with differ, yet these processes ought to complement each other in practice. It is possible and indeed desirable to be strong in both individual and collective relations.

11 Purcell, J. (1988)

10

EXTENDING POLICY INFLUENCE: ORGANISED BUSINESS AND SOCIAL DEVELOPMENT

INTRODUCTION

The process of industrialisation in developing countries exacerbates the inherent conflict between employers and employees over competition for a share of scarce resources. In these emergent nations, employer organisations, on behalf of industry and commerce, have a vital responsibility and opportunity to service as agents for channeling nascent industrial conflict through agreed structures and procedures and for co-ordinated policies for the development of human resources. Furthermore, labour legislation, manpower development and strategies for the effective utilisation of national manpower resources, are important areas which necessitate employer influence on state HR policy.

The paucity of social benefits provided by the state in many developing societies also requires a greater cohesion between employer associations, organised labour and the state, than seems to be the case in highly industrialised countries. In this regard, employer bodies in Southern Africa need to explore opportunities for further dialogue with union groupings, with the aim of creating a forum for negotiating joint accords at the national level. A restructured National Manpower Commission could potentially meet this need. This requires unity of action on the part of employer associations to give expression to pragmatic social policy programmes and thereby match the emphasis by many unions on community involvement. Social policy items on the management–union agenda could include social security, housing, pensions and provident funds, sick-pay, medical benefits and unemployment benefits.

FACTORS RELATING TO NATIONAL HUMAN RESOURCE DEVELOPMENT

Structured conflict is usually defined in terms of competition for economic resources, social status and political power, and should not necessarily be seen as bad or destructive. Employer organisations and trade unions in developing societies have tended up until now to focus on competition for economic reasons only. This conflict has been regulated mainly through the mechanism of collective bargaining between employer associations and trade unions in countries such as South Africa, and also between individual companies and trade unions, for instance in South Africa, Nigeria and the Sudan.[1]

Infrastructural and human resource development is of great importance in developing countries and may, indeed, occur before a significant degree of industrialisation has evolved. Many African countries share a number of socio-economic characteristics that are potential sources of conflict and affect the role of employer organisations. Common features include:

- a relatively recent process of industrialisation, with rural economic activity, often of a subsistence nature, frequently predominant;
- high levels of illiteracy and poor education affecting the quality of the workforce;
- high unemployment and underemployment;
- lack of investment in the kind of industrial and human resource development which could contribute to growth;
- disparities in the distribution of wealth and opportunity, with widespread poverty;

1 Horwitz, F. M. (1986a)

- varying degrees of political and economic stability;
- ethnic, cultural and language diversity, which contributes to a complex and diverse social fabric; and
- perceptions of 'relative deprivation': the discrepancy between people's own expectations and the material 'goods' they actually obtain.

Developing societies therefore experience a range of particular social conflicts that influence the development role of individual employers and employer bodies.

TRANSNATIONAL BARGAINING

In this broader context, what are the main characteristics of industrial relations in developing African nations?

Initially, a multitude of trade unions emerged in the early phases of industrialisation, with industrially based unions only developing much later in the 1970s and 1980s. The processes of industrialisation and political independence may be viewed as being interdependently related to the organisational development of trade unions. In this early stage, like trade unions, employer and trade organisations also tend to be fragmented.

Over time, a number of employer bodies have developed into fully fledged employer organisations. They provide consultancy and educative services to members in the industrial relations sphere, and attempt to influence national social and economic strategies. In the process there is a shift from company and plant-level negotiations towards centralised, industry-based structures for collective bargaining, accompanied by government regulation of minimum wages and conditions of employment. Employer organisations vary in respect of member commitment to progressive HR and industrial relations policies. The most enlightened policies and practices tend to be found in companies who are linked to multi-national corporations.

A sound policy framework is vital for effective regulation of HR development and the creation of an acceptable body of employee rights. A system of collective bargaining cannot be developed without a joint input from local employer bodies and organised labour. At the same it is unrealistic to believe that the creation of national manpower policies in a developing economic region can take place totally indigenously or in isolation.

The socio-economic interdependence of the various development regions in Southern Africa is a product of geopolitical realities. This is also the case in highly industrialised western countries such as Canada, where several American-based trade unions are integral participants in the Canadian industrial relations system.

Labour agreements between South Africa and the main labour supplying states in Southern Africa — Botswana, Lesotho, Swaziland, Malawi and Mozambique — are very similar in their content. The vast majority of the black workers employed in the South African mining industry (88,8% in 1982) were from South African homelands and independent neighbouring countries.[2] Therefore it makes sense to advance similar labour relations frameworks across constitutional boundaries in the region, to facilitate greater industrial stability and socio-economic development. The potential for the establishment of cohesive employer and trade union strategies and policies is likely to be weakened by the pursuit of a set of exclusive and indigenous policies in the sub-continent.

CONTRIBUTING TO NATIONAL DEVELOPMENT

It is inappropriate to compare productivity indices of first-world industrialised countries with the third world, or with other economies like South Africa, which is a mixture of both the first and third worlds. When South Africa's performance

2 Whitseside, A. (1984)

is compared with third-world countries, its gross domestic product (GDP) ranks among the top achievers. South African per capita GDP for 1980 was R1 071 and was obviously high in comparison to those of Zambia (R298) and Kenya (R165). However, it does not compare favourably with the per capital GDP for most first-world countries, which was over R5 000 in 1980.[3] Social inequality and disparity in wealth, as determined by the Gini coefficient, indicates that South Africa has one of the highest disparities in wealth in the world. In the Western Cape, for example, 22 % of blacks have formal housing. Nationally, only 16 % of black people have electricity, although South Africa produces 60 % of Africa's electricity.[4]

The developing nature of South Africa's economy and of other intermediate developing nations inhibits their successful competition in international markets. An important area of social responsibility for the business sector — and by implication, organised labour organisations — is to supplement state efforts in the spheres of schooling and general education, housing, health and welfare and social security schemes such as pensions. In other words, the demands posed by social expenditure, though an unavoidable and necessary aspect of business operations in developing regions, inevitably add to labour costs and undermine market competitiveness.

If developing countries are to compete successfully on international markets they will have to raise productivity levels, through devoting considerable efforts to improving the general level of education and technical skills training of the population. The development of co-ordinated training schemes on an industry-specific bases and sometimes across industries where certain common skills are required, is an area where employer and union organisations can make an important contribution. Besides the productivity advantages, all of

3 Etheredge, D. (1984)
4 Emanuel, T. (1991)

these efforts are also crucial for economic growth, attendant job creation and improved living standards and prosperity. Employer associations and trade unions can assist in national development by establishing training education programmes for their workers, thus raising productivity levels. This requires a commitment by organised business and labour to centralised collective bargaining structures and the idea of seeking bilateral accords.

In many African countries, low economic growth is related to the fact that a major proportion of the economically active population is employed in non-wealth-producing public sector organisations. In South Africa, for example, 30 % of the economically active population is employed by the state. Consequently, the process of wealth generation in developing countries tends to rest with a small private sector. It must meet the immense challenge of generating sufficient wealth to be itself socially responsive, while sustaining and increasing state welfare, education and health services through taxation.

ENGAGING CHANGE

Business is a corporate citizen and has a responsibility to exercise influence on macro-political decisions affecting its interests.[5] Organised industry cannot alone be responsible for improving the socio-economic fabric of society. Employer organisations have to be influential enough on government to achieve changes in critical areas of policy and statute which affect the social and economic imperatives of a developing society. Successful political change is more likely to occur with economic growth, and higher growth is more attainable with such change.

As any plural society reflects various conflict and power interests, there is also a need for organised business to extend dialogue and interaction with organised labour to expand the

5 Godsell, R. (1985)

'traditional' industrial relations agenda. Large corporations should direct resources so as to support more actively the functions of employer associations and should be involved in social projects in conjunction with trade union leaders, and important bodies such as the Urban Foundation.

There is, therefore, a fairly unique responsibility in respect of employer organisations in developing societies. In societies such as Nigeria, the Sudan and South Africa, they have only recently begun to exert more overt and expressive lobbying activities with government to influence political, social and economic change. Greater policy co-ordination between various employer associations and organised industry as a whole will become even more crucial in a 'new' South Africa. Human resources issues such as training and development are rightly becoming part of a new agenda and possible social accords between employer and trade union organisations. Social responsibility can no longer be a cinderella activity, dispensing coroporate largesse. As argued by Emanuel (1991), it is an integral part of socio-economic reconstruction in South Africa.

DEVELOPING INTERDEPENDENT RELATIONSHIPS

Whereas the modern industrial state tends to develop beyond a single centre of power, in developing societies, the state is frequently perceived as omnipotent. Developing societies in the Southern African context should place greater emphasis on developing interdependent relationships between employer organisations and trade union federations. There are indications of tentative moves being made in this direction in South Africa. The establishment of regular national dialogue between employer organisations and union federations may enhance the quality and pace of social development, improve industrial relations stability and generate opportunities for greater mutual understanding and co-operation.

The responsibility for creating an effective labour relations system through developing appropriate legislation should be a joint one, combining the resources, knowledge and experience of the trilateral parties to the socio-economic system, ie organised capital, labour and the state. If the free market economy is going to survive in developing societies, the interactive role of employer organisations with labour and the state in respect of regional development plans and social programmes should be recognised.

Employer organisations and organised labour could sustain and extend meaningful dialogue beyond 'traditional' items on the collective bargaining agenda to include socio-economic, and community and legislative issues, as occured on recent labour legislation. More full-time industrial relations expertise and leadership of national stature are needed to make a dynamic and effective contribution, through developing strategic policies and influencing national-decision-making.

SOCIAL RESPONSIBILITY AND INFLUENCING CHANGE

South Africa is essentially a market economy, albeit with state intervention, participation and regulation. There has been a substantive identification of free enterprise with the apartheid ideology by most Black people. The opposition of organised industry and commerce to apartheid in recent years arose more out of enlightened self-interest than altruism. However, a probable consequence of failure by employers collectively to take visible public stands on human-rights issues affecting their business and which flout progressive HR and IR policies, is the perception by employees of collusion by employers with the state. Inaction would therefore be perceived as constituting in itself, a political statement by an employer or employers.

Business should consider its position in raising human rights violations in society in general, and in ensuring fair labour practices in the work-place. However, a distinction can be made between the exercise of corporate social responsibility projects (which essentially entail the development of particular groups, communities or facilities) and concerted business action to remove racial discrimination in opportunities, institutions and decision-making. There is a critical difference between traditional social responsibility projects and business contribution to the fundamental transformation of South African society away from apartheid[6]

While individual corporate acts of public criticism against state policy may have some symbolic value, they do not constitute a viable strategy for influencing state policy. Similarly, exhortations for greater unity among employers are vitally necessary, but must seek to develop both a clear vision and organisational cohesion.

Business/political relationships reflect enormous divisions in South Africa. These include ethno-political differences and differences relating to competitive business interests. Coherent goals and strategies are required from a concerted leadership effort among organised business to transcend traditional differences and obtain mandates from employers, if the development of South Africa's human potential is to be a serious national policy goal. Multi-level co-ordinated approaches can be developed. These would acknowledge he interdependent contribution to change of: (1) well-conceived IR and HR policies; (2) corporate social responsibility programmes; and (3) concerted collective mobilisation of employers through visionary leadership at employer association level and through employer bodies such as the Urban Foundation.

Previous chapters indicate various policy imperatives at organisational level (Chapters 3–8) and also highlight questions relating to possible joint bilateral approaches at em-

6 Bernstein, A. (1988)

ployer and union federation level (Chapter 2). In a similar context Bernstein (op cit, p 43) refers to the need for a formation of alliances which reflects a formal coaliton of a broad range of interests. The prospects for cohesive co-ordinated policy influence may be enhanced in this way. Given the will, and leadership, such coalitions may be able to transcend some of the differences limiting employer unity, so problematic. However, coalitions or alliances will prove effective only if they are broad enough to obtain viable mandates which represent powerful interests, even if aspects of these interests differ. Alliances also have to recognise and acknowledge conflicts of interests before attempting to obtain consensus on specific issues.[7] It may also be more viable for interest groups seeking to form alliances to identify issues on which concerted action can be taken than to try and achieve congruent values.

In sum, within organisations, senior managers will need to rethink and articulate the core values of their organisation, and develop pragmatic policies and implementable strategies. Business as a corporate citizen has a responsibility to exercise influence over decisions affecting its interests and should play a fundamental role in excising apartheid and transforming political structures.

A pluralist society reflects various conflict and power interests. An organised employer lobby should therefore enter into regular dialogue and dynamic interaction with interest groups such as political parties and organised labour, and endeavour to formulate joint or bilateral strategies for influencing state manpower and labour policies.

Further adaptive responses

Whether for altruistic reasons, or simply to seek adaptive and responsive strategies of economic survival, organised business as a key stakeholder in the survival and prosperity of

7 Boraine, A. (1989)

society has an important role to play in achieving a just society. As actors in the political economy, redefinition of traditional roles of HR managers is needed.

HR/IR specialists have to reconcile productivity goals with employee needs for fair employment and labour practices and equitable wage policies. They will need to find pragmatic and socially responsive strategies, particularly for influencing business strategies and facilitating change in corporate culture. However, organisational change cannot occur in a vacuum. Environmental demands are critical variables which affect business decision-making and strategic effectiveness.

The immense and complex challenges facing IR/HR policy makers in South Africa do not reflect a stark choice between achieving a living wage and higher employment, but the search for a relative balance between equitable wages, employment security, job creation and continued profitability.

In coping with or indeed shaping change, it will become increasingly important for management in organisations to renew strategies and carve out new relationships with key interest groups. The securing of long-term interests and development of human potential could be facilitated by a pro-active role for business leaders and organised commerce and industry in forging bilateral relationships with trade unions, labour federations, community and political organisations. To facilitate greater legitimacy, the styles of managerial leadership require a shift away from autocratic and paternalistic modes, to management by consent.

In particular, it is important to raise managerial capability for:

- conceptual and abstract thought;
- an analytical, rather than 'cocktail party' approach to contemporary issues in the political economy;
- interpersonal and negotiation skills; and

- managing participatively to facilitate a shift towards participative organisational structures and processes.

SOCIAL POLICY

Through joint employer and trade union agreements in industrial councils, supplementation of the state's efforts on social policy programmes can occur. This requires greater unity of action and the resolution of differences on the part of employers' associations to give expression to pragmatic social policy programmes. While the feasibility of seeking common approaches between organised business and labour on economic policy is difficult, there does seem to be more recent evidence of a common resolve to seek the removal of the apartheid system, release of detained leaders, labour legislation and on certain social issues, such as unemployment and housing.

Three is a need for employer organisations and the state to seriously review their social policies in respect of unemployment insurance and medical schemes. There is virtually no effective economic cushion to alleviate the emotional and physical trauma of prolonged periods of unemployment as in Western countries such as the United States and the United Kingdom. This necessitates the consideration of job creation schemes by the state, business sector, and the labour movement, given the imperative for addressing the issues of structural unemployment and redistribution of wealth.[8] The feasibility of joint projects and collaboration in this area together with organised labour should be fostered. It is interesting to note that the Institute of Personnel Management (Southern Africa) has, in this regard, initiated a project on unemployment and job-creation involving HR people.

8 Wilson, F. and Ramphele, M. (1989)

MANAGEMENT'S ROLE: INTERNAL IMPERATIVES[9]

Faced by uncertainty both within and outside the organisation, management is tested to find a way to respond to the demands of the time. Although the conflicts within and outside the organisation are interrelated, management's role in respect of each will need to be different. Inside the company, management must create a working environment free from discrimination, racial differentiation and victimisation, in which all employees have equal opportunities to compete for available positions and have equitable recourse for the resolution of problems, conflicts and grievances which arise from time to time. Management should earn the trust and co-operation of its own employees as a precondition for undertaking any other roles in the wider society.

Management's roles outside the organisation are the most difficult and controversial in that the resolution of the problems often lies outside the customary jurisdiction of managerial authority. The role management can play is mainly dependent on the issue and employee/employer interests. The following roles can be considered by management.

The initiator

Management's role is one of identifying problem areas which have the potential to disrupt relationships between the company and workers and to take steps to prevent these problems from arising.

The honest broker

Management's role is primarily a facilitative one where it assists the two parties in conflict to come to an appropriate

9 This is an excerpt, gratefully acknowledged, adapted from AECI's *Policy Guidelines on Community Involvement*, which forms part of its broader HR and IR policy

agreement, for example, unions competing for membership; community organisations and the state.

The campaigner

This role is primarily a lobbying role where management takes sides in the conflict and seeks to effect a settlement with a third party by negotiating jointly with its employees, for example, the detention of trade unionists.

For management to play either of the latter two roles it is assumed that they have reasonable acceptance within the workplace and that existing company conditions of employment and work practices have some legitimacy with employees. Before deciding to become involved as honest broker or campaigner, managements are advised to consult with employees. A number of South African companies have taken initiatives in seeking to address community conflict and development issues. These include AECI, Middelburg Steel, and SA Nylon Spinners.

CONCLUSION

Unlike those in most first-world societies, employer associations in developing societies such as Nigeria, the Sudan and South Africa have only recently begun to display more overt and expressive lobbying activities with government in respect of influence on political, social and economic change. This lobbying and influencing function is an accepted major role of employer organisations in highly industrialised countries.[10]

As any heterogeneous society reflects various conflict and power interests, there is a need for organised business to enter into a dialogue which is aimed at achieving a just society. Business engagement in influencing change should, however,

10 Horwitz, F.M. (1986a)

be strategically focused and continuous, and not merely issue-related.

Divisions within and between employer organisations reduce their political influence. While some would argue that this influence is limited, and this may well be so, the South African business sector has in the past been perceived by employees as being tardy in this regard.

The differing interests between managers and employees, sometimes requires difficult trade-offs within an organisation. These trade-offs are essentially between the business goals of efficiency, growth and investment on one hand, and employee needs for security, equity, job satisfaction, personal growth, and economic well-being on the other. Organisations constantly make trade-offs, either implicitly or explicitly, between the interests of the owners and those of employees, as well s between various employee groups. This essentially pluralist approach to management also reflects a 'stakeholder interest perspective'. This approach suggests that, in order to provide a more coherent meaning and purpose to managing people, a critical analysis of the interests (common and differing) of key stakeholders and their relative influence is necessary. An understanding of contextual variables such as socio-political, economic and legislative issues, as well as situational variables, such as managerial ideologies and work-force characteristics, is required.

Therefore, a vital aspect of extending HR management influence is that which focuses on the interrelationship and interface between business and macro-level socio-political and economic processes. It also underlines the need for a re-orientation away from exclusive managerial definitions of organisational problems. In conclusion, HR and IR policy approaches in South Africa require both an internal and external focus. This should extend further than the effective acquisition, development, rewarding and participation of employees individually and collectively, to involvement in external social and community issues. The quality of life of communities in which employees live, and an ability to exert independent influence on social and economic change, will prove vital challenges in the 'new' South Africa.

11

DEVELOPING POLICIES AND PROCEDURES: PRACTICAL GUIDELINES

INTRODUCTION

The term 'policy' is used a great deal in any organisation, but often loosely and inaccurately. It is sometimes confused with procedures, objectives and occasionally with strategy. This is not surprising as these concepts are closely interrelated and affect each other. Policies also tend to evolve and emerge slowly and often hesitantly as organisations grow and the need for guidelines to action and practice develops. Because of their implications and their long-term nature, managements are often reluctant to commit themselves, particularly with regard to setting their policies down in writing. There are many pitfalls in this area and commitment to policies should not be lightly undertaken.

At the same time, while opportunism may be a natural approach in the early days of any organisation, no organisation can continue for long without clarifying its policies and defining them. What starts as a feeling that this is the way we want to do things, and a belief that it is the correct way for our organisation, will gradually crystalize into a series of written statements which are of tremendous importance to the development and future of the organisation.

A clearly defined HR and IR policy is fundamental to the development of sound employment relationships in an organisation. The main purpose of a policy is to provide a clear statement of the organisation's values, basic principles, objectives and standards regarding its employees. A policy promotes consistency in management and can reduce uncertainty about the organisation's intentions. It provides a framework for decision-making for managers who are responsible for the day-to-day conduct of IR, managing and developing human resources. An effective IR and HR policy is *integrated into the organisation's corporate business strategy* and reflects the interaction of IR and HR policies with policies in other areas, such as production, marketing and finance. Participation of line managers in policy formation is vital if successful policy performance is to occur. Whether the policy and strategy are developed proactively or reactively is a function of the interaction between constraints and choices — as is the case with all management decisions. Constraints may arise from limitations on power to achieve desired goals as a result of pressures within the macro-environment and the organisation itself, while choices are influenced by the values of decision makers.[1]

The nature and content of HR and IR policies may vary according to the unique characteristics of particular industries, markets, technological factors and the stage of development of a company, organisationally. Generally, however, the principles contained in policies can be universal. The objectives and strategies developed may differ between companies and industries.

Items which can be included in an IR and HR policy can be grouped as follows:[2]

1. the relationship between management and employees, including recognition of the right to join a trade union which may act on their behalf, and the basis on which trade unions are to be recognised for collective bargaining and representation;
2. the determination of terms and conditions of employment through appropriate institutions of collective bargaining and joint consultation;

1 Salamon, M. (1987a)
2 Salamon, M. (1987a)

3. the approach to employment and development to be adopted in ensuring that an organisation has the required level of trained and experienced people; and
4. principles relating to effective communication with employees;
5. the role of procedures in regulating conflict, including grievance and disciplinary procedures.

Organisational differences in the *content* and range of policies and procedures and the managerial process which develops them, can be attributed to the following factors:[3]

1. the *authority* relationship between line management and specialist staff;
2. the extent to which consistency in decision-making and action is being sought (*standardisation*);
3. the codification of policies, procedures and practices in formal written documents (*formalisation*); and
4 the degree to which the organisation has autonomy in its IR/HR decision-making (*centralisation/decentralisation*).

The IR/HR specialist and departmental line management have a key role as the link between strategic and operational decisions. Their contribution is an interactive one with participation of line managers in the IR and HR strategy formation process, being vital in order to ensure its managerial legitimacy. Decision-making within management on IR and HR matters is therefore a collective responsibility requiring the involvement and commitment of both IR and HR specialists and line management at policy and operational levels. Jointly agreed procedures which are negotiated with employees through trade unions have the benefit of establishing a regulatory framework. This means that norms and standards of behaviour are co-developed through a negotiating process. The 'rules of the game' become more formal, so reducing

3 Gill, C. and Concannon, H. (1977)

uncertainty and anxiety amongst managers, supervisors, employees and the union. This social framework is an important means of institutionalising IR conflict.

IMPETUS FOR POLICIES

The impetus to develop (new) policies and procedures or redefine existing ones, is generated by some pressure for change being exerted on the organisation (Salamon, 1987). These pressures include:

1. developments within the organisation, such as the advent, growth or change in the pattern of unionism; a belief amongst management that existing policies and procedures or aspects thereof, are inadequate to cope with current or future IR and HR problems; and changes in the managerial 'style' and culture of the organisation;
2. developments external to the organisation, but still creating internal pressures, for example, changes in the organisation's economic, technological or operational needs; and
3. developments external to the organisation, including changes in labour and employment legislation, fresh nterpretations of existing law, changes in government policies or general development in the fields of IR and HR management (eg new initiatives and techniques). In the South African context, international pressures for change, such as codes of employment practice in the 1980s, and support of international trade unions for unions involved in local disputes, have had important policy implications.

CHARACTERISTICS OF A POLICY

A policy statement is usually distinguished by the following characteristics:

- it deals with *general principles* or practices rather than specific rules or situations;
- it is *long range* in its conception and application;

- though it is usually developed by *top level management,* it should *involve participation at various levels;*
- it must have the approval and commitment of the highest level of authority in the company;
- it should not be violated or lightly set aside, but can be *subject to change and review;* and
- it *should be in writing* and *available* to all concerned.

NEED FOR POLICIES

1. Since they express the general intent of the organisation, policies are *guides to decision-making and action.*
2. They *provide controls and limits* within which action can be taken.
3. They help to *ensure continuity* without imposing absolute uniformity.
4. They have a *co-ordinating function* and *assist* towards unity of purpose.
5. They facilitate *decentralisation and delegation* of both authority and duties.

POLICIES DO NOT DEVELOP IN A VACUUM

It may be the founder of a company, who, through imposing his own values, beliefs, and attitudes in the organisation, lays the basis for future policies (eg: Raymond Ackerman of Pick 'n Pay, Henry Ford, Marks of Marks & Spencers, and Head of Head Ski Company, are examples). The influence of the founder may live on long after he has left, and provides the basis for the distinct personality or profile which each organisation tends to develop. Original policies developed by an owner-manager may, however, soon become outdated and may reflect an inappropriate frame of reference and values.

Other factors involved in policy development are company experience, prevailing practices in a community, changes in management and direction, and changes in general management approaches and philosophy.

A POLICY STATEMENT

Consider the significance and implications of the following policy statement:

> 'It is the policy of this company to select and develop staff on the basis of merit, irrespective of race or gender.'

Such a statement has far-reaching implications for both the organisation concerned and the community in which it exists. There can be little doubt that policy statements are of basic importance in the functioning of any organisation.

Objectives set out 'what' the organisation hopes to achieve.

Strategy describes the overall plan for the achievement of these objectives. Policy, by setting out basic principles and beliefs on how the company should operate, and within what limits, plays a fundamental role in determining the quality of the company's operation.

MAIN COMPONENTS OF INDUSTRIAL RELATIONS POLICY

1. Broad, clear objectives, e.g. the development of mutual confidence, and co-operation, and regulation of industrial conflict.
2. Relationship with corporate objectives
3. Defining HR and IR policy. The common and differing elements must be identified, particularly if IR is to form part of a broader HR policy (a fairly common approach).
4. Rationale
5. Framework
6. Principles, e.g. recognition of freedom of association, promotion of common and acknowledgement of differing

interests, adherence to agreements, effective policy communication to all levels.

7. Standards — universal applicability, inviolate nature, stated in broad terms to ensure consistency.
8. Guidelines and procedural distinctions
   - relationship and recognition of Unions
   - relationship with employers' associations
   - employment practices
   - Grievance procedures
   - Dispute procedures
   - reward structures
   - training and development
   - strike handling
   - retrenchment, e.g. alternative cost-reduction measures seeking avoidance of retrenchment
   - upward and downward communication
9. Monitoring and evaluation mechanisms, including a specification of roles and responsibilities of key individuals and groups.

PARTICIPATION IN POLICY FORMATION

People at work increasingly want to contribute directly to decisions affecting their interests. No matter how large or small the company may be, there is a need for some form of structure(s) which need not necessarily be too formal in operation, for allowing employees through their representatives/shop stewards to participate in decisions affecting their interests at the enterprise level. The decisions concerned might include the following:

- ❑ representation on grievance and disciplinary procedures;
- ❑ communication structures;
- ❑ health and safety matters;
- ❑ retrenchments and methods of avoiding retrenchments e.g. short-time working;

- welfare matters, e.g. catering and mess facilities;
- pensions fund administration; and
- working conditions arrangements.

PROCEDURES

Procedures are the day-to-day instructions and methods by which policies are implemented.

They have the following common characteristics:

1. They state specifically and in detail what steps must be taken, thus facilitating action.
2. They are more open to change and may be adapted to local requirements.
3. They enable action to be taken with or without reference to superior authority.
4. They formalize and simplify day-to-day decision-making.
5. They help to maintain uniformity of action at different levels and in dispersed organisations.

STAGES OF DEVELOPMENT

One can expect both policies and procedures to be affected by the stage of development which a company has reached.

In a first or entrepreneurial phase, the owner-manager usually has very definite (though often inadequate) policies on how he/she wishes the company to operate. These, however, are not always clearly formulated, are seldom in writing, are not well communicated, and may often be deliberately withheld on the basis that the less the employees know the better. Procedures are often poorly developed and are replaced by the changing whims and instructions of the owner-manager.

As the need for system and structure grows, procedures develop in the early stages of a bureaucratic phase, as a means of extending authority down the line. Proliferating procedures are one of the marks of bureaucracy. Organisations tend to become procedure-bound, as procedures supercede the requirements of the situation.

More clearly conceived policies tend to emerge towards the end of this phase as the limitations of procedures become apparent. Policies tend to be carried in the heads of top management who are often reluctant to communicate them because of the commitment involved.

The need for clearly stated policies, available to all, is, however, imperative at all stages of organisational development including the move towards more flexible, and more participative management. If there is to be increased autonomy for both departments and individuals, and if there is a shift towards greater decentralisation, clear policy statements are essential, to allow a certain freedom of action while indicating the necessary limits/parameters.

LIMITATIONS OF POLICIES

Policies can reflect inappropriate values, may be misdirected, or inadequately thought through. They are also not enduring, and may need to be changed as the socio-technological, legal, and political environment alters.

Organisations cannot dispense with policies, but nor can they be taken for granted. They need thoughtful attention and maintenance. Policies have a particular importance in HR and IR management. While rapid changes in tactics, strategy and policies are often unavoidable in line management, policies related to employees cannot be changed arbitrarily, if trust and credibility are to be maintained. Care should therefore be taken in drawing up policies to ensure that they can be maintained in both stable and turbulent conditions.[4]

4 From: O'Meara, J. (1975/6) Lecture notes, Higher Diploma in Personnel Management, University of the Witwatersrand, Johannesburg

POLICY FORMATION QUESTIONS

Invariably a discussion of industrial relations and HR policy and its implementation in a particular organisation especially a smaller organisation, tends to invoke controversy and frequently resistance from various levels of management and supervision. This tends to inhibit the resolution of many basic practical problems which concern the efficient running of the organisation.

With the principle of freedom of association being extended to workers of all races since the Wiehahn Commission reports in 1979, black employees rapidly and in large numbers joined an increasing number of trade unions. These developments have presented employers with certain dilemmas. Many employers have, for example, been approached to sign recognition agreements with trade unions which represent a majority or indeed minority of their employees. Frequently these companies have not had the foresight to give advance thought and planning in regard to how they would handle these developments, or indeed to an overall policy regarding industrial relations. A company may not have any formal policies for dealing with labour–management conflicts. An employer might not even be aware of the existence of a union which is organising employees. If the response of an employer when industrial relations issues come to the fore, is to overreact, this can have disastrous industrial relations and financial implications.

The motivation for sound industrial relations and HR policies and procedures should be neither the fact of unionisation or possible unionisation, nor the size of the company. Sound policies and procedures are a prerequisite for enlightened and effective management, organisational effectiveness and employee commitment. Although it may be argued that trade unions have in the first instance sought to organise the larger multi-national companies, increasingly, smaller companies are being unionised and recognition agreements are being negotiated with these companies.

Disruptive industrial relations problems may occur in large as well as small companies. The principles behind fair labour practices as evidenced by a number of industrial court rulings indicates that unfair labour practice actions may be brought against any company, irrespective of size. This underlines the need for proper industrial relations policies and procedures such as disciplinary and grievance procedures, given that the length and detail of these procedures may be different in smaller companies than in larger ones.

Similarly, the traditional exclusive reliance on informal management–employee relations in smaller organisations has increasingly been perceived by employees as being paternalistic and therefore inappropriate. Procedures for regulating the relationship and preventing disruptive conflict, as well as wage agreements collectively bargained with trade unions are increasing in smaller companies. Employers, irrespective of size, are being called upon by the industrial court and unions to demonstrate fairness in their dealings with employees. Evidence of fairness may relate, for example, to giving an employee a proper hearing to ascertain whether a dismissal is warranted, with the employee being permitted representation at such a hearing. Similarly, the need for documentation of any disciplinary action taken is paramount.

Within the wider context of recent industrial relations developments there are a number of policy items which individual employers might consider, particularly so as to define clearly what specific approaches should be adopted on practical industrial relations matters. The definition and implementation of a policy is a vital mechanism for reducing uncertainty and conflict when dealing with industrial relations matters.

Questions to consider when formulating an IR policy include the following:

- ❑ Does the company's managerial values seriously accept the principle of freedom of association and its organisational implications?
- ❑ Does the company have a positive approach to independent representatives of workers? What is its belief about relationships with trade unions?
- ❑ What procedures for regulating the relationship with unions will be negotiated as part of the recognition process?
- ❑ Does the company accept that employees may wish to be represented at local levels by elected shop stewards, who may have both company and trade union loyalties? What view will the company take on negotiating agreements through an industrial council?
- ❑ If workers wish to belong to a trade union(s) not party to the industrial council what view will the company take? What would its approach be if most employees joined the union and it requested recognition?
- ❑ What is the nature of the company's commitment to advancing fair labour practices and equitable conditions of employment?
- ❑ Does the company have industrial relations structures and procedures which effectively handle employee grievances, disciplinary matters and dispute resolution?
- ❑ What is the company view on involving employees in the design of these structures?
- ❑ Are there procedures for upward communication and joint consultation, as well as downward communication?
- ❑ What view will the company take on the right to strike?
- ❑ Are there effective policies and procedures for handling disputes and strikes? Should shop stewards be involved in developing these procedures?

- What approach will the company take on defining bargaining units?
- Are individual managers and supervisors properly trained in industrial relations/HRM concepts, principles and skills?
- To what extent can top management support for HR and industrial relations policies be obtained and sustained?
- Can mechanisms for monitoring and regularly evaluating policies be instituted once implementation has occurred?
- To what extent can the day-to-day individual and informal relations between workers and their supervisors be improved through proper selection, training, development and involvement?
- To what extent are policies communicated to all levels within the organisation?
- How can the organisation be 'conditioned' and a culture and reward system be developed to facilitate policy performance?

RELATIONSHIPS WITH UNIONS

Policy guidelines on the above questions are an important component of a corporate policy. It is often argued that in smaller companies, relations between managers, supervisors and employees are relatively informal and that consequently there is little need for formal policies and procedures. It is indeed vital that policies be designed to be relatively simple, clearly worded and easily communicable. Equally important is the need for these policies to be integrated with other corporate policies and objectives. An organisation may adopt an inappropriate unitarist policy framework view of industrial relations as previously discussed. This rather simplistic metaphor of the organisation as a family, forgets that family relations tend also to have conflicts and differing interests.

An effective management/worker relationship tends to be based on a pluralistic approach which accepts that both conflict and common goals are inherent to the relationship. Industrial relations policies in order to be viable, must accept the inherent conflict of interest between managers and workers and that such conflict should not be considered as abnormal or induced by 'outsiders'. One of the main benefits of sound industrial relations policies is their value in institutionalising conflict, by preventing conflict from becoming disruptive through regulating the employer/employee relationship by mutually negotiated rules and procedures. Many of these rules and procedures may be formulated through industrial council agreements, but others may be relevant only within the organisational context of an individual enterprise. The industrial council or any other similarly created bargaining structures may indeed have a role in formulating basic rules and procedures. Other policy aspects such as those discussed above appear more pertinent for formulation at the enterprise level. There is a growing acknowledgement, not only within the socio-economic sphere, but also in the wider political context in South Africa and other Western countries, that the locus of decision-making should allow greater flexibility at decentralised levels.

A sound relationship with a trade union requires:

- ❑ optimising common goals and acknowledging differing interests;
- ❑ acknowledgement of the union as an independent organisation representing employees' interests individually and collectively;
- ❑ appreciation by the parties of the compromise principle as fundamental to the negotiation process;
- ❑ joint acknowledgement of the rights an commitments of both parties, including mutual commitments;

- active attempts by both parties to develop respect, confidence and relationships with employee representatives and union officials;
- mutual acknowledgement of the peace obligation, whereby industrial action will not occur during the currency of an agreement in respect of terms in the agreement;
- use of industrial action as a last resort, after agreed disputes procedures such as mediation, have been followed;
- negotiation of a work stoppage procedure which accommodates rights, interests and obligations to resolve stoppages as speedily as possible and as near to the point of origin, as possible;
- training and development of employees, representatives, supervisors and managers is both a right and a necessity for sound relationships and effective organisational performance;
- full acceptance by management of the collective bargaining process and of unionism as an institution (strong democratic and responsible unions are seen as an asset to management); and
- full acceptance by both parties of the mutual need to optimise common interests and co-operation.

COLLECTIVE BARGAINING (CB) CLIMATE AND POLICY

The creation of a CB climate based on trust and a willingness to negotiate is vital, if stable IR is to be obtained. A sound bargaining climate reflects the quality of collective relationships between the negotiating parties.

In addition to the points referred to previously, effective collective bargaining also requires the following:

- recognising a representative trade union as an independent bargaining agent which has a legitimate and legal existence independent of the company;

- mutual commitment to negotiate and follow dispute resolution procedures, if no agreement is obtained;
- strike action or lockouts to be considered as a last resort, with protection of job security for employees if a strike or lockout follows use of agreed dispute procedures; and
- circumspect and considered use of legal recourse is advised, and only used if no other avenue for reconciliation exists.

The role of the state in fostering or eroding a productive bargaining climate became increasingly prominent in the light of the state of emergency in the latter 1980's and the detention of unionists. The Labour Relations Amendment Act (1988) had the effect of creating additional concerns amongst employees regarding the rights of unions to strike. These concerns in turn created new demands on employers. Contextual factors such as state policy, legislation and socio-economic developments have an important bearing on the quality of relationships at plant-level as they affect perceptions of employees. The climate of bargaining is very much a function of co-operative relationships at the work-place and the development of trust with trade unions. Relationships between unions can also have an affect on bargaining climate. If union rivalry occurs, this tends to make the collective bargaining process more difficult.

Good faith bargaining policy

Good IR practice, reinforced by industrial court jurisprudence, requires a demonstrable willingness to negotiate, particularly with representative unions. A number of industrial court decisions have placed an onus on both an employer and trade union to negotiate.

Bargaining in bad faith includes the following:

- use of tactics aimed to deceive, divide or to avoid negotiation;
- unilateral change of agreements;
- refusal to deal with the other party's negotiators;
- unilateral withdrawal from an established bargaining structure;
- establishing unreasonable preconditions;

The law may compel a party to bargain, although it cannot force the parties to reach an agreement.

Bargaining in good faith requires that:

- negotiators are representative of their constituents;
- they have mandates;
- they report back regularly to their constituents;
- issues must be negotiable;
- intentions must be sincere and demands by either party be honest;
- an element of give and take occurs — possitional bargaining may give way to negotiation around needs and principles;[5]
- demands or proposals are realistic;
- agreements should be in writing, signed and adhered to;
- tactics do not override bargaining objectives and processes of trying to reach agreement;
- mandates should be flexible enough to allow movement;
- parties be properly prepared with arguments and substantiated proposals; and
- sharing of sufficient information to enable the parties to understand and intelligently discuss the issues raised. Information sharing should be sufficient to facilitate negotiated compromise, and should occur on an ongoing basis rather than at the time of wage negotiations only.

5 Burton, J. (1990)

The objective is to have an enduring agreement. One needs to consider long-term relationships and the consequences of present bargaining behaviour for future relationships with employees. The impact of proposals and contingent agreements, on all interest groups should be considered. Successful negotiations also depend on identifying the real needs and interests of the other party and not merely looking at the proposal itself. Linking on a merit basis, of issues which are relevant to each other, can facilitate agreement.

Alternatively stated, certain broad policy principles can be identified, which contribute towards co-operative relationships,and industrial peace.

BARGAINING STRUCTURES

Circumstances may call for a creative approach to the establishment of appropriate bargaining structures and levels. There are important considerations in determining appropriate bargaining structures. As a result of agreed priorities, some industrial councils have been restructured to accommodate both union and employer needs. There is a more recent tendency for trade unions to seek centralised bargaining at industry level as membership growth occurs and as they develop organisationally, in the context of seeking a pervasive living wage. This is a very important development for employer IR policy. Centralised bargaining versus decentralised bargaining, or an agreed two-tier structure, is a strategic and economic matter, which also concerns the balance of power in the employment relationship. It has been found that policy choices on collective bargaining levels may, however, be influenced by unitarist or pluralist frames of reference (Horwitz 1985). Some newer industrial council agreements, for example the Cape Textile Council, contained negotiated items such as union shop arrangements and strike procedures, commitments of both sides regarding bargaining levels and shop steward rights. The shift in union strategies towards centralised bargaining also reflects the COSATU goal of industrial unionism, i.e. one-union per industry.

Some employers have concerns about centralised bargaining on three grounds:

1. Large groups of companies may operate in diverse and often unrelated markets with wide variances in market requirements and cost structures.
2. They view centralised bargaining as a threat to employer control, and prefer to negotiate at decentralised levels so as to prevent broad mobilisation of union power.
3. Related to 2 above, is the argument that organisational structures themselves may be decentralised and that IR systems and processes should also reflect this.

Trade unions view the above approach as a 'divide-and-rule' one, which fragments the union's ability to have wider influence, and influence at a higher level. As previously mentioned, this issue is a serious policy matter related to both power and business strategies. Centralised bargaining also has definite advantages. Better wages and conditions are negotiated for more people. Social benefits such as pension, provident funds and medical schemes administered centrally can be more cost-effective for individual employers and employees. These benefits and others may be lost if an industrial council is folded through employer withdrawal. Centralised structures, therefore, provide a private social security system to augment inadequate state provision. Centralised bargaining facilitates the establishment of joint accords between employers and trade unions at national level in issues such as labour law, and training and development. In so doing it creates a forum for mutual influence at leadership level on public policy issues. Finally there is comparative evidence that unprocedural industrial action is lower in countries with centralised bargaining structures. It is vitally important to negotiate (rather than legislate) a bargaining structure which meets the needs of all parties, as shown for example, in the dispute between Nampak and the Paper, Pulp, Wood and Allied Workers' Union in 1990.

Causes of industrial peace[6]

- Full acceptance by management of the collective bargaining process and of unionism as an institution. Strong unions are considered as asset to management.
- Union fully accepts private ownership and operation of the industry; recognises welfare of members depends on successful business.
- Union is strong, responsible and democratic.
- Company stays out of union affairs, does not seek to alienate workers' allegiance to their union.
- Mutual trust and confidence exist between the parties.
- Neither party has a legalistic approach to solution of problems.
- Negotiations are problem-centred — more time on day-to-day problems than on abstract principles, or positional bargaining.
- Widespread union-management consultation and highly developed information sharing.
- Grievances are settled promptly, at local level whenever possible. Some flexibility and informality occur within procedures.

DISCRIMINATION AND EMPLOYMENT PRACTICES

The codification of Unfair Labour Practices in the Labour Relations Amendment Act (1988) specified that discrimination on the grounds of race, gender and other factors constitutes an unfair labour practice. Discrimination in terms of equal pay for work of equal value was also considered by the industrial

6 Text of Footnote

court in the *Sentrachem* v *SACWU* case (1987). A vast array of employment practices will be under increasing scrutiny regarding fairness and equity. This includes areas such as selection criteria, aptitude testing, job grading and evaluation systems, job advancement and training opportunities, as well as fringe benefit policies, such as pension funds. Here, it is necessary to clearly define the principles of fairness and equity and to ensure that policy and practice are congruent.

Training and proper communication of company policies, employment practices and HR systems such as job evaluation, are vital. Job evaluation systems are sometimes perceived as an instrument of managerial control, rather than as a vehicle for creating internal equity and fairness in the relative ranking of jobs. There is a need for education of employees in this regard and also for involving employees and their representatives in the job evaluation process where appropriate. Management should also take more trouble to ascertain employee perceptions of important issues and avoid acting on untested assumptions. A useful approach is to correct identified discriminatory practices proactively, rather than wait for employees or trade unions to raise them. It is nevertheless likely that disputes on discrimination in employment practices will become increasingly prominent with industrial court action occurring more frequently, e.g. regarding racial discrimination in facilities and promotion.

SOCIAL RESPONSIBILITY AND COMMUNITY INVOLVEMENT

This broad heading covers a range of corporate policy issues. The type of issues that arise are important in determining policy management might consider. Questions asked may consider the following:

1. Does the issue affect employees and their dependants?

2. What are the potential benefits to the employer and the community?
3. Will/can employees and their unions participate in the programme?
4. Are there conflicts of interests involved?
5. How can these be resolved?
6. Is there merit in other employers or an employer organisation becoming involved?

Two vital areas which are very current in this regard are employer policies on provident and pension funds, and housing provision. As there are specific concerns regarding these areas amongst employees, trade unions require greater participation, jointly with employers.

In the case of pension schemes, this is an internal organisation matter, although the practical implementation, therefore, for low-earning employees, is often a difficult problem. This is reinforced by job insecurity, whereby a dismissed employee may obtain very little back from a pension fund. Employee concerns also relate to control over deferred income, a need for ready capital, and a dissatisfaction with small pensions, poor withdrawal benefits and administrative problems in getting a pension cheque regularly.

As a result of these and other problems, some unions and employers have negotiated flexible retirement schemes with employee participation on the boards of trustees, as in AECI for example. Control over investment of funds seems to have been better addressed by provident funds, although there is no reason why pension funds cannot resolve these problems if employers are equally open to negotiating the substantive and procedural components of pension funds and have employee participation on the boards of trustees.

Similarly, regarding social responsibility programmes, there is an increasing tendency for employers to become involved on a larger scale in community projects — ie on a broader basis than focusing on their employees alone. Crucial in this regard, is the co-determination of needs and priorities between employers, community organisations and trade unions. the pooling of employer resources through organised employer bodies, e.g. the Urban Foundation, could also enhance effectiveness of employer programmes.

Housing together with social responsibility programmes, has emerged as an area for debate regarding benefit fund investment and the channelling of accumulated funds into socially useful areas. Real problems exist regarding the artificial shortage of land and finance for solving the housing problem in particular. Employers can play a role in assisting resolution of problems in this area, by collective lobbying of government to set more land aside for housing development and abolishing discriminatory practices. The land shortage is an artificial problem and can be resolved by political decisions.

It is possible, therefore, that the range of collective bargaining issues is likely to expand to encompass 'non-traditional' concerns. A wider variety of social policy issues are likely to be raised by employees, with requests to consider and negotiate cost effective benefits.

RELATIONSHIP WITH EMPLOYER ORGANISATIONS

The role of an employers' association in developing guidelines regarding industrial relations and HR policy for member companies is an important one. However, the considerable variety of organisations in a particular industry or industrial sector, can make it difficult to generalise about the most appropriate system for industrial relations for the industry concerned. The line-up of parties, both employers and trade unions, is a crucial variable in determining the kind and level of industrial relations structures which might be considered most appropriate. What is also very important is whether a common or shared approach can be developed by the parties. This may indeed influence the type of structures and policies to be developed at industry, sectorial and enterprise levels.

HUMAN RESOURCE AND INDUSTRIAL RELATIONS PRACTICES

Policies should consider the implications of established policies and practices (e.g. induction, selection, training and communication systems), as well as proposed new policies and practices in areas such as job advancement and performance appraisal.

A variety of quantitative and qualitative mechanisms can be used to evaluate policy performance. Particularly important is the need for feedback about the operation of IR/HR policy to those responsible for its formation and reformulation (Figure 11.1).

- ❑ Performance of line management, job description, performance objectives and appraisal thereof
- ❑ Training follow-up
- ❑ Grievance forms keeping statistics
- ❑ Disciplinary decisions
- ❑ Audit questionnaires/interviews with employees
- ❑ Contact group meetings between supervisors, managers and personnel/IR specialists
- ❑ Labour turnover and absenteeism
- ❑ Hours lost, labour withdrawal
- ❑ Production and efficiency/Quality

Figure 11.1
Monitoring/evaluationg policy performance

GUIDELINES FOR MONITORING OF HUMAN RESOURCE AND INDUSTRIAL RELATIONS POLICY OBJECTIVES.[7]

Aims

The evaluation of the effectiveness of HR department performance against objectives may be a subjective process, but it should be systematic and valid. It is important for members of line management to assist by providing feedback to the HR department on the 'users'' perception for the department's effective performance in key areas. The involvement of line managers may be appropriate if they have been consulted in the identification and formulation of key HR objectives.

Principles

1. The performance of a human resource function should be assessed on the extent to which objectives are met and on the efficiency with which advice, services and guidance are provided, given that both intra-organisational and external factors may facilitate or inhibit achievement of these objectives. Relating the relevance of environmental changes, such as legislative, economic and political developments to the organisation is crucial. The HR function is therefore required to monitor trends within a company such as the maintenance and analysis of records and statistics on labour turnover, absenteeism, sickness, disciplinary problems, grievances and disputes. These indices, if sensitively analysed, may assist in identifying potential conflict areas and developing strategies for their resolution.
2. The evaluation of HR department objectives should not be confused with 'audits' of organisational climate and sur-

7 Adapted from AECI Ltd's *Guidelines on Personnel and Industrial Relations Policy Objectives* (1986)

veys of employee attitudes. These latter activities may form part of a specific objective of the HR department. They are activities and not objectives. Caution should be exercised in using surveys, as they may be seen as undermining the role of existing procedures, and trade unions in representing employee interests.

3. The effective utilisation of human resources and the development of sound industrial relations is a line management function. A critical measure of the effectiveness of a HR function is the extent to which it has succeeded in gaining line management commitment to effective human resource utilisation, development and managing industrial relations as an integral line management responsibility, on which the line managers' performance is assessed.

KEY ROLES

Key roles for evaluating the HR function are:

- ❑ consultancy
- ❑ service
- ❑ guidance.

Evaluation checklists can be designed for these activities.

Consultancy role

The advisory role relates to policies, strategies, procedures and systems.

Policy Areas may include, inter alia, the following:

1. Employment — the level of staffing the company wishes to employ, the provision of equal opportunity and reasonable job security.
2. Compensation — the level and flexibility of remuneration and benefits and the extent to which these are competitive:
   - the extent to which pay systems are negotiated and information shared.

3. Career and promotion — the attitude of the company to providing long-term career prospects and to promoting from within.
4. Training and development — the scope and responsibility for training schemes and the extent of company investment in training and development; assisting managers in developing appropriate programmes and with manpower and career development plans.
5. Industrial relations — policies on union recognition, role of shop stewards, collective bargaining and dealing with grievances, discipline and redundancy.
   - The advice on HR and Industrial Relations policies should be seen as practical, positive, persuasive and communicated clearly and in ways easily understood by line managers.
   - Specific proposals, either written or orally made, must be succinct and well argued, defining the problem clearly, why and how it should be solved, with target dates, responsibility, allocation and cost-benefit implications.
   - The successful working or outcome of advice is important. Examples include advice on dealing with an industrial dispute, disciplinary matters or employment practices.

Advice on *Strategies* may include the following:

1. *HR planning* — the actions required to satisfy short and long-term organisational needs.
2. *Industrial Relations* — the actions required to develop a co-operative relationship with trade unions and to minimize industrial unrest.
3. *Communications* — the actions required to improve the effectiveness of communications as a two-way process.

Advice on *systems and procedures* such as those relating to industrial relations, recruitment, training and development, performance appraisal, communications and wage and salary administration, can be evaluated by monitoring the effectiveness of these systems and procedures. Do they run smoothly? Are they being used properly by managers and trade unions? Are they used frequently? Have they been effectively implemented? Are they practical? Do they receive a lot of criticism? A project approach regarding the implementation of strategies and procedures is useful. Such an approach should set out its aims, benefits, completion target dates, cost budgets and a mechanism for monitoring progress on implementation.

The extent to which problems are anticipated, with realistic proposals for their resolution and pro-active and initiative-demonstrating abilities are shown, is vital regarding evaluation of performance.

Service role

This role concerns the setting of standards for particular areas and a degree of quantification may be desirable for some of the following:

- *Recruitment*: speed in filling vacancies, advertising costs, recruitment cost per head, calibre of recruit, number of unfilled vacancies.
- *Employment*: reduction in turnover and absenteeism rates.
- *Training*: throughput of training schemes, time taken to develop and introduce new courses, training time to achieve job competence, and transfer of learning to the job.
- *Management development*: availability and advancement of trained managers to provide for management succession.
- *Industrial Relations*: nature and number of disputes, extent to which grievances are freely raised and level of resolution, time taken to progress grievances through each stage, frequency and nature of disciplinary cases, manner in which grievances and disciplinary issues and employee relations are handled.

- *Communications*: speed with which information is disseminated, frequency and relevance of communication, extent to which feedback is used to check understanding.
- *HR costs*: expenditure in relation to budget, cost of HR function per employee.

Subjective judgements may be useful to provide a qualitative assessment of the efficiency of the service and the speed, willingness and degree of success achieved by members of the HR function. Willingness and ability to help achieve organisational goals are vital measures of effective HR department performance.

Guidance role

The guidance role may be evaluated by senior management in respect of the way in which the HR department exercises functional control in accordance with the powers delegated to it. Some examples include: the extent to which procedures are used by managers in the decision-making process, good calibre employees are recruited, and the incidence of managerial action resulting in labour disputes.

POLICY PERFORMANCE SUMMARISED

A coercive relationship, where work is completed only because of fear-induced compliance, is not conducive to sound industrial relations and organisational stability. Ultimately, stable relationships are based on both sound shop-floor human relations in regard to the interaction between individual workers and supervisors, as well as on well-formulated structures and procedures which deal with workers as a collectivity. The latter approach is known as the labour relations approach. Both these elements are important complementary ingredients in any IR/HR policy.

When an organisation has traditionally operated in terms of a paternalistic, unitarist management philosophy, employees if taking up problems through trade unions, are no longer regarded as part of the 'family or team'. The 'comfortable' traditional approach of paternalistic management tends to deploy certain ideologies or rationalisations which begin to defend the old way of managing workers. Suddenly, employees are no longer members of the happy family. They and the trade union which seeks to represent them are seen as adversaries or even as enemies. There is no doubt that an adversarial employer/trade union relationship is, from a practical point of view, inimical to co-operative relationships and therefore to a productive, well run organisation. The choice is potentially one of confrontation or accommodation through an open approach to employees.

Chapter 3 deals with organisational determinants of policy performance in detail. Systems can play a vital part in evaluating the effectiveness of policy implementation (Figure 11.2). Here the specification of people management responsibilities in job descriptions and as a requirement in the selection process for supervisory and management staff is vital. Proper training and development together with thorough communication of policies at all levels with the full participation of managers and supervisors, can contribute to the effective operationalisation of policies. As discussed in Chapters 3 and 4, it is necessary to develop selection, appraisal, reward and promotion criteria which reinforce the people management component of management work. At the core of an effective policy are basic questions about the extent to which clearly defined values about people are internalised into both HR systems and behaviour in organisations.

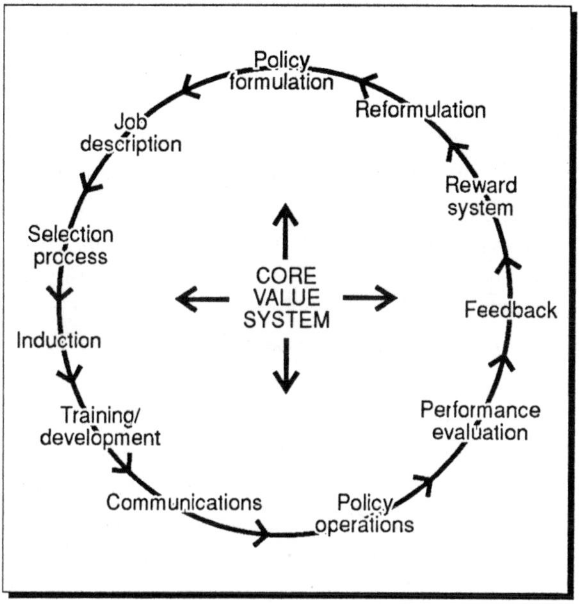

Figure 11.2

Espoused and Operational Model

Source: Adapted from Davie, B. et al. (1987)

12

CONCLUSIONS: STRATEGIC ISSUES IN MANAGING PEOPLE

INTRODUCTION

Both employer initiatives and public policy regarding the structure of the political economy are important factors which will impact on industrial relations and HR strategies in the latter part of the 1990s. A strategic approach attempts to optimise the effective management, development and involvement of human resources to achieve competitive edge and organisational effectiveness. This requires excellence in both individual and collective components of the employment relationship.

THE POLITICAL ECONOMY

The need to identify both causes and outcomes of economic *inequalities* is important. There are vital policy options in respect of a likely change in patterns of public expenditure, collective bargaining, and other new directions in respect of wealth redistribution. A larger proportion of expenditure on lower income groups is a likely priority for a future government. The particular needs of training, education, and housing are paramount. Meaningful participation of black people in the economy is both an important process and outcome of addressing inequalities.

Although reference is often made to the benefits of a mixed economy, the vexed question as to the *direction* of the mix needs to be addressed, ie the extent of state intervention or voluntarism is a fundamental policy matter not yet addressed in depth. This will have a profound effect on the future role of collective bargaining. The social and economic imperative of black economic power not being limited to collective power of blue-collar workers, but empowerment and stakeholding through development, managerial advancement, ownership and control is an important strategic theme. The central issue in this regard is not necessarily black inclusion, but rather the policy of governance in organisations, ie access to and control of power and authority. While the nationalisation option for removing gross inequalities is rejected by employers, there is a need to explore creatively other options (including the future role of collective bargaining) for addressing these fundamental problems. Riordan (1990) suggests four policy directions for redistribution. These include urbanisation, the form and focus of government expenditure, investment in human capital and incremental distribution over a broad front. Economic growth through internal and external investment is a fundamental prerequisite for a well-balanced redistribution policy.

LEGAL ENVIRONMENT AND RELATIONSHIP-BUILDING

The possibility of legal intervention in industrial relations will require substantively well conceived employer and trade union influence on the state. Industrial relations will remain 'political' in the sense that employer and trade union organisations would wish to influence state policy either jointly (bilateralism) or independently. Such influence would include the following issues: socio-economic policy, extension of labour rights, basic protections, levels of bargaining and harmonisation of labour laws geopolitically. The resolution of the historical paradox of the majority of workers possessing IR rights without political rights will pose crucial strategic questions for the trade union movement. However, although there is much fluidity and uncertainty in this regard, employer strategies for marginalising trade unions would be ill-advised.

Not only is it important to get the basics of IR and human resource management right, but it is also vital to encourage creativity and innovation in people management. This challenge means enhancing *both* collective and individual relations. Although the processes of law-making may change, to become more or less deterministic, the need for building better race relations — a 'culture of non-racialism' — on the shopfloor, is a vital challenge. Removal of legislated discrimination will not necessarily lead to the elimination of prejudice and social dicrimination. Managing diversity represents an opportunity for harnessing the creative potential in South Africa's work-force to achieve both individual and organisational goals.[1]

FROM CONFLICT TO CO-OPERATION

IR does not comprise management and trade union relations only, but also includes human resource priorities. These can be categorised into (1) *individual development* including training, literacy skills and echnical, managerial and professional development; (2) *social development* which includes education, housing and health care. However, individual and collective relationships are not mutually exclusive. More debate is needed on the role of trade union involvement in corporate social responsibility programmes which involve redistribution of wealth to employees and their communities. In focusing on skills shortages and poor productivity, some very creative practical ideas, including greater flexibility in work design, and the use of skills and rewards, are necessary. The distinction between strategies at different levels is appropriate. The role of trade unions in assisting in addressing the skills shortage should, however, be considered. This is an oppor-

1 Horwitz, F.M. (1990)

tunity, as is the case in respect of union participation in pension and provident fund boards of trustees, for integrative bargaining and problem-solving.

The traditional IR agenda focusing mainly on materialist economic gains through collective bargaining is likely to be expanded. The 'new' agenda will focus more attention on social and development issues. Employers should be receptive to this, as an enhanced quality of life may have economic benefits for both employers and employees. Identifying and enhancing common goals and interdependent interests is a vital challenge in moving away from adversarialism to a co-operative relationship necessary for economic growth.

One of the most difficult and traumatic barriers to creating a climate for successful negotiation and a culture of democracy at all levels of society, including business organisations, is endemic violence, the intensity of which has increased since President F.W. de Klerk's dramatic speech in February 1990. Although there are several causes of violence employers must take the initiative in finding solutions, as stability is essential for wealth creation. A political constitutional settlement and the removal of apartheid, will not necessarily eliminate conflict in various sectors of society. Conflict resolution processes will become even more important in dealing with the tensions of apartheid's aftermath.

INDIVIDUAL AND COLLECTIVE RELATIONS

The distinction between individual and collective relations has become increasingly popular in managerial industrial relations thinking in the past three years. It offers a valid basis for IR policy formulation based on both pluralist principles and the human resource management emphasis on employee development, growth and involvement. The distinction between collectivism and individualism gives a rationale for providing status and identity for individuals in organisations.

However, it is the mix between individualism and collectivism in practice which is important. Increasingly trade unions are seeking to become involved in human resource issues such as training and development and social responsibility programmes. This is indeed necessary. In practice the distinction between collectivism and individualism may become increasingly blurred even if an organisation acknowledges and is effective in *both* spheres.

MANAGING CHANGE

Underlining the challenges ahead is the leadership role of managers in helping organisations to shape their environment and not merely adapt to it. This will require a paradigm shift for many managers and IR specialists who have revelled in the reactive, fire-fighting and maintenance aspects of IR work. It will require a shift away from the frequent resort to legal remedy, towards relationship-building at collective and individual levels. This necessitates a strategic approach to managing people in organisations. A strategic emphasis will require a long-term policy perspective seeking to enhance competitive edge through effective human resource management, development and participation. It will also seek to achieve enduring organisational change which aligns internal demands and resources with the priorities in the external environment.

BIBLIOGRAPHY

Adam, H. and Moodley, K. *South Africa Without Apartheid.* Cape Town:. Maskew Miller, Longman 167, 180–181. 1986.

Adler, N. (1980): 'Cultural synergey: the management of cross-cultural organisations.' In W. Burke and L. Goodstein (Eds.), *Trends and issues in organisation development,* San Diego, California: University Associates.

Allen, V. *The Sociology of Industrial Relations*. Longman: Lond, 40–42, 1971.

Anshoff, I. H. *Corporate Strategy.* McGraw-Hill: New York, 1965.

Anstey, M. 'Redundancies: Unemployment and Social Responsibility.' *IPM Journal,* 1 No: 10, 16–19, 1983.

Anstey, M. 'Values — what do they mean for management and the Floor?' Address to the annual Conference of the Institute of Personnel Management (Southern Africa), Johannesburg, 2, 6, 21. September 1986.

Armstrong, M. *Handbook of Personnel Practice.* London; Kogan-Page; 1982.

Armstrong, M. 'Human resource management: a case of the emperor's new clothes?' *Personnel Management,* (August), 31, 1987.

Armstrong, M. *Personnel and the Bottom Line.* London: IPM, 11–21, 1989.

Austin, J. and Ickis, J. 'Managing after the Revolutionaries have won.' *Harvard Business Review,* No. 3, 103–108, 1986.

Barker, F. 'Manpower Development: critical element in the unemployment equation.' *Human Resource Management*, 26–30, Jan, 1989.

Barnard, C. *The Functions of the Executive*. Harvard University Press, 1938.

Barnard, C. *Organisation and Management*. Harvard University Press, Cambridge, 15, 26, 1948.

Bean, R. *Comparative Industrial Relations*. London: Croom Helm Ltd, 15, 1986.

Beaty, D. and Harari, O. 'South Africa: White managers, black voices.' *Harvard Business Review*, No 4, 98–105, 1987.

Beer, M. Organisation change and development: A systems view. Santa Monica, CA: Goodyear. 1980.

Beer, M., Spector, B., Lawrence, P., Quinn Mills, D. and Walton, R. *Managing Human Assets*. The Free Press, London, Chapt. 2. 1984.

Bendix, D.W.F. and Verster, E. 'Workerism and populism in the South African Labour movement of the eighties'. *Industrial Relations Journal of South Africa*, 6, No. 4, 21–22, 1986.

Bendix, R. *Work and Authority in Industry*. Harper Books, 10–14. 1954.

Bernstein, A. 'What business can do.' *Finance Week*, 41–43, June 1988

Bethlehem, R. *Economics in a Revolutionary Society*. Craighall: A D Donker (Pty) Ltd, 118–119, 1988.

Bird, A. 'ESOPS — part of a strategy to smash democracy.' South *African Labour Bulletin*, 13, No. 6, 45–49.

Bluen, S., Godsell, G. and Malherbe, M. 'A survey of in-company Industrial Relations Structures.' *Manpower Journal*, 2, No. 2. 5–7 September 1982.

Bluen, S. and Fullagar, C. 'Psychology and Industrial Relations. ' In Barling, J. (Ed.) *Behaviour in Organisations*, McGraw-Hill: Johannesburg 619–659, 1986.

Blunt, P. *Organisation Theory and Behaviour: An African Perspective.* Longman London, 39–42, 1985.

Boraine, A. 'Building broad alliance: unity and contradictions.' *SA Labour Bulletin,* 13, No: 8, 34–39, 1989.

Bot, M. 'Backlongs in technical education.' *Race Relations News.* April 1989.

Bramham, J., in Cascio, W.F. *Applied Psychology.* 1978.

Brewster, C. and Richbell, S. 'Getting Managers to implement policies.' *Personnel Management,* 35, December 1982.

Burgess, M., quoted in *IPM Journal* 8, No: 1, 29–30, 1989.

Burton, J. *Conflict Resolution and Prevention.* London: MacMillan, 1990.

Camay, P. 'Labour and Capital: The issue of equity.' *Financial Mail,* 38–39, 29 August 1986.

Cascio, W. *Applied Psychology in Personnel Management.* Reston Company, 158–159, 1978.

Chalmers, R. 'Industrial Relations: core of management.' *Sunday Times, Business Times,* 6, September 4, 1988.

Charney, C. 'Industrial Relations: The new breed.' *Management,* 41–43, 1982.

Charoux, E. *Integration of Black Managers into South African Organisations.* Juta & Co., Cape Town, 67, 1986.

Clack, G. 'Industrialisation and Industrial Relations: An Analytical Framework'. *South African Journal of Economics,* 3: 113–126, 1964.

Clarke, L., MacGregor, K. and Saunderson-Meyer (Eds). *The Independent Trade Union Guide,* 121, 1989.

Clegg, H.A. *Trade Unions under Collective Bargaining.* Blackwell: Oxford, 2–4, 1978.

Cock, M. 'We can't afford this.' *The Argus,* 6, 11 June, 1988.

Cordova, E. 'Workers participation in decisions.' *International Labour Review,* 121 No: 2 126, April 1982.

Coser, L. *The Functions of Social Conflict.* London: Routledge and Kegan Paul.

Craig, A. 'A framework for the analysis of industrial relations systems, in *Industrial Relations and the Wider Society*, B. Barret, E. Rhodes and J. Beishon (Eds) London: Collier MacMillan, 8–18, 1981.

Cunningham, P. 'Bargaining under emergency regulations.' *IPM Journal*, 6, No. 1, 20–22, May 1987.

Daniel, R. 'Quality circles have a key role in South Africa.' *Engineering Week*, 8, 23 February 1984.

Davie, B., Mitchell, L. and Scott, D. 'Espoused and Operational policies in three Groups of Companies.' MBA dissertion, Graduate School of Business, University of the Witwatersrand, 1–2, 8–19, 21–22, 55–59, 1987.

Denzin, N. *The Research Act*. Chicago. Aldine Publishing Company, 21–22, 33–39, 1973.

Douwes Dekker, L. 'The Right to Strike.' *Research Paper Series*, Graduate School of Business Administration, University of the Witwatersrand, No: 5, 6–9, January 1985.

Douwes Dekker, L. 'Joint Control of Frontiers of Change'. *South African Journal of Labour Relations*, 9: No 3: 6–9, 1985.

Douwes Dekker, L. 'Industrial Relations: Interests, Values and Trade-offs.' *Industrial Relations Journal of South Africa*, 6, No. 3, 41–46, 49, 53, 3rd Quarter, 1986.

Douwes Dekker, L. 'Industrial Relations: Interests, Values and Trade-offs.' *Industrial Relations Journal of SA*, 6, No: 3, 41–49, 53, 1986.

Douwes Dekker, L. 'South Africa's developing Industrial Relations System.' *South African Journal of Labour Relations*, 10, No: 4, 46, December 1986.

Douwes Dekker, L. 'Tripartism.' *South African Journal of Labour Relations*, 11, No: 4, 18–19, December 1987.

Douwes Dekker, L. 'Workers Participation in South Africa.' *Industrial Relations Journal* 7: No 4, 1–2, 1987.

Dror, A. 'A Comparative view of enterprise-level Workers' Participation in Personnel Policy.' Paper presented to the Second European Congress on Industrial Relations, Herzlia, Israel, 13–17 December 1987.

Drucker, P. *The New Realities*. New York: Heinemann, 1990.

Du Plessis, P. quoted in *Sunday Times, Business Times*, 10, November 11, 1988.

Dunlop, J. *Industrial Relations Systems*. Holt: New York, 1958.

Dupisani, A. 'The laager.' *Sunday Times*, 2, 24 July 1988. Economic Participation in South Africa. *Project Free Enterprise Final Report*, School of Business Leadership, University of South Africa, Chapter 5, 1986.

Economic Participation in South Africa. Project Free Enterprise, Final Report. School of Business Leadership, University of South Africa, Chapter 5, 1986.

Emanuel, T. 'An ANC view on social responsibility.' Institute of Personnel Management Address, Cape Town, 28 August 1991.

Etheredge, D. 'South Africa: The unproductive society.' *Topical Opinion*, SA Institute for Race Relations, 1984.

Evans, P. 'A Generalist Conception of Human Resource Management.' *Human Resource Management*, 23, No 4, 347–355, 1984.

Farnham, D. and Pimlott, J. *Understanding Industrial Relations*. London: Cassell Ltd, Fourth Edition, 358–362, 1990.

Festinger, L. *Theory of Cognitive Dissonance*. Stanford University Press, 9–11, 1957.

Financial Mail. 'Black Advancement: Mood of Scepticism,' 701, February 1981.

Finnemore, M. and Van der Merwe, R. *Introduction to Industrial Relations in South Africa*: McGraw-Hill; Johannesburg, First edition. 35, 1985.

Finnemore, M. and Van der Merwe, R. *Introduction to Industrial Relations in South Africa*. Lexicon Publishers: Johannesburg, Second Edition, 57–58, 1989.

Flanders, A. *Management and Unions*. London: Faber and Faber; 172, 1970.

Flanders, A. 'Industrial Relations: What is Wrong with the System?' in *Industrial Relations and the Wider Society*, B. Barrett, E. Rhodes and J. Beishon (Eds), Collier MacMillan: London, 21–25, 1981.

Fombrun, C. The External context of Human Resource Management.' In Fombrun, C., Tichy, N. and Devon, M. (Eds.) *Strategic Human Resource Management*, Wiley and Sons, New York, 17–18, 1984.

Fowler, A.: 'When the chief executives discover HRM.' *Personnel Management*, (January) 3, 1987.

Fox, A. 'Industrial Relations: A Social Critique of Pluralist Ideology'. In *Industrial Relations and the Wider Society*, B. Barrett, E. Rhodes and J. Beishon, London: Collier MacMillan; 302–322, 1981.

French, W. *The Personnel Process*. 4th Edition. Houghton-Mifflin Company, 211–217, 225, 1983.

Giles, E. 'Stress in your own back yard.' *Personnel Management*, 26–28, April 1987.

Gill, C. and Concannon, H. 'Developing an explanatory framework for Industrial Relations policy.' *Industrial Relations Journal*, 7, No 4, 15, 1977.

Gluckman, M. *Custom and Conflict in Africa*, 1973.

Godsell, R. 'Work Station Participation.' *IPM Manpower Journal*, l, No. 7, 16, 1982.

Godsell, R. Personal Interview with F.M. Horwitz, February and April 1985.

Godsell, R. 'Focus on IR.' *IPM Journal* 8, No: 1, 10–11, June 1989.

Golden, C. and Parker, V. *Causes of Industrial Peace*. Harper: New York, 1955.

Goold, M. and Campbell, A. *Strategies and Styles*. London: Basil Blackwell, 1990.

Grundy, K. *The Militarisation of South African Politics*. Oxford University Press, 34, 58, 1988.

Guest, D. 'Workers' participation and personnel policy.' *International Labour Review*, 125, No. 6, 687–688, December 1986.

Guest, D. 'Human Resource Management and the American Dream.'*Journal of Management Studies*, 27 No: 4, 377–394, July, 1990.

Hall, J. *Power Management Profile*. Houston, 12, 1988.

Hall, R. 'Some changes in management practice.' *Industrial Relations Journal of South Africa*, 6 (2nd Quarter), 1985.

Handy, C. *The Age of Reason*, London: Arrow Books, 97–100, 132, 1990.

Harbison, F. *Human Resources as the Wealth of Nations*. New York, Oxford University Press, 1973.

Harbison, F. 'Collective Bargaining and American Capitalism.' In *Industrial Conflict*, A. Kornhauser, R. Dubin and A. Ross, (Eds), McGraw Hill: New York, 272, 1954.

Harvey, L. 'Nine Major Trends in HRM.' Personnel Administrator, 31, No: 11 102–109, 1986.

Hax, A. 'Methodology for Developing a Human Resource Strategy.' *Working Paper Series*, Sloan School of Management, M.I.T. 1638–85. March 1985.

Henneman, H., Schwab, D., Fossum, J. and Dyer, L. *Human Resource Management*. Homewood: Illinois, 7–10, 74, 1981.

Hersey, P. and Blanchard, K. *Management of Organisational Behaviour*. Prentice-Hall Inc: New Jersey, Fifth Edition, 8, 1988.

Heymans, S.C. 'The Politics of Creation.' South African Institute of Race Relations, *Topical Briefing*, 1, 17–18, January 1988.

Hilgard, E. *Introduction to Psychology*. (7th Edition). Harcourt: New York, 1979.

Hill, A. 'The Strategic approach to human resource management.' *IPM Journal*, 6–9 January 1987.

Horwitz, F. M. 'Workers' Participation in Management Decision Making.' *Industrial Relations Journal of South Africa*, 2, No. 4, 14–19, 1982.

Horwitz, F. and Anstey, M. 'Some Considerations on the implementation of a Code of Ethics in Industrial Relations.' *South African Journal of Labour Relations*, 8: No. 3, 22–33, 1984.

Horwitz, F. M. 'Manpower Planning and Redundancy.' *Industrial Relations Journal*, 26–34, 2nd Quarter, 1984.

Horwitz, F. M. 'An investigation of employer and trade union propensity to establish new types of collective bargaining.' *South African Journal of Labour Relations*, 9, No. 3, 53–62, September 1985.

Horwitz, F. M. 'Training and the implementation of Industrial Relations Policy.' *South African Journal of* Labour Relations. l0, No 3, (December) pp. 87–92, 1986.

Horwitz, F.M. 'The Corporate Citizen — Organising emplyers.' *Indicator*, No: 3: 8–12, 1986.

Horwitz, F. M. 'The Challenge facing the management of human resources' *Industrial Relations Journal*, 7, No: 1, 33–41, 1987.

Horwitz, F.M. 'Managerial Strategies in a Siege Economy.' *Indicator*, 4, No: 3 67–70, 1987.

Horwitz, F. M. 'Industrial Relations Policy: Towards Strategic Operationalisation'. *Proceedings of European Regional Congress on Industrial Relations: Abstracts*, 38, 1–34, Israel 1987/8.

Horwitz, F. M. 'Personnel Management or Human Resource Management.' *IPM Journal*, 6, No: 12, 4–8, 1988.

Horwitz, F. M. 'Determinants of effectiveness in industrial relations.' *South African Journal of Labour Relations*, 13, NoL 1, 5–15 March 1989.

Horwitz, F. M. 'Espoused and operational industrial relations policies.' *Industrial Relations Journal of South Africa*, 9, No: 1, 1–12, 1989.

Horwitz, F.M. and Rip, G. 'Human resource development: a component of business strategy.' *Human Resource Management*, 5, No 2, 27–30, 1989.

Horwitz, F.M., Malan, L. and Sakinofsky, I. 'Industrial relations in the Western Cape.' *Indicator* 6, No: 2, 116–119, 1989.

Horwitz, F. M. 'Human resource management: an ideological perspective.' *Personnel Review*, 19, No: 2, 10–15, 1990.

Horwitz, F. M. 'Productivity Improvement and the Development of Human Resources.' *IPM Journal*, 8, No 9, 4–14, 1990.

Horwitz, F.M. 'Determinants of effectiveness.' *SA Journal of Labour Relations*, 15, No: 1 3–21, 1991.

Human, L. and Hofmeyr, K. *Black Managers in South African Organisations*. Juta & Co, Ltd, Kenwyn, 58–59, 1985.

Human, L. 'The Story of Eric Matau: A reply to Edward W Jones, Jr.' Unpublished manuscript, Centre for African Management, Graduate School of Business, University of Cape Town, 8–18, February 1987.

Human, P. 'Some Preliminary Thoughts on Industrial Democracy in South Africa.' *South African Journal of Labour Relations*, 1, No 2, 5–7, June 1986.

Human, P. and Hofmeyer, K. 'Attitudes of South African Managers to the Advancement of Blacks in Business.' *SA Journal of Labour Relations*, ll, No: 3, 53–68, 1987.

Human, P. and Human, L. 'Towards a better understanding of management Development in South Africa.' Unpublished paper, 6, 12, 14–16, 1989.

Human, P. 'Do Multi-Nationals Make a Difference?' Paper presented at conference on Multi-national Culture: Social Impacts of a Global Economy. New York, Hofstra University, 1988.

Hutton-Wilson, D. 'HR strategies for the 1990s.' *Human Resource Management, 23–24, July 1990.*

Hyman, R. *Strikes*, Fontana: London, 91–92, 164, 1981.

Hyman, R. *Industrial Relations, A Marxist Introduction* MacMillan Press: London, 10–16, 26, 31, 1983.

International Labour Organisation (ILO) study, reported in *The Argus* 5, May 13 1989.

Jackson, D. 'The disappearance of strikes in Tanzania: incomes policy and industrial democracy.' *The Journal of Modern African Studies*, 17, 219–251, 1979.

Jowell, K. 'Industrial Relations and the potential for peaceful change in South Africa.' Address to AECI Industrial Relations Conference, Johannesburg, 8 March 1988.

Kanter, D. and Mirvis, P. *The Cynical Americans*, San Francisco: Jossey-Bass, 1989.

Kellerman, A., in Joubert, D. *Sociologiese Begrippe*, Pretoria: Academica, 1–50, 1980.

Khoza, R. 'Africanisation: Implications for the Human Resources Profession.' *African Business*, 13: 13–15, Oct. 1986.

Kilmann, R and Herden, R. 'A systematic methodology for evaluating the impact of interventions on organisational effectiveness.' *Academy of Management Review*, 87–98, July 1976.

Klein, L. *A Social Scientiest in Industry*. Gower Press, 27–28, 1976.

Knipscheer, K. and Horwitz, F.M. 'Espoused and Operational policies.' *Working Paper Series*, Graduate School of Business, University of Cape Town, No. 87–18, 1–56, 1987.

Kochan, T. 'Recent Developments in Work Place Representations.' Paper presented to the Second European Congress on Industrial Relations, Herzlia, 13–17 December 1987.

Kochan, T., Katz, H. and McKersie, R. *Industrial Relations and Labour Relations Review*, 41 No: 3, 451–455, 1988.

Krause, G. and Nel, C. 'Management lacks competency in a participative system.' *Human Resource Management*, 20, February 1986.

Krauthammer, C. 'Deep down, we're all alike, Right? Wrong?' *Time*, 29, August 15, 1983.

Lamprecht, A. 'Industrial justice and industrial democracy in South Africa.' *IPM Journal*, 6, No 1, 23–25, May 1987.

Le Roux, P. 'The economics of conflict and negotiation' in Berger, P. and Godsell, R. *A Future South Africa*, Human and Rousseau, Tafelberg, 202, 1988.

Leach, I. American Chamber of Commerce, Address to the Conference: 'Power and Wealth in South Africa, the Economic System under Review,' Johannesburg: 22 November 1987.

Leatt, J. 'Business Ethics.' Address given at Graduate School of Business Administration, University of the Witwatersrand, Johannesburg, 31 August 1983.

Leatt, J. 'The role of Management education in a future South Africa.' Address to Seminar on Management Education, Graduate School of Business, University of Cape Town, January 16, 1989.

Legge, K. *Power, Innovation and Problem-solving in Personnel Management.* London: McGraw-Hill, 48, 50–51, 1978.

Lewicki, R. 'Ethical Concerns in Conflict Management.' In *Conflict Management and Industrial Relations*, G. Bomers and R. Paterson (eds), Kluwer Publishing, 423–428, 1982.

Lipton, M. Special report for the Economist Intelligence Unit, London, 'Sanctions and South Africa: the Dynamics of Economic isolation', quoted in *Financial Mail*, 47, January 22, 1988.

Lynch, J. *Making Manpower Effective*. Pan Books: London, 12–14, 29, 150–151, 1974.

Manpower/Industrial Relations Survey, *Financial Mail*, 25, September 16, 1983.

Marginson, P. 'How centralised is the management of Industrial Relations?' *Personnel Management*, 54–57. October 1986.

Marginson, P. 'Managerial Strategies and Industrial Relations.' Paper presented to the Second European Congress on Industrial Relations, Herzlia, Israel, 13–17 December 1987.

Marginson, P. and Purcell, J. The Management of Industrial Relations in UK Multiplant Enterprises. Paper presented to *International Industrial Relations Association*, 7th World Congress in Hamburg, 1986.

Marsden, R. 'Industrial Relations: A Critique of Empiricism.' *Sociology*, 16: No. 2, May 1982.

McGrath, M. 'The racial differential.' *Indicator*, 6, No: 2, 35, 1989.

McGrory, V. 'Wage gap narrows.' *Human Resource Management* 5, No: 4, 3, 1989.

Miller, D. 'Social Partnership in West Germany.' *British Journal of Industrial Relations*, XX, No: 1 51–52, March 1982.

Miller, D. Address at Graduate School of Business, University of Cape Town, June 14, 1989.

Mintzberg, H. 'Power and Organisation Life Cycles.' *Academy of Management Review*. 9, No: 2, 207–224, 1984.

Mulder, D. In Hofstede G. and Kassen, M. (Eds) *Reduction of Power Differences in Practice*, 79–86, 1976.

Muller-Jentsch, W. 'Industrial relations Theory and Trade Union Strategy.' Paper presented to the Second European Congress on Industrial Relations, Herzlia, Israel, 13–17 December 1987.

Naidoo, J. 'Labour and Capital: The issue of equity.' *Financial Mail*, 39, 29 August 1986.

Naisbitt, J. *Megatrends.* Warner Books; New York, 103–141, 1984.

Napier, N. and Peterson, R. 'Putting Human Resource Management at the linemanager level.' *Business Horizons*, 27, No 1, 2–4, 1982.

National Procuctivity Institute. *Annual Report*, quoted in *Business Day* 4, April 26, 1989.

Nel, C. 'Economic Participation in South Africa,' Project Free Enterprise, University of South Africa School of Business Leadership, 24–26 1986.

Nel, C. 'Total productivity.' *IPM Journal* 8, No: 2, 19, 1989.

Nel, P.S. 'An Empirical Analysis of Employers' Industrial Relations Policy.' *Manpower Journal*, 3, No 6, 27–36, October 1984.

Newall, I. 'Productivity bargaining.' *Human Resource Management* 25, 1989.

Nichols, T. *Ownership, Control and Ideology.* London: Allen and Unwin, 1969.

Nord, W. and Durand, D. 'What's Wrong with the Human Resources Approach.' *Organisation Dynamics*, 13–17, (Winter) 1978.

O'Brien, Conor Cruise, *The Seige*, Paladin Books: London, 423, 1987.

O'Neill, D. and Lynass, M. 'Shop steward training: Does management have a role? *SA Journal of Labour Relations*, 10, No: 2, 35, 1986.

Oppenheimer, H. 'Visions of the Future.' *Sun*, 13, March 1988.

Oram, S. 'Industrial Relations and Ideology.' *Employee Relations*, 6, No: 2, 22–26, 1984.

Orpen, C. 'Role of qualitative research in Management.' *SA Journal of Business Management*. 18 No: 4, 250–253, 1987.

Owens, J. and Nema, L. 'The role of manpower planning in the Corporate planning process.' *SA Journal of Business Management*, 19, No: 22, 45–55, 1988.

Pansegrouw, G. 'Strategic human resource management.' *IPM Journal*, 8–15, October 1985.

Park, S. J. quoted in Schregle J. 'The German Model of Institutionalised Workers' Participation.' International Industrial Relations Association Congress, 177, September 1986.

Phillips, J. and Seers, A 'Twelve ways to evaluate HR management.' *Personnel Administrator*, No 34, No: 4, 54–58, 1989.

Pieterse, D. 'Industrial relations training: dynamic approach needed.' *Human Resource Management*, 5, No: 2, 36–37, 1989.

Poole, M. *Industrial Relations: Origins and Patterns of National Diversity*. Routledge and Kegan Paul: London, 4, 99–100, 1986.

Purcell, J. and Sissons, K. 'Strategies and practice in industrial relations.' In G.S. Bain (Ed) *Industrial Relations in Britain*, Oxford: Basil Blackwell, 1983.

Purcell, J. 'Management of Industrial Relations in the Modern Corporation.' *British Journal of Industrial Relations*, XXI, No: 1, 11, 1983.

Purcell, J. 'Managerial Control through collective bargaining.' In Thurley, K. and Wood, S. (Eds) 1983.

Purcell, J. 'The Impact of Corporate Strategy on Human Resource Management.' Management Research paper, Templeton College, 1988.

Race Relations News SA Institute of Race Relations Publication 53, No: 2, 9, August 1991.

Rees, D. 'Productivity: causes and cosequences.' *Leadership* 27–28, 1986.

Reshef, Y. and Murray, A. 'Towards a Neoinstitutionalist Approach to Industrial Relations.' *British Journal of Industrial Relations*, 20: 1, 85–95, March, 1988.

Rhodes, D. 'Succession Planning — Overweight and Underperforming.' *Journal of Business Strategy*, 62–64, December 1988.

Riordan, R. 'The redistribution of wealth in South Africa.' *IPM Journal*, 9, No: 2, 25–29, 1990.

Robbins, S.P. *Organisation Theory*. 2nd Edition, London, Prentice-Hall, 26–50, 1987.

Russel, S. 'Sullivan signatories drop by half', Business Day, 2, 20 January 1988.

Salamon, M. *Industrial Relations Theory and Practice*. Prentice Hall: London, 10–11, 17, 1987.

Salamon, M. *Industrial Relations*. Prentice-Hall: London, 392–396, 400, 406, 1987.

Schein, E. 'Increasing Organisational Effectiveness.' In Katz, R. (Ed) *Career Issues in Human Resource Management*. Englewood Cliffs: Prentice-Hall, 4–17, 1982.

Schlemmer, L. 'Political adaptation and reaction.' *Social Dynamics*, 2, No: 1, 3–18, 1976.

Schlemmer, L. 'Focus on IR.' *IPM Journal* 8, No: 1, 1989.

Scholtz, G. The role of labour relations specialists. *South African Journal of Labour Relations*, No: 3–4, & 7–22, Dec 1988.

Schregle, J. 'The German Model of Institutionalised Workers' Participation in the International Context of Workers' Participation.' International Industrial Relations Association, 7th World Congress, Hamburg, 173–177, September 1986.

Shackel, G. *Expectation, Enterprise and Profit: The Theory of the firm*, George Allen and Unwin, London, 1970.

Silverman, D. *The Theory of Organisations*, Heinemann, 47, 1970. Wiley, 1956.

Simon, H. *Models of Man*, New York: John Wiley, 1957.

Sorsa, K. *Industrial Relations Effectiveness*. MBA dissertation, University of the Witwatersrand, 1991.

South African Labour and Development Research Unit, Industrial Council Wage Rates, University of Cape Town, 1986–1987.

Steers, R. *Organisational Effectiveness*. Glenview, IL: Scott & Cox.

Strümpfer, D. 'The Group as a unit of change.' *IPM Journal*, 5, No: 8, 18–20, December, 1986.

Syce, D. 'Conflict models in Africa.' Address to the SA Association for Conflict Intervention, University of Cape Town, 18 September 1989.

Templer, A. and Hofmeyr, K. 'Perception of human resources management practices and organisational effectiveness.' *South African Journal of Business Management*, 1, 7–12, March 1989.

Thurley, K. and Wood, S. 'Business Strategy and Industrial Relations Strategy.' In Thurley, K and Wood, S. Eds, *Industrial Relations and Management Strategy*, London, 1983.

Thusing, R. 'The functioning of Institutionalised forms of Workers' Participation seen from an Employers' Association point of view.' International Industrial Relations Association, 7th World Congress, Hamburg, 169, September 1986.

Van der Merwe, P. 'The Labour Scene: a road full of challenges.' *Human Resource Management*, 14–16, January 1989.

Van der Walt, T., quoted in *Sunday Business Times* 11, June 4, 1989.

Viljoen, J. 'Worker Participation in a South African Context.' *South African Journal of Labour Relations*. 10, No 1, 55, March 1986.

Watson, T. *The Personnel Managers*. London: Routledge and Kegan Paul, 18–19, 1977.

Watts, J. 'Black managers and their colleagues.' Phd thesis, University of Natal, 1985.

Webster, E. *Cast in a Racial Mould*. Ravan Press: Johannesburg, 122, 125, 255, 1985.

Webster, E. 'A new frontier of control?' *Carnegie Conference Paper*, No: 111, South African Labour and Development Research Unit, University of Cape Town, 1984.

Weiss, M. 'Institutional forms of workers' Participation with special reference to the Federal Republic of Germany.' International Industrial Relations Association 7th World Congress, 3, 11–12, September 1986.

Welsh, D. 'Universities' role in a divided society.' *The Argus*, 2, 19 May, 1988.

Whiteside, A. 'Labour Relations between South Africa and Neighbouring States.' University of Natal Economic Research Unit, 1984.

Wickens, P. *The Road to Nissan*. London: Macmillan Press, 1988.

Will, M. 'Personnel Policy Statements, Attitudes and Labour Relations.' *Industrial Relations Journal*m 2: No 2 1–7, 1981.

Wilson, F. and Ramphele, M. *Uprooting Poverty*. David Philip: Cape Town, 276–281, 1989.

Witte, J. *Democracy, Authority, and Alienation in Work*. University of Chicago Press, 82–85, 1980.

Zaleznik, A. *The Managerial Mystique*. New York: Harper & Row, 90, 94–95, 180–181, 194, 1990.

INDEX

S

T

U

V

Z

CONFLICT MANAGEMENT

PROFESSOR D DE VILLIERS

This is a pathbreaking text on one of the most important aspects of industrial relations written by one of South Africa's leading academics from the School of Business Leadership at UNISA. It is of value to anyone affected in any way by employer-employee relationships and, indeed, interpersonal relationships in every sphere of their lives.

Publication 1992

NEGOTIATION
Theories, Strategies and Skills

PROFESSORS H I J SPOELSTRA & W E PIENAAR

Although various approaches and theories of negotiation are acknowledged, the authors of this text clearly view negotiation as a process wherein the development of alternatives is strongly emphasized. Verbal and non-verbal strategies and skills in negotiation receive detailed attention. The book explains how power can be deployed during negotiation and how attitudes and behaviours can be changed through the use of a few step-by-step recipes.

COACHING & THE BLACK MANAGER

Dr J A E CHAROUX

Dr Charoux provides an easy to read book which also turns out to be easy to use and easy to keep using. It is a manual for managers who strive for the best results from, and the best results for, their subordinates. The context is South African. Current changes and stresses are taken into account and this book might well prove to be a valuable building block for a new South Africa.

INDUSTRIAL RELATIONS AND ORGANISATIONAL DYNAMICS
Cases & Text

SONIA BENDIX & FRED JACOBS

The cases contained in this publication reflect real situations through which readers and trainees can engage in pro-active, preventive learning experiences. Although a number of cases reflect traditional industrial relations situations and problems, the text reaches much further, examining the underlying dynamics of organisational and management-worker interactions which so often lie at the root of major conflicts. This title is published in two editions - one for students, the other for practitioners.

RETRENCHMENT AND REDUNDANCY
Some Practical Guidelines

A W DU PLESSIS & C DE W VAN WYK

The current economic situation in South Africa has ensured that retrenchment and redundancies have moved to the forefront of the list of contentious issues confronted by trade unions, employers, and employees. This book is an essentially practical tool for use by industrial relations specialists and legal practitioners. Its immediate relevance is ensured by the inclusion of the latest relevant Industrial Court cases concerning retrenchment and redundancies in South Africa.

Publication October 1991

EMPLOYMENT
Practical Guidelines

P D GERBER

The fragmentary nature of the legislation regulating the practice of employment (and its attendant conditions of service) highlighted a need for a concise and practical handbook suitable for use in the employment process. It was inevitable and necessary that this book, which details the application of employment practice in the South African business environment, should see the light of day.

ENGLISH AND AFRIKAANS EDITIONS AVAILABLE

MANAGEMENT TITLES FROM JUTA

WORLD CLASS! STRATEGIES FOR WINNING WITH YOUR CUSTOMER

A D MANNING

Completely Rewritten and Updated

As South Africa re-enters the mainstream of world business, local businessmen face an unprecedented stream of new threats and opportunities. Whether they choose to export or trade in this market, they'll be up against aggressive world class competitors. To survive and thrive, they'll have to radically rethink and reshape their strategies and rebuild their business systems. This book is a must read for this new age of competition. It's the only South African book with a global focus, and the only one that addresses the all important issue of customer satisfaction. This new edition is completely rewritten and updated. It's jammed with even more facts, ideas, workshop programmes and checklists to help you win with your customers in a new age of competition. It's a how-to-do-it manual that explains the latest competitive strategies, and shows you how to make positive change a way of life in your organisation.

TRENDS TRANSFORMING SOUTH AFRICA

A D MANNING (EDITOR)

This title provides an unique collection of views covering a wide range of issues, from some of the leading experts in key fields. It ranges across politics, economics, the youth, labour, education and technology, illiteracy, international status, AIDS, and the environment. Leading South Africans provide key scenarios for the future — a future in which these issues will have to be addressed if there is to be any real peace or prosperity. This book is essential reading for all South African businessmen and women — indeed for anyone with a stake in the future of this country.

INDUSTRIAL MARKETING

C VAN VEIJEREN

Background on industrial marketing is combined with a description of the strategic marketing planning process in this book which enables the reader to put it all together into an integrated strategic marketing plan. While implementation and the need for a strategic planning system that will ensure continuous rejuvenation are dealt with in depth, the interfaces between industrial marketing and competitive strategic marketing are explicitly considered. This is both a handbook and reference source for the practitioner and the student or academic.

Publication December 1991

MARKETING TO BLACK TOWNSHIPS

R MORRIS

Robin Morris offers penetrating insights into the rapidly growing Black market. He also provides a detailed programme which focuses on distribution and sales maximisation. The book is sales driven and the concepts that are discussed and analysed are all designed for one purpose — the long term growth of sales and the securing of a profitable position for any given product. Robin Morris eliminates the complexities inherent in this huge domestic market and shows the reader just how accessible, how affordable, and how lucrative it actually is.

Publication December 1991

THE MARKETING DECISION-MAKER

L F PITT & D BROMFIELD

The organisation, management, and control of information is a prerequisite for business success. These processes are fundamental to marketing. Effective marketers and customer-oriented organisations require not only information, but information that is timely, organised, useful, and in a form that can be understood and manipulated so that decisions can be made. Information technology has revolutionised the handling of information. This book focuses on the harnessing of technological developments to enable marketers to gather, and use, information to retain competitive superiority.

STARTING MANAGEMENT SCIENCE

D R SNADDON

This book is an introduction to management science and, while it does not compete with large introductory texts, its treatment of the subject is far from superficial. It calls for active participation — problems and tutorial questions graded from simple to those of an examination standard are utilised as 'cues' to think. It is a necessary and valuable addition to the literature available to lecturers and students.

EDUCATING & DEVELOPING MANAGERS FOR A CHANGING SOUTH AFRICA

LINDA HUMAN (EDITOR)

At a time when the development of managers for all sectors of the South African economy has become a crucial issue, many organisations and individuals are dissatisfied with their progress. This book provides an understanding of why our thinking in relation to management education and development has to change. It questions, and often rejects, traditional values, attitudes and practices relating to the development of people and puts forward exciting, new ideas.

GETTING IT RIGHT
The Manager's Guide to Business Communication

ADEY & ANDREW

This work is more an introduction to business practice than a book about theoretical communication. Management, marketing, advertising, and industrial relations are approached from the perspective of business communication. Each chapter has a summary of concepts and terms, as well as case studies that test the understanding of these concepts. The syllabi of the diplomas of various professional institutes, including that of the Communication Course of the Diploma in Busineess Administration as examined by the SA Institute of Management, are covered.

MARKETING MANAGEMENT

MARX & VAN DER WALT

Written to suit South African conditions, the style of this text is easy, while figures and tables are used liberally to explain complicated concepts. While characterised by a practical approach, the content is scientifically founded. The twenty chapters are divided into four parts. The first is a general introduction providing a broad perspective; the second deals with the marketing environment; the third with marketing decisions and the fourth part, including topics such as the product life-cycle, marketing warfare, strategic marketing, product portfolio etc, deals with the integrated marketing strategy. This work is also available in Afrikaans.

Women of Europe

Women MEPs and equality policy

Women of Europe

Women MEPs and equality policy

ELIZABETH VALLANCE

and

ELIZABETH DAVIES

The right of the University of Cambridge to print and sell all manner of books was granted by Henry VIII in 1534. The University has printed and published continuously since 1584.

CAMBRIDGE UNIVERSITY PRESS

Cambridge
London New York New Rochelle
Melbourne Sydney

Published by the Press Syndicate of the University of Cambridge
The Pitt Building, Trumpington Street, Cambridge CB2 1RP
32 East 57th Street, New York, NY 10022, USA
10 Stamford Road, Oakleigh, Melbourne 3166, Australia

First published 1986

Printed in Great Britain at the University Press, Cambridge

Library of Congress catalogue card number: 85-19005

British Library Cataloguing in Publication Data

Vallance, Elizabeth
Women of Europe : women MEPs and equality policy.
1. European Parliament 2. Women legislators—Europe
I. Title II. Davies, Elizabeth
305.4′3329 HQ1233

ISBN 0 521 26562 2

SE

For our mothers,

JEAN McGONNIGILL

and

KATHLEEN DAVIES

Contents

Preface

It is a strange fact of social life that, in spite of great changes in the last twenty years in attitudes to women in Europe, and in the roles they have developed both in domestic life and at work, they are still universally underrepresented in all positions of public power and influence. National politics has been particularly resistant to their encroachment and, although in one or two countries there has been a fairly steady increase in the proportion of women members of parliaments, in most of Europe this has remained very low. Women, who are over 50% of the electorate in all member states, may make up 25% of the Danish Parliament and some 19% of the Dutch, but Ireland's 8%, France's 6% and the UK's 3% do not give such a hopeful picture. It seemed interesting to the present authors, in the light of this, that women were consistently better represented in the European Parliament than in their national assemblies, and they set out to establish the reasons for this. Were they to do with the kinds of women who stood, or with perceptions of the European Parliament itself, or with the nature of European politics?

At one level then, this book is a study of the women MEPs, of who they are and how they got there. It is also, however, an investigation of whether women make a difference in politics and to what extent they introduce women's concerns into the political arena and press for women's interests in a systematic way.

The book begins by looking at the women in the European Parliament: their numbers, and personal, professional and political backgrounds and experience. It goes on to show that they are not exclusively or even predominantly concerned with women's interests. In spite of this however, a great deal of equality legislation affecting the rights of all European women has come through the EEC in recent years and women in the Parliament have contributed importantly to it. This legislation, its history and its effects on women in the member states, is examined and finally some suggestions are made for the future.

In the course of this research, both the authors conducted interviews in

Strasbourg, Brussels, London and Dublin, and all the quotations from MEPs and national representatives derive from these unless otherwise stated. The figures in the book are largely for the Parliament of 1979–83, but those for 1984 have been included where possible. The relatively small number of women in both national and European politics presents a difficulty when it comes to showing them as a percentage of the membership of committees and political bodies of all kinds. One woman more or less may modify the percentage fairly dramatically thus giving the impression of a significant change in representation. To avoid this, numbers as well as percentages have sometimes been given, which although stylistically clumsy, is rather more accurate.

Although the book is a joint effort, some chapters were written by one of us rather than the other. Chapters 1, 5, 7, and 8 are by Elizabeth Vallance and Chapters 2 and 6 by Elizabeth Davies. Chapters 3 and 4 we wrote together. In addition to the books and articles we mention in the references, we have made extensive use of various publications directly relating to Europe or the European Parliament. *The Official Journal of the European Communities* is much like a European Hansard, containing the proceedings of the Parliament, and is published by the EP. Parliament also publishes reports of its own committees (such as those of the Committee of Enquiry into the Situation of Women in Europe) and the Commission produces reports on legislation and proposed legislation. Many of these documents are available from the Commission's Office in London or can be found in a European Documentation Centre (EDC), forty of which have been established at British university, polytechnic and other libraries. Also available in EDCs are copies of the Commission's publication on women, *Women of Europe* (which can also be obtained free from the Commission) and the Parliament's *European Parliament Briefing*, *European Parliament News* and *The Week*. In their Law Reports, *The Times* and *The Financial Times* carry details of ECJ cases, including the ones on sex equality to which we have referred. The legal journals which we found most consistently helpful were *Public Law*, *The European Law Review* and *The Common Market Law Review*. Finally, the regular publication of the Centre for Research on European Women, *CREW Reports*, is an invaluable source of up-to-date information on all aspects of European policy affecting women.

Many people are crucial to the production of any book and this one is no exception. We would like to thank all of those, from every country in the European Community, to whom we have talked in the course of our research. Among them have been MEPs and members of national parliaments, civil servants (both national and European), lawyers, academics, and representatives of trades unions, employers and equality agencies (in particular the British Equal Opportunities Commission and the Irish Employment Equality Agency).

Elizabeth Vallance is grateful, too, to the European Commission for the award of their research grant in 1983/4, which allowed her to develop in more detail the implications for women of existing European equality legislation. Elizabeth Davies would like to thank the Peter Kirk Memorial Fund for a small grant in 1981, which began her interest in the European Parliament.

We are very grateful to June Neilson for permission to use some of her figures on women's interventions in the European Parliament. These appear in Chapter 4. Our special thanks too, to Jean and Bill McGonnigill for their patient and meticulous proof-reading.

Finally, writing books is disruptive of personal life, yet it is those closest to us whom we normally expect to provide the background and encouragement which makes such projects possible. Elizabeth Vallance would like to thank Iain, Rachel and Edmund Vallance for their understanding and Jane Vallance for her domestic support. Elizabeth Davies is grateful to Patrick Carmichael, Cathie Brown, Tim Gorvett and especially to Steven Wibberley, who all lived with this book and offered much thought and help.

E.M.V.
E.M.D.

Abbreviations

ACAS	Advisory Conciliation and Arbitration Service
CAC	Central Arbitration Committee
COREPER	Committee of Permanent Representatives
CREW	Centre for Research on European Women
DGV	Social Affairs Directorate
EAT	Employment Appeal Tribunal
ECHR	European Convention on Human Rights
ECJ	European Court of Justice
EDA	European Democratic Alliance
EDG	European Democratic Group
EEA	Employment Equality Agency
EEOC	Equal Employment Opportunities Commission
EIB	European Investment Bank
EITB	Engineering Industrial Training Board
EMS	European Monetary System
EOC	Equal Opportunities Commission
EP	European Parliament
EPA	Equal Pay Act 1970
EPD	Equal Pay Directive
ESC	Economic and Social Committee
ESF	European Social Fund
ETD	Equal Treatment Directive
ETUC	European Trade Union Confederation
ILO	International Labour Organisation
JRG	Joint Review Group
MEP	Member of the European Parliament
MP	Member of Parliament
OECD	Organisation for Economic Co-operation and Development
PPE	European People's Party

SDA	Sex Discrimination Act 1975
SSD	Social Security Directive
TD	Irish MP
UNICE	European Employers' Union
WISE	Women in Science and Engineering

1 Where are the women?

> We have built a house in the modern style. Maybe we are altogether more in the modern style here. Christiane Scrivener, MEP

> There's no place to hang your sword. Joyce Quin, MEP

> Somewhere that someone who's not too successful . . . gets shunted off to. Rita O'Hare

One of the best attested facts of modern social enquiry is the under-representation of women in electoral politics. Women, who make up in most countries more than half the population and therefore more than half the electorate, are invariably a much smaller percentage of the political leadership. There are many reasons given for this, primarily revolving around the social role of women themselves and the nature of political life. Women in the European Parliament to a great extent conform to this picture. They are proportionately much less well represented than men and many of the reasons for this have to be sought in the same factors as inhibit women's national participation. Yet they are also significantly better represented in the community than in the national context – a fact which might, on the face of it, seem surprising considering the remoteness of European political issues, the extra travelling, the language differences, and so on. One of the questions we will look at in this study is why it is that women seem, if not to have taken Europe by storm, at least to have made a rather greater impact in that political theatre than on their home scenes. Another important question will be whether that impact has made for a greater representation of women's views and interests in the political forum.

What keeps women out of politics?

Before looking for the reasons why women have done rather better politically in Europe than they have nationally, it is worth reviewing the explanations offered for their under-participation in politics world-wide. First of all, it is not simply a European phenomenon. Women in Japan are only 2% of the lower House of Parliament, in America and Australia they are 4%, in India and Canada 5%.[1] Figures from inside Europe but outside the community, 5% in Spain, 6% in Portugal for example, reinforce the image of women as largely uninvolved in the political arena.[2] The easy explanation is to say that it is mainly a result of domestic pressure. Most women have children and are expected thereafter to spend some years rearing them. They do not therefore have the time or inclination to join the external male world of which politics is clearly a part. On its own, however, this explanation is weak. Many women after all do have jobs in the world beyond the home and in some professions, women are much better represented than they are in politics. About a quarter of doctors in Europe, for example, are women; 15% of dentists; 12% of academics.[3] And outside the professions, increasing numbers of women are in paid employment, even while they have small children. Women in Europe as a whole make up some 36% of the work force, and 56% of married women of working age have a job, in spite of recession and the increase in female unemployment.

Again, women no longer on the whole have large numbers of children, spread over a longish period of time. Simple, available contraception means population trends are down and are indeed now, in some countries of Europe, below replacement, so that one or two instead of six or seven children are the norm, with a great increase recently in the number of only children.[4] Women, in other words, are no longer caught in a cycle of breeding and caring for offspring for the greater part of their active life, but rather can expect to be in the world of work for most of it. In the UK, the Equal Opportunities Commission (EOC) calculates that women who have completed their child-bearing and child-rearing roles still have, on average, over twenty years of working life.

Marriage and divorce have also changed their forms. Marriage, which used to be, in the vast majority of cases, for life, is now less likely to last than ever before.[5] This may partly be due to the relative longevity which better medical care and knowledge have brought, so that 'till death us do part' was liable to mean a much shorter period sixty years ago than it is likely to be now. There have also of course been very great changes in social attitudes to divorce recently. The stigma is no longer there: modern society is posited largely on an individualistic basis where we are encouraged to 'be our own person' and where it is thought despicably weak rather than ineffably noble to remain tied to a relationship which has ceased to be fulfilling. Whatever the reasons, the divorce rate has at least doubled in every European country since 1960: in the Netherlands it has tripled and in the UK it has increased five-fold.[6] Many women, then, are in the position of being out in the public world of work because they are the main or the only bread-winner of their families. By 1978, for example, 725,000 women headed one-parent families in Britain.[7] Marriage can no longer be seen as a cosy cocoon within which a woman will be cherished and maintained in return for keeping house and having children, and whereas the women who grew up to this expectation in such a social ethos might be expected to leave politics to men, as part of their world 'out there', it becomes increasingly unrealistic for women brought up in the less secure world today to ignore the issues which impinge so directly on their daily lives as workers, providers and tax-payers. And the fact that women themselves are aware of their changed position here is reflected in the number of women members of all the major political parties. It sounds scarcely plausible to suggest that 'women have no political interest' when, in the UK, Conservative and Labour parties as well as the Liberals and the SDP all claim a female membership of between 45% and 60%.[8]

On its own, then, the suggestion that it is self-evident why women are not much represented in political life – because they are simply too involved in domestic life – is less than convincing. And yet, when the domestic role is seen in the wider context of women's socialisation and education, it is clear that women are largely presented, and encouraged to see themselves, as the providers of care and comfort, the dispensers of domestic harmony rather than the social and political decision-makers. Girls are brought up in just this way to regard themselves as soft, yielding and uncompetitive, supporting rather than challenging the male. In preparation for their domestic role, girls are typically encouraged not to be assertive, opinionated, combative or too self-possessed. As a recent Department of Employment paper puts it, 'boys are trained to be achieving, independent, competitive and self-sufficient, (while) . . . girls are trained to be comforting, dependant, co-operative and group oriented'.[9] From birth, girls are brought up within this stereotype and by school age they are beginning to show all the signs of having internalised the value of the role which society has designated for them. Probably largely as a result of these expectations, girls do not go on in such numbers as boys to higher education. This is not, it seems, because they are less intelligent, or less adept at taking examinations – indeed the opposite appears to be the case – but because they have already acquired an image of themselves as less bright, less able, less academic than their brothers. Although research done both by the DES and by ILEA confirms a pattern of girls doing better than boys in CSEs and O-levels, by the time it comes to A-levels, more boys are entering for public examinations and by university level, some 30,000 more boys apply and 20% more boys than girls get there.[10]

Girls with lower expectations therefore tend to acquire fewer qualifications and fewer qualifications mean lower-status jobs. Whatever else it is, politics is a middle class occupation drawing its participants overwhelmingly from the professions, and women, with their lower educational achievement, tend not to be well represented in, for example, the law, business and the media, from which backgrounds so many politicians come.

It is therefore simplistic to assume that it is women's domestic role *per se* which inhibits their involvement in politics. Of course most women do look after children; they tend therefore not to be able to give the same total commitment to a job outside the home as men, whose support systems – cleaning, cooking, child-minding and so on – they provide. But the education to that role, the maintenance of standards of the 'eternal feminine' and their effects on women's self-image, development and aspirations are crucial too.

If the diffuse influences of women's social role are important inhibitors of their political participations, so too is the nature of politics itself. It surely is the archetype of a male pursuit – assertive, opinionated and requiring a high degree of toughness, self-confidence and competitiveness. While most men are brought up to aspire to something of these qualities, whatever their ambitions at work may be, for women they are much more ambivalent. When, for example, do toughness and self-confidence become brashness and lack of femininity? Self-assurance can quickly be read as coldness in a woman, and ambition is supposed to be reserved for her husband's progress rather than her own.

There is a deep uncertainty among many people – men and women – about the ultimate suitability of the political life for women. Would a 'proper' woman really want to be involved in this kind of enterprise? If she's not committed enough, she's an inadequate candidate, while if she is single-mindedly committed, she's clearly not a typical woman and her femininity is in question. Since at least the time of the suffragettes, casting aspersions on the femininity of female political aspirants has been the classic way of putting them down, and although there clearly are numbers of women successful both in their political and personal lives, the uncertainty lingers, in folk memory, to be revived from time to time when women come up for selection as candidates.

Even the most successful of political women have to ride this storm – to be prepared to counter questions about their domestic arrangements and whether their children will be adequately cared for. Lady Young, who became leader of the House of Lords, says that after selection interviews she often felt she'd been asked so much about such details that 'there was no time to talk about politics and they must have thought I didn't know anything about it'. Audrey Wise, Labour MP from 1974 to 1979, found a way of dealing with a similar situation by agreeing to answer such questions only if they were also put to the other two candidates on the short-list – both men but with children very much younger than her own twenty-year-olds. And even once they have made the break into electoral politics, the ambivalence of their positions can remain. Sheila Faith, ex-Conservative MP and now MEP, for example, recalls how she was told that her husband's frequent presence at constituency events had given the impression that she was excessively dependent on him. When she started to go alone however, the rumour was that her marriage was unstable.

Such stereotyped reactions of women candidates are still very common and they are perhaps not so surprising. Politics is historically a male game. Its roles and arrangements, its way of proceeding, were created by men, relating to each other in ways in which they, and not women, feel comfortable. They are men too, of fairly limited and specific backgrounds – as Barbara Castle MEP says, 'the products of institutions' – the professions, the unions, the large business corporations, and in the case of Britain, the public schools. The processes and structures, as well as the ethos of politics, then, are overwhelmingly male. The historic house in which the representative assemblies of the European countries sit are themselves in most cases remembrances of times past, of histories in which women played, until recently, very little active and public part. Even the statues in parliaments throughout Europe recall and honour those who are almost invariably male. The outcome of all these attitudes and circumstances is a very real uncertainty among some people about the suitability of women for public life. Women and power still appear to be dangerously incompatible, and where is power more overtly and publicly wielded than in politics? And the effects of the assumed dissonance between women and the wielding of power are felt not only by those who do the choosing of candidates, but by women themselves. Many who might feel capable of making a contribution – on a local or national, or even international level – may be inhibited from doing so by their awareness of other people's uncertainty, which thus undermines their confidence and their will to proceed.

Discrimination can take many forms and the most overt may not be the most damaging. The female candidate who reported going to a selection conference on a warm summer day and being greeted, as a very first question, with, 'Do you have a bikini?', at least knew what she was up against! (And it is not necessary to be a humourless man-hater to feel that such a starting-point, intentionally or otherwise, sought to put the only woman on this particular short-list into a position where a relationship of equality had been pre-empted. She was now primarily a pretty lady who could, with the greatest gallantry, be patronised.) Rather it is the more insidious forms of sexism with which it is so difficult to deal. Questions about whether she will be able to stand up to the physical rigours of political life or is psychologically tough enough to survive or can make appropriate domestic arrangements would be unlikely to be put to a man. Again, the suggestion in the end that 'we (the enlightened selectors) would accept a woman candidate, but the electorate aren't ready for such novelty and will discriminate against her', betrays either disingenuousness or ignorance. It is sometimes simply an indirect way of dismissing women candidates out of hand (often in the belief that a married man will give the constituency 'two for the price of one' where his wife gives her time and support freely to her husband's career). If, on the other hand, such a comment about electoral discrimination is made in good faith, it betrays a woeful ignorance of reality. All the considerable evidence now available shows that, although it is true that, given an abstract choice between a male and a female representative, a fairly high proportion of the electorate will still opt for a man, once the candidate is chosen and endorsed by the party, electors will not change their party allegiance to avoid voting for a woman.[11] And in the European elections of 1979, the electorate cannot be said to have discriminated against women: 16% of all candidates were women and women were 16% of those who were successful. Further, in both Holland and Denmark many women actually benefited from high numbers of 'personal votes' given by the electors to popular candidates.

There are, as has been said, proportionately rather more women in the European Parliament than in national parliaments. This was not always the case. The European assembly until 1979 was composed of delegates from national parliaments. There were 198 of them and only 11 were women; one each from the Netherlands, Germany, Denmark and Luxembourg, three from Italy and four from the UK. With the first direct elections in 1979, 66 of the 410 new MEPs were women and in 1984 that number went up to 75 out of 434 (Greece having acceded to the Treaty of Rome in the meantime, so increasing the number of representatives by 24). The proportion of women in the European Parliament in 1984 varies between a low of 8% (Greece) and a high of 37% (Denmark), but in all cases it is higher than the percentage in the equivalent national legislatures. Still it might be thought that women surely face largely the same difficulties in entering the European political arena as they do in their national contexts. The same sexism, the same ambiguous attitudes to women and power, the same educational and professional disadvantages must plague them in their quest to become MEPs as in the attempt to be accepted as national candidates. Indeed there might even seem to be further problems for the women with European aspirations. The travelling between home and constituency and the Parliament could seem even more daunting in the European case than it is often depicted as being in the case of Westminster, for example. There it is sometimes said that women faced with the constant triangle of home (and husband's place of work), constituency and London can be demoralised to the point of giving up. How much more daunting the complications of home, constituency, Brussels and Strasbourg. And yet, the hours are less taxing, more structured. It is possible to plan ahead for the parliamentary time in Strasbourg and the committee time in Brussels – and the weekly plane journeys can hardly be thought much more tiring than the long haul to a domestic constituency in Scotland or the West Country. MEPs too do not have to live in their constituencies and although there is no rule that MPs must do so, most find it expedient to have at least a base and many have their

Table 1. *Women in the European Parliament 1979/84*

	Total membership (1984)	Women members				Women in national legislature	
		1979	1984	1979	1984	1979	1984
Belgium	24	2	4	8%	16%	8%	5%
Denmark	16	5	6	31%	37%	23%	25%
France	81	18	17	22%	21%	4%	6%
Germany	81	12	16	15%	19%	8%	10%
Greece (1984 only)	24	—	2	—	8%	—	4%
Ireland	15	2	2	13%	13%	4%	8%
Italy	81	10	8	12%	10%	8%	8%
Luxembourg	6	1	1	17%	17%	10%	14%
Netherlands	25	5	7	20%	28%	14%	19%
United Kingdom	81	11	12	14%	15%	3%	3%
All	1979 410 1984 434	66	75	16%	17%	9%	10%

homes there. The MEP's involvement with the constituency is less direct (constituencies for Europe are distinctly larger than for national electoral purposes – e.g., in Britain there are 81 constituencies for Europe compared with 650 for Westminster). And although MEPs do tend to hold surgeries to offer constituents advice and to listen to opinions and problems, they are not expected to be 'on show' in their areas to the extent of a national representative and are consequently not so well known. A recent poll showed that only 7% of the UK electorate knew even the name of their MEP.[12] The pressure to be a 'good constituency member' is probably less strong on European representatives, then, leaving them more freedom to arrange their lives around travelling and parliamentary participation.

But are there any positive advantages for women standing in the European rather than the national context? To begin with, the whole structure of the European Parliament is rather different from national politics. In the British Parliament, the French Assembly or the Danish Folketing, members of opposing parties confront each other in a direct and hostile way. In the case of Westminster, even the form of the Chamber of the House of Commons, rectangular, with opponents facing each other directly across the floor, encourages debate and direct face-to-face argument. With a few notable exceptions, women have not been spectacularly successful in this context. They are more at home, on the whole, in the quieter world of committee discussion than in the hurly-burly of the debating chamber. In

Europe the gently curved chamber of the Parliament contains loosely allied political groups. There is little debate and almost no confrontation. Statements are made, and translated, but much of the spontaneity of national assemblies is gone. It certainly seems that women prefer this down-to-earth environment, where histrionics are not at a premium. As one Liberal candidate said, 'In the debating context, women tend to be overshadowed by men: committee work produces compromise rather than confrontation and women prefer this.' Even those who clearly have no trouble dealing with the cut and thrust of debate themselves recognise that most women are perhaps more reticent. Says Lady Young, 'women take to the Committee system more easily', and Dame Shelagh Roberts, with experience as both a national and European candidate, believes, 'women don't like confrontation for confrontation's sake', even, she says, when they may be just as capable of scoring debating points as men. The argument seems to find international agreement: 'Women don't like confrontation as much as men – that's the only real difference between them. Women prefer to find agreement, to discuss and find practical solutions', says Christiane Scrivener, a French Liberal. Comtesse d'Harcourt and Madame Dienesch, her fellow countrywomen, agree that women are 'less aggressive' and 'more sensitive'. And Eileen Lemass, who was a member of the Irish Dail, says, 'women don't have such a fighting instinct'.

It would, of course, be simplistic to suggest either that political women have no desire or ability to be opinionated in defence of their beliefs or that any political framework can be devoid of confrontation and a certain level of aggression. The point remains, however, that the European Parliament is run largely on committee lines and that it is rather difficult to have a real up-and-downer with an opponent whose words one may have to wait to hear on the translation service! The passion of debates is clearly somewhat mediated. The processes of the Parliament too tend to depend on clause-by-clause study of proposals in committees, leaving little opportunity for the use of the debating techniques of questioning and advocacy. Once proposals reach the floor of the chamber from committee, most political disagreements have already been thrashed out. Parliamentary 'debates' therefore are largely set-piece, speech-reading affairs, mainly conducted for the benefit of the media. This mode of operating may well appeal to many women although, as several of them were quick to point out, this need not mean that they are incapable of dealing with personal conflict. As the Irish TD, Mary Flaherty, says, 'Women may dislike confrontation but women *politicians* will have a good deal of experience of it.' And, as Joyce Quin, a Labour MEP, says, some women clearly like the excitement of debate – and she mentions Barbara Castle as an outstanding example of this.

If the processes and arrangements of the European Parliament itself are an encouragement to greater female participation, the method of getting there may also be something of a help. A national general election campaign is a highly competitive affair involving constant hustling, selling yourself, your image and ideas. It is this aspect of politics which has put off many able women who might in the past have sought a political career. Baronesses Falkender and Wootton are among those on record as saying they found the electioneering aspect of national politics the most distasteful.[13] In the particular circumstances of 1979 in Britain, where the European election followed so quickly after the General Election, the low level of interest in the former was predictable and, it was believed, unusual. However, only in Belgium, Italy and Luxembourg were the turn-outs for the 1979 European Elections near to general election levels, and in 1984 Britain repeated almost exactly the same turn-out as in 1979. This lack of engagement has made for campaigns with little media coverage, little involvement of the electorate and little need therefore for the candidates to maintain a high profile. Indeed, as Joyce Quin says, trying to interest the electorate in Europe was 'a bit like banging your head against a brick wall'.

All of this is perhaps symptomatic of the major reason for more women coming forward and being given a chance in the European arena, and that is the rather ambiguous status of European politics in general and of its Parliament in particular. To many people it seemed – and still does – a somewhat remote institution with undefined powers and little importance. The European Parliament, after all, does not legislate. Its relationship to the Commission and the Council of Ministers is confused for most people. The EEC itself is mistrusted by many Europeans as either irrelevant or interfering, and membership of its representative assembly is consequently devalued. As Madeleine Taylor, the Irish TD, says, 'People often haven't a clue what's going on in the European Parliament.' National politics, on the other hand, are immediately and visibly significant. And it is not only the electorate who feel like this; many people at Strasbourg also believe that the competition for Europe is less intense than that for national candidature. Says Norvella Forster, 'Men are very ambitious for Westminster and many therefore don't try for Europe.' Madame Pruvot, a French MEP who ran on the same list as Madame Veil, puts the point in a nutshell, 'In France there is a very ambivalent feeling about Europe – to such an extent that my male colleagues were less interested and so left more room for women.' It is a view shared by Lady Elles, the British Conservative MEP: 'Men tend to believe that their careers must be in the national parliaments, whereas many women who have not been able to get into national parliaments have found a place in European politics.'

Politicians already established in national life, too, were undoubtedly unwilling to give this up to stand in Europe, and although most parties (with the exception of the British Labour Party) allow dual mandate – that is, membership of both the European and national assemblies – the pressure of running both jobs is considerable and probably impossible if any kind of national office is held by the candidate.[14] This means, says Mrs Lemass, the former Irish TD, now MEP, 'All the important people from the national parliaments were not interested. We had people going from here [Ireland] because they were not in the national parliament . . . if they couldn't make it to the national parliament, they would try for the European. In selection, it was a question of who can we afford . . . prominent people in the political scene were already Ministers and Deputies and they obviously weren't going to give that up to run for Europe.' Europe was seen in many cases as a 'consolation prize', says Rita O'Hare, Head of Sinn Fein Women's Department, '. . . as somewhere that someone who's not too successful here gets shunted off to'. Although this is an extreme view, it is echoed in modified form by most MEPs, who agree that the presence of more women in Europe is at least partly a result of less competition there from ambitious men. This would certainly be supported by experience in British national politics, where women are selected overwhelmingly where men are less keen to stand, that is for the minority parties (the Ecology Party in 1983 fielded some 23% female candidates as against the victorious Conservative Party's 6%)[15] or for the marginal or hopeless seats. Only one of the Conservatives' 191 safe seats went to a woman (Mrs Thatcher) in 1979, and half their women candidates stood in seats absolutely safe for the Opposition. The Labour Party, too, having given only eight of their 209 safe seats to women, then ran 45% of their remaining female candidates in completely hopeless constituencies.[16] The argument has also been made that, since there was relatively less competition for European than for national seats, they became, in many member states, more or less the gifts of the parties to their functionaries and supporters. Women who often find it difficult to get into national politics, but are frequently loyal party workers, therefore figured heavily in the nominations. As one writer has it, 'by sending them to Strasbourg the party leaders could let them have their "place in the sun", ostensibly advance them to prominence and thereby prove the non-discriminatory character of the party, without giving them any real power'.[17]

Another factor which may have had the effect of encouraging rather than inhibiting women is the very newness of the European Parliament. Unlike national parliaments with their long histories of male hegemony, the European Parliament has no tradition of excluding women. It was not built, like Westminster, on the model of a men's club, and there is, as Joyce Quin puts it, 'No holy of holies where women aren't supposed to go . . . and there's no place to hang your sword!' (Her reference is, of course, to the existence of just such accommodation for leaving weaponry in the cloakrooms of the Palace of Westminster.) Something of this feeling emerges when MEPs emphasise the modernity of the European Assembly in its form and procedures which are untrammelled by long, largely male, tradition. Even its architecture is unforbiddingly new: 'We have built a new house in the modern style', says Christiane Scrivener, 'Maybe we are altogether more in the modern style here.' It is a notion echoed by Madeleine Taylor when she claims that 'There aren't the same entrenched ideas and traditions in the European Parliament.'

And 'newness' extended to the electoral process in 1979. Before that time, MEPs had been the delegates of their government, selected from existing national members. Only in the first direct election were representatives putting themselves up for a constituency vote. There were therefore no already existing MEPs to overcome, and this may have encouraged women to take a chance. The parties were looking for able candidates – and many of the most experienced were, for reasons already mentioned, unwilling or unable to stand. As Shelagh Roberts says, 'In Britain, there were 270 constituency parties looking for new members and no incumbents to beat.' Many women realised they were in with a chance. Never before, and probably never again, will there be so many political vacancies at one time.

If one is looking for structural factors which may have affected the representation of women in the European Parliament, that most often suggested is the electoral system itself. In all the countries of the Community, with the exception of Britain and France, some form of proportional representation (PR) is adopted for national elections and it was therefore natural that this should be continued in the European elections. France, which elects its National Assembly by a second ballot (non-proportional) system nonetheless adopted PR for the European contest. Britain, which has a single-member first-past-the-post electoral system for national elections, has so far stuck to this (except in Northern Ireland) for the European elections of both 1979 and 1984.

The Treaty of Rome specifies the development of a common system for European elections, and this is still being discussed in the Parliament. In 1981, the Seitlinger report on the basic elements of a uniform electoral system appeared and was much debated.[18] British members, both Labour and Conservative, rejected the move to a proportional system in Europe, largely because it was seen as the beginning of a slide to PR in national elections, which both parties oppose. The discussion however was presented in terms not so much of PR or not, but of the kind of proportional system which might be suitable for all Europeans to adopt. The advantages of the Danish system with a low threshold over the German system with a high one, or the difficulty of local identification in the French regional list system, were assiduously debated. The British were able to take advantage of the fact that several member states, and in particular the Danes, seemed unprepared to compromise and were willing to veto anything but their own system; and in the end, in the 1984 election, as in the 1979, no uniform system was used. Britain (excluding the three Northern Irish seats) used its usual single-member method while the other member states used various forms of PR.

It is suggested by many MEPs that most proportional systems are particularly helpful to women. The argument goes that in a single-member, first-past-the-post system like the British, the tendency is for selectors to choose a candidate most likely to appeal broadly to the electorate, so as not to alienate any section more than necessary. The result is that they will generally choose the standard, successful product – who is, on past record, overwhelmingly middle-class, middle-aged and male. Women are disadvantaged in this system because there is no political incentive in the majority of cases to choose them and so they tend to be squeezed out of the better seats.

In a proportional system, on the other hand (and there are many forms of PR), a number of candidates, rather than just one, are presented to the electorate. Here, there is every political incentive for parties choosing candidates to appeal as widely as possible across the electoral spectrum and to field candidates appealing to different sections. In any electorate which, like all the European ones, is more than 50% female, it would probably be a grave error, in today's climate, for parties to fail to field a reasonable number of women. As Simone Veil says, 'Party leaders knew that women were necessary to their electoral support and therefore their success.' More women are therefore selected for winnable seats on this method and hence more will be elected. As Vernon Bogdanor succinctly puts it, 'Whereas under a single-member constituency system, it is the *presence* of a candidate who deviates from the identikit norm . . . that is noticed, in a party list system, it is the *absence* of a woman . . . that will be commented on and resented'.[19] In the national context, there is certainly prima facie evidence for this argument. Britain, with its first-past-the-post system, has the lowest political representation of women (3%) of any European country, in spite of what might be seen as a reasonable record in the field of women's rights. Certainly the Danish women and the Dutch women are convinced that PR is helpful to them and that the party lists on which they figure give them the chance to attract personal votes and votes for their party, both of which count in the final assessment. French women MEPs too believe that PR in the European elections helped them to achieve the much higher representation in Europe (21–2%) than they achieved in the non-PR assembly elections (4–6%).[20] Indeed the French Socialist Party pledged itself to have 25% women on its lists – and in winnable positions (i.e., not all at the unelected bottom of the list) in the direct elections. François Mitterrand proudly claimed, 'Our party declares itself the most feminist in Europe',[21] and with some justification: of the 22 French Socialists elected to the Parliament in 1979, six (over 27%) were women.

In the case of Britain however, the argument apparently becomes less clear. In spite of the first-past-the-post electoral system, women still did very much better in both European elections (14–15% of MEPs) than in the general elections (3% of MPs). In 1979, part of the reason for this may be found in the background against which the European election was fought. The general election was held only the month before and the turnout for Europe, at 32% the lowest in the member states, seemed to reflect this 'voter fatigue'. People had had enough of politics, and European politics was particularly remote, with one of the two main parties (Labour) fighting the election on a 'take Britain out' platform. This added significantly to the already ambiguous status of European participation and the low interest among existing or aspiring male politicians in standing for the Parliament. These factors, and not the electoral system, probably had the greatest influence on the number of British women who were elected to Europe in 1979. In 1984, in spite of the fact that no general election was taking place contemporaneously, the turnout in the UK was nearly as low (again 32%) as on the previous occasion. (The average in Europe was around 60%, with some member states reaching 80% or 90%.) Again, the relatively low status of the Parliament among the politically interested undoubtedly left more room for women candidates, and this was again reflected in the number of them elected. Indeed, women may be making an eminently rational choice in going for Europe if their aim is simply to get into politics beyond the local level. For it is clear from the figures that, in Britain at any rate, their percentage chances of success are very much greater there. In 1984, for example, 14% of the Labour Party's candidates for Europe were women while 15% of its MEPs were female. In the Conservative Party, the record is hardly much worse, 15% of their candidates being women, producing 14% of the Conservative MEPs. Overall, even when the minority parties (which, true to form, ran a high proportion of the women candidates with no returns) are taken into account, women made up some 17% of all candidates for Europe and produced a relatively high 15% of British MEPs. High, that is, when compared to recent British general elections, where in 1979 women made up 8% of candidates but were returned as only 3% of the House of Commons, and in 1983 when they were 10.5% of candidates, again for a paltry 3% return.

PR electoral systems, then, are probably a factor in the relative success of women in contests for the European Parliament. In a country like France, the electoral system allowed for the Socialist Party, already committed to women, to put them in high on the list. President Giscard's Union pour la

France en Europe was headed by Simone Veil, and five women altogether were elected for the party. In Denmark, women were moved up the lists by the electorate's 'personal' votes for them, allowing them in the end to make up 37% of the MEPs returned. As the case of Britain shows, however, PR is not the sufficient condition of greater female representation in Europe, and factors such as the lower prestige of the Parliament itself, and the consequent limiting of male competition, clearly have an important effect.

Women predominate among the staff of the Parliament: a majority of the large number of interpreters, for example, are female. Although this may, as one MEP suggested, make women 'feel more at home', it also has the effect of making them very aware of the preponderance of women among support staff and in lower grades.[22] As at Westminster, it is often assumed that all women in the Parliament are secretaries. In Europe, at the top of the scale, there has only ever been one woman in the Council of Ministers (Colette Flesch of Luxembourg) while Simone Veil has been the only woman President of the Parliament. The women have become increasingly aware of sexual inequality reflected in the operation of the Parliament and, more particularly, of the Commission, which Yvette Roudy, now France's Minister for Women, described as 'like a club for men only, depriving itself of the vital and complementary approach to the affairs of life which women might contribute'. Such reactions were common in the Parliament's debate on women's rights in January 1981 (see Chapter 5), when Shelagh Roberts summed them up thus: 'I think it is the duty of governments and the Commission to practise what they preach and I have seen in the latest appointments to the Commission that somebody is not practising what is being preached in the field of equality for women.' And she could just as well have been talking about 1984, when again no women Commissioners were appointed.

Some aspects of life in the European Parliament must appeal to both men and women. It is much more comfortable and better appointed, for example, than most national Parliaments. All MEPs have their own rooms – unlike, say, Westminster, where members may have to fight even for a desk. They are well served with personal secretarial help, paid for by the Parliament, in addition to their group secretariat, and the back-up information services are exceedingly good – libraries and computer facilities are readily available in Strasbourg – which may be particularly appealing to women with, in many cases, less experience, self-confidence and money than men. To have such facilities on tap makes life less complicated and better organised. Again, whereas national Parliaments often have somewhat unreliable agendas, making it difficult for members to plan in advance, the European Parliament has a much clearer schedule. Although it may look impossibly complicated for a woman to run a home life and a life in Europe, it is possible to establish a routine of three days there and four days home. MEPs know in advance when they will be in Strasbourg for their Parliament weeks and when in Brussels for their committee weeks and can plan their lives accordingly.

In spite of the fact that women are universally under-represented in political life, and that European politics might seem even more remote from their experience and their grasp than the national variety, some reasons can be advanced to explain why women have made at least an initial impact there. Much of the rest of this study will be devoted to explaining what that impact has been, in looking not only at the kinds of women they are, how they got there and what they have done; but also at what influence they have had on the Parliament's decisions (particularly with regard to women) and through those on the policies of the member states.

2 Introduction to the EEC and the European Parliament

> People haven't a clue what's going on in the European Parliament
> Madeleine Taylor, TD

> The Parliament is only five years old and five-year-olds don't do very well at a lot of things.
> European civil servant

The EEC grew out of the desire of European politicians after the Second World War to ensure peace and co-operation and to try to prevent further European conflict. In 1946, Winston Churchill speaking in Zurich, called for the establishment of a United States of Europe, apparently envisaging full political and economic co-operation between the nations of Western Europe; a co-operation which would eventually see the transcending of national borders and become a fully integrated federal union on the model of the United States of America.[1] Whilst most politicians were agreed that some far-reaching co-operation was necessary, their reasons for this differed. Some saw it as necessary in order to rebuild the individual nation-states after the war; others were committed to a European ideal, transcending national barriers. The vision of the way forward and the priorities involved also differed; some believed political co-operation was a basic requirement, others favoured economic union.[2] As a result, two European organisations developed – the Organisation for European Economic Co-operation, which concentrated on economic co-operation between nation-states, and the Council of Europe which emphasised political integration. Quickly however, both of these came to be dominated by the idea of co-operation in order to rebuild individual nation-states, and aspirations for a politically united Europe began to fade.

But the original founders and theoreticians of the EEC believed in the United European ideal. They wanted in the end to create a single European political and economic identity. With this in mind, in 1950, Robert Schuman, the French prime minister of the time, proposed the pooling of production and consumption of coal and steel within a European organisation. Schuman's plan was a reaction to the refusal of the British and Scandinavian governments to go beyond very limited measures of intergovernmental co-operation and to accept a European Coal and Steel Community (ECSC). This was seen by Schuman, on behalf of the French government of the time, as the beginning of a full economic community which was to lead to political integration. The British government refused to join the ECSC, arguing that it was not prepared to accept the transfer of control over its coal and steel industries; nor was it prepared to accept economic, let alone political, integration as a goal. Thus the Treaty of Paris was signed in April 1951, by the six original member states only (France, Germany, Luxembourg, Belgium, Netherlands, and Italy) and the ECSC began work in 1952. The ECSC, in contrast to the Council of Europe, was not a mere debating chamber, but had real power to supervise the coal and steel industries of its member states. The idea of supranationalism was apparently beginning to become a reality.

Another development affecting the argument about political integration also began in 1950. Churchill in his 1946 Zurich speech had proposed the idea of 'a European army in which we all will play a full and honourable part'. The Americans, following the outbreak of the Korean war, insisted on a German contribution to the defence of the central European front. But Germany had been disarmed in 1945 and France refused to agree to German rearmament or to its becoming a member of NATO. The Germans, on the other hand, refused to be rearmed unless they were given equal rights in European defence decisions. In an attempt to reach a compromise, the French government, through René Pleven, proposed a European army controlled and financed by all the European countries.[3] Thus, the six nations of the ECSC agreed to establish a European Defence Community (EDC) in 1952, and five of the six national assemblies ratified this. But the French National Assembly finally refused in 1954 and the EDC collapsed. At the same time, the possibility of creating a European Political Community (EPC) was being discussed. Such a Community was to include a directly elected Parliament, and would encompass all areas of member states' activities, including defence and foreign policy. However, the EPC was seen as dependant upon the EDC, and when that fell, so too did the idea of a political union.

While the ECSC and Euratom Treaties are very specific, covering particular industries, the Treaty of Rome is general in scope, covering all industries not included in the other Treaties. The ECSC Treaty also details policy quite specifically, while the EEC Treaty is concerned mainly with creating a framework for decision-making, leaving the creation of policy to the institutions it set up. Consequently, EEC institutions are required to play a highly creative role; for example, Articles 100 and 235 of the EEC Treaty allow the institutions wide discretionary power to legislate in areas not specifically covered in the Treaty in order to attain an objective of the Community. As we shall see, this became a significant power in relation to women's interests. In 1957, all three Communities had different institutions, although those of the EEC and Euratom had identical powers and functions. The ECSC institutions, too, had different names to those of the EEC – for example, the ECSC High Authority was equivalent to the Commission. They also had greater power to legislate. In 1967, the institutions of the three Communities were merged by the Merger Treaty, and now the Commission serves all three Communities but still exercises slightly different powers for each.

The United Kingdom had been invited to join the discussions leading up to the Treaty of Rome, but it had dropped out at an early stage. In line with Britain's policy of support for European co-operation to build up national prosperity, but not supranationalism, the government agreed to participate in the European Free Trade Association (EFTA) which involved economic agreements, mainly regarding trade, between the countries of western Europe.

However, the EEC soon proved to be more successful than EFTA. By 1961, the British government under Macmillan had begun to change its attitude and to seek entry into the EEC. At the same time, similar negotiations were underway in Denmark, Ireland and Norway. Initially, General de Gaulle and the French government blocked British accession, and for a time boycotted the EEC in an effort to protect what they saw as French interests. With the death of de Gaulle in 1970 and the perseverance of the four countries, the EEC finally agreed to their accession in 1972. Norway dropped out when a referendum showed that a majority of the electorate opposed entry; but the other three joined the Community in 1973. In 1975 Greece applied for membership following the fall of the Colonels and the re-establishment of democracy, and finally joined the Community in 1981. Although the Greek Socialist Party (PASOK) was elected in 1981 on a platform of withdrawal from the EEC, this was not pursued and the issue has been quietly forgotten. In 1977, Spain and Portugal applied for membership, and they will join the Community in January, 1986.

As the original Community of Six became the Community of Ten and is soon to become Twelve, so its functions have dramatically altered. The original Six member states were similar in their economies and their political structures; they were, in short, advanced, industrial, democratic, western European countries. Italy was probably the least industrially developed of the Six. With the accession of the less developed southern European countries, however, policies which can be adapted to suit all the member states have and will continue to become more and more difficult to find. Take the case of women's rights: the state of women's equality in Denmark, both legally and in practice, is far more advanced than in Greece. To impose, say, targets in public sector employment in member states on how many women they employ, promote, etc., requires the establishment of a common minimum level that would be acceptable to all Ten member states. However, this would probably be far below the norm in Denmark, and could actually lead to a fall in numbers of women employed, to conform with the target, rather than maintaining a higher number. In Greece, on the other hand, such a target, to be acceptable to the other countries, might be well beyond the realms of the possible at this stage. In recognition of this kind of difficulty, the Commission has started to apply different deadlines for its legislation in different countries. For example, Greece was supposed to have implemented the Equal Pay and Equal Treatment Directives by its accession in 1981, but the date has been pushed further forward a number of times. The general problem remains, however, and will not be solved simply by differential deadlines. It highlights a weakness often quoted by the Community's critics: that problems which differ in detail from country to country cannot successfully be dealt with by common measures. Yet the Community is based on common action and if this is its weakness, it has also been its strength. In an effort to take account of such difficulties, a two-tier Community has been suggested, which would hinge mainly on differential deadlines but would at least formally take notice of the fact that the Ten countries have rather different problems and often very different priorities.[4]

The Community now has more scope to legislate than was originally envisaged in 1957. Issues such as consumer protection, environmental protection and women's rights have been defined as objectives of the common market, and the Community has been able to legislate on these.[5] Such issues were not conceived by the original draftsmen as within the Community's scope at all. Unfortunately, while the scope of legislation has increased, its effectiveness has probably decreased. As the Community grew in membership, so legislation that was acceptable to all member states became more and more difficult to agree. Consequently, national interests began to be raised more often, as member states felt that their interests might be infringed. Since all important decisions must be unanimous, any member state can veto a decision which it takes to be against its national interest. The 1984 six-month stalemate over the budget is a good example. The Europe of the Six might have achieved some form of true common market; the Europe of the Ten must defer so much to divergent national interests that it probably never can.

The European Parliament

The European Parliament began life as the Common Assembly of the Coal and Steel Community. In contrast to the Consultative Assembly of the Council of Europe, which was primarily a debating chamber, the Common Assembly had real political power based on its right to supervise the High Authority, the main executive arm. The Assembly consisted of seventy-eight delegates of member states, designated by, and members of, their national Parliaments.[6] Article 20 of the ECSC Treaty calls them 'representatives of the peoples of the member states brought together in the Community' and Article 21 allowed for the possibility of their being 'elected by direct universal suffrage'. So some kind of democratic mandate has always been envisaged. The main power of the Common Assembly was that of being able to force the High Authority to resign by a vote of censure, which gave the Assembly a rather greater power of supervision than the present Parliament enjoys. The High Authority took most of the decisions that the Council, which is not responsible to the European Parliament, takes today. The Assembly debated the High Authority's annual report, could question members of the High Authority and also controlled its own budget and staff. From the beginning, the Assembly tried to extend its powers and aimed to achieve complete political control of the High Authority. It also went some way towards overcoming purely national interests when, in 1953, three European political groups – the Christian Democrats, the Liberals and the Socialists – were formed. From that time on, members sat, and often voted, by political group rather than national delegation.[7]

After the signing of the Treaty of Rome, it was decided not to create three separate assemblies for the three Communities, but rather to transform the Common Assembly into a new single body for the three Communities – the European Parliamentary Assembly. In 1962, the Assembly renamed itself the 'European Parliament', in an effort to claim greater legitimacy and therefore more power. Its 142 members were still, between 1957 and 1972, all delegates from their national Parliaments. In 1973, Danish, Irish and British Conservative members joined and the numbers swelled to 183. British Labour members waited until a referendum was held in 1975, confirming accession, and then took their seats with the Socialists, increasing the numbers to 198. In 1979, after twenty years in existence, the Parliament's first direct elections took place, so that members were no longer delegates from their national assemblies, but directly elected as Members of the European Parliament (MEPs) by the Community electorates. Finally, in 1981, twenty-four Greek members, also directly elected, joined the Parliament to make a total of 434 members.

Article 137 of the Treaty of Rome requires the Parliament to exercise 'advisory and supervisory powers'. Those powers can be summed up under three headings: legislative, budgetary and supervisory. The legislative powers are the least developed of all, and this is the main reason why the Parliament is often considered as unimportant. In accordance with the Treaties, the Commission initiates legislation, which the Council then approves or otherwise, after consultation with the European Parliament on certain areas of legislation.[8]

The Treaties originally made the Commission the major partner in the decision-making process, but with the 1966 Luxembourg Accord, which requires the Council to be unanimous in all important decisions, the Council has in reality become the most important member of the decision-making process. In practice, the Council consults the European Parliament on almost every piece of legislation, whether it is required to or not; and the Commission also usually consults the Parliament before drafting legislation. The Parliament is always consulted on Regulations and Directives, which are general pieces of legislation, defined in Article 189 of the Treaty of Rome. Regulations, once passed, are immediately binding on all member states and citizens. They are directly applicable and so need not be converted by the states into domestic legislation, but have the same kind of binding effect as domestic legislation. For example, once a Bill has received the Royal Assent in Britain it immediately takes on the status of an Act and becomes part of British law. In the same way, once a Regulation has been passed by the Council, it immediately becomes EEC law and must be upheld in all the member states. Directives bind member states on 'the results to be achieved' but do not lay down the means by which the results are to be achieved. Member states are under a duty to pass domestic legislation, if it does not already exist, enacting whatever result is specified in the directive, by a certain deadline. If, after that deadline a member state has failed to make the necessary provisions, then individual citizens may still be able to rely on the directive if it is 'directly effective', that is, if the directive is clear, precise and unambiguous and leaves no discretion to the member state.[9]

But, as we shall see with regard to equality legislation, such claims to use European law direct are not uncontested by member states. In addition to regulations and directives, the Council can also make decisions, recommendations, opinions, declarations and resolutions. Decisions are binding upon the individuals to whom they are addressed, but are not generally applicable. The Commission, for example, may give a decision that a member state is acting in contravention of the Treaty and this is legally binding upon that member state. The other orders are not legally binding.

The European Parliament debates proposed legislation and expresses its opinion in the form of a resolution. Resolutions are usually based upon reports from the relevant committee that has examined the legislation. The resolutions often propose amendments to the legislation but the Council is under no obligation to adopt these, which therefore have persuasive value only. It suits the national interests of the different governments to maintain final legislative power in the hands of the Council. If the Parliament had that power, then legislation would be based not solely on national interest but on wider political ideas. National interests might cease to be paramount. However, Parliament's options are usually taken note of by the Council as it is thought to be more in touch with the electorate and their concerns than are the Commissioners or the representatives of governments in the Council. Parliament also plays a role in publicising legislation which might otherwise remain largely unknown in the countries of the Ten; although it is often argued that it would be more effective in this area if it developed greater direct power, since only then would the media pay it real attention.[10]

The budgetary powers of Parliament are the most recently developed, having been finally thrashed out in 1970. Every year, the Commission submits a draft budget for the following year to the Parliament. The budget is in two sections: expenditure which necessarily results from the Treaty and that which does not (i.e., non-obligatory items of expenditure). Items such as agricultural policy expenditure are amongst the obligatory items which make up 85% of the total budget. The remaining 15% discretionary area includes the Social Fund, the Regional Fund and the Research Fund. Parliament debates the budget and may amend both items of expenditure. On compulsory expenditure, if Parliament's amendment does not involve any further expenditure, it will be assumed to have been passed unless the Council specifically rejects it. If an increase in expenditure is suggested, it is assumed to be rejected unless the Council expressly agrees to it. Amendments to non-compulsory expenditure are assumed to be passed unless expressly rejected by the Council. Parliament then redebates the budget, and may again amend non-compulsory expenditure, although compulsory expenditure is now settled. Finally, Parliament has the right of veto on the total budget, and may refuse to pass it. This it did in 1979 and 1984. However, being without a budget does not immediately bankrupt the Community, since each month's expenditure will then be determined by the expenditure of that month in the year past. Review of the budget, and the right of veto, are Parliament's most effective powers.

There remain Parliament's supervisory powers, developed from the original supervisory powers given to the Common Assembly in 1952. Parliament has the right to question the Commission's representatives and individual Commissioners, both in its plenary sessions and in the relevant committees. This question-time has been most often and effectively used by the British MEPs, who are used to the procedure in their domestic Parliament. Council members may also consent to being questioned, although they are not obliged to do so. Parliament may pass a motion of censure on the Commission which would result in dismissal of the whole body, but since it has no say in the new appointments, its power here is limited. It cannot be used against one individual Commissioner and, unless Parliament wished to make a point by pursuing a process of dismissal, re-appointment and re-dismissal, it would be ineffective in that the same members could simply be reinstated by their governments. The power has never therefore been used, although motions have occasionally been tabled, and even voted upon, when MEPs have a grievance against the Commission that they wished to publicise.

The Parliament's main functions then, are to publicise the work of the EEC and to provide fresh ideas in the decision-making process, although its opinions have no formal legislative standing. However, since Parliament is usually heeded by the Commission, when its opinions do not contravene national interests, this means that there is a persuasive value in its opinions. Consequently, it can have a fair amount of influence where national governments are not politically committed to a particular outcome, for example in some aspects of social policy, whereas over jealously defended interests like agriculture Parliament has little or no influence at all.

Direct elections

Article 138 of the Treaty of Rome requires the Parliament to 'draw up proposals for elections by direct universal suffrage, in accordance with a uniform procedure in all member states'. Proposals were originally submitted by Fernand Dehousse in 1960, and adopted by the Parliament. But the French government refused to discuss the matter, and so direct elections lay for discussion before the Council throughout the decade. Finally, in 1976, the Council agreed that direct elections should take place in 1978, and the Parliament should then consist of 410 members. The members were allocated by national population, but with greater proportionate emphasis on the smaller countries.[11] The four large member states – Britain, France, Germany and Italy – each received 81 seats. The Netherlands and Belgium got 25 and 24 respectively; Denmark 16; Ireland 15 and Luxembourg 6 (Greece now also has 24). National assemblies were slow to ratify the Council's proposal, and so the elections were delayed until June 1979. But, by that time, a uniform system could still not be agreed upon. It was hoped then that the second elections, in 1984, would take place according to a common system, but again by that time, member states had failed to reach agreement and the same disparate electoral systems were used.[12] All the member states, except Britain, used some kind of proportional representation. In 1979, Britain used proportional representation in Northern Ireland, which, as one single constituency, elected 3 MEPs by the single transferable vote (STV). The rest of Britain was divided into 78 constituencies of around half a million voters each and members were elected by the usual first-past-the-post system. Other countries also tended to use some adaptation of their national electoral system. Both Italy and Ireland divided the country into large constituencies and used STV. Belgium was divided into two constituencies, one Flemish and one French, and elections within those were on regional lists. The remaining member states – Denmark, Luxembourg, France and the Netherlands – all had national party lists, and in Denmark and the Netherlands it was possible for voters to express a preference for particular candidates on the list, who would accordingly be moved up. Women candidates seemed to benefit from this system. France was the only state to depart much from its national system, since for national elections the French use a first-past-the-post (second ballot) system. As we have seen many French MEPs see the list system as a main reason for there being more women in the European Parliament than the Assemblée Nationale.

Around three-quarters of the electorate, some 110 million people, turned out to vote in 1979. Britain experienced the worst turnout at 32%, while the highest, of around 90%, were in Belgium (where voting is compulsory) and Luxembourg (which held a general election on the same day).

The vote predominantly went to the Centre–Right candidates, who held a majority in the Parliament. This was particularly marked in Britain where 60 Conservatives and only 17 Labour MEPs were returned. In 1984, the turnouts were around the same levels, with Britain again recording the lowest vote. Again a Centre–Right majority was returned, although the Socialists and Communists did better than in 1979, and the new European right did well, particularly in France, and, to a lesser extent, in Italy.

The Parliament's first duty once in being is to elect its President. The oldest MEP opens the session and presides until a President is elected. The President holds office for two and a half years, halfway through the Parliament's life, when another election takes place. In 1979, Louise Weiss, the oldest member at eighty-eight, opened the session and Simone Veil was elected President. In 1982, Piet Dankert, a Dutch Socialist, succeeded her. In 1984 Pierre Pfimlin (French, EEP) was elected, after Jacqueline Thome-Patenôtre had opened the Parliament. Both Veil and Pfimlin, reflecting the majority view, are Centre–Right members, Veil being a Liberal and Pfimlin a Christian Democrat.

Both in 1979 and in 1984, the Parliament's first major act has been to reject the Community budget. In 1979, this was a protest against the level of expenditure on agriculture. In 1984, it was a protest against national interests and the refund to Britain agreed by the Council at Fontainebleau. In both cases, it also seems to have been a reminder to the Council that the Parliament exists and is not afraid to use the few teeth which it has. It is no coincidence that these budgets were rejected immediately after the Parliament had been directly elected: having fought a campaign and been elected by the people of Europe, MEPs seem to want to prove that this gives them real power and that Parliament is important after all.

Organisation of the European Parliament

The President, once elected, presides over plenary sittings of the Parliament, with the help of the Vice-Presidents.[13] Occasionally, this involves making political declarations to the members, but normally the President is simply responsible for the smooth running of the debate. S/he is also responsible for directing Parliament's activities and supervising its administration, for example by ensuring that all motions have been put on the plenary agenda, and that members are notified of motions in time. The President has the right to declare a budget finally adopted or rejected, in accordance with the views of the Parliament. This means that s/he is involved personally in all the budget negotiations and preparations before it is finally voted on by the Parliament. S/he also represents Parliament externally to other Community institutions, to governments of member states, and to non-EEC states. Simone Veil in particular played an active role as the European Parliament's ambassador to many countries outside the Community. She helped establish the reputation of the Parliament world-wide as an important barometer of European thinking on many issues. Piet Dankert saw his role more as an internal one, and concentrated on representing the Parliament within the EEC and member states, helping to build the profile of the Parliament within Europe, as a body whose opinions were representative and should be respected.

The President is assisted by the Bureau, which consists of twelve Vice-Presidents and five Quaestors. Its main duty is to administer the plenary sessions and sittings of committees, checking the dates, places, membership and so on. The Quaestors in particular are concerned with attending to members' needs, dealing with their travel arrangements, allowances, insurance, working conditions etc. In 1979, Danielle de March was the only woman on the Bureau other than Simone Veil. Since then, she has been joined by Lady Elles, Maria Luisa Cassanmagnago-Cerretti and Nicole Pèry who in 1984 were all elected (or re-elected) Vice-Presidents of the Parliament. There are now no women Quaestors, although Colette Flesch was elected as one in 1979.

The main political power lies with the Enlarged Bureau, which consists of the Bureau plus the chairs of all the political groups. This body, which is responsible for the internal management of the Parliament, requires broad consensus between the political groups; for example, in deciding the provisional agenda of the plenary sessions (although this must be finally agreed by the plenary itself), authorising committee reports and the setting up of sub-committees, making decisions on relations with other Community institutions. In 1973, Sir Peter Kirk, leader of the then European Conservative Group (now the EDG) said 'the place is virtually run by five men – the leaders of the five main political groups. We must constantly decide how business should be handled.'[14] There are now nine, rather than five, political groups, but the real power remains with them, and all but one of the leaders are still men.

Any assembly which, like the Parliament, does not work on a system of governmental majority with a minority opposition but instead contains many shifting alliances, must rely on political consensus for the smooth running of business. As has been said, there are now nine political groups in the European Parliament. The members sit with their group, around the President in the form of a semi-circle. The Chamber itself is called the Hemicycle. The groups sit from left to right: thus the Communists are on the President's left and the Liberals and European Right on his/her right.

The parliamentary groups

The Communists and Allies Group has forty-one members, nine of whom are women.[15] The group is dominated by French and Italian Communists, with some Greek support, and is led by Giovanni Cervetti. A few French and Italian members, who are not strictly members of Communist parties, work as allies. The French and Italians are frequently divided by major differences of political philosophy, and often vote separately and express different viewpoints in debates, rather than having one official spokesperson for the whole group. Italian Communists are not afraid to assert their independence from the Moscow political line, whilst French Communists are still more sympathetic to the Soviet Union. Consequently, Italian Communists push for moves towards European integration, whilst French Communists oppose supranationality and are sceptical about the Community. The two parties are most united on international issues that do not involve the Soviet Union, but the prevailing ideological tensions have adversely affected the Group's ability to play a major part in the Parliament.

The Socialist Group is the largest single group in the Parliament, with 130 members. It is dominated by the German SPD, the French Socialist Party and the British Labour Party. It has twenty-seven women members and Barbara Castle (former leader of the British Labour Group), Eva Gredal, Yvette Fuillet and Gisele Charzat are all members of its Bureau. The Group was the only one until 1984 to have had a woman chair – Mme Strobel, between 1964 and 1967. Since 1979, the Group has been chaired first by Ernest Glinne (Belgium) and now by Rudi Arndt (Germany). The Group has always been well organised against the Centre–Right majority in the Parliament, as was proved by the successful election of Pieter Dankert as President in 1982, when the Centre and Right collapsed in disarray. There are ideological

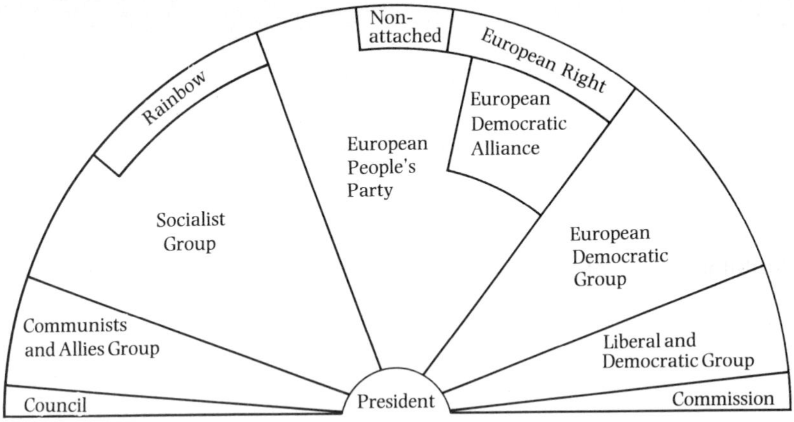

Fig. 1 Plan of the European Parliament chamber (1984). (For party composition of the Groups, see Appendix 2.)

conflicts within the Group, especially over the Labour Party's anti-EEC stand, and more 'social democratic' beliefs of the German SPD, in a mixed economy for example. Danish Socialists, too, share the British Labour Party's fears of further European integration. But the major split in public is between the French Socialists and the rest of the Group, the former tending to insist on having their own spokesperson and on putting their own views before those of the Group as a whole.

The European People's Party (EPP) is based on the federation of Christian Democrat parties in the Community. It has 110 members, thirteen of whom are women. The Group is dominated by the German and Italian Christian Democrats. It is led, as it has been since 1979, by Egon Klepsch (Germany), and has no women amongst its vice-chairs. The EPP has acted as the main political balance to the Socialist Group, perceiving itself as occupying the centre ground, and debates are often polarised between the EPP and Socialists. Their alliance with the European Democratic Group and Liberals has usually guaranteed a Centre–Right majority. They believe themselves heirs to the founders of the Community, and the most dedicated 'Europeans' in the Parliament. Above all they consider themselves pragmatists. The Centre–Right alliance proved successful in 1984, when Pierre Pfimlin (France, UFE (united right-wing)) was elected President of the Parliament.

The European Democratic Alliance (EDA) consists of twenty-nine members, including six women. Before 1984, they called themselves the European Progressive Democrats (DEP). They are dominated by French Gaullists and Irish Fianna Fail, an unlikely alliance of parties which seem to share little more than that both draw their inspiration from important historical figures. The arrangement suits them both, since debates and all the workings of the Parliament are based upon parties being represented by groups, and their alliance gives them this status. Their chair has, since 1979, been Christian de la Malène (France, DIFE (Défense des intérêts de la France en Europe)) but two of the four vice-chairs are now women. The Gaullists are vigilant to protect the national sovereignty of France, and try to ensure that the Parliament's powers are restricted so that it does not encroach on the rights of national assemblies. They are united with Fianna Fail in representing agricultural interests, supporting the Common Agricultural Policy (CAP) and advocating high farm prices.

The European Democratic Group (EDG) is possibly the most united of all the groups. This is because it is overwhelmingly dominated by a single national party – the British Conservatives – who hold forty-five out of the fifty seats in the Group. All but one of the members of their Bureau are British Conservatives, the only other party in the Group being Danish. In 1979, Sir James Scott-Hopkins was elected leader, and Sir Henry Plumb took over in 1981. The Group's main interest is trying to reform the CAP, and to establish an effective system of financial control over the EEC expenditure. They often vote tactically with the EPP, which ensures a Centre–Right majority on most occasions, while preserving each Group's independence and with it the advantage of additional speaking time, etc. The Group maintains close contact with the British Conservative Party headquarters, but can be autonomous, and has been known to go its own way on occasion. However, normally it is content to protect what the Conservatives, and particularly a Conservative administration at home, perceive as British interests.

The Liberal Group (Lib), which is led by Simone Veil, now has thirty-one members. The Group is drawn from seven of the ten member states, and its different parties have very different stands. Unlike British Liberals, who are not represented in Europe, the Liberals from the Benelux countries, for example, tend to support big business in a way that might be identified as right-wing conservative. However, the Group is united by a concern for human rights and a dislike of bureaucracy. They also place a high priority on developing the Community, especially in its external relations, and stress the importance of a uniform proportional electoral system for the next elections, since British Liberals would then be likely to be elected to the Parliament.

Between 1979 and 1984, there was a small group with eleven members known as the Group for the Technical Co-ordination and Defence of Independent Groups and Members (TCDGM). They had four women members, and chair and secretary-general of the group rotated every four months. The anti-EEC Danish Folkebevaegelsen and the Italian Radicals dominated the Group, but its members shared few common aims, and joined together largely in order to benefit from the speaking time, committee posts, etc., allowed only to groups. It represented a number of independent viewpoints. Since 1984, many past members of the Group have now joined with the Belgian and German Green parties to form the Rainbow Group. Else Hammerich is one of the co-chairs of the Group, which continues the TCDGM tradition of rotating posts.

Also since 1984, the Group of the European Right has been set up, comprising ten members of the French National Front, five of the Italian Social Movement and one pro-junta Greek. This far right group is being boycotted by the Socialists and Communists in the Parliament and even the other right groups are attempting to distance themselves from it. There is only one woman member (Martine Lehideux) of the Group, which is led entirely by men, and dominated by the French National Front leader, Jean-Marie Le Pen.

Although there is a broad Centre–Right alliance majority in the Parliament, voting on most issues is rather unpredictable. The chamber is not divided into an enduring majority/minority; rather the groups are continually making different alliances, or voting with new partners for ad hoc reasons. For example, in the 1981 debate on women's rights, the resolution was opposed by some Christian Democrats and other members on the right because it advocated the provision of abortion facilities. The Communists joined them in voting against it, but because it failed to mention exploitation. And voting is not always just by groups. Norvella Forster says 'We vote sometimes by Groups and sometime the Brits vote together and sometimes we gang up on the Socialists and sometimes on the Christian Democrats.' A classic example of voting by nationalities came in July 1984, when the Parliament rejected the Fontainebleau agreement, which gave the UK a budget refund; all the British members, regardless of party or group, voted in favour of the agreement.

Working arrangements of Parliament

Parliament's work is based upon a four-weekly cycle. It sits in plenary session for a week, then spends around two weeks on committee business, leaving the fourth week for constituency matters, group meetings and so on. The plenary sessions meet in Strasbourg, where the big set-piece debates also take place, as do the elections of Parliament's officers. The debates are based upon resolutions, submitted by one of the committees, with a report by that committee. A report is usually on a proposal by the Commission, although sometimes reports are made on Parliament's own initiative, such as the 1981 report on the position of women in the Community. The report is normally introduced by its author, after which spokespersons of groups are allocated speaking time according to the size of their group. The spokesperson for each group will have been on the committee which discussed the report. Representatives from the Commission, or other Community institutions, are generally invited to speak and then the debate is opened to the floor. Amendments, which can be tabled by any member, are taken, following which explanations of votes are called for before the substantive resolution is finally voted upon. Questioning of Commissioners, and any explanations the Commission or Council wishes to make, also take place in plenary session, as do opening addresses by new Presidents of the Commission or Council, introducing their programme.

There are seventeen committees of the Parliament, each with around thirty members. Each political group is allocated a specific number of seats on each committee, depending on the size of the group. Further, within groups, each party is allocated seats depending on its size. Committee chairs are also allocated by group. The real debate on Commission business takes place in committee and Commission members regularly appear before committees, being questioned in detail about their policies. A report can take many months to draw up as it will be drafted and discussed by the committee in great detail before being presented to Parliament. The committees meet for about two or three days each, every month, in Brussels. In 1980 an ad hoc committee on women's rights was set up, with the task of producing a report on the position of women in the Community. After the 1981 debate, the Committee became the Committee of Enquiry into the situation of women in Europe and produced a series of detailed reports (which will be dealt with in more detail in a later chapter) on specific aspects of women's position in the Community. In 1984, it was given a permanent place as the Committee on Women's Rights, although there is a suggestion that a committee with a wider brief, looking at human rights and equal opportunities, might be desirable. Such a committee would investigate the whole issue of racism and discrimination but, for the moment, the Women's Committee has a specific, more limited remit.

The European Parliament also sends delegations to non-EEC countries, (e.g. to Israel, the Gulf states, the United States etc.), and again seats are allocated by group. These delegations have been important in drawing the attention of non-EEC countries to the European Parliament as well as informing MEPs of the world outside Europe.

Other community institutions and their work

The Commission of the European Communities was set up in 1957, under the Treaty of Rome, although the ECSC had, as has already been mentioned, a comparable body but with greater power in the High Authority. In 1966 the institutions merged, and now there is the single Commission, responsible for the EEC, Euratom and ECSC, although it retains the greater powers when dealing with coal and steel matters.[16]

The Commission has fourteen members, two from each of the larger states and one from each of the smaller, and meets in Brussels. Commissioners are appointed by their governments, but are independent of them and explicitly required not to act merely as their governments' creatures. They are appointed for four years at a time. Between 1980 and 1984, Gaston Thorn was President of the Commission; he was succeeded by Jacques Delors. The Commission initiates Community legislation, after much consultation with experts as to the details. It also administers, on a day-to-day basis, the decisions of the Council, and it enforces legislation in the member states, being responsible for declaring them in breach of their Treaty duties and bringing actions against them in the European Court of Justice if they fail to comply. The coal and steel agreement gives some power to the Commission to pass legislation itself, without consulting the Council, but generally it has little direct influence over the passing of legislation. Rather, it is its power of initiative which is considerable and much envied by the Parliament. Effectively, the Commission decides the scope of the Community actions when it decides upon the scope of legislation. Although the Commission cannot achieve anything if the Council opposes it, the role it plays in conciliating all the consultative bodies, and in drafting and redrafting proposals as negotiations continue, means that the Commission has a large measure of control over the final form of legislation. Although the Council has an important role in agreeing to or voting legislation, the Commission's power to initiate policy is equally important. For example, without pressure from the Commission and its continuing interest in the development of the equal pay clause in the Rome Treaty, the three directives on women's rights would probably never have been drafted. The Commission is accountable to the Parliament in that Commissioners must allow themselves to be questioned by Parliament, where Commission proposals are closely scrutinised. Ultimately, too, Parliament has the ambiguous power already referred to, of dismissing the whole Commission.

The Council of Ministers is the decision-making body of the Communities, having the power to pass or reject legislation.[17] The original Treaties obliged the Council to take most of its decisions by majority, which meant that national interests would have to take second place to Community interests and one nation could not block a proposal. However, since the Luxembourg Accord of 1966, which resulted from the French boycott of the Council, most decisions have been taken unanimously, it being agreed that the 'vital interest' of even one member state cannot be over-ruled. This means, in effect, that any member state which feels unjustly treated can veto a whole proposal. The Luxembourg Accord shifted the balance of power from the

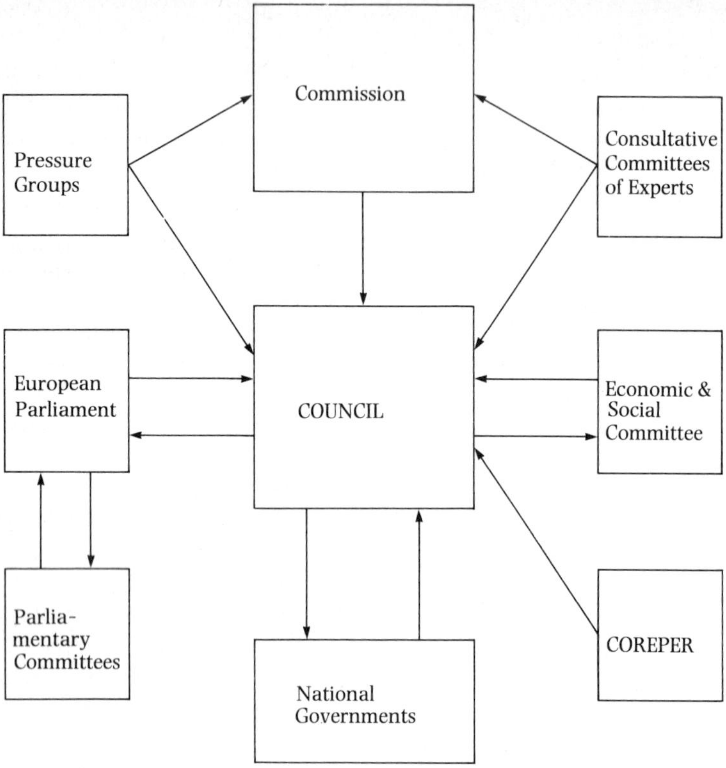

Fig. 2 The consultation and decision-making process in the EEC.

Commission to the Council. The Council ceased to act as a group and became more liable, as individuals, to Commission pressure. Previously a Commission proposal could be changed only by a majority of member states; now the Commission must ensure that its proposals will receive unanimous backing by being acceptable to all governments. The initiative is often with the Commission, and they frequently take it.

The Council consists of one member of each government, theoretically the Minister of Foreign Affairs. In fact, there are a number of specialist Councils, which the specialist ministers from each country attend. These deal, for example, with social affairs, energy, legal matters, etc., and are co-ordinated by the Council of Ministers for Foreign Affairs. In addition to the usual Council meetings are the meetings of heads of governments of the member states, which occur two or three times a year, and which work out general policies for the Community and also discuss the budget.

The Council is aided in its work by the Committee of Permanent

Representatives (COREPER) which helps it prepare decisions, and effectively takes decisions itself on what are judged to be technical, uncontroversial points. The members of COREPER are national civil servants.[18]

It is perhaps worth mentioning at this point the European Court of Justice (ECJ), for although Parliament has no formal relationship with this, the ECJ has the task of ensuring that the Treaties and other Community legislation are interpreted and applied uniformly in the member states.[19] It consists of eleven judges (one from each member state plus one extra) and five Advocates-General. The Advocates-General represent the public interest in cases and give their opinion after the case has been heard, before the judges consider their decision. The Court decides cases of alleged non-observance or infringement of Treaty obligations. The Commission or a member state can bring a case against another member state which they believe to be in breach of their Treaty obligations, either in defying a provision of the Treaty, or in failing to implement directives and other secondary legislation under the Treaty. Individuals can also bring actions directly against Community institutions challenging the legality of their actions. The Court also acts as a final Court of Appeal on matters involving EEC law; domestic lawyers who are doubtful as to the validity or interpretation of questions of EEC law can refer them to the Court. The Court's judgements are binding, and there is no right of appeal, so that domestic courts are bound to implement its decision.

The Economic and Social Committee (ESC) is another consultative body of the EEC whose opinion must be sought on certain types of legislation before they can be passed by the Council. It has 144 members drawn from employers' organisations, trade unions, and consumer bodies, who provide expertise and advice. The Commission usually consults the ESC informally when drafting legislation, but it is also formally consulted by the Council.

Finally, on the financial side, the Court of Auditors supervises the Community accounts of revenue and expenditure, to ensure sound financial management and the lawfulness of the accounts. The European Investment Bank operates on a non-profit making basis, providing loans and financial guarantees for projects in less developed regions of the Community and in non-EEC countries associated with the Community, where national means are not available. It deals in 'ecus', the EEC currency, which is part of the European Monetary System.[20]

Conclusions

The European Parliament scarcely conforms to the traditional notion of a Parliament. It has no legislative power, and no ruling party or formal opposition. Its decisions are made by compromise and consensus in committee, rather than forced by party political voting power. Most MEPs believe that the Parliament should be given legislative power, and indeed will have to be given that power if public confidence in the EEC is to be retained. The Parliament, they argue, is the only democratically elected institution of the EEC and it therefore seems anomalous that the non-elected executive should also be, to all intents and purposes, the legislature. Others, who are opposed to strengthening the EEC, believe that to give the Parliament legislative power would mean the end of national sovereignty since there would then be no argument against its legislating on any subject. As things stand, legislation by the executive (the Commission, with veto held by the Council), allows opponents to argue that the EEC should legislate as little as possible, and interfere only minimally in domestic legislation which is, after all, unlike the EEC variety, made by democratically elected representatives. The logic of giving the Parliament legislative power is that the EEC would eventually become politically supranational, as its founders dreamed, and domestic boundaries, both geographical and legal, would be irrelevant. But very few politicians, and probably fewer citizens, want a United States of Europe; most want only some kind of economic and political co-operation to the advantage of their national interests.

Opinions vary as to the importance, both actual and potential, of the Parliament without legislative power. National MPs have a low opinion of it: Ann Taylor (British ex-Labour MP) thinks 'it's a talking-shop, and a dangerous talking shop at that, since it gives the EEC an unjustified democratic legitimacy'. Martine Frachon (French Socialist deputy) said, more politely, but in the same vein, 'It's only a discussion chamber', while Eileen Lemass, now an MEP herself but originally an Irish TD, suggests 'there's always an image that politicians in the EEC are on the gravy train'. MEPs themselves, perhaps predictably, take a less pessimistic view. Christiane Scrivener, for example, believes the Parliament 'has enormous moral importance and does as much as a national Parliament' in spite of lack of legislative powers. But other MEPs are most concerned by the lack of public interest in the Parliament. Marie-Jane Pruvot says, 'Many people know nothing of it and are completely indifferent', although Christiane Scrivener blames this on the media: 'the public are very pro-European. What is sad is that the media are not interested in fundamental political problems, but are only concerned with individual problems'.

Certainly, although the Parliament is of little formal importance in the Community, it does have a kind of moral or persuasive power over the Council. Frequently, it suggests amendments to proposals that the Council would have been unlikely to introduce on its own initiative. And it has more time to concentrate on issues which the Commission and Council may regard as less politically important. The most obvious example is in the area of women's rights, where the 1981 resolution passed by the Parliament served as a basis for the Commission's Action Programme. Ivor Richard, the Social Commissioner, readily admitted that it was largely the feminist pressure from the Parliament which resulted in the Action Programme for women. The same example, however, shows how little Parliament can do beyond this in controversial areas. The Council of Ministers, especially the British government's representative, are opposed to most of the provisions in the Action Programme and have refused to pass them. So, while the European Parliament can usually introduce an issue, once national interests are involved it has no sanctions against Council intransigence.

The Parliament's peripatetic nature, too, probably makes its life more difficult than need be. To have plenary sessions in Strasbourg, committee and other meetings in Brussels, and half the administration in Luxembourg makes no logical sense and is a strain on all those concerned. Were the Parliament in one location, journalists would find it much easier to cover. To be taken seriously, the European Parliament wants publicity for its work, since very few of its electorate are much aware of it or its deliberations. A single site would make it easier too for pressure groups to lobby MEPs, and if the Commission and Council were also lodged in the same place, an appearance of coherence and continuity would be given to European policy-making, which is currently often difficult to identify.

The European Parliament can exercise some influence when nobody is vehemently opposed to what it is saying. For a time, between the late 1970s and 1982, this was the case with women's rights, in that the male Commissioners and Ministers seemed content to accept suggestions for the extension of equality provisions from the Parliament. Now, in a recession, Ministers are less happy to consider any proposal that requires public spending. Ultimately the European Parliament is a discussion chamber with the influence and publicity potential of an important pressure group, but with no legislative clout. To give Parliament legislative rights would mean member states acknowledging the EEC's democratic legitimacy, thus creating a power which would limit dramatically their own sovereignty. At least for the moment there seems little likelihood of their being prepared to do that.

3 Who are the women?

> Women do tend to be the white blackbird. Norvella Forster, MEP

> The only thing that beats women is a defeatist attitude.
> Elaine Kellett-Bowman, MP

The direct elections of 1979 saw a large increase in the numbers of women in the European Parliament. The highest number (although not proportion) came from France, which returned eighteen women out of eighty-one seats, or 22%. In 1984, seventeen French women were elected, 21% of the total of French seats. The dramatic French success can be attributed very largely to the Socialist party's policy of positive action (five out of their twenty-one successful candidates were women), by which they had insisted that around a quarter of the party candidate list should be female. The success of French women is particularly striking when compared with the proportion of women deputies in the French National Assembly (6%). As has been said, French women attribute the difference here largely to the use of the list system in the European elections, as compared with a first-past-the-post method in national elections. Voters, as Simone Veil says, when presented with a list of entirely male names, will notice that the women are lacking and wonder why.[1] So the central party must put a respectable number of women on the list, in order to avoid alienating an electorate more than half of which is female. The success of Simone Veil, and the publicity surrounding her as former President of the European Parliament, has also helped to encourage French parties to put women forward, and in 1984 she headed the UFE (united right-wing) list.

Denmark has always been the country with the highest proportion of women MEPs – 31.2% in 1979 (five out of sixteen MEPs) and 37% in 1984 (six out of sixteen). Similarly, it has always had the highest proportion of women in its national parliament (25% in 1984). Denmark uses a list system for national elections, and voters can also express preferences for individual candidates within the list. Women have always done well under this system and have frequently moved up the list to more favourable positions by the voters' choice. In Holland, which uses a similar system, there has always been a high proportion of women both in the national assembly (19% in 1984) and in the European Parliament. In 1979, Holland elected six women in its twenty-five seats (24%) and in 1984 seven women were elected (28%). A similar gain was made in Germany in 1984 where three of the sixteen women elected came from the Green party, in which women are well represented at the national as well as the European level. The German socialists (SPD) chose a woman, Katherina Focke, to head their list, on which she and seven other women were returned.

Modest gains were also made in 1984 by Belgian women (up two) and British women (up one). Ireland, Greece and Luxembourg all retained the same proportion of women MEPs as they had elected last time (i.e. 13%, 8% and 17% respectively). Italy, like France, recorded a slight fall in women elected, from 10% to 8%, but this was more than compensated for by the gains elsewhere to give the increased overall figure. In the Parliament, the Communist Group has the biggest share of women members, over 21% of members, while the Christian Democrats have the worst record, with only thirteen of their 109 members being women, some 12%.

In the 1979 Parliament, sixteen women were also members of their national parliaments, and exercised a 'dual mandate', as did 109 men. In 1984, as the directly elected Parliament has become more established, and taken on more work, fewer MEPs have remained members of their national assemblies. Many of the MEPs who did exercise the dual mandate in 1979 had sat in the European Parliament before direct elections, selected from their national bodies, and wanted to provide some continuity into a directly elected Parliament. Elaine Kellett-Bowman was one such MEP who, having held dual mandate since 1975, decided not to stand for the European Parliament again in 1984 as she believed that her function in providing continuity was by then fulfilled.

What then are the backgrounds of those women who have served as elected members of the European Parliament? Are they old or young? Are they married with children? Do they all come from similar social and educational backgrounds? Are they the products of political families? And how do they compare in these respects with their male colleagues or with women in national politics?

Family backgrounds

The extent to which politicians tend to come themselves from political families is a fact often commented on by researchers.[2] All countries have their political dynasties and some of the members of these have found their way to Europe. Sile de Valera, for example, is grand-daughter of Eamon de Valera, Ireland's first Taoiseach, was brought up surrounded by high-level politics, and continues in the family tradition. Antoinette Spaak had a similar experience as daughter of the famous Belgian minister. Others are daughters of lowlier political luminaries, local councillors, or just families who were interested in politics and involved, say, in their local party (for example, Joyce Quin's family). This has made them accustomed to hearing politics discussed, less reticent about public speaking and joining in political debates, and generally more knowledgeable about local and national issues. They tend to know how meetings are conducted, to have met national or local political figures and to have acquired, almost by osmosis, information and experience most people have to struggle to obtain. In addition, of course, the daughters of national politicians find their name is well known, and easily attracts attention from the media. In short, the political arena is more familiar, less intimidating and easier to enter.

Families may help in another way too. It has often been pointed out that women are sometimes the inheritors of their male relatives' political clothes. Melville Currell, for example, talks about 'male equivalence', meaning the situation in which women get into politics as the 'equivalent' of a man to whom they are closely related.[3] The commonest example of this is that of women elected to the United States senate. In the same style, Mrs Gandhi followed in the footsteps of her father, Nehru, and Mrs Bandaranaike inherited her position in Sri Lanka from her husband, who had been prime minister before her. There is strong evidence of this syndrome in the domestic politics of the English-speaking countries, as Walter Kohn shows in his cross-cultural study. This is partly, he suggests, because by-elections are held there to fill any vacancies between elections and 'there is a temptation to take advantage of the name of the former member'.[4] But in countries whose electoral systems do not involve by-elections (all the European member states except the UK) this will not happen. There is, in any case, no example so far of women replacing their husbands in the European Parliament, although national political connections in family backgrounds have already been referred to, and at least one woman, Elaine Kellett-Bowman, has sat in the Parliament alongside her husband.

As yet, there has hardly been time for the development of European political dynasties, but it will be interesting to see if, as the Parliament matures, they can be identified and if more women will be drawn into European politics by this route.

Socialisation

For others, it was their work which naturally led to political involvement. Christiane Scrivener was asked by Giscard d'Estaing as a result of her commercial success to become Secretary of State for Consumer Affairs, and Simone Veil to become Minister of Justice because of her status as a lawyer. Both finally became European parliamentarians. Some women became involved through a historical experience: in particular, for the French, the

Second World War and the Resistance. Marie-Jane Pruvot says 'It pushed me into an active part in the defence of my country', while Simone Veil's concentration camp number is still visible, tattooed on her arm.[5] Marie-Madeleine Dienesch, on the other hand, wanted to change what she saw as unjust legislation on families and the position of women. A few cannot attribute their interest to any specific event or cause: Shelagh Roberts, for example, can only say that even as a small girl 'I used to harangue audiences and meetings in my bedroom'! For the national as well as the European politicians, motives for political participation are similarly manifold, but professional experience is often given the greatest weight. Medical and psychiatric work kindled Berthe Fievet's interest in French national politics. Like her, many women became involved through a desire to change society, especially for women. Florence d'Harcourt, the French deputy, chose politics quite specifically because 'I wondered what I could do to attain equal rights and equal treatment. Politics was the answer because deputies legislate – it was the best way to improve the laws.' Nuala Fennell joined the Women's Movement 'knowing virtually nothing about politics', but 'having experienced all the stresses and frustrations of life as an Irish woman, I knew it from first-hand'; and she went into politics to change it. She is now Minister for Women in the Irish government.

Individual events occasionally politicised these women too: Bernadette McAliskey, the British ex-MP, says she was apolitical until 1968 and then 'all that I was and didn't know I was, found a voice in the civil rights movement'. Marie-France Lecuir says 'When I was fifteen or sixteen I discovered that my country [France] was in an unjust war' – the Algerian war – and this gave her a motive for political involvement.

Whatever their reasons, both the European and national politicians find politics absorbing: 'politics *is* everyday life', says Martine Frachon, French deputy, while Baroness Young, minister in the British Conservative administration, thinks 'Nobody who is in politics can understand why people outside are not interested in politics, just as those who are not involved cannot understand that interest.'

Political education

Once bitten by the political bug, the early careers of women are rather similar whether they end up in Europe or on the national scene. Nearly all have a history of some voluntary party work at constituency level which then led to national involvement. In many cases this local party work was started during a period when they were cut off from their professional life while their children were young. During this time they raised their families and laid the foundations of their political careers.

Rather more than a third (36%) of women MEPs concentrated at this stage on party work, either local or national, whether in the youth movement, like Heidemarie Wieczorek-Zeul who was chair of the Young Socialists of the German SPD, in voluntary work like Susanna Agnelli, or as a party office holder like Winifred Ewing, who was Vice-President of the Scottish National Party. Some were involved in women's organisations within their parties, like Johanna Maij-Weggen of the Dutch Christian Democrats. About another fifth (21%) were involved in inter-party, and sometimes international, women's movements – Marie-Madeleine Dienesch, Lady Elles and Paula Gaiotti de Biase were all, for example, connected with the European Union of Women. A few made their way through academic life or political journalism – Louise Weiss, for example, edited *New Europe* for twenty years and Elsa Hammerich was a professor of sociology.

Many women (20%) found party work led into local government, which has always traditionally been a route into wider political arenas. Examples include Susanna Agnelli, Bodil Boserup, and Colette Flesch. A few (under 5%) came up from the inside, as it were, having been employed by the EEC; Carla Barbarella, for example, worked for the Council of Ministers for seven years and so was fairly knowledgeable about the legislative process when she entered the European Parliament. Some others, around 4%, rose like Eileen Desmond and Danielle de March through the civil service, and 3% came up through trade unions (Maria Baduel Glorioso), business associations (Christiane Scrivener), farming associations (Simone Martin), or consumers' organisations (Janey Buchan chaired the Scottish Gas Consumers' Council).

Many then used these routes to become involved in national politics. The women MEPs have included ex-ministers like Barbara Castle, Katherina Focke and the French women Simone Veil and Christiane Scrivener, as well as MPs like Eileen Desmond, Elaine Kellett-Bowman and Hanna Walz.

The preponderance of national politicians is probably, of course, largely the result of having had the first direct elections as recently as 1979. Since the European Parliament had previously consisted of national politicians delegated on a 'dual mandate', rather than independently selected, some selectors may still be inclined to continue that tradition and choose national politicians, past or present, where these present themselves, on the basis that they have the political experience to be effective. This legacy from the former European Parliament may well diminish in future elections and the Parliament come to be seen more as an independent political goal.

The women MEPs have, in most cases, travelled along broadly similar routes to those of women in the national assemblies in the member states of the EEC. A great many national politicians come in through local government work, as did, for example, Peggy Fenner, Madeleine Taylor and

Martine Frachon. Others rose through unions (Joan Maynard) and similar associations. Party work was important to them (Betty Boothroyd) as is work with women's organisations inside or outside their party. Many, like Florence d'Harcourt, were active in groups like the European Union of Women. Lynda Chalker began in the youth section of her party, while Bernadette McAliskey attributed her spectacular rise simply to 'coincidence and accident'. The routes vary, then, but they are limited and virtually all the women, national or European, have travelled some of them.

Domestic backgrounds

Most women MEPs are married (over 71%) and have children (53%). The average age of the women MEPs is about forty-nine; in 1983 two were over seventy and one was under thirty. Given that most MEPs (women as well as men) are over forty-five, their children tend to be grown up, or at least independent, so that the difficulties of combining rearing children with political life do not occur to any great extent. For some, however, this remains a problem, and Mrs Maij-Weggan spoke of the difficulty of leaving even young teenage children for long periods of time, while Mrs Pantazi was clearly torn between her own political commitments and the demands of a three-year-old daughter. Some women had postponed political involvement until their children grew up.

Lady Elles, for example, thought that 'It was very important for my small children to be at home myself to enjoy them. I can sit on committees till I'm eighty, but I can't enjoy my children at that age.' Others combined family and job by relying upon the support of their husbands. Marie-France Lecuir said, 'It would have been absolutely impossible and I would have renounced politics if my husband had not taken part.' Most, by the time they reached Strasbourg or national assemblies, had children who were old enough to be left. Even then, however, the husband 'must not be averse to women working', thought Louise Weiss. The single women thought their independent state a great help when campaigning or indeed just in organising life, and this view was particularly echoed by some of those who had continued to be involved with their career once elected. Norvela Forster, for example, was sure that, 'If I'd had family as well, I don't suppose I would have taken this on. As it was, I had my Company to consider.'

Comparing the European figures with those for the British House of Commons at roughly the same time (1983), a rather smaller percentage of women MPs were married (59%, including one who was divorced and subsequently re-married).[6] On the other hand, a higher percentage than in Europe had children (63%), although only two women had children under ten. The average age of the Westminster women was much the same as the

European equivalent (forty-eight years) and only two of the MPs were under forty and one over sixty.

Clearly, the differences between national and European women members is not great on the domestic front. They have often chosen to wait until their children are raised before getting into politics in a serious way. Otherwise, they are, fortuitously or by design, childless. The advantages of being single are perhaps obvious: there is no divided loyalty between one's own aspirations and one's husband's job or the continuity of one's children's education. And single women, even if they may lack the solid support of another individual – 'someone', as one said, 'to pour you a gin after a bad day' – have fewer domestic duties to deal with. Consequently, they find organising a political life less complicated and can often progress further. Even so, they are still handicapped compared to married men. Eileen Lemass, a widow, complains 'I'd be coming home to the house with not even a meal prepared, where a man would come home and his wife would be there to greet him and his washing would be done and the house would be clean.' On the whole, women, whether married or single, still have to provide most of the domestic support systems for themselves; and it remains true that what most women, in European or domestic politics, could do with, is a wife.

Educational and professional backgrounds

Most women MEPs are graduates (62%) and within that category most qualified in law (nearly 24%) or economics (10%). Arts and political science are next (around 7% each), followed by languages and the sciences. Academic qualifications to degree level are common for political men or women, both nationally and in European politics. In the UK, for example, in 1983, 63% of women in the House of Commons were university graduates. What stands out, not surprisingly, is the higher percentages of linguists amongst MEPs, more than half of whom speak at least two European languages fluently. Lady Elles, for example, was educated in Paris and Florence; Christiane Scrivener learnt her fluent English at the Harvard Business School. Obviously, a high proportion of both male and female MEPs are competent linguists and some speak three or four of the official seven Community languages well.

So far as their professional backgrounds are concerned, the largest proportion of women are teachers or academics (23%). Examples are Joyce Quin (who taught international relations), Sile de Valera, and Henriette Poirier. Many specialised in EEC affairs, teaching politics, economics or languages, and most gave up their jobs when elected. Many of the women had journalistic backgrounds (15%), again often with special interests in the Community. Examples include Ann Clywd, Yvette Roudy and Luciana

Castellina. 10% of the women are lawyers, some with an international specialism, but others are national practitioners, for example Gloria Hooper, who is a solicitor. A further 4% are businesswomen, usually with EEC economic interests. (Most of Norvella Forster's company's business came from the EEC.) Both law and business interests may be continued whilst an MEP, although the law may be more difficult. Norvela Forster stressed that she gave 25% of her time to her company, but it may be easier for a businesswoman to delegate decisions and maintain continuity at work than it is for a lawyer. Business and the law are both acknowledged as careers which are good backgrounds for political involvement and ambitions. Such overlaps between one profession and another have been referred to as 'professional convergence' and the argument is sometimes made that the most obvious example of the training gained in one context being useful in another is that of law and politics.[7] Not only is the legislative experience common to both, but the lawyer is used to representing people, to putting a case and to arguing forcibly in public – all of which are useful political abilities. Nearly 16% of all MEPs were legally trained, which compares fairly directly with the 17% in the British House of Commons. Of the women in the House in 1983 13% (i.e. three) were legally trained, although one of them had never practised. Women are not as well represented as men in the law: in Britain, for example, only about 8% of practising barristers are women, and 5% of solicitors.[8] This means that far fewer women than men get this particularly relevant professional experience.

In business too, women are rather scantily represented. In Britain only around 1% of the membership of the Institute of Directors is female and in the 1983 House of Commons only one woman (4%, exactly the same percentage as in Europe) could have been said to come from a business background. Only two women held directorships while in the House (9%) compared with well over a quarter of the men, and whereas over 17% of the men were consultants to business, no women at all were employed in such a capacity. This lack of initial connection and on-going relationships with business clearly limits not only the experience which women have, but the support which they can expect from powerful industrial and commercial lobbies.

If relatively fewer women than men came in with legal or business backgrounds, this seems to be compensated for by the high proportion who are teachers (taking in all levels). In the House of Commons in 1982, the proportion of women teachers was even higher (at 32%) than in the European Parliament. Teaching is one of the so-called 'articulate professions', where individuals are experienced in talking to and instructing others, and to this extent it exhibits a certain professional convergence with politics. A fairly large proportion of men (i.e. 13%) in the European Parliament have a teaching background too, but the great majority of them (thirty-two out of the forty-five) came from the university or college lecturing end of the profession, where the experience acquired probably has the greatest overlap with political life. But again, this is an area in which women are rather poorly represented. (In Britain, for example, in 1983, women made up only about 11% of university teachers.)

In Europe, in addition to the usual professional backgrounds, in 1982, there were also two women each, from the secretarial, social service, interpreting and farming spheres. One woman (Mechtild von Alemann) had been a librarian, another an ambassador (with EEC experience again – Marie-Madeleine Dienesch was the French Ambassador to Luxembourg). Only one woman (Louise Herklotz) describes herself as a housewife, and one, Jacqueline Hoffmann, as a welder. She is especially unusual. Working class women are usually disadvantaged, even more than working class men, by less education, little experience of public speaking, fewer political connections, etc. There are no women who could be described as working class in this way in the House of Commons, for example, although there have in the past been a few who have worked up through the union movement. Such women suffer the problems of being women as well as those of being working class. They are often less self-assured and clearly less at home with the middle and upper class lifestyle and ethos of Parliament. They also come from backgrounds where promoting women tends to be disparaged or looked on with suspicion and where women themselves rarely have any money of their own. For such women, too, childcare is a greater problem than it is for the more affluent middle classes who can afford help, and housework is more often exclusively a woman's job in working class than in middle class households. This domestic burden may well be more important in limiting the early political involvement of working class women than even their educational chances or personal self-confidence. Men from similar backgrounds, after all, are significantly better represented in the European Parliament, where over 7% of them have been manual workers or trade union officials.

Case studies

In order to illustrate some of the points raised by these statistics, we made case studies of three British women MEPs, with different political opinions and of different ages and backgrounds. Joyce Quin is a Labour member, aged forty, unmarried, and came into the European Parliament having been an international researcher for the Labour Party, interested in the EEC. Barbara Castle, now in her seventies, was until June 1985 leader of the Labour Group in the Parliament, and the best-known British MEP. She has had a long and distinguished career as a parliamentarian and a Cabinet Minister in Labour governments. Elaine Kellett-Bowman is sixty. A Conservative, until 1984 she held the dual mandate – that is, she was elected to both Westminster and Strasbourg. She was in the European Parliament as a delegate before direct elections, but did not stand again for Europe in 1984 and now concentrates on Westminster.

All three women came from families who were actively involved or unusually interested in politics. Joyce Quin's mother was active in the Labour Party and her great-uncle was an MP. The family has always been closely involved with the Fabian Society and she was eventually nominated for candidacy by the Fabians. Elaine Kellett-Bowman's father was always interested in politics and encouraged her involvement. She herself became passionately committed to the Conservative Party under Anthony Eden, and her education merely fuelled her political ambition: 'I always wanted to get into Parliament and I knew that sooner or later I would.'[9] Barbara Castle's father was a devoted socialist who had an enormous influence not only on his daughter, but on many young people in Bradford at the time. The family lived politics, and Mrs Castle recalls: 'One of my earliest memories, in fact, is of other people's children eating and sleeping in the house; in the 1920s the children of miners on strike; in the 1930s Spanish refugees. There always seemed to be someone sleeping on the sofa.'[10]

Barbara Castle's commitment to Labour Party politics distinguished her at her middle class girls' school: 'Those who were Labour were just a handful at school so we had to stand out against the crowd and be jeered at because we were interested in politics, which wasn't considered quite ladylike by some of my friends.'[11] This only increased her commitment. After school, Barbara Castle and Elaine Kellett-Bowman went up to Oxford, where both read PPE. Barbara Castle went on to become a journalist and civil servant, all the time working actively within the party. When she got married, it was to another Labour Party activist, Ted Castle. She was gaining experience and serving her apprenticeship before becoming an MP. Elaine Kellett-Bowman on the other hand, although determined at some stage to be a politician, took no formal steps in that direction. She trained as a social worker and then with her husband, Charles Kellett, became a farmer. Joyce Quin read international relations and French at university, then went on to become a university lecturer and a researcher for the Labour Party's international department. She thus had a background in both European languages and politics and was always particularly interested in the EEC, unlike the other two when they were setting out.

In 1978, Joyce Quin was speaking to the Fabians about the common market, when she was suddenly asked whether she would consider standing for the European Parliament. She was, she says, taken by surprise, but agreed. Barbara Castle's break into politics had come thirty-five years before at the Labour Party Conference in 1943. As a young delegate from St Pancras she hit the headlines with a speech proclaiming 'Young people are tired of being told about jam tomorrow. They want jam today.' Soon after that, Bradford, her home town, asked her to stand for selection. Elaine Kellett-Bowman became involved in helping in the 1950 and 1951 election campaigns, without really thinking where it would lead. When her husband suggested she should try to become a parliamentary candidate she thought that, with three small children, this might be impossible. But she persisted and went on to become Chairman of North Wales Young Conservatives, a borough councillor and a parliamentary candidate, all within a month of each other.

None of the three thought they had encountered any real difficulty in being selected, and certainly all denied any discrimination against them on account of their sex. Barbara Castle who had in fact been nominated by the women's section of the party began her speech by telling the selection conference that they should forget the fact that she was a woman. 'I told them', she says, 'that they should judge me as a socialist. The thing to do with patronising attitudes is to forestall them.' Bradford at the time had two constituencies, which, she feels, may have affected their willingness to select a woman for one of them. 'They had their man in one; they could afford to take a risk with me', she says. Joyce Quin thought that she had very little difficulty at selection and that her sex was a positive advantage. The selection committee wanted a local candidate and she was from the area although she had worked away from it for some time. She had no factional support within the party, but there were no women Labour MPs in the north-east and the party wanted to change its cloth-cap image. The fact that she was the only woman who stood for selection meant that they 'certainly weren't unfavourably disposed towards me', and she felt she got support from women involved in the selection.

Barbara Castle entered Parliament in 1945, and almost immediately became Parliamentary Private Secretary (PPS) to Harold Wilson, and then to Stafford Cripps at the Board of Trade.

Elaine Kellett-Bowman's life took a tragic and dramatic turn in 1959 when she suffered a car crash in which she lost her husband, her face and her memory. Her face was painstakingly reconstructed by surgeons from a photograph but her memory was more difficult to regain. She found herself running a farm, and 'not remembering how many bags of fertiliser I had ordered'. Recuperating, she entered a competition to find Britain's Number One Country Housewife. She won, and went on a tour of the United States, still with little memory, but finally, she says, 'if you're used to public speaking, that sees you through'. She was advised that intense concentration might help and so she enrolled to study for the Bar. Bit by bit, her capacity to remember returned. Her children were, she says, a great help, rather than a hindrance to her: when Bar finals came up, the elder ones took care of the youngest child, so that she would not be disturbed, and they still try to be with her for elections. Joyce Quin is unmarried, and Barbara Castle, although married, had no children. Her husband, the late Ted Castle, was always extremely supportive: 'I always wanted to be an MP, or else a barrister or an actor. But I decided in 1945 that Barbara's properties were greater; her contribution would be bigger. Then I was defeated in the Abingdon by-election of 1953. Some of my friends think it is tragic and to me it's disappointing, but I can truthfully say that I've never been jealous of Barbara's parliamentary success. I live a vicarious parliamentary life, and move in the circles I like to move in.'[12] (Ted Castle finally got into Parliament by being given a life peerage for his own political work. His wife, however, never used the title and still remains 'Mrs Castle'.) Elaine Kellett-Bowman entered Parliament in 1970, when Barbara Castle had already been Minister of Transport, Minister of Overseas Development and Secretary of State for Employment. In 1975 she was one of the MPs selected to sit in the European Parliament. She enjoyed this and believes that much of her work there was relevant to her constituency. Thus when direct elections were held in 1979, she stood for Europe, as well as retaining her seat at Westminster. The schedule was punishing, but she thinks Europe gave another dimension to her political involvements. When she first arrived in Strasbourg she was asked to sit on the Legal Affairs Committee, but refused because it was not relevant to her constituency. She sat on the Social Affairs and Regional Affairs Committees and found that it helped to be well acquainted already (what she describes as 'well run-in') with the European Parliament. She thinks the dual mandate works and is useful, especially in committee business. 'I could ask questions of Ministers in the House of Commons and then of Commissioners in Strasbourg – and relate them to each other.' The hours, too, are complementary since 'Strasbourg works mainly in the morning and early afternoon, and the House of Commons in the late afternoon and evening, so it is possible to combine both.' Sometimes she has 'a bit of a hectic week', as for example in May 1983 when there was a crucial vote in Strasbourg, so that she drove down from Lancaster (her constituency), flew over, voted and flew back to London that evening. 'It's hard work,' she says, perhaps somewhat under-stating the case, 'but what isn't hard work that's worth doing?'

Joyce Quin and Barbara Castle both stood for the European Parliament for the first time in 1979, Joyce Quin beginning her Parliamentary career and Barbara Castle changing focus in her late sixties. Joyce Quin describes the campaign as 'extremely hard work – like banging your head against a brick wall all day, every day for three weeks and at the end being absolutely exhausted'. With large constituencies of half a million voters each, and a general election just passed, interest in the European Parliament was minimal and candidates were appealing to an electorate who were, Joyce Quin points out, 'uninterested in the EEC and tired of voting'. The ambiguous Labour Party policy on Britain's EEC membership also created problems for Labour candidates.

Barbara Castle has always been a conviction politician, and in the European Parliament her main preoccupation has been to carry on her party's fight against the EEC. Of course, some people will argue that the European Parliament is simply a form of retirement for her, where she can still get the cut and thrust of politics, on which she thrives, without the sheer exhaustion of life in the Commons. Yet she has given much of her vast experience in this new capacity, and proved herself an extremely competent leader of the Labour Group in the Parliament, re-elected leader by acclaim in 1984 after she successfully led the Group to an increased share of British seats in the elections.

Elaine Kellett-Bowman did not stand again in 1984. She put up in 1979, she says, to create a bond between Westminster and Strasbourg which she hopes now exists and which she played some part in creating.

Joyce Quin does not think the European Parliament is of great importance, actually or potentially. Its main role, she believes, is publicising and investigating national and constituency problems. She is doubtful whether the Parliament will ever legislate, and sees it as more of a training-ground for national politics than an embryonic European legislature. Several French Socialists, for example, now in government, were originally MEPs, and the training they gained and the awareness they developed in Strasbourg of the political situation in other European countries were very valuable when they came onto the national political scene. In the British case too, numbers of Euro-MPs admit to a strong interest in becoming Westminster MPs. As for the Germans, the SPD MEPs in particular she regards as being much more interested in the decision-making process in Bonn and debates in the Bundestag than in the deliberations at Strasbourg. Each German MEP on a European committee, for example, must report to the relevant national counterpart. She herself claims to have 'no driving ambition' towards national politics, although she admits she envies 'the less nomadic existence and smaller constituencies of those at Westminster'.

Joyce Quin thinks there is a general problem for the Parliament in creating and maintaining public interest. MEPs are not as well known as Westminster MPs and the national and local media are less inclined to give automatic coverage to European politics than to the national variety. A lot depends, she believes, on the personality and hard work of the individual MEP. Joyce Quin certainly does not find that her constituency neglects her, probably because she so clearly does not neglect it.

None of the three has any pat answers as to why the European Parliament should have a higher proportion of women than national assemblies. Elaine Kellett-Bowman attributes the French numbers largely to their use of the list system in elections, but Joyce Quin does not think the list system is the answer: 'The electoral system itself doesn't determine the number of women elected . . . In all countries of western Europe there is a recognition that Parliaments should strive to have a much greater proportion of women than they have at the moment, and that was just reflected in the selection of candidates.' She also notes the success of the French Socialists in employing positive discrimination, which, she says, 'can work if you have enough able women'. But, she stresses, there are other factors affecting women's candidacy, such as national traditions, the process of emancipation in different countries and national attitudes to women. She thinks that among the women in the Parliament there is 'some esprit de corps; like any minority there is a certain feeling of kinship that you have something in common', although she would not over-stress its importance. There was, among the women, a fair amount of support for Simone Veil's Presidency for example. Joyce Quin thinks that women like Mrs Thatcher and Mme Veil can be an encouragement to women politically by showing that 'they can be received absolutely on equal terms and treated as fully fledged politicians'. She attributes the reasonably large proportions of women in the Parliament partly to the modernity of the place: 'the whole ethos is very modern and informal with equal access; there's no smoking-room or club atmosphere about it at all. National Parliaments are often handicapped by the sheer weight of tradition. The European Parliament seems much more a product of an equal society.'

Each of these women, although with rather different political experiences, shares a common core of intellectual and social background. They are all middle class; all come from politically interested families; all are highly formally educated in the 'articulate professions' which so typically spill into politics. All of them, too, put in a political apprenticeship in the service of their parties at either the local or national level. The two who are married stress the importance of a spouse's support; one who has children did her local, preparatory work when they were small. All of this very much confirms the picture which emerged from the figures in the earlier part of the chapter.

What, then, do these women think about the European Parliament, its significance, its powers and its future? Barbara Castle clearly hopes that, at one level at least, it has no future. She is leader of a group which is committed to taking Britain out of Europe and, as such, she would never agree to any extension of its existing powers. She is critical of its operations, of its spending programme and of its legislative pretensions. She sees it as necessary to be there simply to protect British interests in the period before formal withdrawal. She does not see her own brief as negative, however, for although she has no further political ambitions nationally (indeed, she must feel she has fulfilled them all), she takes a professional pride in leadership and, as one of her colleagues says, has 'contributed greatly to the coherence of the Labour Group's position on domestic and European matters'.

Elaine Kellett-Bowman thinks the European Parliament is developing in an interesting way: 'The French will vote the French ticket across the borders of all political parties. The British quite often band together, but not always. This is to be expected. We're not a Federation. You're expected to go for national interests.' But the Conservatives, who co-operate with Danes in the European Democratic Group, have managed to cross national boundaries: 'we see eye to eye on everything except fishing', she says, and she thinks the Parliament is 'all the time becoming more influential, mainly through control of the budget'.

This is perhaps the inevitable view of a conservative European. She has, however, made her choice between Strasbourg and Westminster and the latter has won. That is where the influence is and there legislative power is a reality rather than an inspiration. She believed that, at a certain stage, the connection between the national and European levels had to be made. She was part of the forging of that connection; it is now up to others to build on it.

All three women are involved full-time in politics and have few domestic responsibilities. Barbara Castle and Joyce Quin have no children; Elaine Kellett-Bowman's are all grown up. None of them feels they had any major difficulty in being selected, or in fighting the campaign, because they were women. They are all deeply committed to their jobs – whether they see this as primarily about constituency work, forging links between Westminster and Strasbourg or attacking the EEC. Yet their analyses of the European Parliament and of women politicians' role, as we shall see in the next chapter, are rather different. Elaine Kellett-Bowman believes that any woman can succeed if she works hard enough, and cites her own efforts and success as proof. Barbara Castle used to take a similar line, but has come to believe that things are more difficult than that for most women. Joyce Quin is well aware of the problems women face, but sees too that there are no easy solutions.

4 Women in Parliament

> There are misogynists in all countries — Marie-Jane Pruvot, MEP

> Women . . . do better at social welfare. Men go to war and kill each other; women want to preserve life. — Eileen Lemass, MEP

The last chapter gave a profile of the women who become MEPs, their social, educational and political backgrounds. This one will look at what they do when they get to Strasbourg. First, however, it is necessary to have some idea of the Parliamentary round into which all MEPs have to fit. What is the life of a MEP really like? Is it, as its critics like to suppose, just an unending series of discussions in French restaurants – on the gravy train? Or does it merely consist of travelling long distances at all hours, in all weathers, to Brussels and beyond?

The first thing to note is the physical strain from the number and length of meetings and the necessary travel. Parliament sits in full plenary session once a month for a week (or twice a month for two half-weeks of half-sessions). So an MEP is called upon to be in Strasbourg twelve or fourteen times a year, generally for a full working week (from Monday afternoon to Friday afternoon). Since 1979, the Parliament only holds plenaries in Strasbourg; before that time, plenaries used to alternate between Strasbourg and Luxembourg, which made the sense of discontinuity even more acute.

MEPs are also normally called upon to sit on one or two Parliamentary committees. Each committee meets at least once a month, sometimes twice, in Brussels, for two or three days, and members are expected faithfully to attend these meetings. Parliamentary political groups also meet for two or three days, in the week immediately preceding each session. The Conservatives in the European Parliament are lucky here; their Group, being overwhelmingly dominated by the British Tories, meets in London. But Labour members of the Socialist Group usually have to fly to Brussels again.

On top of this, most MEPs who do not hold other offices within the Parliament will be appointed to one of the many delegations of the Parliament which maintain contacts with countries who trade significantly with the EEC.

Michael Palmer is so aware of the physical strain involved that he says, 'It is really a job for a young, robust person.'[1] For British MEPs, continually travelling between Brussels, London, the constituency and Strasbourg, this often means catching planes at disagreeable hours, early in the morning or late at night, perhaps in difficult weather conditions, with many hours liable to be wasted hanging around when there is fog or snow. But neither Brussels nor Strasbourg are more than an hour's journey by plane from London, and for MEPs with constituencies in the north of Britain, catching a plane for Brussels from their nearest airport can be quicker than a train to London and Westminster. Peggy Fenner, whose Westminster constituency is near London in Rochester, Kent, thought that, when she was in Europe, by comparison the travelling was bearable: 'The planes to Brussels', she says, 'were about as quick as trains to London, and, unlike Westminster, MEPs are not required to be there every day.' The problems of meeting in both Strasbourg and Brussels lie less in the amount of travelling involved than in the difficulties of being so far from home, and not in any fixed place. This means that MEPs have to stay in hotels, rather than buying or renting their own apartments as many Westminster MPs do. Michael Palmer says 'it is tiring not to be able to go home at night after a long day of travel and work, but to have to put up with hotel life during sessions for several days at a time. And although the restaurant food is excellent in the working centres of the Parliament, a diet of cream sauce and fried potatoes is not good for your figure or your health.'[2] The dual site of the Parliament perpetuates such problems, whereas if Parliamentary meetings were all in one city, MEPs could establish themselves more easily. As it is, travelling between Brussels, Strasbourg and the constituency means the constant transporting of paper and people with the consequent personal and professional disruption.

Several MEPs still exercise the dual mandate – 125 in the 1979–84 Parliament. 'That', admits Peggy Fenner, who was appointed to the Parliament from Westminster, 'is tiring'; and Elaine Kellett-Bowman, who held a dual mandate in the directly elected Parliament, agrees. Many MEPs, of course, do have other careers and involvements outside the European Parliament. Several Conservative MEPs are also members of the House of Lords, which may be less demanding than the House of Commons, but still imposes the strain of having three cities in which to operate, besides the constituency. Other members continue to pursue their careers as lawyers, journalists, etc., and all do a fair amount of work outside their formal commitments as Parliamentarians. All MEPs, for example, are called upon to do some party work – speaking about the EEC to conferences and seminars of their party, campaigning for the party at election times and so on. In the background, and never letting you forget it, is the constituency. MEPs usually have to spend any time when they are not in Brussels or Strasbourg, or on other Parliamentary business, on constituency work, which requires being readily available to perform official engagements and hold surgeries. Although it might be thought that MEPs find this part of the job less demanding than their Westminster equivalents, as they are in general less well known, they do represent around half a million electors each. Constituents' demands on their time, therefore, are liable to be high, especially in areas where local interests are involved.

Finally, of course, MEPs need some kind of personal and family life, and this has to be planned for. To live this constant round of engagements and travelling, and still find time to see one's family often, means allotting diary space to them. They must, said several MEPs, be 'booked in', just like any other engagement. This may sound sadly lacking in spontaneity, but it is the reality for many busy people, and without such planning MEPs could become completely taken over by official engagements. For some, family life can be combined with constituency work, at the weekends. However, Lady Elles thinks that one of the great advantages to women in the 1979 selection and election of candidates was that MEPs were not required to live in the constituency, so that women did not have to persuade their husbands to move, and possibly even to leave their jobs. She herself lives in London and represents Berkshire. Similarly Barbara Castle's constituency is Manchester, but she spends most weekends on her farm at High Wycombe. However, MEPs who do not live in their constituencies are faced with travelling not just between Brussels, Strasbourg and London, but their constituency and their home. It hardly makes for a stable life, and they have to be very well organised to ensure that their time is efficiently used and strain minimised.

Parliament's business is organised on a four-week rota. The first week of the month will be devoted to a plenary session of Parliament held in Strasbourg. The MEPs usually arrive at around midday on Monday, and sit from 5 p.m. to late in the evening. On Tuesday and Wednesday, Parliament will sit from 9 a.m. till 1 p.m., and then again from 3 p.m. to 7 p.m. Those hours do not sound unreasonable when compared, for example, with Westminster, but meetings take place continuously throughout the day, lunch-breaks are not sacrosanct and there are often political groups meeting between 7 p.m. and 8 or 9 p.m. MEPs do not stay in their seats in the chamber during the whole of the session. They mill around the concourse to lobby or be lobbied, attend interest group meetings, or sit in their offices listening to the debates on headphones while answering their mail. On Tuesday and Wednesday in a typical week, for example, Gloria Hooper attended an Ecumenical Discussion Group working lunch on Tuesday, and then at 4 p.m. went to a meeting of the All-Party Parliamentary Disablement Group.[3] On Wednesday morning at 11 a.m. she attended a meeting of the intergroup (the informal meetings of MEPs interested in a particular area or issue) on small businesses, and at 11.30 a meeting of the intergroup of the liberal professions. She had a working lunch with representatives of a chemical firm to discuss the issue of lead in petrol and finally had an evening meeting with the Mail Order Trades Association. All these meetings took place while the plenary session was continuing, and an MEP not only has to spend some time in attendance in the chamber, but has to prepare the speeches he or she may give there. British MEPs in particular, too, have always made much use of Parliamentary question time, which requires preparation if it is to be effectively used. On Thursday, political groups meet at 9 a.m., and the session does not start until 10 a.m., but with a break for lunch, it usually sits until midnight. On Thursday, Gloria Hooper chaired a meeting of the intergroup on retailing, and on the same day Joyce Quin attended an animal welfare intergroup in the morning and a debate on shipbuilding (a constituency interest) in the afternoon. On Fridays, the MEPs vote on the motions they have spent the last three days discussing. Attendance at the voting is usually fairly low and no meetings are organised for Fridays, MEPs preferring to return to their constituencies. During all these meetings, debates and political group discussions, MEPs must also meet constituents and pressure groups who come out to Strasbourg to lobby, while keeping up their contacts with the press and other media in attendance. Joyce Quin, for example, reckons she meets and talks to around 200 people a week specifically in the course of the job.

The weekend, most MEPs said, is usually spent in the constituency or with the family and friends. Few weekends are completely free however. Joyce Quin caught the 6.45 a.m. plane from Strasbourg, one typical Friday morning, to return to Newcastle in order to attend an 11 a.m. conference of Euro-MPs and candidates there. By 2.30 p.m. she was in Sunderland at a local Disablement Centre reporting on her progress in negotiating EEC grants for the disabled. At 4.15 she returned to Newcastle for a television discussion on the European election, and at 6.30 met party workers. On Saturday she was in Lowestoft as the Labour spokesperson on fisheries policy, and on Sunday, a 3 p.m. meeting in Jarrow was followed by a reception for a party of West German councillors whose town is twinned with North Tyneside. She also found the time to catch up on her mail, write a speech and prepare her reports for constituents on the results of her interventions with the EEC on their behalf. In addition, she must encourage visits from EEC officials and visitors from other member states to her constituency, in order to impress on them the need for funding in the area.[4] The demands are heavy and unending. Joyce Quin is unmarried and childless, and therefore perhaps freer than most, but all MEPs are under pressure to give more and more time to the job, thus missing out on personal relaxation, without which their efficiency will inevitably be impaired.

The second and third weeks of the month are taken up with committee meetings in Brussels. Committees usually last over two days, but whilst MEPs are there, they also conduct a great deal of informal business. The 'typical week' Shelagh Roberts let us see was a fortunate one for her since the three committees on which she sat were scheduled consecutively. Thus on Monday afternoon, Tuesday afternoon and Wednesday morning she attended a Transport Committee public hearing, with a reception on the Tuesday evening for the witnesses taking part. On Wednesday afternoon, she flew to London to attend a constituency meeting, caught up with her mail, and on Thursday afternoon returned to Brussels to sit on the Committee of Enquiry into the Situation of Women which finished on Friday afternoon. Lady Elles, on the other hand, having begun the week on Monday and Tuesday with House of Lords business in London, and EEC work including a meeting with a minister at the Foreign Office, flew to Brussels on the 8 a.m. plane on Wednesday. Later that morning, she attended various meetings and addressed a seminar on EEC competition law. She was at the Political Affairs Committee meeting in the afternoon and had dinner in the evening with the European Community Youth Orchestra. The Political Affairs Committee continued all day Thursday and into Friday morning, but she also found time on Thursday to meet members of the Youth Orchestra again and to interview an official from Luxembourg. On Friday morning, she flew back to London and drove to Southampton, where she addressed the Hampshire branch of the European Union of Women, after which she drove on to Windsor for a constituency meeting, finally returning to London in the evening.

The fourth week of the month is largely taken up by political group meetings in London or Brussels, for at least two or three days. Sometimes, however, these meetings take place further afield. For example, Barbara Castle's 'typical week' included a meeting of the Socialist group in Madrid on Monday and Tuesday, before she flew on to Strasbourg (via Frankfurt) for a part-session of the Parliament.

In addition to all this, MEPs who hold offices in Parliament will also be expected to attend meetings of, for example, the Bureau of the Parliament (in the case of the President, Vice-President and Quaestors). Perhaps the most difficult and time-consuming job, however, and one which nearly all MEPs take on at some time or another, is that of being a rapporteur for a committee. When a committee is investigating a particular subject, for example, the position of women in decision-making institutions (on which Mrs Macciocchi reported for the Committee of Enquiry into the Situation of Women), it will appoint a rapporteur, who is expected to take evidence from the hearings which the committees hold, and write reports based on a combination of that evidence, and her own personal knowledge, experience and research. Most rapporteurs have some knowledge of the subject they are asked to study, but the job still involves turning oneself into an expert in the appropriate area. The report will be drafted, and redrafted, criticised and discussed by the committee, before finally, one or two years after the process of investigation was begun, being discussed by the Parliament in a plenary session and voted upon. The job of a rapporteur is thus a long-term and demanding one.

Recognising the constant pressures and punishing travelling schedule, what makes anyone want to become an MEP? The salary is often mockingly cited as the reason, but it is no higher, before expenses, than national members' salaries, and many MEPs have given up highly paid professional jobs in order to serve in the Parliament. There is certainly some challenge to the job itself. MEPs provide a communication channel between the needs of their constituents and officials of the EEC; the most successful of them can bring funding to their areas and be a powerful lobby for regional and national interests. International politics are also discussed in the Parliament, and for anyone who wants to put their point of view forcefully, there is a chance to talk about such issues in a forum which may at the least exercise some kind of moral influence on world events. There are also chances of promotion within the Parliament. Simone Veil made the office of President an internationally-known and respected one, flying all over the world to meet national leaders and discuss international issues. The chairs of the various political groups exercise a good deal of political influence in controlling the debates and work of the Parliament. And in the committees, especially as an official of a committee, MEPs get the chance to become expert in important policy areas.

All of this means that the Parliament is an excellent training ground for national politics, and this is probably where many members' real interest lies. Several of the present French Socialist administration, for example, were originally members of the European Parliament, and have brought a valuable knowledge of Europe to their international work as government ministers. In the British case, Euro-MP Ann Clywd has gone on to become a Westminster MP, and Beata Brookes's struggle to be selected for Westminster is well known.

Looked at from the other direction, Strasbourg may seem like a stepdown in terms of the power, public attention and prestige received by politicians at national level, yet people who have been at Westminster, and become vitally involved with politics, can find it a consolation prize if they lose their Westminster seat. For example, Sheila Faith's constituency was lost in the redistribution of boundaries and she failed to get back to Westminster in 1983. She was then elected to the European Parliament in 1984. Europe may also be a winding-down process for those who, like Barbara Castle, are retiring from Westminster, but do not want to leave politics altogether. The life of an MEP, for all the travelling, is still less strenuous and less demanding than, if not that of a Westminster backbencher, then certainly that of a minister.

The salary, of course, is not inconsiderable. Members are paid at the same rate as members of their national assemblies, which meant that, in 1979 salaries ranged from under £10,000 a year (Irish members) to over £24,000 a year (French members).[5] However, all MEPs also receive an allowance for every day they attend Parliamentary meetings. This pays generously for an MEP's hotel and subsistence costs, which are high in both Brussels and Strasbourg. MEPs also receive travel and secretarial allowances, which, Michael Palmer says, help to relieve the disparities between the salaries received by MEPs of different nationalities.[6]

Since all allowances are tax-free, MEPs are fairly well-off, especially as many of them continue at one level or another with their professional life, although, of course, this is more difficult with some careers than others. On the other hand, many MEPs who have no prior journalistic experience suddenly discover a flair for writing and find a ready market for their offerings.

For all the travelling and unhealthy restaurant food, the working hours and conditions are still much more civilised than those of Westminster. The House of Commons sits from 2.30 p.m., all night if need be. MPs have to fight for desks, and, if they are lucky, a share of a room and a phone. In contrast, Strasbourg may continue on one day to midnight, but few MEPs will attend that debate and there are no three-line whips. In addition each MEP has his or her own office in the Parliament building, within easy reach of the chamber.

The most irritating part of most MEPs' lives seems to be the illogicality and inconvenience of having three seats for the Parliament: Strasbourg, Brussels and occasionally, Luxembourg. With one established seat, MEPs would still have a fair amount of travelling between Parliament and their constituencies. With three seats, the irksomeness of travelling is not the only cost. MEPs are mostly unable to have a permanent office in each place of work, and have to move papers and assistants around too. During plenary sessions in Strasbourg, half the Parliament's staff remain in Luxembourg, where the administration is situated. Thus either the Parliament is conducting its plenary sessions at half efficiency, or there are twice as many staff employed as need be. Besides, there are huge costs involved in moving staff, equipment and documents between Luxembourg, Strasbourg and Brussels. 15% of Parliament's budget is spent on maintaining this peripatetic existence (£12 million in 1979 terms). Parliament is often unable to supervise the Commission effectively, since Commissioners have to make special trips to Strasbourg rather than being readily accessible to MEPs on the spot.

Pressure groups find it difficult to know where any MEP is at any one time, which makes lobbying more difficult than it might be. Again, the large pressure groups which have established offices in Brussels have to join in the perpetual motion by sending delegations down to Strasbourg every month.

There would be no need to collect all the Community institutions in one city. The Court of Justice, the Auditors and the Investment Bank work very effectively in Luxembourg. But the main decision-making institutions – the Parliament, the Commission and the Council – should logically all have permanent offices in one place, and Brussels would seem to be the obvious seat of the Parliament. Around three-quarters of its four-week schedule already takes place there and the Commission and Council are located there. It has an international airport and international atmosphere, and good rail links with other member states. The main reason this does not happen is that vested national interests oppose it. The EEC is big business and Belgium, Luxembourg and France all want the revenue and prestige involved in housing it. Sites can be changed only with the consent of the entire Council of Ministers, made up, of course, of representatives of national governments. Now that large, modern premises have been built in both Strasbourg and Luxembourg to house the Parliament, it seems unlikely that either government will ever agree to making those buildings redundant.

Women's membership of political groups

Women's political affiliations have always been widely discussed. When the whole question of women's suffrage was being debated in Britain before 1918, some Labour Party men opposed votes for women, arguing that women were politically more conservative than men. This may be true to some extent in the case of the electorate, although commentators now tend to think that it is age rather than sex which is the crucial variable in voting patterns here. Women are on average more long-lived than men and it is this which puts them in what has been called a 'generational cohort' more likely to be conservative.[7] It seems hardly to be the case, however, that women representatives, national or European, are more frequently of the right than of the left: if anything, the opposite is true. Nearly 87% of the women deputies in the 1982 French National Assembly are Socialist or Communist, a far higher proportion than the PS's overall majority. In Britain, before the 1983 election, the Labour Party, although in a minority in Parliament, had more women MPs (thirteen) than the majority Conservatives (nine). Left-wing parties have always traditionally been seen as more welcoming to women candidates than right wing ones. In spite of fears about women's conservatism, left-wing parties were often associated with the early battles for women's suffrage: in Britain, Keir Hardie, George Lansbury and Fredrick Pethick-Lawrence, all radical politicians, were early protagonists of votes for women. The argument went that the left, supposedly dedicated to the principle of equality, must realise that this ought to apply between the sexes as much as between the classes. In Britain, Labour women MPs were the first women to be elected on their own name and merits, and not as substitutes for their husbands, and sixty-one women MPs were returned for the party between 1918 and 1981, whilst the Conservatives, over the same period, elected under forty.[8] Some commentators have also suggested that women have certain concerns which are more radical than conservative. Thus, they argue, women have a more moralistic attitude to politics, are more idealistic, more likely to be pacifist and more concerned to reform the world.[9] While there is some evidence that women tend to be concerned with such issues, the main reason for the preponderance of women elected on the left is probably that the left, being less traditionally minded, and more prepared to see women in other than their traditional roles, is more willing to accept them.

The numbers of women MEPs in the different political Groups in the European Parliament certainly seem to reflect this. (See Appendix 2 for the number of women in each political party and Group.) The Rainbow Group is possibly the least traditional and most innovative of all the Groups, consisting of members of the Ecology and Green Movements. These movements have, in recent years, challenged the role of political parties as being merely election machines. They have set themselves up to achieve certain goals outside the Parliamentary structure, both nationally and on a European level, whilst also trying to work within elected assemblies. They use the methods of political protest, and direct action, and their preoccupations are largely to the left of the political spectrum, with e.g. ecology, nuclear weapons, and the structure of society. It is perhaps not surprising, then, that the Group has the highest percentage of women MEPs – 25%, or five women out of twenty members.[10] The Group does not have a leader, but rather four Co-Chairs, including one woman.

The trend towards the left continues with the Communist Group which has 21%, or nine women, including Bodil Boserup as its Treasurer. To have one woman official is not a particularly impressive record, however, given the Communist Group's high proportion of women members, and such a situation reflects the criticisms generally raised about Communist Parties, that they are male-dominated, old-fashioned and predominantly concerned with the industrial working class in highly unionised heavy industries, a section of the population who tend almost exclusively to be male. The Communist Party is perhaps more concerned with economic analyses than personal politics, and has never consistently raised in the Parliament the question of women's equality. That said, the first woman Vice-President of the Parliament, Danielle de March, was a Communist, and among the party's women members is Vera Squarcialupi, one of the most vociferous advocates of women's rights in the Parliament.

Next in order among the Groups is the European Democratic Alliance which has 20% (i.e. six) members. These include Winnie Ewing and Nicole Chouraqui, who are Vice-Chairs of the Group. The Group has also included the only two women since 1979 who have presided over Parliament while it elects its President. The oldest Member of Parliament traditionally takes this role, and in 1979 and 1982, Louise Weiss had this honour. Again, in 1984, Jacqueline Thome-Patenôtre, although newly elected, was the oldest member and took on the job.

Back on the left again, women constitute 20% (27 members) of the Socialist Group. This high percentage is partly explained by the position in the French Socialist Party, which insisted, both in 1979 and 1984, on employing positive discrimination for women when drawing up its list. Women had to constitute at least 25% of the list, and to be in acceptably high positions on it. This policy was successful, and in 1984, 5 out of the PS's twenty MEPs were women. The Group also promotes women most assiduously. Barbara Castle and Eva Grendal are both Vice-Chairs along with six men. Barbara Castle was until recently leader of the British Labour Group in the Parliament; Yvette Fuillet, who is Treasurer, is another enthusiastic campaigner for women's issues; Gisele Charzat sits on the Bureau of the Group, and Nicole Pèry is a Vice-President of the Parliament.

In the Liberal and Democratic Group over 19% (i.e. six) of the membership is female. They have promoted a high proportion of women, and three of the six are office-holders of the Group. Simone Veil, who was first President of the directly elected Parliament, is Chair of the Group; Tove Nielsen is one of the three Vice-Chairs and Colette Flesch is the Treasurer. Colette Flesch was also a Quaestor of the Parliament between 1979 and 1981.

The centrist parties have rather poorer records as far as promoting women is concerned. The European Democratic Group has 16% (i.e. eight) women, six British Conservatives and two Danes. One woman, Diana Elles, is on the Bureau of the Group, and is also a Vice-President of the Parliament.

The European People's Party has 12%, or thirteen women MEPs. There are no women among the office-holders of this Group, although Maria Luisa Cassanmagnago-Cerretti is a Vice-President of the Parliament. Finally, the new Group of the European Right has only one woman among its seventeen members (5%).

Office holding in Parliament, on committees and on delegations

When the question of promoting women within Parliament arises, the success of Simone Veil immediately springs to mind. She was President from 1979 to 1981, earned the respect of MEPs from all parties and is frequently the one woman, and sometimes the one MEP, of whom people have heard. Yet Simone Veil, like Margaret Thatcher, is an exceptional individual. 'Women like them are merely leading the way for other, average women who may later on be able to follow that path which they have opened', says Marie-Jane Pruvot.

As has been said, one female Vice-President was elected with Simone Veil – Danielle de March. She has since been replaced by Lady Elles, Maria Luisa Cassanmagnago-Cerretti and Nicole Pèry, making three women Vice-Presidents out of twelve. In 1979, there was one female Quaestor – Collete Flesch – out of five. There are now none. All the Group leaders, except Simone Veil, are male. The numbers of women promoted are small in absolute terms, but there are still, of course, relatively few women members of the Parliament, however many more there may be in Strasbourg than in national assemblies. With the competition from men, and no reserved places for women, it is probably not surprising that women are not promoted in greater numbers. In fact, although the sample is too small for any proper statistical analysis, the proportion of women promoted overall is on a level with their proportion in the Parliament, at around 17%.

Most commentators are agreed that while political women seem to be promoted as frequently, or possibly even rather more than men, they are often promoted into the less prestigious jobs, or to those which are concerned with social or educational issues, supposedly requiring 'feminine' skills.[11] In Britain, for example, Margaret Thatcher is Prime Minister, but there are no women in her Cabinet and her only experience of high office before becoming leader of her party was as Minister for Education. The last Labour Government (1974–9) had two women in the Cabinet, Barbara Castle at Social Services and Shirley Williams, first at Prices and Consumer Protection and then at Education and Science. In France too, three out of the five women ministers in the 1981 Socialist administration are responsible for Women's Rights, Youth and Sport and Consumer Affairs, all 'women's interests'. It is sometimes assumed, therefore, that women have not taken up key offices, such as the Home and Foreign Offices, the Treasury or Defence, because their interests and talents lie in welfare and education, for example. There may be some historical justification for this in that women used to be prominent in matters concerning the family, children and social welfare. So the impression has been created that women are more tender-hearted, socially concerned and generally more interested in people than are men. Women have often seemed keen, too, to take up individual grievances and problems rather than concentrating on broader issues of policy; yet this is not to say that they are uninterested in the wider political questions. There is considerable evidence that all MPs and MEPs, both men and women, are primarily concerned with constituency issues, and with their own specialisms which may, or may not, be those traditionally connected with their gender.[12] Some women in the European Parliament think that women really are best suited to certain issues. Eileen Lemass says, 'Women are more sympathetic and do better at social welfare. Men go to war and kill each other: women want to preserve life.' Some women, on the other hand, shy away from protective areas, afraid of being thought unable to deal with what may be seen as 'real' or 'hard' issues. Norvella Forster, with her business background, has served on the Economic and Monetary Affairs Committee. Joyce Quin concentrates on constituency interests in Agriculture and Fisheries. Some, like Marie-Claude Vayssade, have done both. She was on the Women's Committee but was also Chair of that on Legal Affairs. On delegations to non-EEC countries, women are rather unevenly represented. Are they, as the figures suggest, particularly interested in ACP (African, Caribbean and Pacific) countries and not in China? There seems no obvious reason why women's participation should vary from seven in the Latin American delegation to none in the Swiss. Overall, on delegations, women receive rather less than their fair share of places (around 15%, when women represent 17% of the Parliament's membership). There have only ever been two women Chairs of delegations, Eva Gredal to the USA and Ann Clywd to Portugal, and four Vice-Chairs, Annia Krouwel-Vlam to Israel, Johanna Maij-Weggen to the Nordic countries, Ursula Schleicher to Malta, and Mechtild von Alemann to Spain. Women have been largely concentrated on the delegations to the ACP countries, Greece and Latin America, but, the MEPs believe, by chance rather than design.

The men's response

Although some of the women consider their male colleagues as allies, many of them claim to have noticed some hostility among the men to working with women politicians, particularly if they believe the women to be feminists. Marie-Jane Pruvot says 'Two and a half years ago [before she had entered the European Parliament] I would have disagreed with any suggestion of prejudice; now I must say yes. Certain men react in a hostile way, many are ironical and only a few react really positively. Of course, there are misogynists in all countries.' Shelagh Roberts thinks, 'A small minority have no patience with the concept [of women's rights] at all. They think everything is perfect as it is and it shouldn't be changed.' Norvella Forster thinks that 'men tend to gang up a little on women. Women do tend to be the white blackbird.' And Louise Weiss recalled how things had changed since she was fighting for the vote seventy years ago when 'men used to say that women's hands were not for gunpowder, but for men to kiss, and this was applauded. Today a man would be laughed at for saying that.' The men who react negatively to the idea of women politicians are often also the ones who oppose any extension of women's rights. But men who take that extreme position tend to be relatively few: it's not politic, and it is therefore rather difficult to find a man willing to make any such statements publicly. This leads many women to say, like Joyce Quin, that they have never noticed 'any male vs. female hostility'. Yet the real problem for women probably lies not so much in the small number of men who are overtly hostile but in the great majority who are apathetic. They may not make sexist remarks, it is no longer socially or politically acceptable to do so, but they will not put themselves out to support women's rights, or to help their female colleagues to do so.

The story is the same in national parliaments, where the men's support tends to be, at the most, luke-warm. In France, for example, the commitment of the Mitterrand Socialist government to far-reaching legislation on women's rights was eroded bit by bit and only achieved to a limited extent by the efforts of Yvette Roudy and her female colleagues. In Britain too, when the liberal abortion law of 1966 has been challenged from time to time in the House of Commons, it has been the women there who have had to organise the opposition. The men were mainly passively supportive of them, but unwilling to give the issue their time.[13] In the European Parliament, many parties are proud of the high proportion of women MEPs in their ranks. But most men pay little or no attention to women's issues, and Joyce Quin complains that 'in the day's debate we had on women's rights [in 1981], it tended to be women speaking all the time to a largely female audience'.

There are no attendance figures kept of debates, but every one on women's rights had seen a woman speaker comment, at some point, upon the low level of attendance among the men. Men reckon they can leave the women to get on with sorting out their own affairs, and most do not even bother to come and listen, far less contribute. Martine Frachon, French Deputée in the Assemblée Nationale, describes many men's reactions to women politicians there, not as hostility, but 'a lot more pernicious than that, it's a tendency, a tendency perhaps to patronage'. Women complain of a tolerance, a friendly but irritating condescension towards them, which although it may occasionally be useful if played up to, is certainly not an indication of equality. Sheila Faith pointed out the familiar problem that men (and constituencies) 'expect a little more of a woman than they would of a man'. A woman always has to prove herself in their eyes, to play herself in, where a man may be given more automatic acceptance. Among the men, Derek Enright did not notice any hostility towards women: 'the men's attitude is pretty reasonable; we all just work together as people'. Richard Balfe agreed, and pointed to the great respect for Barbara Castle, in particular, among the men in the Socialist Group. Alf Lomas took much the same line, but acknowledged that the men might find it difficult to make time fully to support the women. Although there is no reason to doubt these men's good faith, it is difficult to see how any politician, in the present climate of opinion, could say anything very different. It is undoubtedly the case, however, that although most men are probably fairly indifferent to women's rights and interests, some feel challenged and insecure by what they see as the female invasion of politics and policy. 'It's not the most successful, secure men who are afraid of the influx of women, but the less successful, who see their own position under threat', says a British male MP. And, in politics of all areas, where the insecure can quickly become paranoid, the feeling of being under threat may turn indifference into positive opposition.

Perceptions and self-perceptions of women MEPs

It is sometimes suggested that political women are their own worst enemies, that they are unsupportive of each other and unable to work together. This, however, did not emerge from our interviews with the women MEPs. About half of them thought there was some kind of fellow feeling, an esprit de corps, between them. Most did not rate it highly, but were aware of mutual support; as Joyce Quin put it: 'Like any minority there is a certain feeling of kinship and you have something in common.' Some of this fellow feeling among the women in the European Parliament may have been generated by Simone Veil's Presidency. Christiane Scrivener says she feels 'there was a good atmosphere around Mme Veil'. Lady Elles says, 'an esprit de corps can, although doesn't always, develop. Anybody in politics becomes ambitious, even unconsciously, and another woman is always a rival, not as a woman but as another politician. There can be a certain solidarity among women at some levels; at the highest levels however, there's just as much rivalry as there is among the men.' Be this as it may, many women seem to have a sense of solidarity with others of their sex, and co-operation in the Parliament on women's issues, often across political groups, has at some points been impressive.

Another persistent ideal about women in politics is that they are more diligent than men. Both women and men tend to regard them as such. Lady Elles, for example, believes women politicians are more conscientious 'because they have to be that much more assiduous in order to achieve success'. Or, as Beata Brookes puts it, 'like a woman driver, a woman politician will try that bit harder to show that she's at least as good as a man'. From the beginning, the odds are against her; and given an equivalent woman and man, a selection committee will tend to choose the man. To overcome this, a woman has to present them with no choice, by being clearly the best candidate. The argument goes that women, brought up in this hard school, will continue to make more effort than their male equivalents and that this will be reflected in their performance in Parliament. One way in which this theory might be tested is to look at the committee record of MEPs in the Official Journal of the European Parliament and see if women are indeed, in this area at least, more assiduous than men. In 1979, over a quarter of the women sat on more than one committee, as opposed to just under a fifth of men. Of course, both male and female MEPs tended overwhelmingly to sit on just one (270 men and 45 women sat on only one committee), but no woman (except Simone Veil as President) was not a member of any committee, whereas ten men had no committee places at all. Two women sat on three committees – Vera Squarcialupi and Annie Krouwel-Vlam – whereas no man did.[14] And of course, once the ad hoc committee on women was formed in 1980, several women served on that as well, and this increased again their committee duties. So women do appear, in this way at least, to be rather more diligent than men, in line with the general belief and expectation.

Women and 'women's issues'

Women politicians have traditionally been caught with even greater demands on their time than men. Not only do they have their usual constituency, Parliamentary and party work to do, but they also find they are expected, by women themselves and by male MEPs, to represent women. Somehow an extra constituency, composing 52% of the population, is to be represented by the female 17% of the Parliament. Not surprisingly perhaps, some MEPs react against this. Elaine Kellett-Bowman, for example, says, 'I don't think of us as women MEPs, just MEPs', and refusing to define herself as a woman anything, denies her special responsibility to other women. Some MEPs are equally worried about being defined as 'women MEPs', which somehow implies that they are not 'real MEPs'. But many recognise a problem here and argue that if women MEPs do not take up women's issues and interests, these will simply be left aside. Men will not make the time for them, however much it may be argued that they should in an ideal world. Whether they like it or not, too, women are often left with the 'housekeeping' roles. It was Janey Buchan, rather than one of the male members, who provided homely advice for the new MEPs in 1984. 'Can I suggest you get a kettle?', she wrote, and also placed 'great stress on the benefits of having a pillow'.[15] It takes a very conscious rejection of this female caring role to react as Maureen Colquhoun, the British ex-MP, did when a male colleague greeted her with relief as a woman in the House who could now 'do something about the food in this place'. She promptly told him he would have to see to that himself, as she intended to be Chancellor of the Exchequer!

There are two main types of issues that can be defined as 'women's interests': firstly, those areas which directly affect women as women – for example, equal pay. Secondly, areas in which women have involved themselves as an extension of their traditional roles as homemakers and carers for children and men – issues such as education, consumer protection and health and welfare. These subjects are sometimes seen as 'soft', although they require no less skill and ability to manage than foreign policy, the economy or defence. Both nationally and in the European context, women politicians have often been unwilling to take on these issues, not wanting to be seen in women's traditional role and thus be professionally undervalued. But party leaders have tended to appoint women to those ministries rather than others and there is no point in refusing Education and insisting on Defence if you want promotion. Similarly, although no doubt the issue is sometimes discussed within the Group more democratically, Group Chairs in the European Parliament appoint their Group's membership of committees, and women predominate in the 'soft' health and welfare type of committees.

Out of eight women who have held Cabinet rank in Britain, four of them at one time or another have been Secretary of State for Education (it is interesting that this was Mrs Thatcher's only Cabinet experience before becoming Prime Minister). Even Barbara Castle, probably the woman to have fared best in breaking out of this mould as Minister of Transport and Secretary of State for Employment, was back heading Social Services in 1974–6.[16] The same picture becomes clear in the European Parliament when committee membership is studied. In a Parliament where women made up 16% of the total membership, the committee on Social Affairs and Employment in 1979 had twenty-seven members, nine of whom were women (i.e. 33%). Environment, Public Health and Consumer Protection also had twenty-seven members, eleven of whom were women (41%). The committee on Youth, Culture, Education, Information and Sport had eight women among its twenty-five members (32%). On the other hand, at the same time, the committee on Transport had twenty-five members, all of whom were men, and the committee on Economic and Monetary Affairs had thirty-seven members with only one woman among them. By 1984, although the balance of women's representation was still predominantly social, they were now on all committees of the Parliament. Their proportion on the 'social' committees, too, has gone down, while on some of the 'harder' ones, it has gone up. For example, Social Affairs is now 23% female, Environment and Public Health 26% and Youth, Culture and Education 16%. Transport on the other hand, has gone up to 12% and Economic and Monetary Affairs is now 14% female. The position on committee chairs too, is perhaps becoming more encouraging for women. In 1984, six out of seventeen committees are chaired by women, one of those, of course, being the committee on Women's Rights which is now led by Marlene Lenz. Of the other five, two are in traditional 'female' areas – Environment, Public Health and Consumer Protection, is now chaired by Beate Weber, and Youth Culture, Education, Information and Sport by Winnie Ewing. But the remaining three are in more technical areas: Shelagh Roberts is Chair of the Committee on External Economic Relations (having previously been Chair of Transport), Marie-Claude Vayssade heads the Committee on Legal Affairs and Katharina Focke, that on Development and Co-operation. But these women are still the exceptions. In 1984, women continue to be best represented on the same committees, and there seems no reason, apart from tradition, why this should be so. Why should not men take an equal interest with women in education or the environment? The only committee where women actually outnumber men – and it is probably right that they should do so – is that on Women's Rights, where women continue to make up some 70% of the membership. It is arguable that they, rather than men, have a greater understanding of the nature of the discrimination against them and also the interest and commitment to try and change it. But there is no obvious reason why women should be thought, because of their sex, to have a better understanding of other areas.

Women's specialisms are not, however, indicated only by their membership of committees: it is also important to find out in which areas they intervene in Parliament itself. To do this, we took one year (1979–80) and analysed the interventions of each woman as recorded in the index of the Official Journal of the European Parliament. These interventions show that women tend to be preoccupied not so much by 'women's issues' or by a specifically 'feminist' approach, as by their own specialities, on which they may be spokesperson for their Group. Speaking time in the plenary is so scarce that it is unusual for anyone other than a Group leader to be called unless s/he is selected as spokesperson on a particular issue. An examination of the Official Journal shows that MEPs' specialities tend to relate to their committee membership, and a high proportion of women therefore specialise in consumer and welfare issues. Thus Maria Luisa Cassanmagnago-Cerretti, who in 1979 was a member of the Social Affairs and Employment committee, the Environment, Public Health and Consumer Protection committee, and the EEC–ACP Consultative Assembly intervened almost exclusively on questions relating to those three issues.[17] Similarly, Barbara Castle, with no consumer or welfare background, but on the Agriculture Committee, spoke most on agriculture, and Mrs Wieczorek-Zeul made 40% of her interventions on her committee specialism (External Economic Relations). Group discipline is such that when women speak in this context, they tend to put forward the political policy of their group rather than any more personal or specifically 'female' point of view. For example, even in the 1981 women's debate, in which Group discipline was noticeably lax because of the controversy over abortion, Shelagh Roberts, on behalf of the EDG, criticised the report on women for 'overstating the case' and suggested that 'we should limit our aspirations'. This was probably her own personal view, but more importantly it was the position of her Group and in accordance with Conservative philosophy. Similarly, in the 1979–80 session studied, Hanna Walz, for example, made 36% of all her interventions on Group policy issues.

Parliament does not, of course, only debate internal Community policy, but spends much of its time examining current international issues. The shooting down by Russia of the South Korea plane in 1983 was such an occasion. In spite of its formal powerlessness in the context, Parliament was burning to discuss this most controversial international incident of the season. On such issues, too, women make their contributions, whether speaking in a debate or merely signing a resolution, but again, their interventions are very predictable politically, putting the Group line rather than any specifically and identifiably feminist position. MEPs sometimes intervene too on constituency issues. The level of interventions here tends to depend on individual MEPs' interests and on specific circumstances. For example, in 1982, Italy suffered an earthquake and France heavy flooding, both of which were sufficiently serious to encourage a number of French and Italian MEPs, both male and female, to raise them in Parliament. Many constituency problems are too limited in scope, or too detailed, to bring up on the floor of the chamber and are most appropriately dealt with by lobbying for grants or putting questions to the Commission rather than by discussion in Parliament. Some MEPs, however, specialise in wider issues which yet specifically affect their constituency. For example, Joyce Quin's speciality is now shipbuilding, although she had no particular knowledge of this before 1979, simply because she represents Tyne and Wear which still depends heavily on that industry. Beata Brookes often brings the problems of Wales before the Chamber, and perhaps most outstanding among the British MEPs in this regard is Winnie Ewing, who intervenes more often on constituency matters than on anything else (30% of all her interventions in 1979–80) and who is continually raising the issue of Scottish independence. While it is clear, then, that women tend to intervene proportionately more than men in social welfare 'women's' areas, these tend to be just the ones in which women are given specialisms within their Groups, and in which, therefore, they might be expected to feel competent and be given the time to contribute. Overall, MEPs, both male and female, tend to put the Group line, intervening mostly in such terms, though also occasionally on constituency interests.

There is also the view of 'women's issues' not as social welfare but as those areas which exclusively or largely affect women and their treatment in society. As has been mentioned, many women MEPs worry that, if they are seen to be stressing the women's view much of the time, men will simply leave them to discuss discrimination among themselves. Christiane Scrivener says 'It's very important not to allow any segregation on this; it's dangerous because one day you may be out of politics and women's issues will be forgotten about.' Women's issues, in other words, are too important to allow men to avoid the burden of agitating about them, and indeed, if women let men give them that burden, then soon men themselves will forget all about women's interests. Yet, women are afraid that if they continually raise women's issues, they will be labelled as 'women politicians' who have no real expertise or technical competence. Whilst it is common for politicians to have special knowledge of and support for all sorts of social groups, somehow for a woman to specialise in the interests of women is seen as less important than, say, a knowledge of the interests of fishermen or miners. While this view prevails, it is perhaps surprising, not that so few, but that so many ambitious women are willing to put their own credibility at risk, particularly with their male colleagues, by pursuing the interests and rights of their sex. Not all the women, however, feel it is incumbent upon them to support women's rights. Elaine Kellett-Bowman, for example, doesn't believe women need special support for legislative programmes. She thinks that 'the only thing that beats women is a defeatist attitude, which was much more prevalent a few years ago than it is now'. She did not approve of the women's ad hoc Committee, or the Committee of Enquiry. Their members put in too many amendments to debates and went far beyond their briefs. In this context she particularly criticises the 1981 women's debate as 'too wide; abortion was not in the terms of reference and should never have been included'.

Barbara Castle's attitude towards women is rather ambivalent. She claims, 'I've always thought of myself as an MP, not as a *female* MP. Being a woman here is something I'm not even conscious of. I never had any conscious determination not to take up women's issues in the European Parliament – I have just not been particularly interested in them.' Yet in national politics, her position was rather different. She wanted to take on the men's specialisms and beat them at their own game. 'I refused the maternity benefits committee and stuck out for sewers and drains', she says. These citadels had to be taken and she knew she could take them. She was always vaguely contemptuous of 'women's concerns' or of any suggestion that she might not be a match for the men in their own terms. In 1966, she gave a press conference as Minister of Transport and presented herself as 'this woman who can't even drive'. When asked if she was now going to learn to drive, she replied, 'No, and no for the sake of matrimonial harmony. One family, one car, means one husband, one car.' Says a journalist who was there, 'One could sense the approval of every man in the room; the women there bristled slightly.'[18] She was prepared to use those kinds of tricks against her own sex to get the men of the press on her side. She always rather despised too the Labour Party Women's Conference, attending it only out of a sense of duty. However, during the 1970s, she says she was struck by the number of young women there who were making political speeches on important issues. She recalls how once, 'on the train back, one of the delegates said to me how much she had enjoyed it because she could never get to ordinary party conferences, since her GMC always sent a man. And I suddenly realised: I had always had a launching pad in a highly intellectualised and political background. You can't just say to any woman who hasn't been brought up in that kind of environment – go ahead and do it. That's a kind of elitism.'[19] In 1970, Barbara Castle was the driving force behind the Equal Pay Act, and during her introductory speech in the debate noted 'We women members (of parliament) would scoff at the idea that we were too frail to do all-night sittings. Indeed I have noticed that we usually look fresher than the men at the end of them.' She has never approved of women confining themselves to women's issues, fearing not only that the 'serious' areas then get left for the men; but that women, as she puts it, 'get enclosed in the antechambers of power [instead of] going for the centre, going for the top'. She admits that she is still not interested in the Women's Committee, because, as she believes, 'Power lies where the money is . . . so if you want to follow the money, you have to get on a technical committee like Agriculture.' (Mrs Castle is on the Agriculture Committee.)

Shelagh Roberts is realistic about the difficult conflicting pressures on women MEPs: 'Women want to be forced into women's issues – they have other interests and their electorate is larger than just the female. But if women don't press those issues they tend to get overshadowed. Men have other priorities.' The figures on intervention on women's issues confirm this. In the early 1970s, when there were only 5% or so women MPs, interventions on women's issues tended to be below 1% in the case of both questions and resolutions. In 1979, when sixty-six women were suddenly elected where there had been only eleven before, the proportion of questions on women rose from zero to over 2% of the whole, and of resolutions, from 0.6% to 6%.[20] This higher level of activity has continued since 1979, and since 1980 seems to have been co-ordinated firstly by the ad hoc Committee on women's rights and then by the Committee of Enquiry into the Situation of Women In Europe. Most prominent in continually raising women's issues in the Parliament have been some of the best-known members of these women's committees – among them Anne Marie Lizin, Maria Luisa Cassanmagnago-Cerretti, and Yvette Roudy. Question Time is probably most productive as far as the women are concerned, because it is easier to table questions than debates, resolutions, etc. In 1979, fifty-two questions were asked concerning women and this level of activity was maintained in 1980 and 1981. Since 1981, the reports of the Committee of Enquiry into the Situation of Women, which is discussed in the next chapter, have provided ready-made resolutions which have made up around 5% of the total resolutions before Parliament. It was probably as a result of this pressure (and Ivor Richard, the Commissioner on Social Affairs, has suggested as much), that the Commission introduced its Action Programme for Women in 1982.

But, as has already been shown, even these women who are prominent in this area in fact spend only a small proportion of their time on women's issues. When their total personal interventions are analysed, it emerges that Anne Marie Lizin, for example, made most of her contributions in Parliament on her speciality – energy. Similarly, Maria Luisa Cassanmagnago-Cerretti contributed most on Social Affairs and Employment, and Yvette Roudy on Group political issues. Even Johanna Maij-Weggen, who was seen as the champion of women's rights in the Parliament after her huge report in 1981, spent five times as much time on environment, public health and consumer protection than on women's affairs. Yet these women have the reputation of continually raising questions affecting women, to the exclusion of any other political interests they may have. This shows how women are 'labelled', in just the way so many of them fear, for showing even a modicum of sustained interest in the rights and concerns of their own sex. Although this analysis of interventions demonstrates that women are not in any sense exclusively concerned with the interests of women, and, as has been said, there is little evidence of a specifically 'feminist' view on political issues such as defence or economic policy, there is yet strong evidence of a much greater involvement of women than men in the whole area of sex equality. For example, only 15% of the women but 92% of the men (in the 1979–80 session) made no interventions at all here. Of the twenty-eight men who did intervene, nineteen did so only once (none more than twice) and of these, seventeen were merely signing a motion.[21] To this extent, women do make a difference in politics by keeping equality issues in particular before Parliament. This pressure, largely by the women, has meant the encouragement of a mass of secondary legislation on sex equality by the EEC, and it is the story of this legislation, the influence of women MEPs on it and its effect on women in the Community, which we will now take up.

5 Women for women: the historical context

> Men used to say that women's hands were not for gunpowder but for men to kiss . . . today a man would be laughed at for saying that.
>
> Louise Weiss, MEP

The commitment of the European community to the interests of women and their rights was initially more or less a matter of historical accident, but it is nonetheless firmly established. There is little doubt that without the pressure exerted by the Commission and the European Parliament, particularly since the 1970s, national governments in Europe would either have rested on their existing equality laurels or, more probably, as often happens in the course of recession, actually left legislation to lapse or be overtaken by events. Instead, at the least, the Community has encouraged, and in some cases forced, member states to explore the limitations of their laws and practices, to remedy these in line with changing conditions and to widen the scope of their equality programmes.

The Treaty of Rome

To begin at the beginning, however, is to go back to the Treaty of Rome. It seems ironic perhaps that this agreement, so largely framed in terms of trade and industrial development, should have become the basis of equality policy in Europe. However, Article 119 of the 1957 Treaty claims the 'principle of equal remuneration for the same work as between male and female workers'. On the face of it, since all member states agree to this article on joining the Community, all thereby outlaw sex discrimination in the workplace. In practice, of course, it has not been as simple and far-reaching as this, and it is only by pressure from committed individuals and groups to test and extend the law that it has developed beyond more than a formal statement. For the inclusion of the commitment to equal pay was hardly, in the fifties, an indication of the advanced feminism of these early Europeans. Rather, perhaps predictably, it had its origins in economic concerns. The French government was set to introduce minimum wage and equal pay legislation nationally, and French industrialists feared that this would erode their competitive position unless others were compelled to bring in similar measures. They seem to have believed that they already complied with the treaty requirements whereas others did not, and while they may have been right at the time, the inclusion of Article 119 opened the way for all sorts of secondary equality legislation, far beyond the purely economic sphere, in which France was no more advanced than any other Community member. It is this secondary legislation, consisting largely of Regulations, Directives and Decisions, prepared by the European Commission and approved by the Council of Ministers (Article 189 of the Rome Treaty) which forms the real body of European anti-discrimination law, upheld by the European Court of Justice (ECJ). In any case of discrepancy between national and Community law, the latter take precedence over the former. This was confirmed in *Costa* v. *ENEL* (1964) which stated that law 'stemming from the Treaty ... could not ... be overridden by domestic legal provisions, however framed . . . without the legal basis of the community itself being called into question'.[1]

In spite of the fact that the Rome Treaty does not automatically confer rights on private individuals, the European Court has ruled that where an Article is 'clear and precise' in its meaning and is not dependent on some further action being taken by member states, it has 'direct effect', and individuals may claim their rights. Article 119 has been interpreted as having such direct effect and must therefore be applied in all national courts, including labour courts and industrial tribunals, in the ten member states. Out of the Social Action Programme too came a Council Resolution (1974) which expressed the political will to achieve equality in employment and training. From this Resolution came a memorandum, 'Equal Treatment for Male and Female Workers (Access to Employment and to Vocational Training and Promotion and Working Conditions), February 1975'. This was to all intents and purposes a Community programme to improve the situation of working women, and mentioned for the first time the three Directives which were to become the mainstay of Community equality policy.

Almost from the beginning, however, the apparently unambiguous requirements of Article 119 – the implementation of equal pay in member states within four years of signing the Treaty – became contentious. Arguments raged about what 'equal pay for equal work' actually meant; the Commission was non-committal, and without a case the European Court was powerless. Specifically to remedy this last and to test what Article 119 was worth, the Belgian lawyer Eliane Vogel-Polsky set out to find a case to which the Article would apply in order to see if it conferred rights which women could not claim at national level. Belgian trades unions gave no help at this stage, completely rejecting the idea that equal pay was a legal matter in this sense and claiming that women's best chance here was through union negotiated collective bargaining. (They did ultimately support the case.)

The Defrenne case

In the end, Vogel-Polsky found her case when Gabrielle Defrenne, a stewardess with Sabena Airlines, complained about discrimination in both retirement age and the terms of her pension.[2] By 1971, the case had been referred through the Belgian courts to the ECJ and although it was found to be technically outside the scope of Article 119, reading between the lines of the judgment, it was clear that in other cases, which more precisely related to equal pay, the Article could be read as giving women direct rights (although not retroactively). The importance of this case was both in its pointing up of the implications of legal action in this area and in its illustration of the very limited application of the existing law. Neither of these points was lost on the supporters, considerable in number by the early seventies, of sexual equality in the wider social and political sense. Since that time, this goal has been pursued both by pressing for interpretation by the court and encouraging the framing of further secondary legislation to clarify, specify and tighten the original article.

The Social Action Programme

In 1974, the EEC announced its Social Action Programme. At one level, this was a public relations exercise to drum up popular support for the Community, support which had never been strong, but which was by this date at an all-time low. It was believed that the Community should show a human face and give the lie to those who said that it was simply an industrialists' club with no interest in social conditions or the plight of the weak and disadvantaged. The Action Programme therefore concentrated on just these areas, and the Social Affairs Directorate (DG V), which had already begun to campaign for a much more effective equal pay policy, was able to present its proposals on women as part of the package. Whatever the political origins of the programme, its effect was to emphasise the significance of equality for the Community, and in the second Defrenne case, the ECJ tightened up the interpretation of Article 119 considerably. It now accepted that the Article was to be seen not as merely narrowly economic but as having wide social implications, and that it did give direct rights in pay discrimination cases.

The three directives

In 1975, the Council of Ministers reinforced the equal pay commitment of the Treaty of Rome by a Directive on Equal Pay (EPD). This meant that instead of just stating a principle (in this case of equal pay for equal work) the

Directive gave the necessary powers to put it into effect. This was done under Articles 100 and 235 of the Treaty which between them allow for the provision of specific measures to ensure that the objectives of the Treaty are carried out. The Directive specified 'equal pay for work to which equal value is attributed' (Article 1) and put a time limit on compliance with this. The aim of this directive was, in addition to reinforcing the concept of 'work of equal value' (as opposed to merely the 'same' work), the abolition of discriminatory clauses in collective agreements and the provision of protection for employees against dismissal following complaints. In 1976, this was followed up by the Equal Treatment Directive (ETD) which, following the same reinforcing pattern as the EPD, sought to establish that 'there shall be no discrimination whatsoever on grounds of sex either directly or indirectly by reference in particular to marital or family status' (Article 2).[3] As the introduction in the EPD of the notion of 'equal value' was important, so in the case of the ETD was the idea of 'indirect discrimination'. At its most basic, this is simply the situation where a provision applying to both sexes is in effect discriminatory to one. It is, as we shall see, however, more difficult to prove in law than this clear statement would suggest.

The third Directive adopted by the Council of Ministers was that covering Social Security.[4] Adopted in 1978, the Directive covers people in the working populations and deals with, *inter alia*, invalidity and old-age pensions and unemployment and sickness benefits. Occupational pension schemes are specifically excluded from the terms of the Directive. In view of the complexity of the Directive's aims, governments were given a relatively long period in which to comply with its requirements, having until the end of 1984 to bring their legislation into line with the European framework.

The three Directives have considerably extended the scope of the EEC's concern with equality policy, and place wide obligations on member states in this area. Although primarily relating to women in the work force (and it is women as workers who are, via Article 119, 'treaty-based') they have implicitly conceded that for women to have equality at work involves the establishment of equal treatment in related but separate spheres like education and training, pay and promotion and so on. The notion of 'equal value' points up and tries to deal with the problems of job segregation where women seldom do the 'same' work as men and where this has meant low pay in just these 'female' areas where direct comparability with men is not possible. Similarly, the idea of 'indirect discrimination' can show the extent to which the structure of work is dominated by male experience and male requirements in spite of the large and growing female presence. In this context, the integration of women may require not only making room for them, but making changes so that they have a real, and not just a formal, opportunity to participate at all levels.

The European Social Fund (ESF)

In 1978, too, it was agreed that a special allocation within the European Social Fund should be set aside for training projects for women. It was only a small percentage of the total ESF budget but it was dedicated to the provision of courses and the development of projects exclusively for women. This provision lapsed in 1983, since when no 'women's budget' has operated, but it did show in another way the commitment of the Community to equality policy in the 1970s. The passing of the Directives, too, was not merely an easy piece of window-dressing. They needed, at the least, to be monitored and reviewed as implementation proceeded, and this meant the creation of a staff, a budget and consultative committees, all of which were duly established. From this period date the Women's Employment Bureau and the Women's Information Bureau, both of which established contacts with women's organisations and legal experts within all the member states. Such contacts have developed and expanded, and their significance and potential will be considered later.

Direct elections to the European Parliament, 1979

To continue the story of equality legislation and the EEC, we must now change the scene from the Commission and the Council of Ministers to the European Parliament. Before 1979, Members of the Parliament had been delegates of their national parliaments, chosen by national party hierarchies, and always had 'dual mandate'. In June of 1979, the first direct elections to the European Parliament were held in all nine of the then member states. This was significant for women's concerns in at least two respects. Firstly, it meant that the new Parliament could claim a democratic base with the ensuing power and credibility that this brought, and, although it continued to be described as a talking shop in some quarters, its sense of itself was enhanced and its right to demand a voice much strengthened. Secondly, the Parliament now included a relatively high proportion of women, for all countries higher than in their national parliaments. The reasons for this are complex and not entirely explained by the lower status of the European body with its uncertain powers (see Chapter 1), but the result for women was a group within the Parliament committed to their cause.

The ad hoc committee

Almost immediately, in October 1979, the Parliament set up an ad hoc committee charged with the responsibility of preparing for a Parliamentary debate on the situation of women in Europe. To this end, they were to prepare, in collaboration with the Commission, a report on the subject, which the thirty-five committee members (twenty-five of them women) produced in February 1981. During its existence, the ad hoc committee members took evidence from experts, organised a public hearing in Milan, and attended a conference in Manchester on the future of equal treatment, as well as the United Nations mid-decade Conference on Women in Copenhagen.

It is perhaps worth emphasising the importance of these extra-parliamentary gatherings, as they added greatly to the feminist ethos developing in the Parliament through 1980. The Manchester conference in May was arranged by the European Commission and hosted by the British Equal Opportunities Commission. It was the beginning of real co-operation between the equality bureaux of the member states and it discussed many of the ideas which were to find their way into the Maij-Weggen Report and then into the 1982 Action Programme.

The United Nations World Conference of the Decade for Women (1975–85) was held in Copenhagen in July 1980. Its themes were Equality, Development, and Peace, and its International Convention on the Elimination of all forms of Discrimination against Women was, and is, a very wide-ranging document. Its concern not just with women in the work force and in education and training, but with their role in health programmes, in development policy and in welfare provisions, provided a model for the report of the ad hoc committee when it came to be written. Another body, the European Trade Union Confederation (ETUC) was also influential at this point, establishing, in 1979, its own programme for 'the attainment of equal rights and opportunities for women'. The declaration of the Organisation for European Cooperation and Development (OECD) Conference in May 1980 reflected, too, a similar concern with opportunities at work and a desire seriously to tackle the problems women encountered.

The ad hoc committee drew up two questionnaires, one on the place of women in the media and the other on discrimination against women at work. This latter formed the basis of an opinion poll which was later published by the Commission under the title 'Working Women in Europe'.

At the end of eighteen months (its original six month term having been twice extended by the Parliament) it produced a huge report, often referred to as the Maij-Weggen Report after its rapporteur Mrs Maij-Weggen of the Netherlands. The resolution put to the Parliament first recommended the improvement of existing Community measures (i.e. the three Directives) and then went on to suggest that the Social Fund should be used to combat growing unemployment among women. Further action on part-time work, new technologies and social services was recommended, and sections dealt with women's education and training, health care and the special needs of developing countries. Finally, a whole series of recommendations were made, from calling on the institutions of the Community to look at their own employment patterns, and put their house in order by promoting women at all levels, to asking for an enquiry into prostitution and related activities.

The debate on the Report took place on 10 and 11 February 1981 and was, not surprisingly, at times a turbulent affair. In the public gallery sat Mrs Sadat of Egypt and the Grand Duchess of Luxembourg. Simone Veil, President of the Parliament, was in the Chair and Mrs Maij-Weggen began by insisting that 'the disadvantages suffered by women should be eliminated, and balanced and just relations between European citizens must be created'.[5] Others could not agree. Mr Forth (UK, European Democrat Group), for example, was scathing of the report which he characterised as 'a bulky document making utterly unrealistic demands', and he went on to castigate it as 'costly and irresponsible . . . seeking commitments of resources which . . . would cause us to cut back on other programmes in the Community'. Mme Roudy, on the other hand, had no hesitation in pronouncing that 'this resolution is exactly what we need', presenting as it did 'a genuine programme of work for the Commission and the Communities'. The differences of opinion were not only between men and women: several of the female MEPs expressed misgivings about the report. For example, the Communist women felt that it failed to grapple with the real problems, while the women of the right tried to limit the scope of the resolution by introducing amendments. But Mr Enright (UK, Socialist) held that whereas there might be 'theological arguments about other articles, [Article 119] is unequivocal and clear'. He went on to say that men, as well as women, should fight for justice 'and the only way we can fight for justice is to adopt this resolution'. Women participated actively in the debate, making up more than half the speakers. Ninety-six of the 126 amendments were tabled by one or more women, and only twelve by men alone (the remainder being presented by mixed groups). If the value of the debate at this stage seemed mainly at the level of publicising the women's case, this was perhaps not an unworthy result. As Ivor Richard of the Commission was to say afterwards, 'there must be more information so that women will ignore nothing of their rights under the law, a campaign to publicise new ventures and possible action . . . so that every woman will be made aware of the pressure for change'.

The 59 paragraphs of the Resolution included the provision that the ad hoc mandate should be ended for the moment, and the committee reconvened after two years to review progress on the implementation of the measures agreed. During the debate, disagreement had emerged about the value of the committee and whether it should be made a permanency or should simply be allowed to lapse. It was argued against a permanent women's committee that it would allow for the convenient 'marginalisation' of women's concerns which would then cease to be taken seriously by the Parliament as a whole. The alternative view was that if the women's committee ceased to exist, the case for equality would simply not be put in any forceful and concerned way, and there were some women MEPs who feared that when Parliament came to look at progress in two years' time, it would find that little or nothing had been done. This latter view gained sufficient support by July 1981, for Mrs Lizin and 109 other signatories (acting under rule 95 of the new rules of procedure of the Parliament) to request the setting up of a committee of enquiry to monitor the progress of the terms of the Resolution adopted in February. Thus was set up the Committee of Enquiry into the Situation of Women in Europe with eighteen members, each of whom was allocated a particular topic for study and report. The Committee met regularly and took evidence from the Commission, the Council of Ministers and the Commission's new Advisory Committee on Equal Opportunities. In addition to their investigative activities and reports (for details of which, see below), the Committee of Enquiry produced an opinion on the proposed revision of the European Regional Development Fund and, in the vote on this proposal, got Parliament to agree to amendments taking greater account of the interests of women.

The new Action Programme, 1982–5

Since there is no legal obligation on the other institutions of the EEC to implement the resolutions of the European Parliament, it was quite possible that the vote of February 1981, having had its brief moment of glory, would go no further. However, as has been said, the Commission had developed a commitment to equality policy in the seventies, and a small and devoted, if under-funded, staff had been pursuing these objectives ever since. It is perhaps not so surprising, then, that by the end of 1981 many of the provisions of the resolution had found their way into the Commission's New Community Action Programme on the Promotion of Equal Opportunity for Women, 1982–5.[6] This document limits itself to the situation of women at work and takes no account of the Resolution's recommendations on abortion or contraception (both of which had inspired a good deal of disagreement during the original debate in the Parliament). Nonetheless, it is a wide-ranging document which makes a determined effort to achieve equal treatment specifically by strengthening individual rights and by encouraging positive action programmes. It is also strong in its determination to monitor results and to make sure that there is close co-operation between national equality agencies and the Community. To this latter end, the Commission set up an Advisory Committee on Equal Opportunities for Women and Men, staffed by leading members of equality commissions in the Ten, which meets regularly to pool experience and discuss progress. In addition to this Committee, a network of independent experts drawn from all the member states monitors the implementation of the Directives. This committee has been particularly concerned with the concept of 'indirect discrimination' (which one of its members defines as 'the operation of a law, practice, arrangement or requirement which is neutral and equal on its face, but which in practice has a disproportionately adverse impact and cannot be justified by the requirements of the job or basic necessity irrespective of sex').

Apart from monitoring in a very systematic way the progress of Community equality policy so far, the Action Programme covers a wide area of legal and industrial activity affecting women. For example, legal redress in respect of equal treatment is clearly of major importance if women are to gain equality. Yet comparatively little use is made of the existing arrangements for redress through national law. This is partly, as the programme points out, a result of the difficulty of proving discrimination and partly of the fear which women have, particularly in times of high unemployment, of losing their jobs if they complain. The programme recommends examination of the functioning, in some member states, of special advisory bodies giving help to women fighting equality cases. It also recommends consideration of reversal of the burden of proof (i.e. the onus being placed on the alleged discriminator to show innocence), again a practice which is provided for in some cases in some member states.

A further area to be examined is that of protective legislation for female workers. This has for long been a contentious issue between governments, trade unions and some feminists, the latter arguing that the 'protection' afforded to women amounts to their exclusion from lucrative shift-work and overtime, while the unions claim that the exemptions afforded to women, rather than being cancelled for women, should be extended to everybody. The aim of the relevant provision in the Action Programme is to combine these views by calling on governments to abolish 'unjustified protective legislation . . . and to promote equal standards of protection of men and women'.

Social security is to be equalised further than the third Directive suggests (it dealt with *state* pension schemes only and exempted occupational schemes, equalisation of the retirement age, survivors' pensions and family allowances, etc.). This section of the programme also aims at the 'gradual' establishment of individual entitlement to benefits of all women (i.e. not through a husband or male co-habitee). It is this 'individualisation' of benefits for which the developing women's lobby is pressing. The programme goes on to cover such areas as equal treatment for self-employed women, taxation and parental leave, all of which are presented as extensions of existing individual rights.

So far as the positive action element of the programme is concerned, the provision of special budgets and special training for women are mentioned, as is 'integration into working life'. The latter involves the diversification of the jobs women do, particularly into new technologies, thus helping to break down the 'women's areas' which so often suffer from lack of comparability with male jobs and so remain low-paid. In this context, publicity is recognised as crucial. Women must know both that they have a right of access to any type or level of vocational training and what kind of courses and guidance exist. It is in response to this suggestion that the British Equal Opportunities Commission has sponsored its WISE (Women in Science and Engineering) project, to make not only girls but parents and employers aware of the opportunities for women in these areas.

Although these aspects of positive action have to do with special treatment for women, the other side of such a programme is the monitoring of trends in order to assess what progress is being made in desegregation and equalisation. Positive action is not about quotas, as its critics often think; it is not even just about instituting special programmes without which endemic inequality will inevitably continue; it is also about the analysis of trends over time, the setting of targets and the identification of facilities and services which affect women's employment. The gathering and pooling of information and experience is crucial (see Chapter 8) if much time and effort is not to be used up re-inventing the wheel in every case in each country. This is not to suggest naively that programmes are transferable lock, stock and barrel from one context to another. But experience may often be valuable, intelligently adapted, to others.

Mme Quintin, Head of the Commission's Women's Bureau, was under no misapprehension about the complexity and the political difficulty of the Action Programme when she talked to CREW (Centre for Research on European Women) soon after its adoption. Given the economic situation in western Europe as a whole, she said, the Bureau will have to fight even harder to put policies for women into action. She was to be proved right in the next stages of the equality programme.

An indication of the generally less supportive atmosphere for sex equality was perhaps the progress of a spontaneous, so-called Intergroup, comprising the majority of women MEPs, which came into being in the November 1981 part-session of the Parliament. Although it had wide support to begin with, and analysed prostitution, military service for women and co-habitation laws, it soon ceased to attract women across the political spectrum. This was only partly because, as the more conservative women said, it was too extreme in its concerns; it was rather indicative, at a deeper level, of the changing climate of opinion, encouraged by recession, on equality. This meant that governments were unwilling to do more than was absolutely required of them in this sphere, and consequently many of the women MEPs felt that it would be impolitic to spend time on issues which had absolutely no chance of winning wider support, when they needed all their energy to keep the mainstream demands under review. By this time, too, many of the women were deeply involved with a new and official project on equality.

The Committee of Enquiry on the Situation of Women in Europe

After the presentation of the Maij-Weggen Report and the Parliamentary debate, it was assumed that the work of the ad hoc committee was at an end. As has been said, some suggested that it might reconvene after eighteen months or two years to review progress on its recommendations, but this was thought by many to leave too long a gap without any Parliamentary contribution. In December 1981, the Standing Liaison Committee of advisers from member states was constituted as a permanent advisory body to the Commission. Named the Advisory Committee on Equal Opportunities for Women and Men, it was given a budget, and a networking as well as an advisory brief. Soon afterwards, the European Parliament also agreed to set up a committee of its own, the Committee of Enquiry on the Situation of Women in Europe, which would follow the progress of the three Directives and monitor the Parliament's Resolution on women.

At its first meeting, the Committee of Enquiry decided on a list of eighteen themes for investigation (including the application of the three Directives). The other topics to be investigated in relation to women were: the re-organisation of working time; vocational training; new technologies; the European Social Fund; health; migrants and immigrants; the self-employed; employment in Community institutions; the Third World and European aid; information policy; parental leave; taxation; less favoured regions; education; and decision-taking centres. There was also to be a report by Mrs Pantazi on the situation of women in Greece. Most of these were expected by the end of 1983. The rapporteurs, in many cases, questioned not only the Commission but the Council of the European Communities, representatives of member states and appropriate national bodies.

By the middle of 1983, many of the reports had been approved by the Committee, and Parliament was due to discuss their final recommendations in November. By this stage, there was clearly some disagreement between the radical members of the Committee and those who considered themselves to be more realistic. Recession had hit women badly, as the unemployment figures showed, and the Socialist members wanted this tackled in the final report. Others, however, felt that governments could not be expected to take on further commitments involving expenditure at this time. It was largely on this difference of views that the unity of the Committee foundered. Mrs Lizin, whose original request had led to the setting up of the Committee of Enquiry, had what some believed to be the most relevant parts of her report on women in development cut by the Committee. She had called for the adoption of 'administrative rules' by member states to ensure that women were consulted on development projects; this was limited to a recommendation that states 'improve their development aid planning to take account of women's problems'.

In some cases, however, the Committee was firm in its insistence that fundamental changes were needed. For example, they endorsed the recommendation by Dame Shelagh Roberts that the individual and not the family should be the tax unit and suggested that childcare expenses should be tax-deductable.[7]

The final reports were not made to the Committee until October 1983 and the debate was set, rather later than originally planned, for January 1984. Again, political divisions were in evidence when the Committee discussed the report drafted by Mrs Wieczorek-Zeul on the readjustment of working hours which called for the adoption of the Directive on part-time work, as well as a new Directive on the reduction of working time. Although the Committee backed both of these proposals, they were accompanied by an amendment which again reflected the concern of the more conservative women that the Committee's recommendations be realistic in the prevailing economic conditions. Thus Dame Shelagh Roberts and Ms Hooper (both UK Conservatives in the European Democratic Group) suggested that the reduction in hours be subject to 'the need first to achieve movement towards economic recovery in the member states'.

Towards the end of December 1983, the need to finalise the Report of the Committee of Enquiry became urgent, and a marathon eleven-hour session went through over 270 amendments. There, the political divisions, which had at first been almost imperceptible, but then emerged briefly over part-time work and reduction of working time, finally broke to the surface, with the Conservative women acknowledging the uncertainty they had always felt about not only employment issues, but the nature and scope of the whole report. Ms Hooper, true to the Conservative political creed which shuns the utopian vision and the abstract statement of aspirations, felt that the report was much too diffuse. It would have been better, she argued, 'to pick a few priority areas and concentrate on those where the Community has power . . . such as taxation, for instance'. Thus even before the debate, it was clear that the women themselves were divided and the British Conservatives and many of the Liberal group, although they agreed to support the Report as a whole, still said they would table amendments to the resolution. The left-wing women, on the other hand, saw the Report as a compromise, yet one which did make progress and which pointed up and limited the erosion which recession and complacency had wrought on the progress of women's rights. But this was probably an optimistic response when put in the context of the Committee's report on the Commission's actions in response to the 1981 debate and resolution. Fifty-eight requests were made at that time, thirty-four of which appeared to have been ignored, and only six fully met. Others were being considered and another six had been integrated into the Action Programme. It was not surprising, then, that when the debate took place it was in an atmosphere of disharmony among the women which harmed the credibility of their case.

The 1984 debate on the Report of the Enquiry

On 17 January 1984 a one hundred and sixteen point resolution on the situation of women in Europe was passed by the European Parliament by 125 votes to 17 with 55 abstentions. Less than half the Parliament, in other words, even bothered to vote, and attendance during the six-hour debate often went well below this. It was not only the Christian Democrat and Liberal men who dismissed the resolution as a 'lot of left-wing chatter'; their female colleagues too felt that they had been drawn into political polemics by their Socialist sisters.

In much the same way as abortion had been the sticking point for the Conservatives in the 1981 debate, so in 1984 they said they could no longer support the resolution because it had been so changed by amendments. In particular they disliked an addition to the section dealing with the 'dignity and rights of women' which attacked 'the excessive exploitation of employers' and talked of 'working conditions more in keeping with an earlier age; victimisation, insults and harassment of all kinds'. The Liberals and European Democrats (Conservatives) condemned such sentiments as party-political and dissociated themselves from what they characterised as a 'call to the class struggle'. In spite of this, the Committee's demand for a thirty-five-hour week was carried, along with suggestions over a wide range of areas, in many of which the Community has little or no control over member states.

The resolution calls for the adoption of existing draft directives on parental leave, occupational social security (the existing social security directive covers only state schemes), part-time work, temporary work, rights of residence of non-nationals, and the illegal traffic of workers. According to Ivor Richard, the Commissioner for Employment and Social

Affairs, the Commission is committed to pursuing legislation on the first three of these, and discussions are well advanced. This does not mean, however, that quick solutions to problems in these areas are imminent. All governments claim, for example, that standardising occupational pension schemes is complicated and costly; parental leave is expensive and difficult to regulate; and giving equal rights with full-timers to part-time workers is deeply unpopular with employers and might result in job losses. If there are problems in the areas where the resolution follows pretty directly the Commission's line, as above, there are clearly even greater difficulties where it departs from existing Commission policy and demands more radical steps towards equality. For example, it calls for a directive on positive action and one on equal treatment in taxation law, as well as harmonising legislation on contraceptive provision and the reduction of working time. The last two are politically unpopular with member governments, and the Commission itself takes the line that the differing tax bases of the various member states would probably make a directive on taxation law impossible to operate. Positive action, too, is seen as more appropriately dealt with by a recommendation than by a directive.

Such reactions from the Commission to Parliamentary recommendations often lead critics of the Parliament to pour scorn on its lack of legislative power, and to argue that its impotence makes it unimportant. Many MEPs disagree, and claim that the Parliament has, at least, an informal or 'moral' influence, while admitting that its lack of formal legislative powers is frustrating. Parliament is certainly assured a hearing, as the Council is obliged to consult it before legislating, although it need not heed Parliament's advice. However, the Council and Commission seem to respect the fact that many MEPs, sitting as they do on expert committees, are specialist in their various subjects. They are also well aware that MEPs may be more accessible to lobbyists through their constituencies than Commission bureaucrats or members of the Council (who are government ministers). So Parliament's views tend to be held in some respect.

The case of women shows Parliament's influence in another way too. Ivor Richard, the Commissioner for Social Affairs between 1980 and 1984, readily admits that the Action Programme on Women, although emanating from the Commission, was largely based on Parliament's Resolution on the Status of Women passed in February 1981. In some ways, it may be easier for Parliament to influence the Commission on a subject like equality than over more politically contentious subjects such as, for example, agriculture. The European agricultural lobby is large and well organised. Their policies are backed up by powerful member states, and there is a high proportion of farming interests represented in the European decision-making process. So in this area there are already members of pressure groups and vested interests with which Parliament has to compete for the Commission's ear. By contrast, although there is also a relatively high number of women in the European Parliament, few regard themselves as there to represent women and continually to push for women's issues. As we have seen, they have other interests. Apart from the officially appointed Advisory Committee to the Commission, the only pressure group for women at a European level is CREW, which does a valiant job, both in attempting to inform women in Europe and in pushing for the serious consideration of women's interests. But CREW is far less well known or well financed, and much less consulted than, for example, the powerful farming groups, and there are no national governments fighting unreservedly for women's issues. Consequently, when the European Parliament does take up women's issues, the Commission and Council are prepared to listen to it. The Parliament is one of very few voices articulating these interests, and provided the issue is not too contentious its views will generally be listened to. This said, of course, if the Commission perceived any particular proposal as politically unacceptable, it will simply be watered down, as was the Action Programme. And, as with the Action Programme, where member states are opposed even to the more limited version, acting through the Council, they can still prevent legislation being agreed.

In general, the 1984 debate was successful in giving publicity to the idea of equality and in articulating wider aspirations for women. In some respects, too, the resolution gave practical indications of how to achieve these aims. For example, the Parliament backed a proposal to stop all finances from the European Social Fund to states which do not agree to a balanced allocation from the Fund as between men and women. But although such statements and the reiteration of support for existing directives and draft directives are useful, they cannot compensate for the obvious disunity of the women MEPs on equality, or the clear unwillingness of member governments to take on more than the absolute minimum legislative requirements in what they call 'the present economic climate'. The priority given to sex equality, then, is much lower than in the heady days of the mid-1970s, and this is reflected in political attitudes to the whole issue.

Things have come a long way since the Treaty of Rome, but ironically the position for women may be more vulnerable now than it was then, in the midst of post-war expansion. It is now all too easy for critics to point to what has been done and pronounce it enough. Thus is the backlash established; women *have* equality, it is claimed; nothing further can be done by legislation. Whatever happens in the wake of the 1984 elections, it is certain that those who support women's rights, inside the European Parliament and outside, have an even tougher fight on their hands than before.

6 European legislation and the European legal systems

> Whether lawyers . . . like it or not, they are going to have to equip themselves to deal with the social facts which lie behind legislative policies of this kind. In the modern area of legal regulation (such as sex equality) . . . the lawyer cannot limit himself to the logical organisation of rules and principles.
>
> Professor B.A. Hepple

EEC law

To understand how EEC equality legislation has been translated into the legal system of the member states, it is necessary first to describe the Community legal system. EEC law is different from any other type of legal system in existence. Unlike international law, it is binding upon individual states just as their own laws are, and indeed it takes precedence over these. Yet unlike national law, it arises from an international organisation and is consequently an independent legal system, with its own rules and structures, on a supranational level, neither national nor international.

The primary sources of the EEC legal system are the three founding Treaties – the Treaty of Paris of 1951 establishing the ECSC, the Treaty of Rome, and the Euratom Treaty of 1957 establishing the EEC and Euratom Communities. There are also other, more recent Treaties, such as the Merger Treaty of 1965 which brought the three communities under one administration, and the Luxembourg Accord in 1966. The Treaties specify the aims and objectives of the communities, and are generally directly binding on the member states. Article 119 of the Rome Treaty is an exception in that it laid down the binding aim of equal pay for equal work, but left the methods to the discretion of the member states, to be achieved within four years. Articles 100 and 235 are also relevant here, as both articles prescribe the means by which further legislation may be enacted. Article 100 allows the Council to issue directives 'for the aproximation of such provisions . . . as directly affect the establishment or functioning of the common market'. The Equal Pay Directive was brought under Article 100 in an attempt to harmonise the laws in the different member states. Article 235 is wider, and known as the 'everything else' provision, allowing the Council to 'take the appropriate measures to attain, in the course of the operation of the common market, one of the objectives of the Community when this Treaty has not provided the necessary powers'. This allows the Council to legislate for anything that could arguably be within 'the course of the operation of the common market'. Now, with legislation on social provisions such as women's rights and environmental issues, 'the common market' has been very widely defined.[1] The Equal Treatment Directive was introduced under Article 235. Generally the Treaties create rights for individuals which can be enforced, and define principles to be applied for the smooth running of the market and good relations between the member states.

Article 189 allows for secondary legislation to be passed by the Council. The same Article defines Regulations, Directives, Decisions, Recommendations and Opinions. Of those, only Regulations and Directives have general legal force; and Decisions are legally binding on those to whom they are addressed, but are not more generally applicable. (See Chapter 2 above.) Directives are not quite as far-reaching as Regulations since they are binding only as to the end to be achieved, but leave to the member states the means by which this should be achieved. In most cases, this is because the subject of legislation is in a sensitive area, such as the economy, where the member states want to retain some degree of control, or where the situation in the ten states is so varied that different measures are needed in each to implement the order. (This latter tends to be the case with women's rights.) A time-limit is set on each directive and, if no adequate measures have been taken by the member states upon expiry of the time-limit, the Commission may initiate proceedings to enforce compliance. Like a Directive, a Decision is binding in its entirety on those to whom it is addressed, but it relates only to the particular case and does not have general legal application.

Apart from the Treaties, there are other sources of EEC law, such as the general legal principles common to most member states and integral to their individual legal systems.[2] The European Court is still working out the extent to which it relies upon national legal concepts. It recently decided, for example, that fundamental rights are basic principles of EEC law since they are basic principles in many of the member states' legal systems, and as such, cannot be overridden.[3]

So EEC law is common to all member states and can create binding rights and duties on governments and individuals, just as can domestic law. EEC law also takes precedence over domestic law, and where there is a conflict between EEC law and domestic law, the domestic courts have a duty to implement the EEC legislation. This was first decided in *Costa* v. *ENEL*,[4] where the European Court ruled that EEC law 'could not, because of its special and original nature, be overridden by domestic legal provisions, however framed, without being deprived of its character as Community law and without the legal basis of the Community itself being called into question'. Obviously there would be no point in having an independent legal system of Community law if the member states could decide whether or not to recognise its provisions. Such a concept of precedence over domestic law is easily accepted by countries such as the Netherlands, but in Britain, the situation is more complicated. The British legal system recognises only one source of legislation, Parliament, and only that which Parliament decides is unquestionable. This is the doctrine of Parliamentary sovereignty. Treaties can be recognised by British courts if Parliament has ratified them, and thus deliberately incorporated them into the domestic system, but not otherwise. Effectively, a two-tier legal system operates; on the one hand, there is Parliamentary law which is binding; on the other hand there is international law which is not binding, but merely persuasive. Consequently, the primacy of EEC law, where each piece of legislation does not require individual ratification from Parliament for it to be binding, theoretically goes against the idea of Parliamentary sovereignty. Parliament tried to prevent this difficulty by incorporating a general ratification of any legislation the EEC passes into the 1972 European Communities Act Section 2(1) and Section 3(1). In practice, the British courts now always apply European law against conflicting British law, even if the British law has been passed since the European law.[5] And effectively the courts have decided that, unless Parliament passes an Act intentionally conflicting with European Law, they must assume that Parliament did not intend such conflict, and so enforce the European law provisions rather than the British legislation.[6] Although in certain cases this could be damaging, women in Britain are clearly benefiting from the more favourable EEC provisions on, for example, equal pay.

A further concept which has developed in European law is that of 'direct effect'. Direct effect was first recognised by the European Court in 1963 in *Van Gend en Loos* v. *Nederlandse Administratie der Belastingen*;[7] when it was said that

> the EEC constitutes a new legal order of international law for the benefit of which the states have limited their sovereign rights, albeit within limited fields, and the subjects comprise not only member states but also their nationals. Independently of the legislation of member states, EEC law therefore not only imposes obligations on individuals but is also intended to confer upon them rights which become part of their legal heritage. These rights arise not only where they are expressly granted by the Treaty, but also by reason of obligations which the Treaty imposes in a clearly defined way upon individuals as well as upon the member states and upon the institutions of the EEC.

Thus a member state need not recognise a provision of EEC law for their nationals to claim and enforce the rights created by that provision. In *Van Gend en Loos*, the Dutch government had increased import duties contrary to Article 122 of the Treaty of Rome. The European Court held that individual traders could rely upon Article 122 not to pay the illegal import duties, since Article 122 was 'directly effective' and conferred rights upon individuals whether their government accepted it or not.

In 1974, in *Van Duyn* v. *Home Office*,[8] the European Court decided the criteria in terms of which a provision could be construed as directly effective. There are three elements: the provision must impose a clear and precise obligation on member states; it must be unconditional – in other words, subject to no limitation; and member states must not be left with any real discretion with regard to the application of the rule in question. All European law provisions must meet this test in order to be construed as directly effective; no provision is automatically directly effective. Article 119 was held to be directly effective in the second *Defrenne* case in 1976.[9] So now any woman in the ten member states may claim equal pay for equal work through her national courts, which are obliged to let her pursue her case if she has one. However, the European Court has consistently refused to answer the question of whether the three directives on women are directly effective. Although the directives are frequently taken into account by the British courts (for example, by the House of Lords in the *Garland* case),[10] both the Court of Appeal and the Employment Appeal Tribunal have decided that the directives are not directly effective.[11]

European law is enforced by the European Court of Justice and the Commission of the EEC. The European Court has the job of ensuring that in the interpretation and application of this Treaty, the law is observed.[12] As the supreme Court of Appeal for all member states, it attempts to ensure that the law is interpreted uniformly in all the member states. It also sees itself as playing an expansionist role, and has consistently interpreted cases in line with the policy of furthering the common market. For example, introducing direct effect in *Van Gend en Loos* was not done purely and strictly on the facts of that case but also because direct effect was seen as necessary for European law to be adequately enforced, and so the case was decided partly on that basis. The Commission is the police force of the EEC. It has the role of initiating proceedings in the European Court against member states when they are in breach of their Treaty obligations: for example, when they have failed to implement a directive after the time-limit has expired. For example, in *Commission* v. *UK*[13] the Commission took the British Government to court in 1981 for failing to provide the means of determining work of 'equal value'. An infringement by a member state may be presumed and established in one of several ways: a member state fails to inform the Commission of the legal measures that it has taken to adapt national law to Community law, although it is obliged to do so; the Commission may itself rule that the measures taken are inadequate; or an individual may submit a complaint to the Commission against a measure which is said to be incompatible with Community law and the Commission finds that the complaint is well-founded. Once the Court has held that a member state is in breach of its Treaty obligations, the member state then has a duty to rectify the breach as quickly as possible. The Court has no sanctions to impose, but outright refusal to implement EEC law would effectively be construed as a statement against the Community and become a political matter.

The Court also has the task, under Article 177 of the Treaty of Rome, of acting as a supreme Court of Appeal for all member states. Under the Article, domestic courts may refer questions of European law to the European Court to interpret or determine the validity of secondary legislation. Most of the British sex discrimination cases reached the European Court by this route of preliminary references. The European Court merely determines the question of *European* law, and then sends the determination back to domestic courts to apply the interpretation to the facts. The European Court's decision is binding upon that particular case, but does not create a precedent in the normal British sense. However the British courts have effectively used the European Court's decisions as precedents and the European Court itself has said that once a question has been determined, there is no need for a second case to bring the same question to the Court again.[14] Article 177 is thus one means of ensuring a uniform interpretation of European law in all member states.

The Directives on equal pay and equal treatment

The Equal Pay Directive of 1975 (EPD), Equal Treatment Directive of 1976 (ETD), and Social Security Directive of 1978 (SSD), were the Community's first important actions in support of women's rights. Although Article 119 of the Treaty of Rome had guaranteed equal pay for equal work, the Article had never been implemented by the member states and had effectively lain dormant for years. Then, in the seventies, feminist pressure on the Community had resulted in the formation of the Women's Bureau of the Commission and the 1974 Social Action Programme, which had included a general commitment to sex equality. The three Directives were a direct result of this programme. The first two Directives will be dealt with together and the Social Security Directive separately.

All the Directives had to be implemented by the member states by certain deadlines, otherwise states could be taken before the European Court by the Commission and held to be in breach of their Treaty obligations. Once the deadlines had passed, the Commission held investigations into the level of implementation of the Directives in the member states, and then took the decision as to whether or not to bring infringement proceedings. Generally, if a member state was judged not to have implemented the Directives fully, mere notice of infringement proceedings was enough to make it comply. The deadline for the EPD was 1976, only a year after the Directive was passed. It was thought that since the original obligation of equal pay had been passed in 1957, in Article 119, that one year was long enough for the member states finally to implement the requirement. And the report on the implementation of the EPD included the implementation of Article 119 as well. The ETD deadline was set for 1978, and the report was published in 1981. The reports were compiled from questionnaires sent to governments, employers and workers' organisations. The Directives were not seen by the Commission as likely to attain female equality by themselves, but rather as a means of enforcing the practice of non-discrimination in the workplace. The Commission regards legislation as a means of enforcing standards which can play an important part in efforts to change attitudes. 'The Commission is also aware of the distance that can separate such standards from reality', it states in the introduction to the report on the implementation of the ETD.[15] Consequently, it tries to supplement its legal commitment to women's rights by other means, such as providing money from the European Social Fund for women's work, etc. The reports were not only concerned with showing the inadequacies in the laws of the member states, and their failure to implement the directives fully; but also hoped that by pointing up these shortcomings and successes, member states would learn from each other's experience of remedying the problem of unequal pay. The Commission also regards the directives as showing the need for a 'common awareness of the urgent need for solutions to be developed', on certain crucial points.[16]

The ETD in particular was the first broadening of the Commission's action on women's rights. It had been introduced strictly in line with Article 119 of the Treaty of Rome, and was seen as an extension not of the principle of equal pay, but of the wider principle of equality. Consequently the ETD is more general in its terms, and a wide interpretation of it would extend its scope into strictly non-economic matters such as sexual harassment. However, this is clearly not specifically intended in the original Directive which was to apply primarily to the workplace. Yet as it has been interpreted, it has extended women's rights at work and elsewhere considerably, from equal pay to equal treatment in all sorts of other areas.

Most states now have general implementing legislation for the EPD and ETD. Some states, such as the United Kingdom, argued that their earlier legislation (Equal Pay Act 1970 and Sex Discrimination Act 1975) was sufficient to fulfil their obligations under the Directives, although since they were passed without reference to the Directives they were unlikely to do so exactly, and have since had to be modified. Both West Germany and Italy argued that the commitment in their constitutions to equal rights was sufficient as implementing legislation, until the Commission ruled otherwise and threatened infringement proceedings. Luxembourg completely ignored the ETD in particular until infringement proceedings were brought, at which point the 1981 equality law was finally passed. Most states have incorporated the EEC's description of 'equal pay for work of equal value' (Article 1, EPD) into their domestic legislation. Some states, however, have not defined the concept of pay at all (for example, Italy and West Germany). Others have defined pay narrowly, as in the Netherlands, where pay, but not allowances, comes within the scope of the law. Those countries with legislation based on the EPD (such as Ireland), have all incorporated the definition of 'equal pay for work of equal value' into their legislation. Thus those states which failed to satisfy the Commission tended to be those which had some kind of sex discrimination provisions before the EPD came into being, and who argued that those provisions were themselves sufficient implementation.

The UK, for example, relying upon its Equal Pay Act of 1970, allowed for equal pay only for 'like work', which meant work similar to work performed by men, or work rated as being equivalent by a job evaluation exercise. Since job evaluation schemes are not mandatory on employers, there is no set procedure for establishing equal value. This was the subject of an action for infringement by the Commission, and the European Court ruled that the UK was, indeed, in breach of the Directive.[17] Now, new regulations have been passed, by which a tribunal may refer an equal value claim to an expert who will compare the woman's job with a relevant man's. Unfortunately, the new regulations are extremely difficult to understand, and seem to make the job of a woman trying to prove discrimination in pay, if anything, more difficult than before.[18] First she must satisfy the tribunal that it is reasonable to refer the matter to an expert, which effectively means proving her case to the tribunal; and once the expert has reported, she is not allowed to question that report or call evidence, so that, in practice, it seems likely that the tribunal will simply rubber-stamp the expert's report. The EOC considers that the regulations do nothing to remedy the UK's breach of EEC law and hope that a further infringement action will be started.

Denmark is the other outstanding infringer of the EPD. Its general implementing law, based on the Directive and passed in 1976, stated that the principle of equal pay applies only to 'like work' ('samme arbeijde'), and there is no clause regarding work of 'equal value'. Infringement proceedings were initiated by the Commission and the case referred to the European Court in 1983. Denmark considered that the words 'samme arbeijde' implied more than the words 'like work' and included 'work of equal value'. However, the Court disagreed and, in early 1985, found Denmark in breach of the EPD, and ruled that a change in Danish legislation was necessary. Ireland probably has the most useful definition of work of equal value. Ireland passed its Anti-Discrimination (Pay) Act in 1974, a year earlier than the EPD, and it defines work of equal value 'in terms of the demands it makes in relation to the physical effort involved, responsibility, etc.'. So long as a fair job evaluation scheme is involved, this seems a sensible definition.

Article 1 defines the scope of the ETD as 'the principle of equal treatment for men and women as regards access to employment, including promotion, and to vocational training and as regards working conditions'. Most member states have adopted that framework, and applied it to the public, private and self-employed sector. West Germany has applied its law only to the private sector, which is the subject of another action for infringement currently before the European Court. The Commission considers that working conditions should be widely defined, including age limits, parental leave etc., and Italy in particular has incorporated such a wide definition. But most other member states, including the UK, have left working conditions undefined, which in practice means that employers tend to implement as little equal treatment as possible. The Danish law imposes equal treatment only where men and women actually have the same workplace, against which intervention the Commission has also initiated proceedings. Given the sex segregated labour market, it is not difficult to identify certain occupations which are virtually entirely male or female and a requirement to implement equal treatment only if men and women share the same workplace, defeats the main object of the Directive.

Article 2(1) of the ETD defines equal treatment as no discrimination, directly or indirectly, on grounds of sex or by reference to marital or family status. 'Indirect discrimination' was a new concept in 1976, and many member states did not bother to include it in their implementing legislation. Most member states manage to include some of the definition; for example, the West German law mentions indirect discrimination, but not family or marital status, and the British law does not include family status. Other laws do not specifically mention indirect discrimination, but list certain prohibited practices which are clearly examples of indirect discrimination (as is the case in e.g. Italy and Belgium). The Dutch and Luxembourg laws are the most faithful to the Directive, and were both passed in reaction to infringement proceedings. The Danish law is equally comprehensive and also includes discrimination due to pregnancy. Pregnancy is not specifically mentioned in other countries' legislation, and tends to be a grey area. Only the British courts have ruled on this question, and then not to women's advantage, since the Employment Appeal Tribunal held that a pregnant woman could not be compared with men, and therefore could be discriminated against.[19] Again many national laws do not define vocational training, which also leads to dispute, for example, on how much of the education process is included under vocational training.

Article 2(2) (ETD) allows member states to exclude from equal treatment those occupations where the sex of the worker constitutes a determining factor, but requires a periodic assessment of these exclusions to see 'in the light of social developments' whether they are still valid. A narrow interpretation of this provision seems to be within the spirit of the Directive, as in Belgium, for example, where certain occupations in which sex is a determining factor (such as an actor or model) are excluded. In the same way, jobs in countries where local laws or customs make it expedient to appoint someone of a particular sex are also excluded. Belgium also allows for derogations for the police and armed forces, at the discretion of the government. But this discretion becomes much wider and may be exercised with regard to foreign customs, personal safety, unpleasant working conditions, exposure to violence, organisational requirements, moral factors and certain institutions where man and woman are segregated, for example, in prisons. Most of these exclusions are unacceptable to the Belgian Committee for Women's Employment, and infringement proceedings are pending regarding women's denial of access to training as engineering officers. Belgium has no procedure for revision of exclusions. Most member states, like Belgium, allow for much wider exceptions than the spirit of the Directive would suggest. All countries have some kind of derogation for the police and armed forces, and usually take into account concepts such as morality or decency; for example, Denmark allows an exception for sales staff of ladies' underwear. The Germans allow for exclusions where sex is a determining factor in the eyes of the employer so that this kind of discrimination can never be challenged before a court, as the employer can always allege that, as s/he sees it, sex is a determining factor. There are no objective criteria for the employer to meet in order to be seen to be reasonable.

The British list of derogations is the longest, and includes the exclusion of all firms with fewer than five employees from the force of the legislation. The Commission brought the UK government before the European Court on the latter point, and on the prohibition on male midwives.[20] (UK legislation now includes a provision for review, after consultation with the EOC, and male midwives are not allowed, but there are only two training establishments in the country which accept them. The Commission, however, is not planning further infringement proceedings on this issue.) The usual grounds, not within the spirit of the Directive, of decency and safety are also included.

So all member states have interpreted this provision far more widely than was intended. Not all states have provision for a periodic review, and where that provision exists, it is rarely implemented. In most cases, the grounds for exclusion are extensive, including notions of morality and exposure to violence. The Commission considers that such wide use of derogations has severely limited the movement towards equality, and that the powers under Article 2(2) are being generally abused.

Article 2(3) (ETD) allows for exclusions from the principle of equal treatment for provisions concerning pregnancy and maternity. The Commission considers 'it is clear that this Article should be interpreted strictly and that the provisions taken to grant leave or other advantages for purposes of bringing up children come under Article 5 of the Directive and they should accordingly be applied to workers of both sexes'.[21] Consequently, the exclusions should relate strictly to leave for pregnancy and immediately after child-bearing. Any other time off, such as that taken during a child's illness, is considered the joint responsibility of father and mother, and preference should not be given to the mother. The aim here, of course, is to challenge the assumption that it is women who are exclusively responsible for childcare. Article 2(3) is interpreted in this sense in Belgium, France, the Netherlands, the UK, and Luxembourg. The Italian and West German laws include time off for bringing up children, which the Commission considered an infringement, but the European Court has held that denying a man leave on the adoption of a child (in Italy) is not an infringement of the Directive.[22] In another case, however, it has ruled that parental leave should be given only to working mothers, and not fathers.[23] In the light of this, the Commission has now dropped its action for infringement against West Germany.

Article 2(4) (ETD) also allows for exclusions, this time for 'measures to promote equal opportunity', i.e. positive discrimination. Whilst most member states incorporate this exclusion, very few allow for any form of positive discrimination in their legislation. There are a few measures in practice; for example, in France age restrictions in access to employment were eliminated. Most states allow for some type of special training in male dominated occupations, and some funding for training and retraining courses for women, but very little has been done in this direction. Article 3(2) of the ETD allows for exclusions for protective legislation but imposes obligations on the member states to repeal such legislation 'when the concern for protection which originally inspired them is no longer well founded'. These exclusions, like Article 2(2) above, which allows exclusions where sex is a determining factor in a job, are used by member states to legitimise many otherwise discriminatory practices. Most member states have a list of at least twenty occupations from which women are excluded, or in which they require special conditions and protection. Most common are provisions affecting mining, manual lifting, work with dangerous chemicals, night work, maximum working day and week, and Sunday and holiday work. Very little protective legislation has been repealed by any member state. Italy bans women working at night, but otherwise claims that it has no protective legislation. All the other member states have long lists of areas from which women are excluded. The UK Equal Opportunities Commission argues that these straightforward exclusions should be banned and replaced by a list of fair criteria for dangerous jobs – for example, requiring from men and women certain measurable amounts of physical strength for jobs involving much manual lifting of loads.

The remaining articles in both Directives are concerned with enforcing the principles outlined above. Article 2 of the EPD and Article 6 of the ETD require member states to provide an adequate system of legal redress for employers seeking to pursue equal pay and treatment claims.

Most member states merely include discrimination claims within the scope of their labour courts/industrial tribunals. Some also provide conciliation boards before recourse to the courts (e.g. France and West Germany). Others provide specialist opinions to the court, like the Belgian committee of experts instigated in March 1983, which may be called to give the court advice. In Ireland, Equality Officers, who specialise in discrimination cases, investigate the case and make a recommendation which may be challenged before the Labour Court. Most member states allow for trade unions to bring cases themselves, or to assist their members. In Britain, as has been said, the EOC may assist complainants financially and with legal advice, etc. The Dutch and Irish equality agencies may also advise individuals, but may not provide financial help or representation. The burden of proof in most member states is carried by the complainant (i.e. the woman), and not the employer; although in West Germany, once the complainant has proved that actions occurred which were to her detriment, the employer must then assume the burden of proof and show that this was *not* due to discrimination. In France the burden rests on the employer.

Articles 3 and 4 of the EPD (and Articles 3, 4 and 5 of the ETD) require member states to abolish all discriminatory laws and regulations, and nullify all discriminatory collective agreements. Most countries include provisions stating that contrary laws are automatically null and void, as are discriminatory collective agreements. But, in practice, some benefits are still regulated on discriminatory criteria, for example 'head of household' allowances, which are usually paid to husbands, but not wives. Infringement proceedings on this point were initiated against France and Belgium, both of which then amended their rules, so that the Commission shelved the matter. Luxembourg was taken to the European Court over head of household allowances and was found to be in breach; an amendment to the law has now been passed. The nullity of discriminatory agreements can be decided only on a case-by-case basis, with individuals complaining to the Court about the particular agreement. This means that many discriminatory collective agreements still occur, and although officially null, they are not declared so unless taken before the Court, which rarely happens. Case-by-case analysis also does very little to determine the general factors which make agreements discriminatory, for example the under-rating of certain female jobs. Only systematic analyses, such as have been done in Belgium, France and the Netherlands, of differing types of collective agreements and what makes them discriminatory, can do this.

Article 5 of the EPD (and Article 7 of the ETD) forbids victimisation by employers of employees who complain of discrimination. The articles apply only to dismissal, not to other more subtle forms of victimisation, and only regarding the complainant herself, and not, for example, her colleagues who might support her as witnesses in legal proceedings. Most member states require employers who are found guilty of victimisation to pay compensation and/or reinstate the employee. Both Belgium and Ireland reverse the burden of proof in victimisation cases, requiring the employer to prove that he did not dismiss the employee because of her allegations.

Article 6 of the EPD requires member states to ensure that the principle of equal pay is enforced. An adequate and accessible system of legal redress is one method of enforcement, but that must be backed up by more general measures. Four member states – Belgium, France, Italy and Luxembourg – rely on works inspectorates to enforce the provisions at factory level. Ireland and the Netherlands require an investigation by equality officers before an action may be brought alleging discrimination. All countries, except West Germany, now have some kind of government committee on women's rights (such as the EOC), but only the British, Dutch and Irish agencies have wide powers. All three of them have powers to investigate discriminatory practices in private firms, and to assist complainants in bringing actions. The EOC has the widest powers in terms of assistance, both financial and legal. The Irish Employment Equality Agency (EEA) and the British EOC can both refer cases to the courts themselves. In Denmark and West Germany, such administrative control is considered contrary to legal practice, and both sides of industry, in particular the trade unions, have been entrusted with the task of supervision. In these countries, the equality agencies do little more than provide information.

Article 7 of the EPD (and Article 8 of the ETD) require employees to be informed of their rights under the Directives. Most countries display the law at workplaces, and some annex it to their works regulations. Equality agencies usually publicise the provisions through the media, as do trade unions and employers' organisations. Equality agencies and trade unions have also published leaflets and pamphlets outlining and simplifying the new provisions.

Both Directives have problems of implementation. Women's pay is not equal to that of men, and they are still being refused jobs on the grounds of their sex. These problems come from inadequate drafting of the Directives themselves, but also from the unwillingness of the member states to put the principles of equality into practice.

Neither pay nor working conditions are defined strictly enough in either Directive. Member states are left to decide whether pay includes allowances and benefits, and what types are discriminatory; for example, the whole controversy over head of household allowances arose in this way. The

Commission has clearly stated that allowances are included, but has not said which ones. Does 'training' as specified in the ETD apply merely to apprenticeships, or does it take in the whole range of education? Does 'equality of working conditions' mean the outlawing of sexual harassment? How far is pregnancy included in the scope of the ETD? These are far-reaching questions of interpretation which nobody has yet answered. The provisions of victimisation are too narrow, in that they do not cover witnesses who appear for the woman plaintiff, who may just as easily suffer victimisation by an angry employer. The victimisation clause too, defines victimisation in terms of dismissal only, failing to recognise other, more subtle, responses such as refusal to promote an employee who complains of discrimination. Again, discriminatory collective agreements, whilst officially null and void in all member states, have to be declared as such on an individual case-by-case basis. This means that discriminatory collective agreements are still widespread in most member states. Job offers reveal that stereotyped attitudes still exist, for example, in the use of masculine or feminine words in job descriptions (in all languages except English). Discriminatory job offers are least common, however, in member states where there are guidelines clearly setting out how to draw up a non-discriminatory job offer; where agencies may amend any discriminatory job offers; where advertisers and press are fully informed about the law, and compliance with legal obligations is being monitored. In other words the law is adequate here if backed up by the expertise of equality agencies, the political will to make it work, and the dissemination of information to women themselves. But women are still not adequately informed about their rights. And the agencies are not fulfilling the function of full support to women workers in most countries. They are generally seen merely as information bureaux and funded accordingly. In Britain, Ireland and the Netherlands, equality agencies may conduct investigations into firms where discrimination has been alleged, and the British EOC can support a woman all the way through her case, from financial help, to legal advice, representation, and publicity for her cause. But such a level of support is unique, with the result that few women follow through their initial complaints and discrimination continues.

The member states show a distinct lack of political will towards equality. Luxembourg and West Germany were threatened with proceedings for infringement before they drafted equality laws. And the long list of exclusions for occupations where sex is still a determining factor and the existence of much protective legislation in force in the member states are examples of their desire to limit the force of anti-discrimination laws as much as possible. They typically leave loopholes in the law, and give their enforcement agencies and equality commissions as little power as they dare. Trade unions, too, who are responsible for collective agreements with employers, largely suffer from a lack of political commitment to women. If they decided to take women's rights seriously, discriminatory agreements would disappear overnight, women's skills would no longer be downgraded, the list of exclusions and protective legislation would be limited, and employers would have no choice but to agree. But on the whole, however, they still see women as working for pin-money, or at most supplementary income, and, in times of recession, are content to sacrifice women's jobs for the sake of men's.

The sex segregation of the labour market also hampers women's chances of equality. While women still do very largely 'female' jobs, it is difficult for them to find 'comparable' men when claiming discrimination. Usually the problem is not so much that a man doing 'the same' job is paid more (employers are sufficiently aware of the law no longer to do this blatantly), but that female typing skills, say, are downgraded and paid less compared with men lifting heavy loads. Only a job evaluation study, which allocates fairly grades for different skills, and has no sex bias, can overcome this. In Britain today job evaluation surveys are compulsory if a woman claims sex discrimination, but she may have great difficulty even persuading the tribunal that her claim is valid enough for them to undertake the survey. And there is no guarantee that the survey, if undertaken, will be free from bias – for example, giving more importance to, say, physical strength (generally male) than dexterity (generally female) – as there is no mechanism for questioning the report.

One country, Denmark, may seem to be rather outside the influences of the Directives and to raise the question, dealt with in more detail in Chapter 7, of how far legislation is effective in changing attitudes and practices in the area of sex discrimination. At first glance, Denmark seems to have relatively little legislation on either equal pay or equal treatment. This is perhaps surprising since its record is one of the more progressive on women's equality, and it has the highest figure for women's pay as compared with men's. However, the Danish system works much more on collective agreements than on legislation. Industrial agreements are concluded nationally between the Confederation of Employees (LO) and the Confederation of Employers (DA), and these bind nearly all employers. In 1973, two years before the EPD was passed, they came to an agreement on equal pay, which was as detailed as any legislation would have been. It included an analysis, for example, of the definition of pay and remuneration, which was taken to include rates for piece-work and work-related benefits, etc. This agreement was then backed up by the Law of 4 February 1976, which officially implemented the EPD. The agreement has gaps in it, and is not entirely in accordance with the EPD, but Denmark should probably not be seen as failing to comply with the spirit of the European legislation. Rather it had implemented the principle some time before the EPD was passed, and merely failed to predict exactly, in its collective agreement, the content of the Directive. The 1976 legislation simply deals with matters that could not be concluded in an agreement – for example, the form of legal proceedings should an employer fail to comply. Implementation of equal pay in practice is supervised by the LO, and the Danish government believes it would be 'contrary to Danish practice' to have state supervision. The agreement and enforcement mechanisms effectively act as a conciliation process. If any infringements are found, the trade unions negotiate with employers, and no cases have yet had to come before the Danish courts. The recent judgment of the European Court may change this (see p. 94). There are greater problems when it comes to negotiating equal treatment, as opposed to equal pay, as there are separate trade unions for men and women in most industries, and this affects the identification of discriminatory practices. The Danish government therefore passed legislation, in 1978, governing equal treatment, but most agreements are covered in any case by an implied equality clause in all contracts.

The Social Security Directive

Such is its complexity that this Directive, passed in 1978, was given a very long period (6 years) for implementation. It applies to statutory social security schemes (not occupational schemes) and attempts to abolish inequalities resulting from obviously discriminatory concepts, such as that of head of household or breadwinner. It does not attempt to tackle the inequalities arising out of low pay, or part-time work, although women are particularly adversely affected by those factors as well. It attempts to eliminate differences in the notional incomes attributed to men and women (especially married women); differences in retirement ages; the idea that a married woman is dependent upon her husband and so is covered by his insurance for sickness benefits (when married men are very rarely taken to be covered by their wife's insurance); and the assumption that insurance contributions are held to include a widow's pension, but almost never a widower's.

The first *Defrenne* case in 1971 held that pay did not include social security, and thus social security could not be included in the EPD.[24] Social security schemes are, in any case, so complex, that it seemed more sensible to draft a separate Directive on the subject. Social security was originally going to be included in the ETD, but Barbara Castle, British Minister for Social Services at the time, fought against this, and had it delayed. The Directive covers the working population, including the self-employed, the sick, the unemployed and the retired. It does not include survivors' or family benefits. Although the deadline for implementation was 1984, and the Commission would not have begun to investigate the position of the member states until that time, some of the Ten have already begun to incorporate the Directive into their legislation, and to change their social security schemes accordingly.

Belgium, for example, has moved in the direction of the Directive, by passing three Royal Decrees in 1980, covering the areas of disability, sickness, dependency, unemployment, part-time work and pensions. However, the Commission has noticed that the discriminatory concept of 'head of household' is still present in Belgian social security legislation and has already brought an action for infringement. Other member states consider that, in their cases, discrimination has already been eliminated in most of the areas covered by the Directive, and are examining their laws. The Italian government considers that its social security laws are even less discriminatory than the Directive's own provisions. The UK is considering amendments to its provisions on dependants' benefits, married women's claims for benefits, and family income supplement, etc.

The main problem raised by the Directive, apart from harmonising the complexities of member states' social security schemes, is that of indirect discrimination. Should the entire concept of dependency be considered discriminatory since it is the woman who is usually the dependent spouse? Or should the Commission concentrate on encouraging acceptance of the concept of dependant husbands? Although the Directive is limited to statutory social security schemes, it has potentially a wider scope, and is soon to be supplemented by a Directive on occupational social security schemes. It remains to be seen whether member states will implement the Directive to the limits of this potential.

Greece

Greece is a special case with regard to all the Directives, in that it acceded to the EEC only in 1981, at which time Community law became part of its internal law. The Greek government was required to have implemented the EPD and ETD by the accession date; however, the time limit was implicitly extended to 1982 and the Commission is now preparing a report on the situation in Greece in 1984.

The Greek 1975 Constitution guarantees equal pay for equal work (Article 22(1)) and this has been applied by the courts in a limited sense. The Greek courts are still uncertain, for example, how far the concept of pay includes allowances. The concept of 'head of household' was eliminated in 1983. Different job classifications for men and women in collective agreements have been eliminated, but the less well paid jobs are still mainly held by women, however much job titles may appear non-discriminatory now. Bonuses are mainly paid in jobs performed by men, and there still exist overtly discriminatory collective agreements, providing for different rates of pay for men and women.

Equal treatment is also guaranteed by the Constitution (Article 4(2)), which has a much broader scope than the ETD itself. The principles included a wide definition of both working conditions and recruitment conditions (for example, midwifery excludes men). Quotas, and vacancy notices specifying sex, are still allowed. A law on equality in working conditions and promotion was passed in 1984. The Social Security Directive imposes the same time-limit on Greece as on the other member states, and some elimination of discrimination in social security provisions is already taking place. Workers may claim legal redress through the industrial tribunals, with the aid of trade unions, but there is no equivalent to the EOC. There is, however, a general provision forbidding reprisals against workers who have complained of discrimination.

Greece is perhaps one of the best examples of the difficulty of changing attitudes through legislation. By comparison with other member states, Greece is fairly progressive in giving full legal rights to women workers and in complying with EEC law. Yet the actual situation of the Greek woman worker is amongst the worst in the Community. This difference between theory and practice is common where legislation has been implemented but where attitudes have not caught up.

Time and again in all member states the same problems keep appearing with the three Directives. All involve concepts which have not been sufficiently defined – pay, working conditions, dependency, etc. This lack of clarity makes it very difficult for member states to produce precise, workable and practical laws, even if they wanted to; and given the lack of political commitment to equality which most show, women's pressure groups have their work cut out just to persuade governments to take women seriously. Again, there are insufficient enforcement provisions in the Directives as they stand. They require only that 'effective means are available to take care that the principle is observed'.

The UK's EOC is the women's commission with the widest powers in the EEC, but even its funds are small and it is limited in the number of cases it is able to bring. Elsewhere even these facilities are not available. The new Advisory Committee to the Commission may help here in at least identifying quickly cases of non-compliance with the Directives, so making it more likely that those will be chased up and eliminated.

Member states have in general been reluctant to implement the Directives. They have pursued delaying strategies and incorporated as little as possible into their domestic law, usually only under threat of infringement proceedings. They have tried to narrow the scope as much as possible, and, as we have seen, have made provision for large numbers of exclusions. Trade unions are not sufficiently concerned to encourage governments to take women seriously, and equality agencies are not normally given the power to do so.

Whatever the problems, the three Directives are still more progressive and radical than were, for example, the British Sex Discrimination and Equal Pay legislation on their own. It is clear that, certainly in the mid-1970s, the Commission was more susceptible to feminist pressure than were national governments. Consequently the Directives and pressure from the Commission on the member states have achieved something for women's rights, even if a lack of national political will still limits their full potential.

Legal redress in the member states

For one legal system to try to unite ten different systems is a major challenge. EEC law attempts to do just this; to bring together all these legal frameworks, many of which have fundamentally different structures.

One of the major differences is that between case-law systems, such as the English, and codified systems like the French. Case-law operates in England, Ireland and Greece, and is the method whereby cases decided by higher courts are binding upon lower courts so that judges can 'fill the gaps' left by statute. On the other hand, codified systems, which operate in all other member states, are based on Roman law and do not work on the basis of precedent in the same way. Thus each Court is free to decide the case before it solely on the basis of the relevant legislation. The European Court for that reason does not formally set precedents, although, in Britain especially, and generally in the other member states, its decisions can be influential. It does, however, have ultimate authority on questions of European law, and lower courts are bound to follow it. EEC legislation, like much European national law, is based upon codification principles (such an idea of basic Treaties, on the other hand, is anathema to the English legal system), and the Commission is attempting to codify and harmonise all the disparate laws relating to the workings of the common market within the member states.

There is also the problem of whether fundamental rights are entrenched in the constitution. In Britain, there is no Bill of Rights, Parliament being free to legislate on individual rights, as on everything else, by a simple majority vote. Elsewhere, however, fundamental rights are entrenched in a written constitution and so cannot be overturned by a Parliament. For example, Articles 1–19 of the German Basic Law of 1949 list the individual rights of German citizens which cannot be overturned. The German courts have held that not even EEC law may take precedence over these constitutional rights.[25] The European Court has resolved this by holding that fundamental rights, as defined by the European Convention on Human Rights (ECHR), are part of EEC law.[26] The general accessibility of legal redress is obviously important too. It is crucial to the enforcement of legislation for individual women to pursue their rights against employers, in addition to the Commission's keeping a watching brief. Taking employers to court, and winning, can provide important individual remedies. Discriminatory practices can be outlawed in a particular workplace and the woman concerned can be given compensation. Just as importantly, test cases also provide much needed publicity about unlawful discriminatory operations, which may make other employees and employers think about their own practices. All directives stress the importance of the availability of legal redress, but very little has been done by any of the member states to improve the accessibility of the legal system to women.[27]

First of all, a woman has to know, or at least suspect, that she is being discriminated against. This requires a certain level of knowledge about her rights, which are complex and seldom sufficiently publicised. Although any woman may wonder about the legality of certain practices, few would know how to pursue that concern through a court, or how to obtain professional advice or help with costs. In Britain, the EOC plays a useful role in this regard, in that many women now know to contact the Commission if they think a practice may be discriminatory, and the EOC is empowered to provide legal help, etc. Trade unions are also beginning to take the question of equality seriously, and some provide information and legal advice. But although the EOC or a trade union may give advice, help with costs is strictly limited, in the unions by the feeling that funds must be used to the advantage of *all* members (and not just women), and in the EOC by the relatively small sum set aside for legal purposes. Legal aid in all member states is means-tested to such an extent that virtually anyone in paid employment is excluded. More information about women's rights needs to be provided, as well as advice about where to go for further expert help. Adequate advice agencies need to be established in all member states, with sufficient funds to finance test cases and provide legal representation.

Another problem arises from the method of court proceedings themselves. Courts in the member states are divided into those which operate an inquisitorial system, and those using the adversarial method. Four members use inquisitorial systems (Belgium, France, Italy and Luxembourg) while the other six use adversarial methods. An adversarial method is, as its name suggests, a battle between the two parties. Lawyers normally represent both and have only one aim – to win the case for their client. The judge acts as an adjudicator on both the arguments and the evidence put forward by the parties. There is no formal attempt to establish the 'truth', the judge deciding the case on the basis of the most credible argument backed up by the parties' versions of the evidence. In inquisitorial systems, on the other hand, the judge plays a more active role in seeking out the truth, and the lawyers representing the parties have a duty both to help the judge and to do the best they can for their clients. The judge can order the discovery of documents, compel the attendance of witnesses, etc., as s/he feels necessary in order to establish the truth. In adversarial systems, judges are restricted to the material presented by the parties. Chairpersons of industrial tribunals in Britain tend to adopt a far more investigative role than the judge in a county court, but even then there are limits because the tribunal must not give the appearance of favouring one side rather than the other. Since discrimination law is treated, in Britain, as a form of industrial relations law, an inquisitorial method, aimed at establishing facts, might seem more appropriate here. However, relying upon the judge to ask questions is only effective if the judge has an adequate understanding of discrimination law and practice.

Many member states conduct some kind of preliminary investigation, based on the inquisitorial method, before the case comes to Court. France, Greece and Denmark, for example, all have labour inspectors, who have power to obtain information and enter workplaces. This means that a system for seeking out the 'truth' is established while all parties are later given the chance to challenge such a report in court. In Ireland, Equality Officers deal with such cases at the preliminary stages and have become experienced in the complexity of discrimination law, the difficulties in obtaining evidence, and so on.

Indeed, obtaining sufficient evidence is one of the major hurdles facing any woman complainant. Normally, her employer will have all the relevant documents, detailing her record of employment, etc., which she may need to make her case. Some courts make orders for discovery of documents (which involves bringing such papers to court) and give their inspectors the powers to obtain such information. Since the burden of proving discrimination rests with the woman (unless she is alleging victimisation by dismissal in Belgium or Ireland), those documents may well be crucial to her claim. The reversal of the burden of proof would mean that the employer would be bound to produce the relevant documents in denying that he has practised discrimination. Whilst it may seem unfair to inflict upon an individual who has not complained the initial burden of proving his innocence, he would not find it difficult if he kept a record of all employment decisions, reasons for promotion, employing women or dismissing them, etc., and this is beginning to be done in some countries (e.g. France). The reversal of the burden of proof, combined with a statutory requirement on the keeping of records, would allow for fair discussion of all the relevant documents, while not being unduly harsh on the employer. Nor, in light of all the other difficulties facing women bringing cases against their employers, would it open the floodgates to a host of trivial actions, as is sometimes suggested. A woman has to feel very strongly to bring an action against an employer, with all the deterrents that lie in the way now. Reversal of the burden of proof would simply give her a better chance of making her case.

A woman has to decide whether she wants to be represented by a lawyer, or whether she will conduct the case herself. Most member states allow for either at first instance, although most also insist on lawyers appearing if the case goes to appeal. Conducting the case oneself, possibly with legal advice from a body such as the EOC or a trade union, will certainly keep costs down, and will also probably lend an air of greater informality to the proceedings. But attempts to keep proceedings informal are often blocked by the legalistic approach of some judges. Besides, under an adversarial system one party (especially a richer employer) may often choose to be legally represented, which usually offers the other party no alternative but to do likewise.

If cross-examination is involved in the case, lawyers will usually be needed, since this is a skill of advocacy. Besides, discrimination law is usually extremely complex, and even lawyers, unless specialists, find difficulty in understanding it. Rarely would it be possible for a lay person, then, especially one in full-time employment without the time, to grasp fully all the legal implications. Corcoran quotes an Italian lawyer as saying, 'where the claim is for 250,000 lire or under, representation by a lawyer may not be required. But the law is so complex, I doubt whether it would ever be advisable to be unrepresented.'[28]

The complexity of discrimination law presents problems whether or not a woman is legally represented. Very few lawyers are fully conversant with the provisions of national law, EEC legislation and the cases involved. There are, for example, only a few specialist discrimination lawyers in Britain. Discrimination law is perceived in the UK (and every other member state) as an area of industrial relations law, and thus the hearings take place in industrial tribunals/labour courts. Very few judges sitting in industrial tribunals are fully conversant with discrimination law, since their training is likely to be in labour law. Indirect discrimination in particular presents problems. In such cases a woman has to argue that she had to face a condition with which significantly fewer women than men could comply; that she could not comply with it, and thus suffered. Showing that 'significantly fewer women than men could comply' may require the presentation of complex sociological and/or psychological evidence, and depend upon the judge's own experience. Admitting expert evidence is something courts are very loath to do, since they like to believe that the issues they consider are entirely legal ones. Sociological evidence is admissible elsewhere: in America, for example, and Belgium, where the law allows for experts to be called, although they rarely are. The British government's acceptance, in 1983, of the criterion of 'equal value' as the determinant of equal pay has resulted in the suggestion that industrial tribunals receive expert reports on the value of work which is claimed as 'equal'. These reports, however, cannot be challenged before the court and, accordingly, women may be unwilling to use the procedure. In general women will probably continue to have to rely upon the judge's own experience, as Ms Price had to, in *Price* v. *Civil Service Commission.*[29] In that case, the judge agreed that an upper age limit of twenty-eight years for employment was discriminatory, since, in his experience, most women were childbearing and rearing up to and including that age, whereas men were not, and so significantly fewer women than men could comply with the provision. But that was a relatively simple fact for the judge to grasp out of his own experience. More complex would be, for example, evidence relating to women's education as compared with men's. Besides, the experience of a male judge is likely to be quite removed from that of a female factory worker. One solution to such problems might be specialist courts, which admit discrimination law as a specific branch of the law, and do not see it as part of labour law. Another might be some form of class actions, where the plaintiff brings the action on behalf of a whole class (here, of women workers in a certain category). Such devices might also help to overcome the problem of presenting sociological evidence. (See Chapter 8.)

Any woman alleging discrimination will probably want to call her colleagues as witnesses. But these colleagues will often be reluctant to appear if they are afraid of reprisals by their employer. The law on victimisation needs tightening up to include witnesses, and also to protect the plaintiff, who, although she is currently protected from dismissal, is not shielded from other, more subtle, forms of reprisal.

Even if a woman is successful, against all the odds, in winning her case, she is unlikely to be awarded sufficient compensation. Few complainants bring actions just to prove matters of principle; most believe they have been sufficiently badly treated to require realistic compensation. Without effective remedies, the action won is merely a pyrrhic victory. Most member states allow back pay for two or three years to be awarded in cases of equal pay. In equal treatment cases, the number and scope of remedies is vast. Generally, member states can have an act delared null and void, in accordance with the provisions of the ETD; however few award compensation to the plaintiff. In Germany, only minimum damages are available in recruitment and promotion cases, known as 'the postage stamp awards'. In one case, the equivalent of 60p was awarded to a successful plaintiff who had spent at least £20 on legal advice alone. In other countries, such as Britain, Ireland and France, compensation may be awarded for both economic and non-economic damage, but even there actual awards tend to be low. Yet awarding large sums of money against a defendant is not only a compensation to the plaintiff, but can also act as a deterrent. Remedies, therefore, should fulfil two functions, that of compensating, and that of deterring the discriminator. Unfortunately this almost never happens, and a recent case involving German prison staff held that the European Court has no power over remedies, since Article 6 of the EPD was not directly effective; thus, other than in actions brought direct by the Commission against member states, harmonisation of remedies will be difficult to achieve.[30] Lack of effective remedies could bring the whole legislative commitment to equality into disrepute, as employers realise that although the law prohibits certain practices and the courts uphold the law, their decisions have, in many cases, little or no punitive effect.

All member states except Britain, Ireland and the Netherlands allow for limited penal sanctions (as opposed to civil remedies) against employers, usually after investigation by labour inspectors. Such investigations may overcome some of the problems of proof already mentioned, but tend to be discretionary, making it difficult for individual complainants to enforce the sanctions. Although penal sanctions might operate as a useful deterrent, they offer little remedy to the individual, and so may in the end be even less satisfactory than civil proceedings.

There are also problems with appeal in most member states. In Ireland, Italy and Britain, appeals can be made only on points of law, although in other member states they may be made on questions both of fact and of law. In Ireland, the Labour court is not required to give reasons for its conclusions, and this can make it almost impossible to appeal. Time-limits for appeals are generally shorter than those for claims at first instance, so that a woman is required to seek legal advice and take action fairly promptly. On appeal, too, costs can increase massively, and there may be considerable delay involved. In the UK it can take three to four years for a case to reach the Court of Appeal of the House of Lords. And Appeal judges tend to be more conservative than the often younger first-instance judges. This can be especially difficult in cases of sex discrimination, which often rely, as has been said, on a judge's personal experience. In sum, legal redress, to be really adequate, needs a number of radical reforms. Legal aid could be given a less stringent means test, or equality agencies given more funds to conduct and finance cases. Specialist discrimination courts, with specialist lawyers and judges, are required. Those lawyers and judges would then have more knowledge of the complexities of the law, and basic concepts such as indirect discrimination would not have continually to be explained. Such courts would also be more open to receive sociological evidence, which is often vital in proving indirect discrimination. Adequate legal protection from victimisation needs to be provided, for both complainants and witnesses, and this legal protection should be well publicised, so that women know their rights here too. Adequate remedies must be available, which reflect both compensatory and deterrent aspects. Large compensation sums of back pay would be sufficient in this context. The use of equitable remedies might help prevent such discriminatory practices happening again. Investigations before the case comes to court (such as are made by equality officers in Ireland, for example), would overcome the problem of the complainant having to gather information which is in the hands of her employer. It might also be a quick method of remedying discrimination without always having to go through the expense, delay and difficulties of taking an employer to court. The employer might well remedy the discrimination once an investigation was instigated. Changing the initial burden of proof so that it rests with the employer, rather than the complainant (as happens in the United States), might also help. While this may seem an onerous burden, such a shift, combined with a legal requirement to keep records of women employees, would make it much easier to disprove discrimination if it had genuinely not occurred. The most difficult problem still lies in ensuring that women are aware of their rights and can exercise them effectively. This requires, at least, the development of equality agencies in all member states with powers equivalent to those of the British EOC. The EOC may assist research, financially or otherwise, conduct formal investigations into complaints of discrimination, and assist individuals in bringing cases, with advice, legal representation and finance. The EOC ought to be much better publicised, as a means by which women can find out if they have a claim, and, if so, how to pursue it successfully.

But governments should not rely on equality agencies to do all their work for them. They should institute information campaigns themselves, so that every woman worker knows of her rights. They should be responsible for monitoring and surveying, so that firms with discriminatory practices are identified and suffer the sanctions which exist in law. They should include specific non-discrimination clauses in all contracts they make. That they do none of these things in any systematic way is a measure of the weakness of their commitment in this field, in spite of their formal acceptance of community policy and legislation.

7 European legislation and women workers

> There is no problem here, and the problem that there is not is best solved by voluntary agreement.
> Dipak Nandy

> Women themselves have got to grab the microphone and make their contributions.
> Peter Bottomley, MP

Almost without exception, those interviewed for this enquiry believed that the EEC had been 'a good thing' for women. This opinion was often qualified in one way or another, but it was generally agreed that, at the least, European equality policy had put women on the political agenda in a way which made it difficult for member states to disregard them. As Jane Finlay of the British Equal Opportunities Commission (EOC) puts it, Europe 'changed the climate of opinion' on equality, and although this modification of attitudes may not be so apparent elsewhere, it seems generally true that the constant pressure from Europe, the new legislation, the setting of common standards, have all forced politicians to take women's affairs seriously.

In some cases, however, it is argued that governments do not have to be 'forced' by women MEPs; many Greeks, for example, believe that it is their Socialist government's commitment to equality which has really changed things for women there. As Konstantina Pantazi, the Greek Socialist MEP says: 'Legal frameworks are useless without the political will to enforce them', a point echoed by the French Minister for Women, Yvette Roudy, who suggests that it is only really since the Mitterrand government came to power, committed to a policy of sex equality, that the situation is changing for women in France. Partisan comment aside, there is clearly much in the argument that political will is crucial to the success of any policy, and European decisions on their own cannot make changes in women's lives. Sile de Valera, the Irish MEP who produced the Committee of Enquiry report on women in less-favoured regions, is convinced that European policy has contributed to changes in attitudes in Ireland and that, in many less advanced areas of Europe, EEC directives have, at the least, meant changes coming more quickly than they might otherwise have done.

Even the most advanced countries (with the possible exception of Denmark) tend to think their European involvement has been advantageous, if only in keeping the equality issue before politicians during a difficult period of recession. Johanna Maij-Weggen, the Dutch MEP, sees this as an important gain for women in the Netherlands. While agreeing that not all the existing EEC laws are equally valuable in every member state (some may have had good equal pay or equal treatment legislation in advance of the directives), still, she says, 'We need to tackle these fundamental areas in a concerted way. Although the Equal Pay directive was not so important in the Netherlands, the Social Security one is; in Italy, on the other hand, equal pay was a critical issue.' The Danes are probably more sceptical than anyone else about the value of the Community in the context of equality. Ligestillingsradet, the Danish commission on equality, believes that legislation there is well in advance of the European equivalents, a belief supported by the Danish MEP Bodil Boserup who thinks that, by comparison, the Commission's equality directives 'are thirty years out of date'. A more fundamental objection to Community policy here is also put forward by a Danish woman, Elsie Hammerich, MEP, who points out that the Commission is so male-dominated that it is unsurprising that its 'crisis policy' to deal with unemployment and recession recommends cuts in benefits, nursery facilities, caring agencies etc., all of which hit women very hard. She declined to become involved in the Parliament's Committee of Enquiry because she believed it would give the erroneous impression that something positive was being done for women, when this was not the case. However, even in the Danish case, Hella Degn, who heads Ligestillingsradet, believes that the relatively high priority given to equality policy in the Community has been useful in keeping up the pressure for improvement.

The real worry of the Danes, as of all those with more advanced social climates, is that their development will be retarded rather than advanced by a Community policy which is simply the lowest common denominator. As Barbara Castle, the British ex-Cabinet Minister and now Socialist MEP, says, this is a problem for Community legislation in all areas, not just on women. She points, as an example, to the directive on asbestos use which finally got Council agreement only when its requirements were well below those that Britain would have been applying anyway. And, she adds, 'Governments tend to wait for Community policy to be formulated and do nothing themselves in the meantime.'

This latter problem, the 'immobilism' of governments forever waiting only to respond to European initiatives, is not lost on equality agencies all over Europe. One of the few drawbacks to a general equality policy may be the complacency it engenders in member governments, who are liable therefore to 'tread water'. The phrase is Nuala Fennell's, the Irish Minister for Women, and although she is quick to acknowledge the importance of the three Directives, she deprecates what she calls 'the tendency to think all good things come unasked from the EEC'. Many political women are strongly aware of the need to involve women directly in fighting for their own causes, otherwise the result of EEC policy may simply be to make women passive. There is no political advantage to be gained from sitting with one's hand out. Political complacency, then, may be connected to and reinforced by women's own failure to push for their rights, leaving the EEC's great legislative engine to operate in something of a vacuum.

While the Community may not be liable to do much about the way in which governments often respond to its legislative initiatives in a minimal way and at the last possible moment, it ought perhaps to explore the reasons for the rather negative response to its policy from the European woman in the street. The idea of equal rights has found a response very largely among middle-class, professional women who are less affected by unequal pay and probably less likely to be in receipt of unequal benefits. Yet ironically, for the majority of working women to whom such policies should bring real benefits, equality apparently seems a rather abstract notion, a rarified commodity which 'doesn't really affect me'. A partial solution to this problem may be, as will be suggested later, greater publicity of the Community's policy among those whom it affects most. A revolution may sometimes be started from above, but it can only be sustained by its beneficiaries and it may be important at the moment to convince much greater numbers of women of those practical benefits.

If there is a danger of complacency on the part of the member states and indeed of lack of engagement among women themselves, there is the corresponding danger of the Commission's believing that all problems are solved with the passing of a directive. Generally, of course, this is the beginning rather than the end of the fight to compel member states to conform to new regulations. The Commission has shown a greater awareness of this in the last year or so with the establishment of the network of experts (chaired by Angela Byer of the United Kingdom) to monitor and report on the effects of the Action Programme. The work of such a team is crucial not only in tracking what governments are doing over a wide range of policies which affect women, but in pooling experience and information.

The Women's Bureau at the Commission is over-stretched and under-funded. Run by a devoted staff, it constantly tries to cover as wide an area as possible and to this end may encourage national equality agencies to take on investigations and research projects for it. Resources which they spend on such projects, however, are then not available for other purposes directly related to women's equality, and women in the member states may be the losers. Yet in spite of such reservations about the value of a Europe-wide equality policy, it is clear that most workers in the field, be they politicians, civil servants or leaders of women's organisations, believe that Europe is good news for women and that the Directives and the Action Programme have done much both to establish and to consolidate sex equality as a permanent part of the political agenda.

Can the law change attitudes?

At the back of all Community policy on equality lies the assumption that the law can change the way most people think about the roles of the sexes in society and at work. Only if this is accepted will it be thought worthwhile to try to enforce general standards of equal treatment or to institute positive action programmes. This is not however an uncontested position, and there are always those who argue that the law cannot change deeply ingrained behaviour patterns and social assumptions; you cannot, in other words, legislate against prejudice. This has recently become a common line among jurisprudential writers who, while they may lament the impotence of the law here, feel that the overwhelming evidence is that 'Reformist laws that mandate dramatic new patterns of behaviour often do little to bring that behaviour about.'[1] The writer here, Richard Abel, goes on to say that to look for the effectiveness or otherwise of such laws, 'is to pose a non-problem; we know in advance that they will be largely ineffective'. Even if we do not accept this pessimistic line, it is perhaps salutary to remind ourselves of the limitations of legal sanctions in this area. It may not be the case that legislation is worthless in the context of social change, but it is unlikely to be effective on its own. We do well not to expect too much of it and certainly not to believe that by passing a law, we have thereby solved the problem. As we have seen in tracing the legislation in the member states, discrimination and inequality may well continue to exist even when a law has been passed which would seem to outlaw such things. Many factors limit the law's effectiveness in this area; *inter alia* the attitudes of women themselves, the reactions of employers and trade unions, the complexity of the law itself and the economic situation which may inhibit the claiming of existing rights. Added to all these is what Roger Cotterrell calls the 'barrier to effectiveness posed by the conceptual structure of the law itself'.[2] Discrimination law is extremely complicated, its concepts being based, unlike other areas of legislation, on complex sociological theories. As Cotterrell puts it, 'Anti-discrimination law embodies the ostensible interests of the state in going beyond and behind the equal and universal subject of private law to confront the sociological realities of inequalities between individuals and groups. It "lifts the veil" of equality before the law to disclose real inequalities considered harmful to the social fabric.'[3] Further, anti-discrimination law is distinct from other forms of law in that it does not create special legal categories or special legal capacities. The starting point is the existence of certain prejudices which have then to be shown to be the basis of the treatment afforded to a woman and which have to be distinguished from all other possible grounds (e.g. her abilities) in terms of which she might be judged.

All of these complications, and others, make the operation of sex discrimination legislation difficult and unlikely to be entirely effective. Yet, while accepting this, it is possible to give the law a realistic and important place in the promotion of equality. To begin with, the very existence of a law concentrates interest in the area and makes a statement about government policy and intentions. Industrial and business interests will probably be unwilling to give the impression of being discriminatory and will at least have to make their genuflections in the direction of equality. More importantly, however, the law stands as a permanent reminder of official attitudes which cannot simply be ignored, and this may be crucial in the face of changing political priorities or economic fluctuations. For example, the Conservative government in the UK rates sex equality very low on its list of priorities; as one worker in the field put it, 'The government says there is no problem here, and the problem that there is not is best solved by voluntary agreement.' This attitude would leave women in an even more vulnerable position if the law (in this case notably the Equal Pay Act and the Sex Discrimination Act) did not exist to encapsulate the gains made in a rather more liberal area. This may be even more important where the economic climate is against any change which costs money. Here the existence of a law may at least ensure that minimum standards are enforceable, regardless of cost.

It can also be argued that the law exists not so much to change attitudes, a role for which it is admittedly inadequate, but to change *behaviour*. The employer who is forced to give women the same employment rights as men may still have sexist views but s/he cannot translate them into action in the workplace without risking bringing the law into play. Although it would be nice if women could be assured that employers and others were truly committed in their hearts to equality, this is not necessary. What is essential is that if discriminatory attitudes result in discriminatory behaviour, this can be prosecuted.

Attitudes of law-makers and opinion-formers

One area in which attitudes are important, however, is that of the formation of opinion and the creation of legal structures. The views of governments, civil servants and national and Euro-politicians are clearly instrumental in the implementation of policy and its effects on women themselves. Are those involved at all such levels supportive of existing legislation and creative in their pursuit of new developments? Do they see women's concerns as a priority? Is there, in short, the political will to pursue a realistic equal opportunity programme, to be sustained over economic good times and bad? The answers to these and related questions differ from country to country, time to time, department to department, and indeed from individual to individual.

A common theme, however, as has been said, is the unwillingness of all governments in time of economic uncertainty to spend money. Equality programmes, although they may not be very expensive, do require some reallocation of resources, and when money is tight, this is often made the excuse for doing nothing. Another common feeling among member governments is the dislike of European 'interference' in national legislation. No sovereign body, such as a national parliament, takes kindly to the idea that it must in some areas take orders from another (in this case foreign) body. Governments, too, often need to play to a domestic audience which likes to see its leaders stand up for national rights and interests. Mrs Thatcher was popular in the United Kingdom when she fought for a Community budget reassessment which would be in Britain's favour. Mme Cresson provoked a similar reaction in France when she defended French agricultural policies. In an area such as sex discrimination, where the national lobbies may be less powerful than in the economic or industrial sectors, governments are prone to develop weak political will, take the line of least resistance and comply only minimally with any outstanding Community legislation.

This has tended to be the reaction over the past few years of the British, Dutch, Danish, Belgian and German governments. Where more than minimal compliance is apparent, it is often because some other factor or factors have affected the political will of governments. In France, for example, the Socialist government came to power committed to a programme of equality legislation. Already, before the election, they had shown willing by making an all-out effort to get 25% women on their list of parliamentary candidates. This they achieved, and a higher proportion of women was returned to the National Assembly than ever before. Once in office, the government installed their promised Minister for Women and began drafting far-reaching equality legislation. Bit by bit, this commitment seems to have been eroded, and the bill which is still going through the French Assembly is a much weaker instrument than first envisaged; but the case illustrates well the need for political commitment if advances are to be made.

In Italy, the governing coalitions have been intermittently committed to improving the position of women, and this has been reflected in legislative initiatives, some of which are quite radical. In this case, the commitment of the left-wing parties to the poor has been to the advantage of women. In the case of pay, for example, the government compressed differentials between higher and lower paid, and in so doing increased the pay of women, who were so numerous among the lowest paid. A similar commitment of a Socialist government to the least privileged lies behind the policies on women of the Greek government. The new laws which give Greek women equal rights are framed in terms of EEC aspirations in this area, but give no impression of being merely a formal acknowledgment of the various

Directives. It may also be the case in Greece, as in Ireland, that the policy of the Community serves to back up the commitment of the government and give political muscle to its policies. In Ireland, too, it is always possible to remind those who look on equality policy with antipathy that such measures are part of the total package of Community membership, which is of great overall benefit to a country like Ireland.

In general terms, then, governments will use the regulations, recommendations and directives of the Community to their own ends; where those involve strong equality programmes, they will indicate the Community position to back up their own predilections; where this is not the case, they will simply pursue a minimalist strategy while pointing to this compliance as proof of their being against sin. In Britain, the impression of those who are professionally involved in this area is that the latter position tends to be adopted. At the EOC, the general belief is that the political will at the moment is more or less nil. As one worker said, 'They [the government] constantly buy time . . . they prevaricate and do nothing to initiate change.' In the trade unions, the impression is, perhaps predictably, the same. Although many union officials are sceptical about the value of EEC membership for Britain, most are convinced of its value for women. Says Marie Patterson of the TUC, 'It's the only thing that's pushed the government into some action.'

Civil servants often take their line from their political masters, and so it would not be surprising if governmental attitudes were reflected in their actions and reactions. European civil servants are in a rather different position in that they work to a Council of Ministers which does not necessarily have a united view. In the Social Affairs Directorate General (DG V), support for women's equality runs well ahead of what can reasonably be expected to pass the Council, and there, commitment is greater than in national government departments, where equality policy may be only a small part of overall work. In the national case, civil servants serve a government with a mandate for a programme, only a part of which is in any way related to equal rights. They may well see their job therefore as balancing the needs and aims of that programme as a whole. If they identify conflicts, they see it as their duty to point these out to ministers. As one British civil servant put it, 'The government can't let, say, equal pay policy prejudice its whole package on economic growth, and I can't fail to point out any such incompatibilities.'

On the other hand, there clearly are individuals in virtually all government departments who are personally as well as professionally committed to women's equality. And beyond this, departments will take account of policy suggestions coming out of Europe, if only because they may lead to the formation of directives on which the government will have a view and will want to have a say. At this level too, however, there is often some irritation with Europe. In Britain, for example, its rules and regulations are seen by some civil servants as time-consuming and, as one said, 'Not all policies which look good in Brussels "fit" nationally.'

In view of all this it is probably true to say that the strongest and so far most consistent champion of women's rights is the European Parliament itself. As we have seen, it is not the case that the European Parliament is committed, to a member, to this; a glance at the 1981 or 1984 debates gives the lie to that. But there is strong support among many women and some men for the extension of the policy which began with Article 119 and has so far resulted in sex equality being written into the legal system of every member of the Community.

Effects of equality policy on women workers in the Ten

It is one thing to have equal rights legislation duly promulgated throughout the EEC; it is quite another to ensure that women actually have equality. It is very difficult to quantify the success of the three Directives and the Action Programme in this respect. Clearly one of the criteria would be the extent to which women have made use of their legal rights to claim equal pay, equal treatment and the rest, and some of the cases brought to the courts have been mentioned. But it is also worth looking at the current position on equal pay, equal treatment, social security and the positive action recommendations of the Action Programme in an attempt to elicit how women are doing here and what might be the next step.

Equal pay

If the criterion for the success of the Equal Pay Directive (EPD) were simply the achievement of the same average hourly earnings for women and men, the Directive would be a resounding failure in most countries. In Britain, for example, after a high of around 75% of men's earnings in 1977, the female rate dropped to 73% in 1980.[4] Taking manual workers in manufacturing only, the figures are even more disappointing: from 67% in 1975, a rise of only 2% was recorded by 1982.[5] In the same period, Sweden, which is not of course a member state or subject to the EPD at all, improved its rate for women in manufacturing from 85% to 93%.[6]

It has been suggested earlier that there may be greater benefits to be derived from Community membership by the less advanced countries and it is therefore interesting to see how they have fared in this case. Greece came into the Community too late for any meaningful figures to be available. In Ireland, the picture is much the same as that in the United Kingdom. Starting from the rather lower base of 61% in 1975, EOC figures show that this had risen to 68% by 1982. In Italy, on the other hand, the 1975 figure of 79% had jumped to 87% by 1982. This latter might seem a small triumph for the EPD and its knock-on effect in Italian equality legislation; however it appears that the more important reason for the strength of the Italian position here is, as already mentioned, the centralised wage negotiations which take place there. Socialist administrations have tended to encourage the suppression of wage differentials as a way of helping the low-paid, and as women figure so heavily among the worst paid, they have been pulled up accordingly. It is ironic that, in this case, a measure which was not in any way primarily intended to help women should have had a greater effect in this respect than many which specifically aim to do so.

In the other countries of the Community, using the same figures from the EOC (derived from the ILO Yearbook and the SOEC Bulletin), the changes in percentage rates between 1975 and 1982 are minimal. In France, the Netherlands and Belgium, there was an increase of 2%; in Denmark, the increase was only 1%; in West Germany, the figure was constant through every year of the period; and in Luxembourg, the 1975 rate of 61% had actually dropped to 60% by 1982.

The position on pay may be even more depressing, from the point of view of equality, than those figures suggest. In Britain, the average gross weekly earnings of women are even less in comparison with men when overtime pay is taken into account. Since women do almost no overtime, this pushes their average rate down to under two-thirds that of men. And the legislation which exists in all Community countries seems unable to do much to help. In the UK, claims made under the Equal Pay Act have declined from 1742 in 1976 to fifty-four in 1981. By that year, 71% of the cases were withdrawn by the applicant, the vast majority of them without a settlement. In addition to this, a research project by the London School of Economics (Equal Pay and Opportunity Project) found that, although the EPA and the related Sex Discrimination Act (SDA) had initially had the result of narrowing pay differentials between men and women, as the equality legislation had become known to employers and unions, its effects had been minimised.[7] This was as a result partly of the strategies developed by employers so as to conform only to the letter of the law, and partly of the reluctance of women themselves to use the law to advance their case. This latter has been much commented on and women themselves criticised as unwilling to fight their corner. As in other areas, such as political representation, the argument is sometimes made that women are their own worst enemies, that they do not pursue the opportunities which exist to acquire equality. Yet the reluctance which women apparently show in such contexts is now beginning to be recognised as perfectly rational. To decline to pursue a career in politics, say, when women's success rate is clearly so low, in spite of the considerable necessary investment of time and effort, is quite intelligible. Similarly, if the time and effort, and money, involved in taking claims through the courts is not clearly and frequently rewarded by a successful outcome, it is hardly surprising if women vote with their feet and stay away from litigation. This then becomes, as it has in most Community countries, a declining spiral, with fewer and fewer cases being fought, fewer victories and hence even fewer cases taken to law. And yet it is necessary, as the *Defrenne* cases showed, to push the boundaries of the law, to seek clarification of its meaning in particular cases and so to build up some precedents. Some of the ways in which this might be encouraged are dealt with in the next chapter. All the same, changes in the operation of the law are not the whole answer to the problem of unequal pay. As Mrs Gaiotti de Biase showed in her report for the Committee of Enquiry into the Situation of Women in Europe, proceedings brought by the Commission have resulted in modifications in national legislation in all member states one way or another; yet, as she says, 'equal pay has not been achieved in any of these countries'.[8] In a sense, the problem is less one of achieving *equal pay* for women, than of getting them out of the predominately low-paid category. Women work very largely in women's areas, where direct comparability with men is not possible. These female areas are traditionally low-paid, often because employers use female labour part-time, which fits in with most women's domestic arrangements, and pay a lower rate accordingly. Women, it is believed, make only a small contribution to most family incomes, and therefore a 'breadwinner' wage is not necessary either economically or morally. This, of course, even if it were just, fails to take account of the extent to which women's wages are crucial to family incomes, particularly in a situation of high unemployment. It also fails to acknowledge the decline of the traditional two-parent family. Whether through divorce or the decision not to marry, many women (nearly a million in Britain alone) are bringing up a family for which they are the sole providers.

While it is worth having legislation which sets out the aspiration of equal pay, it may be that it has achieved in most countries all that it can at the moment, and that what should now be tackled more rigorously, are the areas of part-time work and protective legislation which discourage women from doing more lucrative overtime shifts. In both of these areas, the Community is ahead of national legislation with its statements in the Action Programme and its draft directive on part-time work (now likely to be limited to a recommendation). In other words, it is the indirect discrimination against women which has to be tackled next. The EPD has not been a great direct success. It has not achieved 'equal pay for work of equal value'. Yet it has progressively opened women's eyes to the factors which underlie their unequal pay, and allowed the possibility of these being tackled in their turn. Without the EPD, it is unlikely that the debate would have been moved along in this way. This is not to sink into complacency; the application of the principle of equal treatment and the identification and eradication of indirect discrimination are huge risks. It is rather to underline the argument of Mrs Gaiotti de Biase, that the Community directives in this area, and in particular the EPD, are simply stages on the way to equality. 'To prevent this stage from becoming a stopping place, action is needed on two fronts: to reform production processes . . . and encourage lasting and profound changes in the prevailing attitudes, primarily through positive action.'[9]

Equal treatment

As in the case of equal pay, looking at the legal take-up on equal treatment rights does not make heartening reading. Little use has been made of the equal treatment laws which now exist in all member countries. In Britain, for example, there has been a marginal increase in cases brought under the Sex Discrimination Act (SDA) since 1977 when 229 applications were made, but in 1981 the figure was still only 256.[10] More worrying still is the low success rate of complainants. Professor Hepple of University College, London, calculates that only about two in every ten women who take their cases to law win them after a tribunal hearing, and although in the county courts the success rate is about three in ten, in the five years 1976–80 there were only thirty-four such cases begun.

As Hepple suggests, this low success rate reinforces the tendency not to make use of the law. As he shows, people 'are unlikely to go to court if past experience shows there is little prospect of success. In turn, the lack of use of the law makes it very difficult for the courts . . . to develop their expertise in this highly complex and unfamiliar field.'[11] It is rather more difficult to find in the case of equal treatment than in that of equal pay, criteria in terms of which the usefulness of the European directive can be judged. At this level, the EPD's efficacy can simply be looked at as an aid or otherwise to the achievement of pay parity. Equal treatment, on the other hand, is by its nature a much more diffuse and complicated concept. It may be useful, however, to find a more or less objective standard which could be taken to represent the influence of equal treatment policy in the Community as a whole. To this end, trends in women's unemployment can be traced over the past few years to see how women have fared in a period of recession when the equality legislation might be needed more than ever.

Between 1979 and 1982, the number of registered unemployed in the Community rose from just over six million to slightly under eleven million. Of these figures, women made up nearly $2\frac{3}{4}$ million in 1979 and $4\frac{1}{2}$ million by 1982.[12] Looking at the figures country by country, it emerges that women's

Table 2. *Women as percentage of total unemployed*

%	Germany	France	Italy	Netherlands	Belgium	Luxembourg	UK	Ireland	Denmark	Greece	All
1979	52.4	53.1	43.9	37.0	62.4	49.3	30.7	22.9	49.3	41.1	44.8
1982	44.3	50.0	48.6	30.6	55.8	46.5	28.9	24.1	42.9	38.9	41.4

Source: Women of Europe, Supplement no. 10, *Women in Statistics* (1984).

unemployment, as a percentage of the total, falls in all but two cases (Italy and Ireland). (See table 2.)

This might appear to be good evidence for the efficacy of the ETD and its associated legislation, which could be seen as protecting women from the worst ravages of the recession. However, when one looks at women as a proportion of the workforce and then at their percentage unemployment, the position is less hopeful. In 1977, women made up 35.9% of the working population in the Community. In the same year, they were 41.8% of registered unemployed. The story is much the same for every recorded year since; women's percentage share of the workforce climbs slowly from 36.1% in 1978 to 36.8% in 1980, while over the same period, their share of the unemployment total jumped from 42.8% to almost 45%.[13] Women, then, are disproportionately represented among the unemployed. And the extent of this is probably not even fully reflected in the figures, which include for example the UK, where married women are often not 'registered unemployed' although they may be out of work. If any jobs are being protected at all, they are men's and not women's, and apparently the equal treatment legislation cannot prevent this happening.

What this extrapolation cannot take account of, however, is what would have happened if the ETD and its associated legislation had not been in force at all. It may not have been able to stop women coming off badly in the fight for jobs during the slump, but it is possible to argue that without the legal framework they might have done even worse. All Community states claim to have done something to ensure women a greater chance on the job market, but, as ever, these efforts differ markedly in scope and effectiveness from place to place. In Belgium, where women make up over 53% of the unemployed while being only 37% of the working population (1982 figures), little is done specifically for them.[14] A community service programme taking in the long-term unemployed has been in operation since 1980, and it is claimed that most of those involved in this are women. There are also some moves to improve the counselling and training of women and to encourage them into non-traditional areas. The European Social Fund helps finance several pilot schemes in such areas. In Denmark, women's share of unemployment, 44%, is virtually identical to their participation in the workforce. Again, some provision is made for training in non-traditional occupations, and women's special needs are taken into account in the encouragement of childcare facilities and of part-time training to fit in with domestic responsibilities. One innovation since 1981 has been the appointment of equality advisers working in placement offices to encourage women to claim their rights and to try to influence the attitudes of employers and of those who give vocational guidance.

In France, women make up almost 50% of the unemployed but only 39% of the working population. There has been some recognition by the French government of the problems which women have in gaining equal access to employment, and efforts have been made to deal with indirect discrimination in such things as age limits in the civil service. It is now recognised that a low age limit for recruitment to certain grades may discriminate against women who have taken time off to have children. These limits have therefore been raised to take account of family situation. Again, the French have tried to encourage women into the workforce by getting rid of what might be limiting conditions attached to some jobs (for example a restriction on the weight of mail bags to be handled by women), and by relaxing protective legislation prohibiting women from working certain shifts. Training in particular is encouraged by the Ministry for Women's Rights, which gives subsidies to adapt premises for use by both sexes where only men have operated before, and provides for childcare services.

In Germany, women account for 43% of unemployed people and 38% of the working population. There exist, however, almost no measures specifically to aid women, the Federal government's manpower policy programme being directed at everyone in the regions most severely affected by unemployment. There are some schemes for women re-entering the workforce, and additional help is available to increase the proportion of women enrolling in training courses, but that is all.

In Greece, women are 30% of the working population but 41% of the unemployed. The 1975 Constitution establishes equality of rights, in the family and at work, between men and women, but few specific measures have as yet been introduced to back this up. Women are now being encouraged to train in traditionally male sectors and child-minding facilities are being set up, although, as elsewhere, not on anything like a national scale. Awareness of women's special vulnerability as a result of childbearing and childcare is apparent in, for example, the motherhood law (1082/1980) which forbids dismissal on grounds of pregnancy. This was further strengthened by new equality legislation (passed in January 1984) to outlaw discrimination, direct or indirect, on grounds of sex or family status.

In Ireland, although women only make up just under 25% of the unemployed, they are also a smaller proportion of the workforce than elsewhere (27%). Ireland has the advantage of a strong equal opportunities body in the Employment Equality Agency (EEA) which is responsible for pursuing and monitoring measures to implement the law in this area. In addition to training schemes to help women into the workforce, a 40% quota for women has been put on places at training centres teaching non-traditional occupations. The EEA has also taken very seriously its role in providing information about rights to Irish women, and gives guidelines to employers instigating equality programmes. The 1977 Employment Equality Act, which set up the EEA, also resulted in the removal of the ban on night work for women and allowed for positive action in occupational areas where women are under-represented.

In Italy, where women are 48% of the unemployed but only 33% of the working population, the law of 1977 (903/77) outlaws discrimination and enshrines the principle of equal treatment. Beyond this, however, measures to achieve equality for working women are few. Action has been taken to recruit women into non-traditional, and specifically manual, occupations, and protective legislation has been repealed to allow women to work night shifts. A certain amount of training through the trades unions has been specifically aimed at women but much remains to be done.

In Luxembourg, women make up 46% of the unemployed and just under 30% of the workforce. In 1980, a committee on female unemployment was set up which recommended some special training facilities for women, but most training still applies to both sexes. The only limited initiative the government has taken is to support schemes for informing parents, teachers and girls about widening vocational choices.

The Netherlands can boast a smaller percentage of women among the unemployed (32%) than in the working population as a whole (33%). Training and retraining measures are high on the Dutch list of priorities for women, as is the creation of temporary jobs to give women work experience. In addition to the usual public sector schemes to open employment to more women, those with the same qualifications as men are now given preference in recruitment to the civil service.

In Britain, too, the official figures show women as a lower proportion of the unemployed (28%), than of the working population (39%). The unemployment figure is often questioned as it is thought to under-represent the number of women who would like work but do not appear in the official statistics. Britain, like Ireland, has an effective equality agency in the EOC, which has statutory powers of enforcement under the Sex Discrimination Act of 1975. The Act also allows for the setting up of training schemes specifically for women. The Training Opportunities Schemes (TOPS) and the Wider Opportunities for Women (WOW) are designed to help women acquire new skills and vocational training. The EOC's 1984 project, Women into Science and Engineering (WISE), promoted information and awareness in areas not traditionally seen as female ones. Rather than simply endorsing the idea of equal treatment, the EOC and the Trades Union Congress have begun to develop draft codes of practice on the ending of discriminatory activity and the promotion of, for example, job evaluation schemes and positive action programmes.

Many of the measures adopted by member states to tackle women's unemployment are clearly inadequate, and the directive on Equal Treatment (ETD) does little to change this. As a recent Commission report says, most of the policies of member states in this area should 'be regarded as social measures, rather than as actions which tackle the root causes of women's unemployment'.[15] The resources dedicated to such policies are minimal, financial incentives to employers for the recruitment of women are few, and job training schemes are very often in traditional female areas, thus reinforcing job segregation. Yet some measures have been useful and the experience of countries with some success, however limited, may be of value to others. In her report to the Enquiry into the Situation of Women in Europe, Mrs Gaiotti de Biase suggests that the existence of equality commissions, such as the British and the Irish, are particularly useful here.[16] It is important that such bodies have wide terms of reference and powers, and although some kind of equal opportunities agency has been set up in all the member states (except Germany) not all have great importance. In Italy, for example, although there is a national committee responsible for equal treatment, its actual powers are minimal. A law designed to set up a body with teeth was presented to the Assembly in 1983, but it lapsed without getting through at the end of the legislative term.

The specific measures which seem most valuable in reducing women's unemployment are those which involve some kind of positive action, to enrol women in non-traditional training schemes, for example, or to provide special facilities (e.g. for childcare, etc.) to encourage women to take up opportunities. But in general, the existence of the first two directives has not been enough to stop women faring worse than men in the recession, much less ensure them genuine equal pay or equal treatment.

Social security

The third Directive, on social security, only came into effect at the end of 1984, and it is therefore impossible yet to assess its full effects. As Mrs Van den Heuvel's report to the European Parliament's Enquiry on Women shows, there is enormous diversity in social security legislation in the various countries.[17] Although there have been some improvements in existing legislation as it affects women's claim to benefits, in many cases the recession has meant that governments have been looking for ways of cutting their spending on social security, rather than aiming to extend it. In Belgium, for example, cuts in unemployment benefits have hit women, who now get less money if they are co-habiting; maternity benefits are paid the month after a child is born instead of, as hitherto, in the same month; family allowances, which used to be raised at ages ten and fourteen, are now raised at twelve and sixteen. All of these modifications affect women more than men, and all of them change the base from which 'equality' is measured. In France, too, action has been taken to decrease unemployment benefits, and in Holland the Minister of Finance is quoted as saying that equal treatment for women in 'individualising' benefits (i.e. paying all benefits as to individuals without reference to co-habitation or family status) would simply cost too much. In the UK the measures introduced in November 1983 under the Social Security Directive are mainly cosmetic. They do not cover all benefits and they in no way challenge the assumption that women are the dependents of men.

The general picture in Europe is of governments trying to find ways of cutting spiralling benefit bills. In this context, not only are they unwilling (and would indeed say, in many cases, unable) to give women access to greater benefits, but they are looking to find ways of limiting the commitments they already have.

The Community's equality policy in the Treaty of Rome is based not only on the pursuit of equal treatment in the labour market, but on the assumption of continuous improvement in social and economic conditions for everyone. In the fifties, sixties and even early seventies, continuous growth must have seemed very likely if not inevitable, and then equality for women meant parity with this ever-improving male condition. In the eighties, however, the question is being asked whether equality has lost much of its appeal in a situation of no growth. In the case of social security benefits, 'equality' may end up by meaning being equalised down to where economic conditions have taken male benefits. There is the related problem that when, as in the case of the Social Security Directive, a long implementation period is allowed and in that time material conditions decline, the 'equality' that was envisaged in the original order will probably no longer be possible as standards and benefits are eroded bit by bit. Yet any attempt to come to terms with this problem by specifying, at the beginning of the exercise, minimum standards which cannot be dropped, is immediately rejected by member governments, who say that they could not commit themselves for the future in this way. In spite of this, there has been a little movement in women's favour in the social security area. For example, in both Ireland and Denmark, the length of maternity leave has been extended, while in Greece, women were given the right as from January 1983 to twelve weeks' maternity leave and benefits, and in Germany (Law 20–12/82) men's and women's rates of contribution to the state pension scheme were harmonised.

The Action Programme

The new Community Action Programme on the promotion of equal opportunities for women runs from 1982 to 1985 and it is not until after the latter date that its achievements will be able fully to be assessed. However, it is possible to see to what extent the member states have so far moved along the paths suggested by the Programme's aims. An interim report on progress produced by the Commission in January 1984 is pessimistic.[18] As far as the first part of the Programme's intention to extend individual rights is concerned, it says, 'very few legislative provisions have really helped to implement the new Action Programme'. Indeed almost the only piece of legislation the report can find in this category is the French law of 1983 (Art. L 123) amending the Labour and Penal codes to prohibit all forms of discrimination in employment. As well as requiring equal treatment, this law also introduces positive action to effect equal opportunities for women. Beyond this, however, the report can point only to the establishment of equal opportunity agencies in the Netherlands, Italy and France, and to a very few other modifications to existing equality legislation.

The reaction of member governments to the Action Programme has been predictably cool. When most states wait until the last possible moment to implement even the mandatory directives of the Commission, it is unsurprising that they are even less inclined to rush to comply with the suggestions of the Programme. All claim that, in the present economic climate, whatever their commitment to equality, they are unable to find more money for further changes. This is hardly a convincing line at the best of times but is particularly feeble in the light of the original Council agreement to promote equality whatever the economic situation and to use positive action to achieve it. It was the apparent existence of such 'political support' which gave heart to Mme Quintin, head of the Commission's Women's Bureau, when she announced the Programme in 1982;[19] it is the evaporation of such support which puts it in jeopardy now.

As far as the second aim of the Programme, that of positive action, is concerned, there has been, at least on the face of it, rather more movement. In the areas of vocational guidance and training, employment and promotion (particularly in the public sector), the encouragement of sharing of domestic responsibilities and changes in attitudes, governments have shown some willingness to promote women's rights. Girls are everywhere in Europe being encouraged to follow technical courses. The British EOC's

WISE initiative has already been mentioned, and the German Federal Labour Office has developed new teaching methods to this end. The French, too, have introduced quotas (up to 25% women) on courses arranged by the National Training Service. Again, women are everywhere being encouraged to go into non-traditional areas, for example metallurgy in Germany and Denmark, banking in Britain and the electrical industry in Belgium. More flexible kinds of work units are also being explored: for example, the Irish government are backing a research scheme on co-operatives. In the Netherlands and in Britain, efforts are beginning to be made to bring women back into the job market after interruptions to careers for family reasons. In Britain, the National Westminster Bank has been particularly active in this sphere.

In an attempt to desegregate the labour market and bring women out of the low-paid, women-only jobs which they largely have, many member states are making special efforts to advise women of opportunities in wider areas. In the UK, training in equality counselling is available for careers officers, and equal treatment practices are outlined in the Department of Employment's advisory booklet. In Germany, training is available to all placement staff, and in Denmark special counsellors have been appointed since 1981 to every labour exchange. Their job is to develop guidance methods which get away from the attitudes which traditionally regard certain kinds of work as male or female. Also, in some regions of the country, counsellors have developed groups to support women who wish to train in non-traditional areas. It is rather too early to say what effect this new form of action will have, but it is an interesting attempt to think through the problem of job segregation and tackle it at source.

In several countries, too, efforts have been made to overcome the reticence of employers to organise training specially for women. In the UK, the Department of Employment stress that it is now usually a simple matter to acquire the dispensation necessary to run single-sex training schemes, and the Engineering Industrial Training Board (EITB) gives financial support to employers who take on women trainees. In Denmark, too, the job creation programme for 18–25 year olds allows for positive action on behalf of women.

It is clear from the report of Mrs Macciocci to the Enquiry into the Situation of Women that women are grossly under-represented in all decision-making areas.[20] Efforts have been made in some countries to counteract this: for example, in the UK, the Joint Review Group composed of employers and trades unions has been examining the position of women in public sector jobs. In France, too, a government circular of January 1983 requires that ministers encourage applications from women and report on the success of their positive action to assess its effectiveness. In order to get more women into positions of responsibility, the Dutch have instigated a positive action programme to increase the numbers of women mayors and senior civil servants.

The small number of women on public bodies which have a strong influence on the formation of public policy is recognised in many countries now, and some efforts are being made to correct this imbalance.[21] In Britain, the EOC has recommended advertising public appointments rather than perpetuating the present system, which tends to proceed on the basis of personal recommendation and the 'old boy network'. In Ireland, the National Federation of Business and Professional Women's Clubs has instigated a Women's Talent Bank to provide names of suitably qualified women for public appointments. The same kind of initiative has been started in the UK by the Fawcett Society, committed to women's equal representation in public life for over a hundred years, which recommends suitable women to the appropriate appointing bodies. Whether governments agree with positive action as a strategy or not, it is clearly a major point of debate among those concerned with women's advancement. At a conference in Athens in September 1983, the whole question of a Commission directive on positive action was discussed. A study by Professor Vogel-Polsky recommended legislation in this area, but the important question remained whether this should be mandatory (i.e. a directive) or simply a recommendation for member states.[22] Members of the European Parliament and of the European Trades Union Confederation (ETUC) favoured a directive, but Ivor Richard, Commissioner for Employment and Social Affairs, suggested instead drawing up a 'code of good practice', probably in the form of a recommendation, to be used as a guideline by member states. Governments, he seemed to be saying, are not ready to support positive measures, and without the political will and commitment, the mere statement of aspirations would be valueless.

Positive action has however been pursued in some countries in a number of industries. Banks, for example, in the UK, Belgium and France have made strenuous efforts to reorganise traditional structures to take account of women's needs. At Thames Television, in the UK, a Positive Action Committee was set up to organise and monitor help for women within the institution. Clearly the results of this kind of activity need to be studied and its more general value assessed. One area in which this experiment could easily take place is in the Commission itself, where the Action Programme promised measures to bring about greater equality between men and women within its own personnel. There has only ever been one woman Foreign Minister in the Council of Ministers (Colette Flesch); no woman has been a European Commissioner, judge or auditor; and in 1983, out of eighty-two staff in the highest levels of the Directorates only four were women. In reply to a Parliamentary question, the Commission has said that women are mostly employed as secretaries and clerical staff, and least in the administrative grades, where they totalled only 230 compared with 2,465 men.[23] Mr Burke, Commissioner in charge of staff policy, has acknowledged the problem here and has appointed (January 1984) an official to head the equal opportunities committee and begin 'the long, long task of changing attitudes' in the Commission.[24]

The effects of Community action, then, are rather hard to determine, although the picture is not one of unmitigated gloom. It may be difficult to point to quantifiable gains but the line has in many cases been held in recessionary conditions and, more positively, the debate has been moved on. It is significant that governments are no longer seriously questioning women's right to be in the workforce but asking how they can most successfully be given an equal chance: positive action is no longer dismissed as the demand of a few radical feminists but is approached in terms of whether it should be pursued mandatorily or by voluntary agreement: indirect discrimination is seen as a reality, even if its definition presents some difficulties in law and politics. Most importantly, perhaps, these areas of positive action and indirect discrimination have emerged as the next significant, if still problematic, issues to be tackled in the sphere of sex equality. It is extremely unlikely that without the constant pressure from the European Community, things would have come thus far.

8 Women of Europe: the future

> Parental leave would provide for institutionalised absenteeism.
>
> UNICE (The Union of European Employers)

> The directive would threaten the competitiveness of industry by disrupting working patterns.
>
> CBI (The Confederation of British Industry) reaction to the draft directive on parental leave

> The directive's value lies precisely in the fact that it would cut down the disruption of working patterns suffered by women.
>
> Angela Phillips, writing in *The Guardian*

In the end, then, do women make a difference in politics? As we saw in Chapter 4, they certainly do not, in the European case, devote themselves exclusively to women's interests or raise only equality issues in the Parliament. Indeed it would be surprising if they did, as they all represent constituents whose interests they have to support before they can expect to be re-elected. They are, in this respect, politicians first and women only incidentally. But their concerted perception of themselves as women, with particular experience and concerns, has greatly affected the emphasis of European politics. As is clearly apparent from the analysis of the women's interventions (Chapter 4), they are just as concerned, if not more so, with constituency issues or their specialist interests, as with specifically women's issues. Yet the increased preoccupation with women and equality since the elected Parliament of 1979, with its large influx of female MEPs, is still striking. For example, the number of written questions relating to women went up from twelve in 1978 to forty-five in 1979. To this extent, women do make a difference. They made a difference, too, in the level and extent of equality legislation passed by the Commission during the 1980s. True, the three Directives were already on the statute books before 1979, but it is very likely that there would have been little or no follow-up in the form of the Action Programme or draft directives if the Women's Committee, in its various manifestations, had not been the focus of concerted effort for the extension of the original legislation. This is not at all to say that other factors were not significant in the legislative activity of the late seventies and early eighties. The time, for example, was propitious: there was still a hangover from the Seventies fashion for women's rights, briefly flavour of the month with many European politicians, while the recession had not yet begun to cut into expenditure programmes. Again, it is arguable that committed individuals in DG V (the Social Affairs Directorate) were at least as important to the equality programme as the Women's Committee. Ivor Richard himself and several members of his cabinet were continuously supportive of the Action Programme and the draft directives, and it is probable that, without their work, agitation from the Parliament would have been in vain. At the least, however, having that constant pressure applied to the Commission by the women in Parliament was undoubtedly politically helpful to DG V, which was able to point to this as evidence of the strong and enduring feeling in the Parliament about women's affairs.

Just as the commitment of some individuals was important to the European equality programme, so too was the desire of some governments to improve the position of their women nationals, and this, it could be claimed, had more influence on the legislation than any agitation in the European Parliament. However, without the framework provided by the Community, it is likely that governments such as the Greek or the Irish would at least have taken very much longer to introduce legislation. People agitating for change in those societies could, as it was, point to the European initiatives and use them as a focus in their own campaigns.

Finally, it is sometimes said that the women in the Parliament have not been so important to developments in the field of equality as the sustained pressure and expertise of national equality agencies (like the EOC) and the specialist advisory committees and networks. Indeed, equality agencies have done what they can to publicise women's rights and to help individual women to pursue their claims through the courts. But they are not strong in most member states, and their resources are desperately inadequate. The advisory committees, too, although they are important in monitoring legislation and providing expert experience, are of limited value unless they have political support. Without this, their engines are idling and all that intellectual horsepower will be unable to move things along.

It is clearly not the case, then, that women, on their own, make a difference. All sorts of factors affect the seriousness of the attempt to make equality a reality: the time, the economic conditions, the political will, the individual actors among governments and their advisers – and the women in politics. More women there are certainly not a sufficient condition of women's being more accounted politically; yet perhaps they are a necessary one: for in politics, nobody fights other people's battles; nothing is an issue until it has been shown to be electorally significant. If women do not fight for the rights of other women, more than one female MEP said, who will? To have more women in such positions of power is to have more chance of keeping the whole area of sex equality in the foreground politically, in good times and in bad. Perhaps, ironically, it is even more important to have women there in significant numbers when recession and slump spell the end of governmental generosity in equality programmes, when such concerns are easily dismissable as frivolous in comparison to unemployment, say. In the halcyon days of the early seventies, when resources were plentiful, equality seemed easy and women had many friends. At that time, the women in Parliament could be looked on as just another area of support for a well-subscribed cause. In the darker times ahead, it may be that that support becomes the central prop maintaining interest in what are now much less popular issues. In this context, women may well make a difference.

Before attempting to identify the areas of policy which need to be tackled now, or the wider strategies which might be considered by women in the European Parliament in the pursuit of equal treatment, it is worth looking briefly at the main factors which militate against change. Much of this has emerged in the previous discussion but it is helpful to bring it together at this point.

The first and fundamental problem here is women's own ignorance of the law. They are, in effect, often unaware of their due. Great debates about the value of class action or the importance of specialised courts are hardly to the point if women don't even know what their legal rights are under the present arrangements. The existing law will not be having an impact with the people it was designed to help. It is middle-class women, often in jobs where discrimination is less likely to bite, who are most inclined to be strongly feminist or, at any rate, to know what the law provides. Many of the women most vulnerable to discriminatory treatment, those in low paid, part-time jobs for example, are not aware of the protection the law gives. Education and publicity are still a vital part of any equality programme, and on this the EP can help. Even if women are aware of some legal protection, they are often afraid that if they challenge an employer, they will have to face reprisals which, in a recession, may mean loss of irreplaceable work. This fear must be reinforced by the very low success rate, already mentioned, of those bringing discrimination cases.

There is fear too on the parts of governments and employers at what they see as the ever-widening scope of European equality legislation. Their fear is two-fold: of loss of freedom and of expense. Governments fear, and often resent, encroachments on their sovereignty, and, in the case of equality law, most member states have been taken by Community policy far beyond what they would have done if left to their own initiative. Employers too often deeply dislike what they take to be the imposition of legal structures between themselves and their employees. Even if these arguments are sometimes rather disingenuous, masking simple dislike of changes in the comfortable status quo, the results are equally debilitating for women's rights. They are manifested in governments' lack of political will and minimal compliance, and in employers' strategies which ensure that the effects of the law are strictly limited.

An unwillingness to spend money in this area is another reaction common to both governments and employers, and in a recession this is often given explicitly as the reason for opposition to policies designed to protect women. These will, it is sometimes claimed, 'price women out of the market' and thus be to their ultimate disadvantage. Alternatively, governments may claim, as the French, Belgian and Dutch have all done on occasions recently, that they simply cannot afford to pursue even those policies to which they had seemed committed. In the same spirit, the British Conservatives in the European Parliament agreed to support the Report of the Committee of Enquiry into the Situation of Women in Europe only if it was recognised that these recommendations could not be pursued except in a healthier economic climate.

Recession has brought other problems too for women. The Treaty of Rome was based on the assumption not only that equality could be achieved but that prosperity would continue and increase. Policies are often introduced, especially in the field of sex equality, with long lead times so that governments can realistically bring existing arrangements into line with new requirements. What happens, however, if, during the implementation period, conditions deteriorate so that equality may mean 'equalising down'? In Belgium and the Netherlands, for example, it is claimed that new discriminatory measures have recently been introduced (for example, reducing unemployment benefits for all who are not head of a household, a move which is clearly at least indirectly discriminatory against women).[1] Although the Commission has been taking legal action since 1983 against the member states involved, this is still not resolved, in spite of the fact that the Belgian government's 1984 austerity programme included more cuts in social security benefits.

If recession is a major problem, in a number of ways, for the cause of sex equality, an even more persistent one is complacency. The general assumption that 'things are getting better' for women can inhibit the serious attempt to look for the real causes of discrimination and do something about them. Existing legislation is pointed to as proof that things have been done, and suggestions that more may be needed are looked upon with suspicion as the outlandish demands of radical feminists. The belief that equality will come of its own accord, given time and the basic legislative framework already in existence, can be combatted in two ways. Firstly, by showing empirically that in specific areas, unemployment for example, women are becoming worse and not better off. Secondly, by convincing those who take this line that progress in such areas is seldom a once-for-all affair. As we come to understand more of the social, political and legal springs of inequality, so our preoccupations with particular structures, institutions or attitudes change. The development of the idea of indirect discrimination is a case in point. Laws which made direct discrimination illegal could not deal with the common case where the vast majority of those affected by a particular, apparently non-discriminatory, action were women. When this situation is recognised, the campaign has to move on to tackle it. Similarly, we should not allow suggestions for such things as specialised courts, changes in the rules on the burden of proof, and positive discrimination programmes, to be dismissed as the endless aspirations of those who can never be satisfied. Rather, they must be presented as what they are, the demands which come out of experience as our understanding of the problem, and indeed the problem itself, changes.

Finally, the identification of the specific policies to be pursued or structures to be modified at this particular stage becomes crucial if real advances are to be made. All the member states of the Community are theoretically against discrimination, and they have legislation to prove it. This is, in most cases however, simply the political equivalent of being against sin. Governments need to be constantly reminded that if they claim to will the end, they must will, and deliver, also the means. It is the job of the Commission, the Parliament and national equality agencies persistently to identify such means.

In this context, then, which 'means' need to be tackled now? There seem to be three main areas: the draft directives put forward in the Action Programme; some of the reports of the Committee of Enquiry into the Situation of Women in Europe; and the development of the idea of indirect discrimination as it has emerged out of the practice of the existing legislation.

Action Programme (draft directives)

When, in 1982, the Commission produced the Action Programme on the promotion of equal opportunities for women, it included commitments to pass certain legislation, to fill the loopholes of the original three Directives and to extend the scope of the Community's legislation on equality. It also included undertakings to monitor trends in women's unemployment, etc., and to introduce programmes of positive action into the Commission's own staff practices, and into member states' public sector employment, besides encouraging private firms to take women on. When the Action Programme was passed by the Council, the UK, West German and Dutch governments insisted on watering it down: taking out promises of action and replacing them with notes, refusing to allocate financial resources to it. Norman Tebbit, the UK Minister responsible for Employment Policy, was adamant that 'efforts to promote equal opportunities must be seen in the context of the general economic situation and existing financial means of governments'. This effectively gives all member states an opting-out clause.

Part-time work

However, the Commission continued to fulfil its commitments and began to draft directives, several of which it seems important to pursue. The Directive on part-time work, for example, guaranteed equal rights in law with full-timers to part-time workers (who tend to be women) regarding working conditions, dismissals, vocational training, promotion, social facilities, medical care, remuneration, holiday pay, redundancy and retirement pay. When discussed by the European Parliament, the directive was strengthened in most respects, although part-timers working less than twelve hours per week were excluded from its scope, thus creating in effect two different classes of part-time workers. The draft Directive reached the Council of Ministers in December 1982, to meet opposition from Denmark, the Netherlands, West Germany, Ireland and the UK. Again Britain's Norman Tebbit intervened and attempted to change the instrument from a directive to the weaker recommendation, which would have no binding force on member states. The Commission rejected this, but the Council then refused to accept even a weakened directive. Mr Tebbit argued that legislation was unnecessary and unrealistic, and that these matters should be dealt with through collective agreements. Greece became President of the Council in December 1983, and initially expressed a strong commitment to the draft directive, but the Council requires unanimity in the passing of directives (under Article 235 of the Treaty of Rome) and the UK and Denmark still held out against it. Negotiations in mid-1984, after the directive had lain on the table for two years, seemed to indicate that it would be dropped in favour of one on shorter working hours. The French President of the Council expressed a commitment to the directive, but nothing was done. The Irish succeeded to the Presidency in June 1984, and gave it their support, but it remains to be seen whether positive steps will be taken. The Commission will continue to refuse to accept a recommendation and is pushing for a directive, but the UK, at least, is adamant that this is not appropriate in the circumstances. It will be particularly sad if this measure is allowed to lapse as it made, in its original form, an interesting distinction between rights and benefits which would have been of general advantage to women workers. The claim was that rights are indivisible, applying to all workers *qua* workers. Benefits, on the other hand, are proportionate depending on the type of work done, whether full or part-time. This assertion of indivisible rights would have been helpful to women who are predominantly in the part-time, low-paid, low status jobs (in Britain, for example, 87% of part-timers are women) where such rights can often be at risk.

Parental leave

The draft directive on parental leave was also prepared by the end of 1982. The directive referred to both parents, whether married or not, and created a voluntary period of parental leave for a minimum of three months from the end of maternity leave, and for up to 2 years. This right was to be non-transferable, so that fathers could not give their leave to mothers but might take it themselves. Re-employment at the end of the period was guaranteed. The directive was committed in principle to pay during the leave, but Belgium, West Germany, Greece, Luxembourg and the UK argued against this, saying it was economically impractical. It also included leave for family reasons (such as taking care of a sick child) for between five and fifteen days a year, again a non-transferable right to induce fathers to take it. The directive got a hard ride from the Commission, was backed by the European Parliament (and by the Economic and Social Committee, which inserted a provision allowing for pay during the leave to come from public funds), but is still awaiting approval from the Council. Like the directive on part-time work, approval seems unlikely. The recent German case, already referred to, in which Herr Hoffmann was refused parental leave by the ECJ, will do nothing to improve the directive's chances of adoption. The European employers union (UNICE) has called the suggestion 'institutionalised absenteeism' and the Confederation of British Industry (CBI) takes the line that such a directive would 'threaten the competitiveness of industry by disrupting working patterns'. As *Guardian* writer, Angela Phillips commended (17/10/84), the great value of the proposal is precisely 'that it would cut down the disruption of working patterns suffered by large numbers of women'.

Occupational social security

The draft directive on occupational social security schemes was adopted by the Commission in April 1983. It outlaws direct and indirect discrimination, including that on grounds of marital or family status, from all social security schemes. This takes in conditions of access, calculations of contributions and benefit entitlements, and the practice of giving women lower pensions because they are expected to live longer. The draft directive does not include provisions on retirement age and survivors' pensions, on the grounds that they are too complicated. For that omission, the Commission was criticised by the European Parliament, which also changed the deadline for implementation to January 1986 rather than two years after Council passes the directive. The European Parliament also reversed the burden of proof in such cases, so that it rests upon the employer to prove a scheme non-discriminatory. Again, the directive is opposed by the governments of the UK and West Germany and seems unlikely at the moment to be passed.

Reorganisation of working time

Finally, the Commission has proposed a recommendation (of no binding force) on the reorganisation of working time. The Commission favours a recommendation since it argues that reorganisation of working time requires a high level of political will as well as flexibility in its scheme if it is to be implemented. Unfortunately, given the reluctance of the member states to implement anything voluntary in the field of women's rights, mere recommendations are most unlikely to change anything. Agreement to a recommendation was probably a compromise by the Commission in order to get the provision through the Council, but this was unsuccessful as the UK still opposes it there, arguing that such matters should be established by negotiation between management and trades unions, not legislation. The recommendation proposes to maintain the present level of wages for fewer hours (not a popular proposal in a period of economic crisis), in order to protect lower-paid workers. It encourages part-time work, and attempts to make working hours shorter and more flexible, which could, in addition to helping women, reduce unemployment. The European Parliament would prefer something stronger than a recommendation and has criticised the Commission for not including sufficiently practical measures. However, even the recommendation is unlikely to be passed by the Council, let alone any more binding instrument.

All these proposals were based on the Resolution passed by the European Parliament after its 1981 debate on women's rights. However, the Resolution had gone further than this, and included many more radical proposals. The European Parliament had called for action in the field of education: for example, for more girls to be encouraged into non-traditional areas, such as engineering, and for more boys to take domestic courses, thus encouraging them to share family responsibilities. It also called for research into effective, safe methods of contraception and safe, available abortions as a last resort, besides appropriate provisions for day nurseries so that women need not be discouraged from having children or from working if they so wish. The Parliament also considered that the ESF should be used to provide funding for centres for unemployed women, and centres for women victims of violence. Finally, it reiterated the plea, which the Commission had been making for years, that protective legislation in the member states should be harmonised.

The Commission did not feel able to incorporate the more radical elements of the European Parliament's Resolution into the Action Programme. It foresaw difficulties enough in getting the adopted proposals through the Council. Still, it could not have foreseen that the Council would refuse to pass anything in the form of mandatory legislation in the way it has done, effectively causing the Action Programme to grind to a halt. In the mid-1970s, when the original three Directives were passed, there was sufficient feminist pressure on governments, and enough financial freedom, to create a suitable political environment and the political will to maintain a commitment to equality; in the recession of the 1980s, however, governments are content to give women's rights a low priority. The European Parliament has continually criticised the Commission for not being radical enough. Marie-Claude Vayssade, who reported on the Action Programme for the Parliament, questioned its not including practical measures on education, health and maternity provisions and its being too reliant on voluntary implementation by the member states, which she called 'a dangerous gamble in a period of crisis'. Indeed, Parliament thought that the Commission should use regulations rather than the weaker directives, so that the measures would be legally binding and enforceable without even having to be implemented by the member states. The Action Programme was seen as a minimum commitment, an attempt to take over the more acceptable parts of the Parliament's Resolution while leaving aside the controversial areas of abortion, contraception and girls' education. It has not so far been particularly effective, and the implementing measures should probably have been stronger. At the most, it was a minimum commitment to women's rights; unfortunately, even this was seen as too strong by the Council, who have consistently opposed all attempts to legislate in this area. So the Action Programme suffers, not so much from relying too much upon member states, as from the Council's refusal to pass any form of binding legislation. The UK government, for example, has been fairly consistently inflexible, and will not accept even non-binding recommendations; and since women's rights are not a major priority for any government, the other member states are not concerned to put political pressure on the UK to conform. There seems a limit to the extent to which the Commission can continually water down its proposals in order to try and make them more acceptable to all Council members. The scope of the Action Programme as it stands is limited enough: given the Council's intransigence, it is further weakened. Only if the UK and other governments could be made to give way to pressure from a strong women's lobby inside Europe and in the member states would the Commission be in a position to implement even its present truncated policy on women's rights.

Reports of the Committee of Enquiry

The themes of some of the reports of the Enquiry are covered in recommendations or draft directives already referred to. This is so, for example, of Mrs Wieczorek-Zeul's contribution on the reorganisation of working time and Mme Le Roux's on parental leave. The importance of these areas is not in doubt, for changes here would allow women much greater freedom in their working lives. However, there are several other reports in spheres where the Community has as yet little official policy but which are vitally important for women at this time.

New technologies

Mrs Spaak's report on the new technologies (topic no. 6 of the Report of the Enquiry), for instance, outlines the possibilities for women's employment in the developing areas of data processing, office automation and robotics. She makes it clear that, unless women are trained for these new forms of work and domestic arrangements modified to take account of them, women could end up once again at the end of the job queue. Education and training must be geared to the use of the new technologies, with mathematics and the ability to use abstract concepts playing a much greater part. Many schools fail to encourage girls in such subjects, leaving them at a permanent disadvantage.

The problem is, of course, more complicated than this. Even when women are offered retraining in these areas, the take-up is often disappointing. Yet, as always, the reasons behind such apparent apathy must be sought. If training schemes are inconveniently located or the hours incompatible with domestic commitments, it is not surprising if women vote with their feet. Again, the wide-ranging implications of technological change become clear when work at home is considered. Travelling to a place of work becomes unnecessary when all that is required is a terminal in the house. Convenient as this may sound for women (and Spaak emphasises that it is predominantly women who will be laid off for work at home) it brings its own problems of isolation, insecurity and lack of protection. All of these factors have to be considered now if women are not to be disadvantaged in the future. Yet very little has so far been done. The trades unions do not pay much attention to women in this context and most of the Community proposals so far have been very general, making no specific reference to the problems of women. One exception is the resolution adopted by the Council in 1983 on vocational training, which suggests that special attention be given to the training needs of women in new technologies. As Spaak concludes, 'The new technologies provide an ideal platform for positive action as laid down in the 1982–85 Action Programme'; without this, the initiative and the potential for women will be lost.

Taxation

Dame Shelagh Roberts of the UK prepared the Enquiry's report on women and taxation (topic no. 15). As she suggests, the three Directives on Equal Pay, Equal Treatment and Social Security all assume the value of the economic independence of women, and it is therefore anomalous that the tax systems of many of the member states have an adverse effect on women's employment and consequently on their potential financial equality and independence.

In most member states, the income of a married woman is treated as belonging to her husband; married women have no privacy in matters relating to income as they usually do not fill in a tax form but have to reveal details of their finances to their husbands who in turn inform the tax authorities. Tax deductions are most often set against the husband's income so that, where income tax is deducted at source by the employer, the wife will have a proportionately greater amount of tax withheld. All of these factors and others have an effect on whether married women decide to go out to work. In the UK, for example, where a working husband and wife get a bigger allowance than when only the husband is working, women are encouraged to go into paid employment. In West Germany, where tax splitting arrangements hold, the reverse is true, and women are often deterred from achieving economic independence.

It does seem important that in this fundamental area women should have freedom of choice, and this requires that the tax system be neutral as between spouses and that, at least in the longer term, taxation of individuals rather than married couples should be the norm. Ivor Richard, just before he left the Commission, promised a policy paper on income tax systems, but agreed that although a directive on this was urgent, it was currently 'difficult to imagine'.

Information policy

It has been a recurring theme of this book that women themselves and society at large must be educated and informed on equal opportunities. This message lies at the heart of Gloria Hooper's report on information policy and women (topic no. 13 of the Report of the Enquiry). The dissemination of information, she says, quoting from the Action Programme, is 'of key importance not only to ensure that women are aware of their rights . . . but also at a more general level to enable a wider public, particularly through the mass media, to accept women as equals in all areas of society and to understand the positive aspects of this development'.

The recognition that women are often housebound and cut off from discussion and other sources of information in the workplace should encourage the use and expansion of the existing network of women's magazines, radio and television programmes and voluntary organisations. In all of this, the national equality agencies such as the British EOC and the Irish EEA have a crucial role to play. The Commission, too, already publishes regular information on women, but more money needs to be spent on this, and the number of staff dealing with women's affairs increased.

It is important too that the media used to inform women should themselves be non-sexist. Women are still often predominantly represented there either as sex objects or as housewives and mothers, and it is men who are seen as experts and power-wielders. This would probably be less likely to happen if there were more women in the higher echelons of the media, both on the creative and managerial sides, and it should be a priority to encourage this.

Women in Community institutions

There is one area in which the Commission itself could give a valuable lead on equality and also promote practically the idea of positive action: that is in the promotion of women within its own hierarchy. Mrs Lenz's report (topic no. 11 of the Report of the Enquiry) makes recommendations on how this might be done. As she points out, the European Parliament has recognised for some time that the ratio of men to women, especially at the top of the employment hierarchy, is very unequal. In 1981 and again in 1982, the Commission affirmed the need to promote equal opportunities for women, but nothing was done, and by 1983 the Commissioner in charge of staff administration, Mr Burke, was saying to the Committee of Enquiry that the numbers of women in the higher grades was still 'ludicrously low'.[2] The Lenz report uses staff statistics for 1981 showing that only 10% of category A staff were women, and only at the lower levels 4 and 5 in this category did women make up as much as 25%. In the lower categories B and C, on the other hand, women occupied between 62% and 90% of posts.

A recent survey shows the figures in October 1983 confirming these trends.[3] The vast majority of the women employed in the Commission were secretaries and clerical staff, and in the administrative grades they numbered only 230 out of 2695. The Lenz report outlines problem areas for women in training, working hours, provision of leave and childcare services, all of which could be dealt with in a positive way. It also suggests monitoring women's numbers and progress in the various grades and as members of committees, on training courses, etc., with a view to establishing targets for women's increased participation.

Indirect discrimination

The Commission promised in the Action Programme to monitor case law on the sensitive issue of indirect discrimination, in an attempt to clarify the concept and ensure a uniform interpretation throughout the Community. Indirect discrimination is defined by the British Sex Discrimination Act as the application of a condition (for example on access to a job) with which substantially fewer women than men are able to comply, where non-compliance will be to their detriment (e.g. will result in not getting the job) and where the condition is not justifiable by the employer. For example, in the case of *Price* v. *Civil Service Commission*,[4] already referred to, the age-limit was indirectly discriminatory since most women could not apply while they were bearing and bringing up children. The British Employment Appeals Tribunal agreed, in the light of their experience, that most women could not comply with the age-limit, and so held it was discriminatory. Indirect discrimination has also been held by the English courts to apply to part-time workers, if they are made redundant before full-time, since, it is agreed, most part-time workers are women.[5] It is fairly easy to see the indirect discriminatory nature of conditions such as age-limits; but indirect discrimination is not always as simple as that. It is part of our social ethos; generally accepted notions, such as that mothers have the main responsibility for bringing up children, are indirectly discriminatory, as is the idea that women should become secretaries rather than builders. Any artificialities which result in women being excluded from jobs are indirect discrimination; as is the fact that women are not encouraged to apply for jobs if they have small children; and that, in languages other than English, jobs are typically described in the masculine gender (unless of course they are secretarial etc!). The fact that women make up a higher proportion of the unemployed than they do of the labour market is at least partly explained by indirect discrimination. Education, too, is indirectly discriminatory in the way that girls are channelled into certain areas of study (domestic science and the humanities) and into achieving less prestigious qualifications than boys. Thus, men often get the better jobs, and women the family responsibilities and the dead-end typing.

It is often very difficult to prove in court that certain conditions are indirectly discriminatory. Ms Price had to rely upon the judge's experience that most women were child-rearing until twenty-eight. European courts do not generally allow sociological and psychological evidence to show, for example, that since girls as a group do less science than boys at school, they may therefore be disadvantaged when it comes to finding work. Normally, British and European courts rely upon the judge's own experience, which, in the light of the restricted class, gender, education and work experience of most judges, is unlikely to be wide enough to include, say, knowledge of the factory floor or of most women's life-styles. As has already been said, American courts first developed the concept of indirect discrimination, and they do admit sociological and psychological evidence, which makes it easier for patterns of discrimination to be demonstrated.

There are some moves now, however, to standardise the definition of indirect discrimination within the Community. The first report of the network of experts monitoring the application of the Equal Treatment Legislation[6] traces for each member state the extent to which indirect discrimination is explicitly acknowledged in its laws and practice. In the UK and in Ireland, for example, it is specifically written into the law. In Germany, on the other hand, the concept is not covered by legal definition. The network report concludes with a suggestion for a standard definition of the notion, including five 'key-conditions' which it is claimed could be applied in all the member states. It is at any rate an important move on the way to specifying the general features of indirect discrimination, Community-wide.

Wider strategies to facilitate change

Having considered some of the factors which militate most against change and the areas which it is suggested need to be tackled further, it is now possible to review the wider strategies which might facilitate change in the direction of equality. These include some legal reforms and 'best practice', where certain institutions or offices have been successful in a particular context and might usefully be applied in modified form elsewhere. They also include some more general recommendations on Commission policy and priorities.

To suggest that we may learn from the experience of others is not at all the same thing as saying that institutions or arrangements can be transplanted direct from one environment or country to another. It was one of the weaknesses of British imperialism to suppose that the Mother of Parliaments could simply be reproduced, as it stood, world-wide. In the case of social and legal structures, the lesson holds. What grows naturally out of one set of experiences may sit very oddly on another. However, when this is appreciated, it may well be possible to gain from studying a successful strategy, even if it is unsuitable for general application, if the reasons for its success are elicited and can be achieved by other means. For example, the

Irish Labour Court has had some success recently in extending the acceptance of the idea of indirect discrimination. It has ruled that, *inter alia*, requirements of mobility, minimum height and upper age limits are indirectly discriminatory. There are, however, problems for the Labour Court even in Ireland, and nobody would suggest copying it throughout the Community. But examination of the way in which the court operates, with the establishment of Equality Officers and the increased acceptance of 'sociological' evidence, begins to suggest that discrimination cases are probably not best dealt with in the ordinary tribunal and court system. Thus, as will be suggested, specialist courts for discrimination cases would probably be useful.

Specialist courts

In Britain, sex discrimination cases are decided by industrial tribunals, with appeal to an Employment Appeal Tribunal (EAT) and then to the Court of Appeal and House of Lords. This means that discrimination cases are treated as industrial relations problems that can be solved by conciliation between the parties, rather than as problems following from attitudes and behaviour created by our society, which affect women's status and treatment.

In Ireland, discrimination cases are also heard by the Labour Courts, but first they are referred to Equality Officers for investigation. This is at the least a recognition of the specific status of discrimination cases: that they are not simply industrial relations problems which can be conciliated, because their causes go far deeper than this. It also means that Equality Officers can build up a specialised knowledge of the complexity of discrimination law, and begin to advise women accordingly. Since Equality Officers are not functioning within the formal proceedings of a court hearing, they may receive sociological and psychological evidence to show indirect discrimination. Again, since they are specialists, they also become aware of indirect discrimination and its cause and effects themselves, and often do not need experts to explain situations to them. In any event, their own experience of women's life-style and problems becomes much wider than that of an average High Court judge. So far, so good. But if either party to the dispute does not agree with the Equality Officer's recommendation, the case is heard before the Labour Court. Since the Labour Court regards itself as an industrial relations conciliation court (and, indeed, nine-tenths of its work is in this area), it does not give reasons for its findings. Thus appeals are very difficult, since there is no reasoned judgment to challenge.

The answer would seem to be specialised courts in each member state, dealing exclusively with discrimination cases, thus developing an expertise in discrimination law and the use of sociological evidence. Such expert evidence should be allowable to prove indirect discrimination. The specialised courts should not be directly linked to industrial relations courts, as this gives a false picture of discrimination law's scope. Discrimination cases are not, like industrial disputes, matters simply of arbitration and conciliation where each side is 'asking four to get two', and negotiating positions are accepted as quite different from realistic final agreements. This approach, therefore, and the tribunal system which has grown up to service it, is not the most suitable for discrimination cases, where other standards and objectives need to be met. The courts should give reasons in their judgments, too, so that precedents are developed where applicable and appeals are possible. In England, such a discrimination court could be a branch of the Employment Appeals Tribunal, with appeal to the Divisional Court. This would mean having lawyers to represent parties, which is not the practice in industrial tribunals: and it would set the functions of the court apart from the conciliatory industrial relations one of industrial tribunals, so that individual rights, which should not, after all, be negotiable, would be secured by legal action.

Collective rights, on the other hand, can be determined by conciliation and industrial relations. For that reason, in the UK, CAC (Central Arbitration Committee) has the power to amend discriminatory clauses in collective agreements. That power, and its equivalent in other member states, might well be strengthened, and arbitration tribunals encouraged to make greater use of it. Since most women are unprepared to take their employers to court individually, it is largely through eliminating discriminatory agreements that they will be treated equally.

Class action

American courts make provision for the use of the 'class action', which allows a common question of fact or law as between each member of a class and the defendant to be taken as one, and determined in one case. The plaintiff, in other words, brings the action on behalf of a class. This might include, say, not only all those women who actually applied for jobs and were rejected but also those who would have applied but for the discriminatory practice. Finding proof of the pattern of discrimination is made easier by admitting evidence of discrimination against any member of the class. Once the practice of discrimination is proved in a class action, the burden of proof shifts to the defendant to show that he did not discriminate against the individual. It is not necessary for each member of the class to prove her individual loss, as a wide range of techniques has been developed for calculating class-wide damages. (The nearest equivalent in Britain is the representative action, which still contains many difficulties in proving indirect discrimination.)

There seems little doubt that provision for class action is to the benefit of women in the United States, and it is tempting to suggest that it be introduced directly into the legal systems of the member states. But there are procedural differences in American law which make this difficult, and the acceptance there of indirect discrimination and positive action means that a whole framework of statistical evidence, mandatory employers' records and specialist legal advice has emerged, none of which exist in any developed form in any member state of the Community (with the possible exception, on some points, of Ireland and France). However, it is now accepted by many lawyers that discrimination law is uniquely complicated and also relatively new. Even those who, like Professor Hepple, are sceptical about the transferability of procedural law, concede that changes in legal attitudes and the acceptance of different forms of evidence are necessary. 'Whether lawyers, including judges, like it or not, they are going to have to equip themselves to deal with the social facts which lie behind legislative policies of this kind. In the modern areas of legal regulation (such as sex equality) . . . the lawyer cannot limit himself to the logical organisation of rules and principles.'[7] Provided it is realised, then, that the introduction of a class or representative action would probably require the development of other provisions, such as employers' records and equality officers, there seems little reason why unions and equality agencies should not be allowed to take action on behalf of a number of women rather than laboriously fighting individual cases.

Burden of proof

Both the 1981 European Parliament Resolution and the Commission's Action Programme agreed that the burden of proof in discrimination cases should be reversed. This means in effect that instead of a woman having to prove discrimination on the part of another, the defendant would have to show innocence of the claimed discrimination. At present in most European countries, the initial burden is on the complainant, except in Belgium and Ireland in dismissal and victimisation cases. In the UK, West Germany and the Netherlands the plaintiff merely has to show a prima facie case that a certain course of events occurred to her detriment and to the benefit of a comparable man. The burden then shifts to the employer to prove that he/she did *not* discriminate, and to prove that his/her conduct was justifiable. However, frequently the court will insist that the plaintiff prove her case *objectively*, which means showing that a certain course of events occurred and that any reasonable person would agree that this was to her detriment. This is not always easy: for example, it is difficult to prove wounded pride and self-esteem as 'detriment', which is why cases of sexual harassment seldom succeed. The employer may merely have to prove his case *subjectively*, that is, to show that he believed at the time that he was not acting in a discriminatory fashion. Even if the tribunal is being fair to both sides, and both must prove their case objectively, there still remains the problem for the woman plaintiff of proving her case. Her employer will have all the information, records etc. that she needs. All she will have is her own recollection of her treatment, the knowledge, say, that a man received promotion where she did not, and the assumption that he was less well qualified than she.

The argument against reversal of the burden of proof is the general legal assumption that who alleges must prove, otherwise the floodgates would be open to frivolous and damaging allegations. However, the disincentives for women to bring actions against their employers are strong enough. Mere reversal of the burden of proof will not alter women's fear of losing their jobs. It may seem unduly hard that someone who has not initiated an action should be burdened with proving innocence. Yet it would surely not be too difficult to impose a statutory duty where one does not already exist on employers to keep records of all their staff, broken down by gender, rates of pay, position, promotions etc., and also of their selection procedure and their reasons for selecting or rejecting particular applicants. Reversal of the burden of proof is clearly not to be recommended in all areas of law, but in discrimination cases the parties tend to be in an unequal situation in the first place – an employee generally against her employer – and some reversal of the burden of proof would help to redress the balance.[8]

The European Court of Justice

The European Court is effectively the Supreme Court for each member state when it comes to matters of EEC law. Given the commitment of the EEC to women's rights, and in particular the European Court's seminal decision that Article 119 was directly effective (in the second *Defrenne*[9] case in 1975) it might be expected that the Court would be progressive when it came to remedying defects in domestic legislation on discrimination. Yet this is not so. Few of the Court's decisions since that time have been clear.

The third *Defrenne*[10] case said merely that retirement ages were not included in Article 119. In *McCarthys Ltd* v. *Smith*,[11] the Court managed to agree that a comparable man did not need to be employed contemporaneously with the woman plaintiff (which is more than the English courts were prepared to hold), but sidestepped the issue of whether the EPD was directly effective, and relied instead on Article 119. *Worringham & Humphreys* v. *Lloyds Bank Ltd*[12] held that the 5% differential pension rights between men and women were included in 'pay', but defined those pension rights so narrowly that the case really affected only those employees of Lloyds Bank who came under that particular scheme. In *Jenkins* v. *Kingsgate Ltd*,[13] the judgment of the European Court was so obscure that the Employment Appeal Tribunal in the end decided the case on the basis of English law. *Garland* v. *British Rail*[14] did extend the concept of pay to cover any consideration, in cash or in kind, immediate or future, provided the worker receives it in respect of employment. Almost alone of the Court's decisions, it managed to be clear and precise in its definitions. In *Burton* v. *British Rail*[15] the Court reverted to form and merely said that differential retirement ages were discriminatory unless linked to a national statutory scheme, which was not much help to Mr Burton.[16] Finally, in *Von Colson & Kamann* v. *Nordrhein-Westphalia*[17] it was held that penalties in the Directives are not directly effective, and so the plaintiffs must rely entirely upon the weak penalties available in German law. It seems strange that the European Court, which prides itself on its progressive interpretations on the extension and harmonisation of EEC legislation, and which was initially radical in its reading of discrimination law in the second *Defrenne* case, should be so reluctant and coy when it comes to the three Directives. It has consistently refused, for example, to rule on whether the EPD and ETD are directly effective, and is obviously tentative about encroaching too much on national sovereignty and domestic legislation in such a sensitive area as women's rights.

But even if the European Court were consistently more favourable to women than are national courts, its judgments would probably have little more effect than they do now. They are already legally binding, and domestic courts are meant to apply them. When member states are found to be in breach, not having implemented directives effectively, they are under a legal duty to comply with the European Court's judgments. Although most member states do comply to some extent, the political pressures exerted on domestic courts are not strong. Thus a domestic court, having been instructed by the European Court, may put a decision into practice, but other courts will not necessarily follow it. There may be a case here for the European Parliament asserting itself by introducing sanctions for non-compliance with court decisions. Many MEPs would like to see Parliament hold back grants to member states who are slow to implement court judgments in this and other areas. In the past, this would have been difficult to operate, as information on the state of play in member states was rather difficult to come by and follow-up on decisions somewhat erratic. This may be changed for the better, however, by the monitoring roles of the Advisory Committee of Experts and the Women's Committee, so that more information will exist on which Parliament could make decisions about the withholding of money as a penalty for non-compliance.

The European Court would also seem the obvious forum in which to try out reversal of the burden of proof and class action. Although class action before the European Court would have to be accepted in domestic courts as well, the burden of proof is merely a procedural requirement and could be introduced for the European Court alone if the Court were willing to conduct such an experiment.

Experience from within the Community and abroad

In her report for the Commission on positive action programmes, Elaine Vogel-Polsky looks at the experience of countries where such projects have met with some success (e.g. Sweden and the United States). She does this not because she believes that schemes are directly transferable elsewhere, but because by studying how they have worked out in practice, we begin to understand the problems which arise, the areas which have to be tackled first and the limitations of initial simplistic approaches. History may indeed teach no lessons, but a review of what has been tried, given a clear appreciation of its setting in a particular time and place, may at least allow us to avoid the reinvention of buckled wheels.

In this context, a number of recent practices within the Community and elsewhere are worth mentioning.

On the question of positive action itself, the experience of Australia might be added to that of Sweden and the United States. There, an affirmative action law began an interesting experiment, with an Employment Opportunity Plan based on statistical data, with staff appointed to institute the changes, set targets and review the plan annually. The fact that this was based on legislation, says Alison Ziller, director of the scheme, meant that employers ceased to ask 'Why should we?' and began to ask 'How can we do it?'[18] After a year, it became, she says, just another public service task, and 'the debate had been changed' from the rights and wrongs of the aim to the methods of its attainment. This insight is in itself valuable, as are the detailed and precise check-lists (five in all) which were developed to facilitate the programme. Again, the claim is not that any such scheme is simply directly transferable, but that, intelligently used, the experience has a general interest.

In Denmark, as has been said, Equality Counsellors have been appointed in labour exchanges since 1983. Their job is, among other things, to encourage women to think of working in non-traditional areas, to make them aware of their rights in the labour market, and to set up introductory courses for women in such skills. The scheme is so new that it is impossible to judge its effectiveness yet, but is clearly a development to be watched and perhaps emulated in the future.

In recent years several countries have appointed ministers for women as a way of establishing their *bona fides* with the female half of the electorate. In some cases, this has been a minister of Cabinet rank, in others, a junior minister (France has had both at different times). There have also been 'special advisers on women's affairs' appointed, for example, in the United States and in Australia. The value of such a post has been very uneven. In some cases they have been largely public relations exercises, and their influence always depends on the kind of resources they acquire. This is really the problem in a period of recession: no government is likely to look favourably on expenditure in what most of them take to be a marginal area. Yvette Roudy, the French Women's Rights Minister, who has more power than most in such an office, told the European Parliament in January 1984 that France was the most advanced country in the world as regards women's rights, but her own attempts to introduce a radical bill on equality were not entirely successful. It was modified in important respects before it was passed by the Senate, by which time, following a reshuffle, Mme Roudy was no longer a full Cabinet minister and therefore in a weaker position to press it with her colleagues. The creation of women's ministers is therefore no guarantee of great advances in women's status. The office is much too vulnerable to the ups and downs of political fashion; but in combination with other devices, it does keep the issue in the public eye as well as constantly before the government of the day.

Both the EPD and the ETD required member states to take administrative action to ensure that the principles of equality are observed, and that all employees know their rights. The UK created the Equal Opportunities Commission to fulfil this function, based on the American Equal Employment Opportunities Commission (EEOC). The EOC provides information to employees in the form of advertisements, brochures, pamphlets etc., advises employers on how best to implement the legal requirements of equality, and can provide legal advice and legal representation directly to individuals. It can bring actions against employers itself, or can finance and provide legal representation for employees to do so. It advises the government on the state of equality in practice, on possible revisions to the law and on new proposals concerning equality. It also conducts regular surveys on equality in practice – in employment, education, job opportunities, etc. As the EOC is well known, legal redress becomes more readily available in practice to individuals who are aware that they can complain to an agency which is there to advise them. Of course there are problems. The EOC is regarded as an administrative agency, another of the government's QUANGOs, and so it is not expected to be too radical. There can be tensions between the staff, who tend to be personally committed to feminism and want things changed quickly, and the Commissioners, who are political appointees, and more likely to support gradualism. (The nominees of radical women's groups have consistently been rejected for these positions.) Again, the EOC tends to concentrate on test cases, which, it could be said, do not do much to further the cause of equality. The Commission too does not really plug into the developing network of women's groups and individuals struggling for equality, but rather cultivates the higher-level structures manned by civil servants and politicians, in an attempt to inspire enthusiasm for equality from above rather than below.[19]

However, the EOC has the greatest powers of all the agencies in the EEC. The Dutch and Irish equivalents may give advice, but not assistance, to litigating individuals, and although all the agencies are supposed to provide information about women's rights, the EOC is probably the most assiduous. An equality agency in every member state would not only be a direct advantage to women in the Community, but would facilitate the pooling of information and experience across national boundaries.

Finally, a number of general recommendations might be made about the extension and development of structures or facilities within the Parliament and Commission. The importance of information and publicity has been underlined a number of times already, but it is worth stressing that while women remain badly informed of their rights, the effectiveness of existing and future policies is strictly limited. A survey done within the member states has shown that only about one-tenth of all women in paid employment know about Community initiatives in this sphere.[20] Methods of disseminating information which have proved successful in some of the member states might well be encouraged in others. The French government, for example, used the mass media to publicise their campaign for occupational equality during 1982–3, and the Dutch now use television and radio broadcasts ('Gesprekken met vrouwen') as a matter of course. This allows contact with women in the home as well as with those at work. Special publicity is also needed for the European Social Fund (ESF) to increase the applications from women. In addition to publicity, there is need for a centralised data bank, not only for researchers but for those who are attempting to determine the next stage of policy in member states. The establishment of the Advisory Committee to the Commission, and of the Network of Experts, should do much to facilitate the exchange of ideas and experience. In the sphere of legal decisions, Jennifer Corcoran has suggested that the Commission publish reports of all discrimination cases heard in member states and details of all Community law developments and initiatives in the area.[21] This would at least allow lawyers and other advisers to know about major cases throughout the Community and perhaps save duplication of time and effort.

Until very recently, it was unclear what would happen to the Women's Committee of the European Parliament. It has produced the Report of the

Enquiry into the Situation of Women in Europe and this had been duly debated by the Parliament in January 1984. Between then and the Parliamentary elections in June of that year, opinions differed among the women MEPs as to what should happen next. Mrs Maij-Weggen, for example, although she supported a permanent women's committee, believed that women 'must not isolate themselves and must be involved in other things'. Some of the women MEPs believed that a separate women's group was inherently discriminatory and would be liable to result in the marginalisation of women's issues. Gloria Hooper, for example, originally took this line, fearing what she called the 'ghetto syndrome', but she came to believe that some such forum was useful for women. The idea was also canvassed that rather than another women's committee being established in the new Parliament, a 'woman for women' should be appointed to all committees to put the women's position and monitor decisions from the woman's point of view. This found some support but was rejected by others, including Simone Veil, who felt that 'it would put an intolerable burden on the women, as well as creating antagonism which would be counter-productive'.[22]

In the event, the new Parliament quickly set up a permanent Women's Committee with twenty-five members, headed by Marlene Lenz of Germany. The committee will examine the development of women's rights in Europe, taking as its base the 1981 and 1984 resolutions, and the implementation, improvement and extension of EEC equality legislation. The permanent establishment of the committee is important in keeping women's rights before the Parliament at a difficult time and as a potent lobby on the Commission and the Council. But it is important to be clear that the mere existence of such a body is no panacea. First of all, other committees, like the important Employment and Social Committee, for example, must be kept informed of women's needs. Also, those who represent women's interests inside the Parliament require the support of those outside.

This raises the crucial question of a coherent and united women's lobby. Tentative efforts have been made since the early 1980s to co-ordinate the experience of those concerned with women's interests. Conferences were held in Manchester (1980), Bonn (1982) and by the ETUC and OECD, but different groupings and individuals attended different gatherings and the movement was not united. With the establishment of the Enquiry, the Commission's Advisory Committee and the European Network of Experts, however, the advantages of co-operation became increasingly obvious. In addition to this, the women MEPs knew that the EEC is dominated by lobbies of all kinds, large and small, representing every conceivable interest group. As well as the huge and well-funded trade union, agricultural and business lobbies, there are groups for consumers and crafts and all the professions. As a recent *Financial Times* article says, 'Lobbying in Europe is seen as a perfectly legitimate activity and there is currently no control on lobbyists or even a register of MEPs' interests.'[23]

There are, of course, difficulties attached to this kind of super-national pressure. To begin with, differing national policies can make agreement on a common group position difficult. Again, there is the possibility of a strong lobby calling out opposition from other groups, the so-called 'countervailing pressure' argument.[24] In addition to these difficulties, a women's lobby has the problem of bringing together the equality aspirations of countries at very different stages of development (for example, Greece and Denmark). Further, traditional women's groups and more radical and recently established ones do not always find it easy to communicate. In spite of this, the Centre for Research on European Women (CREW) has begun the attempt to involve women, from the grass-roots up rather than from the top down, in a new European Network of Women (ENW). Whether this intiative will be successful it is too soon to tell, but already they have held a conference in London (May 1984) to pool information on the Social Security Directive and to decide on a common campaign to encourage governments to comply.

The problem remains of co-ordinating this kind of pressure with that of the more traditional groups and the experts working at both the national and the European level. However difficult, the effort is necessary and urgent. As one British MP puts it, 'Women themselves have got to grab the microphone and make their contribution.' But there will be no advantage to this if all that is heard is a cacophony of unrelated aims and priorities. Some kind of united front, outside as well as inside Parliament, is essential if the interests of women are to continue to be adequately represented on the European scene.

Appendix 1: Women MEPs since 1979

Women MEPs	Country	Group	Dates of service
AGNELLI Susanna	Italy	Lib	1979–84*
von ALEMANN Mechtild	Germany	Lib	1979–84
ANGLADE Magdeleine	France	EDA	1984–
BADUEL GLORIOSO Maria Fabrizia	Italy	Com	1979–84
BANOTTI Mary	Ireland	PPE	1984–
BARBARELLA Carla	Italy	Com	1979–
BLOCH VON BLOTTNITZ Undine	Germany	Rainbow	1984–
BONINO Emma	Italy	Non-Att	1979–
BOOT Elise	Netherlands	PPE	1979–
BOSERUP Bodil Kathrine	Denmark	Com	1979–
BRAUN-MOSER Ursula	Germany	PPE	1984–
BROOKES Beata Ann	UK	EDG	1979–
BUCHAN Janey O'Neil	UK	Soc	1979–
CARETTONI RAMAGNOLI Tullia	Italy	Com	1979–84
CASSANMAGNAGO-CERRETTI Maria Luisa	Italy	PPE	1979–
CASTELLINA Luciana	Italy	Com	1979–
CASTLE Barbara	UK	Soc	1979–
CHARZAT Gisele	France	Soc	1979–
CHOURAQUI Nicole	France	EDA	1979–81, 1984–
CINCIARI RODANO Maria Luisa	Italy	Com	1979–
CLWYD Ann	UK	Soc	1979–84
CRAWLEY Christine	UK	Soc	1984–
CRESSON Edith	France	Soc	1979–81
DALY Margaret	UK	EDG	1984–
d'ANCONA Hedy	Netherlands	Soc	1984–
de BACKER Rika	Belgium	PPE	1984–
DEKKER Suzanne	Netherlands	Non-Att	1979–84
DE MARCH Danielle	France	Com	1979–
DESMOND Eileen	Ireland	Soc	1979–81
DESOUCHES Marie-Jacqueline	France	Soc	1981–84
DE VALERA Sile	Ireland	EDA	1979–84
DIENESCH Marie-Madeleine	France	EDA	1979–81
DUPORT Paule	France	Soc	1982–84
DUPUY Anne-Marie	France	EDA	1984–
DURY Raymonde	Belgium	Soc	1982–
ELLES Diana Louie	UK	EDG	1979–*
EWING Winifred	UK	EDA	1979–*
FAITH Sheila	UK	EDG	1984–
FLESCH Colette	Luxembourg	Lib	1979–81, 1984–
FOCKE Katharina	Germany	Soc	1979–84
FONTAINE Nicole	France	PPE	1984–

Women MEPs	Country	Group	Dates of service
FORSTER Norvella	UK	EDG	1979–84
FUILLET Yvette	France	Soc	1979–
GADIOUX Colette	France	Soc	1984–
GAIOTTI DE BIASE Paola	Italy	PPE	1979–84
GASPARD Françoise	France	Soc	1979–84
GIANNAKOY Mariori–Marietta	Greece	PPE	1984–
GREDAL Eva Wilhelmsson	Denmark	Soc	1979–
GROENENDAAL Jessie	Netherlands	Lib	1984–
GROES Mette	Denmark	Soc	1979–84
HAMMERICH Else	Denmark	Rainbow	1979–
HEINRICH Brigitte	Germany	Rainbow	1984–
van HEMELDONCK Marijke	Belgium	Soc	1981–
HERKLOTZ Luise	Germany	Soc	1979–84
van den HEUVEL Ien	Netherlands	Soc	1979–
HOFF Magdalene	Germany	Soc	1979–
HOFFMAN Jacqueline	France	Com	1979–
HOOPER Gloria	UK	EDG	1979–84
JACKSON Caroline	UK	EDG	1984–
JEPSEN Marie	Denmark	EDG	1984–
KELLETT-BOWMAN Elaine	UK	EDG	1979–84*
KROUWEL-VLAM Annie	Netherlands	Soc	1979–84*
LEHIDEUX Martine	France	Eur Right	1984–
LEMASS Eileen	Ireland	EDA	1984–
LENZ Marlene	Germany	PPE	1979–
LENTZ-CORNETTE Marcelle	Luxembourg	PPE	1981–84
LE ROUX Sylvie	France	Com	1979–84
LIENEMANN Noelle	France	Soc	1984–
LIZIN Anne-Marie	Belgium	Soc	1979–
MACCIOCCHI Maria Antoinetta	Italy	Non-Att	1980–84
MAIJ-WEGGEN Johanna	Netherlands	PPE	1979–
MARINARO Francesca	Italy	Com	1984–
MARTIN Simone	France	Lib	1979–
MOREAU Louise	France	PPE	1979–84
NEILSEN Tove	Denmark	Lib	1979–
OPPENHEIM Jeanette	Denmark	EDG	1984–
PANTAZI Konstantina	Greece	Soc	1982–
PAUWELYN Jeanne	Belgium	Lib	1981–84
PERY Nicole	France	Soc	1981–
PEUS Gabriele	Germany	PPE	1982–
PHLIX Alphonsine	Belgium	PPE	1981–84
PIERMONT Dorothee	Germany	Rainbow	1984–
POIRIER Henriette	France	Com	1979–84
PRUVOT Marie-Jane	France	Lib	1979–
QUIN Joyce	UK	Soc	1979–
RABBETHGE Renate-Charlotte	Germany	PPE	1979–
ROBERTS Shelagh	UK	EDG	1979–

Appendix 1 (*cont.*)

Women MEPs	Country	Group	Dates of service
van ROOIJ Yvonne	Netherlands	PPE	1984–
ROUDY Yvette	France	Soc	1979–81
SALISCH Heinke	Germany	Soc	1979–
SCRIVENER Christiane	France	Lib	1979–
SEIBEL-EMMERLING Liselotte	Germany	Soc	1979–
SIMONS Barbara	Germany	Soc	1984–
SPAAK Antoinette	Belgium	Non-Att	1979–84
SQUARCIALUPI Vera	Italy	Com	1979–*
THEOBALD-PAOLI Yvonne	France	Soc	1981–84
THOME-PATENOTRE Jacqueline	France	EDA	1984–
TONGUE Carol	UK	Soc	1984–
TRUPIA Lalla	Italy	Com	1984–
VAYSSADE Marie Claude	France	Soc	1979–
VEIL Simone	France	Lib	1979–
VIEHOFF Philippine	Netherlands	Soc	1981–
WALZ Hanna	Germany	PPE	1979–84*
WEBER Beate	Germany	Soc	1979–
WEISS Louise	France	EDA	1979–83
WIECZOREK-ZEUL Heidemarie	Germany	Soc	1979–

*Indicates member of pre-1979 Parliament

Appendix 2: Composition of political groups in the European Parliament

Country	Party	No. of MEPs	No. of Women
Socialist Group			
Belgium	Parti Socialiste (PSB)	7	3
Denmark	Socialdemokrater	3	1
	Siumut (Greenland Party)	1	0
France	Parti Socialiste (PS)	20	6
Germany	Sozialdemokratische Partei Deutschlands (SPD)	33	8
Greece	Pasok	10	1
Italy	Partito Socialista Italiano (PSI)	9	0
	Partito Socialista Democratico Italiano (PSDI)	3	0
Luxembourg	Letzeburger Sozialistesch Arbechter-Partei	2	0
Netherlands	Partij van de Arbeid	9	3
Britain	Labour Party	32	5
	Irish Social and Democratic Labour Party (SDLP)	1	0
		130	27
European People's Party Group (PPE)			
Belgium	Christelijke Volkspartij	4	1
	Parti Social-Chrétien	2	0
Denmark	Centrum Demokraterne	1	0
France	Union pour l'Opposition	9	1
Germany	CDU-CSU (Christian Democratic Union)	41	5
Greece	New Democracy	9	1
Ireland	Fine Gael (FG)	6	1
Italy	Democrazia Christiana (CDI)	26	1
	Sudtiroler Volkspartei	1	0
Luxembourg	Chreschlech-Sozial Volkspartei	3	0
Netherlands	Christen-democratisch Appel	8	3
		110	13
European Democratic Group (EDG)			
Denmark	Konservative Folkeparti	4	2
Britain	Conservative Party	45	6
	Irish Official Unionist Party (OUP)	1	0
		50	8

Appendix 2 (*cont.*)

Country	Party	No. of MEPs	No. of Women
Communist and Allies Group			
Denmark	Socialistisk Folkeparti	1	1
France	Parti Communiste (PCF)	10	2
Greece	Communist Party	3	0
	Communist Party, Interior	1	0
Italy	Partito Communista Italiano (PCI)	26	6
		41	9
Liberal and Democratic Group			
Belgium	Partij voor Vrijheld en Vooruitgang	2	0
	Parti des Reformes et de la Liberte	3	0
Denmark	Venstre	2	1
France	Union pour l'Opposition	12	3
Ireland	Independent	1	0
Italy	Partito Liberale Italiano	5	0
Luxembourg	Demokratesch Partei	1	1
Netherlands	Volkspartij voor Vrijheid en Democratie	5	1
		31	6
European Democratic Alliance (EDA)			
France	Union pour l'Opposition	20	4
Ireland	Fianna Fail	8	1
Britain	Scottish Nationalist Party (SNP)	1	1
		29	6
Rainbow Group			
Belgium	Front der Frankophonene und wallonische Sammlungsbewegung	2	0
	Ecologie	2	0
Denmark	Folkebevaegelsen	4	1
Germany	Ecology Party	7	3
Italy	Partito Radicale	3	1
Netherlands	Green Progressive Alliance	2	0
		20	5
Group of European Right			
France	Front Nationale	10	1
Greece	Egen	1	0
Italy	Movimento Sociale Italiano	5	0
		16	1

Appendix 2 (*cont.*)

Country	Party	No. of MEPs	No. of Women
Non-Attached			
Belgium	Independents	2	0
Italy	Democrazia Proletaria	3	0
Netherlands	Coalition of Protestants	1	0
Britain	Irish Democratic Unionist Party (DUP)	1	0
		7	0

Notes

1. Where are the women?

1 Note the figures given for national legislatures are for the election prior to 1979 and that the percentages in some cases may now have changed slightly after a subsequent election.

2 All figures are for the Lower House of the countries mentioned and have been acquired from their embassies or Parliaments.

3 J. Milburn, *Women as Citizens: A Comparative Review* (Sage professional papers in contemporary sociology) (Sage Publications, 1976).

4 In all countries of the EEC, except Ireland and Greece, the birthrate by 1982 was between 1.4 and 1.9 children per woman. See CREW Reports, vol. 4, no. 4 (April 1984), p. 6.

5 See J. Ryder & H. Silver, *Modern English Society*, 2nd edn (Methuen, 1977), pp. 300–2.

6 *Women in Statistics*, supplement no. 10 to *Women of Europe* (1982), published by the European Commission.

7 See *The Fact about Women*, published by the Statistics Unit of the Equal Opportunities Commission.

8 The exact figures are difficult to find, but informed sources at party headquarters claim around 45% for the SDP, 50% for the Liberal and Labour parties and as high as 60% for the Conservatives.

9 *Women & Work, Sex Differences and Society*, Manpower paper no. 11 (Department of Employment, 1974), p. 4.

10 DES figures: see also Polly Toynbee writing in *The Guardian* about the ILEA research, 'So many bright little girls – and so many humble young women' (18.6.82).

11 See, e.g., J. Hills, 'Candidates; the impact of gender', *Parliamentary Affairs*, vol. 24, no. 2 (1981); E. Vallance, 'Women candidates and electoral preference', *Politics*, vol. 1, no. 2 (1981).

12 Conducted by MORI for *News at Ten* (24.3.82).

13 See E. Vallance, *Women in the House* (Athlone Press, 1979), pp. 175–6.

14 Significantly only Mrs Kellett-Bowman and the Rev. Ian Paisley from Britain had dual mandates from 1979–84. Both are backbench MPs, and Mr Paisley attends the European Parliament only when its deliberations affect Northern Ireland. Mrs Kellett-Bowman did not stand again for Europe in 1984.

15 See E. Vallance, 'Women candidates in the 1983 general election', *Parliamentary Affairs*, vol. 37, no. 3 (1984), p. 303.

16 See M. Charlot, 'Women and elections in Britain', in H. Penniman (ed.), *Britain at the Polls, 1979* (AEI, 1981).
17 W. Kohn, 'Women in the European Parliament', *Parliamentary Affairs*, vol. 34, no. 2 (1981), p. 219.
18 Produced by the Political Affairs Committee of the Parliament, PE 64.569 (1981).
19 V. Bogdanor, *What is Proportional Representation?* (Martin Robertson, 1984), p. 115.
20 In the French elections of 1981, women won 6% of the seats, an improvement on their earlier record. This was largely due to the enormous effort made by the French Socialist Party to attract and aid women candidates. When the Socialists won, some of this paid off in a rather higher female representation, but still nothing like the percentage achieved at the European elections.
21 Quoted in *Ici et Maintenant*, August 1980.
22 The situation is similar for women in other international organisations. See, e.g., B. Thom, 'Women in international organisations: room at the top', in C. Epstein and R. Coser (eds.), *Access to Power* (Allen and Unwin, 1981), pp. 169–81.

2. Introduction to the EEC and the European Parliament

1 *Forging Ahead, Thirty Years of the European Parliament* (EP Directorate General for Research and Documentation, 1982).
2 For a full discussion of the different aims and functions of the Community put forward at its inception, see L.N. Lindberg and S.A. Scheingold, *Europe's Would-Be Polity* (Prentice Hall, 1970).
3 M. Palmer, *The European Parliament* (Pergamon Press, 1981), p. 21.
4 E. Grabitz and B. Langeheine, 'Legal Problems Related to the Proposed "2-tier system" of Integration within the EEC', *Common Market Law Review* (1981), p. 330.
5 G. Close, 'Harmonisation of laws: use or abuse of the powers under the EEC Treaty?', *European Law Review* (1978), p. 461. Also, House of Lords Select Committee on the European Communities, 22nd Report, Session 1977/8 (on approximation of laws).
6 For details of the Common Assembly's composition and powers, see Palmer, *European Parliament*, and J. Fitzmaurice, *The European Parliament* (Saxon House, 1978).
7 See further G. Pridham and P. Pridham, *Towards Transnational Parties in the EEC* (Policy Studies Institute, 1979).
8 For detailed description of the Community legislative process, see T.C. Hartley, *The Foundations of European Community Law* (Clarendon Press, 1981), pt 2, p. 67ff.
9 See, e.g., *Van Gend en Loos* Case 26/62 (1963) ECR 1, and *Van Duyn* v. *Home Office* Case 41/74 (1974) ECR 1337. For a discussion on direct effect and applicability, see S.A. Winter, 'Direct applicability and direct effect: two distinct and different concepts in Community Law', *Common Market Law Review* (1972), p. 425; A. Dashwood, 'The principle of direct effect in European Community Law', *Journal of Common Market Studies* (1978), p. 229; A.S. Easson, 'The direct effect of EEC Directives', *International and Comparative Law Quarterly* (1979), p. 319.
10 See Palmer, *European Parliament*, ch. 3.
11 For further discussion of direct elections, see V. Herman, 'Direct elections to the European Parliament', *Common Market Law Review* (1979), p. 209.

12 See the Seitlinger Report on the basic elements of a uniform electoral system (PE 64.569/rev.v.).
13 For a detailed discussion of the organisation of the Parliament, see *Forging Ahead*, especially Pt 5, and Palmer, *European Parliament*, ch. 4.
14 Quoted in Palmer, *European Parliament*, p. 69.
15 All figures, unless otherwise stated, are for the Parliament elected in June 1984. Figures from *EP News*, No. 56, July 1984.
16 See further E. Noel, 'The Commission's power of initiative', *Common Market Law Review* (1973), p. 123; F. Graupner, 'Commission decision-making on competition questions', *Common Market Law Review* (1978), p. 291; Hartley, *Foundations of Community Law*, p. 8; Palmer, *European Parliament*, p. 25.
17 R.H. Lauwaars, 'The European Council', *Common Market Law Review* (1977), p. 25; Palmer, *European Parliament*, p. 26; Hartley, *Foundations of Community Law*, p. 11.
18 See Mangas Martin 'La participation du COREPER au processus de decision communautaire', *Cahier du Droit Européen* (1980), p. 25.
19 L.N. Brown and F.G. Jacobs, *The Court of Justice of the European Communities*, 3rd edition (Sweet & Maxwell, 1983); J.A. Usher, *European Court Practice* (Sweet & Maxwell, 1983).
20 The EIB & EMS are discussed in Hartley, *Foundations of Community Law*, ch. 1, and Palmer, *European Parliament*, ch. 3.

3. Who are the women?

1 Author's interview with Simone Veil.
2 See, e.g., the analysis of women members of Parliament in Vallance, *Women in the House*, pp. 61–3.
3 M. Currell, *Political Woman* (Croom Helm, 1974), pp. 58–9.
4 W. Kohn, *Women in National Legislatures* (Praeger, 1980), p. 238.
5 All references to MEPs' and MPs' opinions are from interviews by the authors.
6 All figures for the British House of Commons are either from authors' interviews with women MPs or from *The Times Guide to the House of Commons*.
7 H. Eulau & J. Sprague, *Lawyers in Politics: A Study of Professional Convergence* (Bobbs Merill, 1961).
8 A. Sachs & J. Hoff Wilson, *Sexism and the Law: A Study of Male Beliefs and Judicial Bias* (Martin Robertson, 1978), p. 174.
9 All quotations, unless otherwise attributed, are from the authors' interviews with the politicians involved.
10 Quotes from Barbara Castle, when not from the authors' interviews with her, are from Melanie Phillips, *The Divided House* (Sidgwick & Jackson, 1980).
11 Ibid., p. 95.
12 Ibid., p. 174.

4. Women in Parliament

1 Palmer, *European Parliament*, p. 100.
2 Ibid.
3 All the following details, unless otherwise stated, come from weekly diaries kindly made available to the authors by some British MEPs.
4 Profile of Joyce Quin, *The Guardian*, 28.5.1984.

5 In 1979, MEPs' salaries were as follows:

Belgium	£19,950
Denmark	£10,876
France	£24,376
Germany	£21,551
Ireland	£ 9,389
Italy	£11,133
Luxembourg	£13,004
Netherlands	£19,273
UK	£10,735

From Palmer, *European Parliament*, p. 106.

6 Ibid., p. 106.

7 See, for example, D. Butler and D. Stokes, *Political Change in Britain* (Pelican, 1969), p. 323.

8 See Vallance, *Women in the House*, Appendix 1.

9 For a discussion of this theme, see Currell, *Political Woman*, p. 47.

10 All figures are for July 1984, unless otherwise indicated, and come from *The Week, 24–27 July 1984*, and *The Results, June 1984*, both published by the European Parliament.

11 See Vallance, *Women in the House*, p. 98 and p. 104.

12 See E. Vallance, 'Women in the House of Commons', *Political Studies*, vol. 29, no. 1 (March 1981).

13 See Vallance, *Women in the House*, pp. 88–9.

14 Figures from the *Official Journal* (1979–80) compiled by the authors.

MEPs	Numbers of committees they attended				Total
	0	1	2	3	
Men	10	270	61	0	341
Women	0	45	18	2	65

15 *The Guardian*, 3.10.1984.

16 See Vallance, *Women in the House*, Appendix 3, p. 186.

17 All details on interventions derived from *Official Journal* of the European Communities, Annex, Debates of the European Parliament, 1979–80, Sessional Index Edition.

18 J. Anderson in *The Guardian*, 7.1.1966.

19 Quoted in Phillips, *The Divided House*, p. 163.

20 Figures from the *Official Journal*, compiled by June Nielson. The authors are very grateful to June Nielson for permission to use these findings.

21 *Official Journal*, 1979–80, Sessional Index Edition.

5. Women for women: the historical context

1 *Costa* v. *ENEL* Case 6/64 (1964) ECR 585.

2 For details of the case see V. Hall-Smith et al., *Women's Rights and the EEC* (Rights of Women Europe, 1983), pp. 27–8.

3 For details of the ETD see Chapter 6.

4 For details of the Directive, see Chapter 6.
5 For a report of the debate see the *Official Journal* of the European Communities, 10–11 February 1981, pp. 33–97.
6 A New Community Action Programme on the Promotion of Equal Opportunities for Women, 1982–1985, com (81) 758, 1981.
7 For all the reports, see EP Working Document 1–1229 183/C, January 1984.

6. European legislation and the European legal systems

1 G. Close, 'Harmonisation of laws: use or abuse of the powers under the EEC Treaty?' *European Law Review* (1978), p. 461.
2 J. Usher, 'The Influence of National Concepts on Decisions of the European Court', *European Law Review* (1976), p. 359.
3 See *Nold* v. *Commission* Case 4/73 (1974) ECR 491, and *Hauer* v. *Land Rheinland-Pfalz* Case 44/79 (1979) ECR 3729.
4 *Costa* v. *ENEL* Case 6/64 (1964) ECR 585.
5 *Re Medical Expenses Incurred in France* Case 2/77 (1977) 2 CMLR 317.
6 *McCarthys* v. *Smith* (1979) 3 CMLR 44.
7 *Van Gend en Loos* v. *Nederlandse Administratie der Belastingen* Case 26/62 (1963) CMLR 105.
8 *Van Duyn* v. *Home Office* Case 41/74 (1974) ECR 1337.
9 *Defrenne* v. *Sabena SA* Case 43/75 (1976) 2 CMLR 98.
10 *Garland* v. *British Rail Engineering Board* Case 12/81 (1982) 2 CMLR 174.
11 See Anthony Lester, 'Fundamental rights: the United Kingdom isolated?' *Public Law*, Spring, 1984, p. 70, note 20.
12 Article 164, Treaty of Rome (1957).
13 *Commission of the European Communities* v. *Government of the United Kingdom* Case 61/81 (1982) 3 CMLR 284.
14 *Da Costa* Cases 28–30/62 (1963) ECR 31.
15 Report on Council Directive 76/207/EEC, COM (80) 832 final, p. 4.
16 Ibid.
17 *Commission* v. *UK* (as above, n. 13).
18 See Julia Neuberger, 'Equality vs Gobbledegook', *300 Group News* (Winter 1983/4), p. 4; Also EOC Opinion, 17 October 1983; Anthony Lester's Opinion, 24 February 1983; Anthony Lester's Opinion, 20 September 1983.
19 *Mrs K. Turley* v. *Alders Department Stores Ltd* (1980) ICR 66.
20 *Commission* v. *UK* (as above, n. 13).
21 Report on Council Directive 76/207/EEC, COM(80) 832 final, p. 62.
22 *Commission of the European Communities* v. *Italian Republic* Case 163/82 OJ C160/7, 25.6.82.
23 Case of Ulrich Hoffman decided 12 July 1984.
24 *Defrenne* v. *Belgian State* Case 80/70 (1971) ECR 445.
25 *Internationale Handelsgesellschaft* Case 11/70 (1970) ECR 1125.
26 See *Nold* v. *Commission* and *Hauer* v. *Land Rheinland-Pfalz* (as above, n. 3).
27 For a detailed discussion of the following, see the Commission's *Report on the provisions for legal redress in member states in respect of Article 119 and the Equal Pay, Equal Treatment and Social Security Directives*. Prepared by Jennifer Corcoran, V/564/84-EN, 1983.
28 Ibid., p. 34.
29 *Ms B.M. Price* v. *Civil Service Commission* (1978) ICR 27.

30 *Von Colson and Kamann* v. *Nordrhein-Westphalia* Case 14/83, see *The Times* Law Report, 25.4.84.

7. European legislation and women workers

1 R. Abel, 'Redirecting social studies of law', *Law and Society Review* (1980), p. 805.
2 R. Cotterrell, 'The impact of sex discrimination legislation', *Public Law* (1981), p. 469.
3 Ibid., p. 473.
4 EOC Report no. 7, 1982.
5 EOC figures derived from SOEC Bulletin 'Wages and Incomes 5 – 1983', 1983.
6 EOC figures derived from ILO Yearbook of Labour Statistics, 1982.
7 Equal Pay and Opportunities, Department of Employment Research Paper No. 20, 1981.
8 Topic No. 1 of the Report of the Enquiry, The application of the first two directives, Document 1-1229/83/C.
9 Ibid., p. 11.
10 Civil Judicial Statistics (quoted by the EOC).
11 B. Hepple, 'Judging equal rights', Inaugural Lecture, reprinted in *Current Legal Problems* (Stevens & Sons, 1983), p. 73.
12 *Women in Statistics*, supplement no. 14 to *Women of Europe* (1984), published by the European Commission, p. 16.
13 Eurostat, Employment and Unemployment 2, 1982.
14 All figures in this section are from the member states' replies to Commission surveys and questionnaires (1981–3) or derived from Eurostat.
15 Women's Unemployment in the Community, COM(83)653, 1983, p. 12.
16 Ibid., p. 13.
17 Topic No. 2 of The Report of the Enquiry, The implementation to date of the Third Directive, Document 1-1229/83/C.
18 COM (83)781, p. 2.
19 See interview in CREW Reports, vol. 2, no. 6 (June 1982), p. 4.
20 Topic no. 18 of the Report of the Enquiry, Place of women in the decision-making centres, Document 1-1229/83/C.
21 See E. Vallance, 'Equality and the formation of public policy', in G. Ashworth and L. Bonnerjea (eds.), *The Invisible Decade* (Gower, 1985).
22 E. Vogel-Polsky et al., Study on Positive Action Programmes, V/30/83-/N (doc. 34).
23 WQ no. 1514/83 put by Jens-Peter Bonde of Denmark, November 1983.
24 Quoted in CREW Reports, vol. 3, no. 10 (December 1983), p. 8.

8. Women of Europe: the future

1 See CREW Reports, vol. 3, no. 6; vol. 4, no. 4; vol. 4, no. 5
2 CREW Reports vol. 3, no. 6, p. 7.
3 WQ no. 1514/83 from Jens-Peter Bonde of Denmark.
4 *Ms B.M. Price* v. *Civil Service Commission* (1978) ICR 27.
5 *Clarke and Powell* v. *Eley Kynoch Ltd* (1982) IRLR 482.
6 Report written by Angela Byre of the UK, November 1983 (V/1775/83-EN).
7 B. Hepple, 'Judging Equal Rights', *Current Legal Problems*, 1983, p. 86.

8 For a detailed argument on this point, see Corcoran, J., *Report of a Comparative Analysis of the Provisions for Legal Redress in Member States of the EEC in respect of Article 119 of the Treaty of Rome and the Equal Pay, Equal Treatment and Social Security Directives* V/564/84-EN.
9 *Defrenne* v. *Sabena SA* Case 43/75 (1976) 2 CMLR 98.
10 *Defrenne* v. *Sabena SA* Case 149/77 (1978) 3 CMLR 312.
11 *McCarthys Ltd* v. *Smith* Case 129/79 (1979) CMLR 44.
12 *Worringham and Humphreys* v. *Lloyds Bank Ltd* Case 69/80 (1981) 2 CMLR 1.
13 *Jenkins* v. *Kingsgate Ltd* Case 96/80 (1981) CMLR 24.
14 *Garland* v. *British Rail Engineering Board* Case 12/81 (1982) 2 CMLR 174.
15 *Burton* v. *British Railways Board* Case 19/81 (1982) 2 CMLR 136.
16 See A. Lester, 'Fundamental Rights: the UK Isolated?' *Public Law*, Spring, 1984, p. 70, note 20.
17 *Von Colson & Kamann* v. *Nordrhein-Westphalia* Case 14/83. See *The Times*, 25.4.84.
18 Information derived from a Seminar held on 6/7/84 at The Royal Institute of Public Administration, on Equal Opportunity in the Public Sector: Lesson from Australia? See also *Equal Opportunities for women in the UK and Australia*, Australia Studies Centre, June, 1984.
19 See E. Meehan, 'Implementing equal opportunity policies: some British-American comparisons', *Politics*, vol. 2, no. 1 (April 1982), p. 14.
20 *European Women in Paid Employment*, supplement no. 5 to *Women of Europe* (1980), p. 39.
21 The Commission's Report (as n. 27, p. 166), p. 83.
22 All quotations are from the authors' interviews with the MEPs concerned.
23 'Knocking at the door', *Financial Times*, 9.4.84.
24 See E. Kirchner and K. Schwaiger, *The Role of Interest Groups in the European Community* (Gower, 1981), p. 5.

Bibliography

European Community publications

Briefing on the European Parliament, Directorate-General for Information and Public Relations, Publications and Briefings Division, 1-2929 Luxembourg.

European Parliament News, Directorate-General for Information and Public Relations.

Forging Ahead, 30 Years of the European Parliament, Directorate-General for Research and Documentation, 1982.

Report on the implementation of the Equal Pay Directive COM (78) 711 final.

Report on Council Directive 76/207/EEC, COM (80) 832 final.

Seitlinger Report on the basic elements of a uniform electoral system (PE 64.569/ rev.v.).

The Week, Directorate-General for Information and Public Relations.

Women of Europe, Directorate-General for Information, Rue de la Loi 200, B-1049 Brussels.

Official Journal of the European Communities (English edition), Annual Index Editions, 1979, 1980, 1981.

Report of the ad hoc committee on Women's Rights (the Maij-Weggen Report), Document 1-829/80–11, The European Parliament, 1981.

Report of the Committee of Enquiry into the situation of Women in Europe, Document 1-1229/83/C, The European Parliament, 1984.

J. Corcoran, Report of the provisions for legal redress in member states in respect of Article 119 and the Equal Pay, Equal Treatment and Social Security Directives, V/564/84 – EN.

Women's unemployment in the Community. COM (83) 653 final. New types of employment initiatives especially as relating to women, study for the Commission by CREW, V/614/82 – EN.

New Community Action Programme on the promotion of Equal Opportunities for Women, 1982–1985, COM (81) 758 final, 1981.

Progress Report on the Implementation of the New Community Action Programme, COM (83) 781 final, 1984.

Official Journal, Debates of the European Parliament, no. 1-266, Report of 10 February 1981, pp. 34–90.

Report on the tasks of the European Social Fund, Document 1-61/83, European Parliament, 1983.

Report by Monique Chalude to the Commission of the European Communities, Women and Job De-segregation in Banking, V/2778 82 – EN, English edition.

Report by Jacqueline Laufer to the Commission of the European Communities, on Equal Opportunities in the countries of the EEC, V/2455/1/82 – EN final, English edition.

Report (edited by Nancy Seear and Margery Powell) of the EEC Seminar on Equal Opportunities in Banking, V/981/82.

First Report of the Network of Experts set up to monitor the application of Community Equal Treatment legislation, by Angela Byer, V/1775/83 – EN, 1983.

Study on positive Action Programmes, directed by Eliane Vogel-Polsky. V/30/83 – EN, 1982, English edition.

Report by Mireille Planteligne et al., on promoting de-segregation in the public service, V/2794/82 – EN, 1982, English edition.

European law

A. Barav, 'The exception of illegality in Community law: a critical analysis', *Common Market Law Review* (1974), p. 366.

'Direct and individual concern: an almost insurmountable barrier to the admissibility of individual appeal to the EEC Court', *Common Market Law Review* (1974), p. 191.

'Preliminary censorship?', *European Law Review* (1980), p. 443.

G. Bebr, *Development of Judicial Control of the European Communities* (Nijhoff, The Hague, 1981).

'"Acte clair" and the Court of Justice', *Common Market Law Review* (1983), p. 439.

J. Bridge, 'Community law and English courts and tribunals; general principles and preliminary rulings', *European Law Review* (1976), p. 13.

L.N. Browne and F.G. Jacobs, *The Court of Justice of the European Communities*, 3rd edn (Sweet and Maxwell, 1983).

G. Close, 'Harmonisation of laws: use or abuse of the powers under the EEC Treaty?', *European Law Review* (1978), p. 461.

C. Collins, 'Article 177 of the EEC Treaty and English interlocutory proceedings', *International and Comparative Law Quarterly* (1974), p. 840.

A. Dashwood, 'The principle of direct effect in European Community law', *Journal of Common Market Studies* (1978), p. 229.

'The Advocate General in the Court of Justice of the European Communities', *Legal Studies* (1982), p. 202.

J. Dinnage, '*Locus Standi* and Article 173 of the EEC Treaty', *European Law Review* (1979), p. 15.

A. Donner, *The Role of the Lawyer in the European Communities* (Edinburgh University Press, 1968).

'The European Court and its functions', *Law Teacher* (1973), p. 139.

'The constitutional powers of the Court of Justice of the European Communities', *Common Market Law Review* (1974), p. 127.

A. Drzemczewski, 'The domestic application of the European Human Rights Convention as European Community Law', *International and Comparative Law Quarterly* (1981), p. 118.

A. Easson, 'The direct effect of EEC Directives', *International and Comparative Law Quarterly* (1979), p. 319.

'EEC Directives for the harmonisation of laws', *Yearbook of European Law* (1981), p. 1.

W. Finnie, 'Fundamental rights in the EEC Treaty structure', *Legal Issues of European Integration* (1982), p. 89.

G. Freeman, 'References to the Court of Justice under Article 177', *Current Legal Problems* (1975), p. 176.

G. Grabitz and B. Langeheine, 'Legal problems related to the proposed "two-tier system" of integration within the EEC', *Common Market Law Review* (1981), p. 33.

F. Graupner, 'Commission decision-making on competition questions', *Common Market Law Review* (1973), p. 291.

N. Gravelis, 'Article 177 EEC and the obligation to refer', *Law Quarterly Review* (1983), p. 518.

V. Grementieri and C.G. Golden, 'The United Kingdom and the European Court of Justice', *American Journal of Comparative Law* (1973), p. 665.

C. Harding, 'The review of EEC regulations and decisions', *Common Market Law Review* (1982), p. 311.

T. Hartley, *The Foundations of European Community Law* (Clarendon Press, 1981).

V. Herman, 'Direct elections to the European Parliament', *Common Market Law Review* (1979), p. 209.

House of Lords Select Committee on the European Communities, 22nd Report, Session 1977/78 on approximation of laws.

F. Jacobs, 'When to refer to the European Court of Justice', *Law Quarterly Review* (1974), p. 494.

F. Jacobs and A. Durand, *Reference to the European Court* (Butterworth, 1975).

A. Lester, 'Fundamental rights: the United Kingdom isolated?', *Public Law* (Spring 1984).

Lord Mackenzie Stuart, *The European Communities and the rule of Law* (Stevens, 1977).

J. Mertens de Wilmars and I. Veroughstrate, 'Proceedings against member states for failure to fulfil their obligations', *Common Market Law Review* (1970), p. 385.

J. Mitchell, 'Sed quis custodiet ipsos custodes?', *Common Market Law Review* (1974), p. 351.

'The rationality of the European Court of Justice', *Three Banks Review* (1975), p. 62.

R. Monaco, 'The limits of the European Community order', *European Law Review* (1976), p. 269.

K. Mortelmans, 'Observations in the cases governed by Article 177: procedures and practice', *Common Market Law Review* (1979), p. 557.

E. Noel, 'The Commission's power of initiative', *Common Market Law Review* (1973), p. 123.

P. Pescatore, 'An infant disease', *European Law Review* (1983), p. 155; on direct effect.

R. Plender, *A Practical Introduction to European Community Law* (Sweet and Maxwell, 1980).

R. Plender and J.A. Usher, *Cases and Materials on the Law of the European Communities* (Macmillan, 1980).

H. Rasmussen, 'A new generation of EEC Law?', *Common Market Law Review* (1978), p. 249.

H. Schermers, 'The law as it stands against treaty violations by states', *Legal issues of European Integration* (1974), p. 93.

'Indirect obligation', *Netherlands International Law Review* (1977), p. 260.

Judicial Protection in the European Communities (Kluwer, 1979).

I. Schwartz, 'Article 235 and law-making process in the EEC', *International and Comparative Law Quarterly* (1978), p. 614.

J. Steiner, 'A chameleon concept', *Law Quarterly Review* (1980), p. 126.

T. St. John N. Brutes, 'The scrutiny of European secondary legislation at Westminster', *European Law Review* (1976), p. 22.

Sweet & Maxwell's European Communities Treaties, 4th edn (Sweet & Maxwell, 1980.
J. Usher, 'The influence of national concepts on decisions of the European Court', *European Law Review* (1976), p. 359.
'The interpretations of Community law by the European Court of Justice', *Law Teacher* (1977), p. 162.
'Language and the European Court of Justice', *Law and Finance Review* (1981), p. 277.
European Community Law and National Law: The Irreversible Transfer (George Allen & Unwin, 1981).
European Court Practice (Sweet & Maxwell, 1983).
J. Usher et al. (eds.), *In Memoriam J.D.B. Mitchell* (Sweet & Maxwell, 1983).
J. Warner, 'Some aspects of the European Court of Justice', *Journal of the Society of Public Teachers of Law* (1976), p. 15.
J. Weiller, 'The Community system: the dual characteristics of supranationalism', *Yearbook of European Law* (1981), p. 267.
J. Winter, 'Direct applicability and direct effect: two distinct and different concepts in Community Law', *Common Market Law Review* (1972), p. 425.

Women

V. Bogdanor, *What is Proportional Representation?* (Martin Robertson, 1984).
N. Burrows, 'The promotion of women's rights by the EEC', *Common Market Law Review* (1980), p. 191.
R. Cotterrell, 'The impact of sex discrimination legislation', *Public Law* (1981), p. 469.
CREW Reports, Centre for Research on European Women, 33, Rue Stevin, 1040, Brussels.
M. Currell, *Political Woman* (Croom Helm, 1974).
G. Drewry and J. Brock, *The Impact of Women on the House of Lords* (Centre for the study of public policy, 1983).
C. Epstein and R. Coser (eds.), *Access to Power* (Allen & Unwin, 1981).
Equal Opportunities Commission (Overseas House, Quay Street, Manchester, M3), *Equality Now*.
Women and Public Bodies, Joint Working Party Report No. 5. (1982).
Research Bulletin, vol. 1, no. 3 (1980).
Towards Equality, A Casebook of Decisions on Sex Discrimination and Equal Pay (1976–81).
H. Eulau and J. Sprague, *Lawyers in Politics: A Study of Professional Convergence* (Bobbs Merril, 1961).
G. Flanz, *Comparative Women's Rights and Political Participation in Europe* (Bowker, 1983).
V. Hall-Smith et al., *Women's Rights and the EEC* (Rights of Women Europe, 1983).
B.A. Hepple, 'Judging equal rights', *Current Legal Problems* (1983).
W. Kohn, *Women in National Legislatures* (Praeger, 1980).
'Women in the European Parliament', *Parliamentary Affairs*, vol. 34 (1981).
A. Lester and D. Wainwright, *Equal Pay for Work of Equal Value* (TMS Management Consultants, 1984).
J. Lovenduski and J. Hills, *The Politics of the Second Electorate* (Routledge and Kegan Paul, 1981).
J. Milburn, *Women as Citizens* (Sage Publications, 1976).
V. Novarra, *Women's Work, Men's Work, The Ambivalence of Equality* (Marion Boyars, 1980).

Women and Employment Policies for Equal Opportunities (Organisation for Economic Co-operation and Development (OECD), 1980).

Equal Opportunities for Women, Organisation for Economic Co-operation and Development (1979).

H. Penniman (ed.), *Britain at the Polls, 1979* (AEI Studies in Political and Social Processes, 1981).

M. Phillips, *The Divided House* (Sidgwick & Jackson, 1980).

Ed. M. Rendel, *Women, Power and Political Systems* (Croom Helm, 1981).

M. Ruggie, *The State and Working Women* (Princeton University Press, 1984).

A. Sachs and J. Hoff Wilson, *Sexism and the Law* (Martin Robertson, 1978).

V. Sapiro, *The Political Integration of Women* (University of Illinois Press, 1983).

J. Siltanen and M. Stanworth (eds.), *Women and the Public Sphere* (Hutchinson, 1984).

M. Stacey and M. Price, *Women, Power and Politics* (Tavistock Publications, 1981).

E. Vallance, *Women in the House* (Athlone Press, 1979).

'Women candidates in the 1983 General Election', *Parliamentary Affairs*, vol. 37 (1984).

'Women In the House of Commons', *Political Studies*, vol. 29 (1981).

Development of the EEC and the European Parliament

P. Allott, 'The democratic basis of the EEC', *Common Market Law Review* (1974), p. 298.

G. Van den Berghe, *Political Rights for European Citizens* (Gower, 1982).

G. Bibes et al., *Europe Elects its Parliament* (Policy Studies Institute, 1980).

J.G. Blumber and A.P. Fox, *The European Voter* (Policy Studies Institute, 1982).

D. Butler and D. Marquand, *European Elections and British Politics* (Longman, 1981).

C. Cook and M. Francis, *The First European Elections* (Macmillan, 1979).

D. Coombes, *The Future of the European Parliament* (PSI studies in European politics, 1979).

H. Daalder and P. Mair (eds.), *Western European Party Systems* (Sage Research Series, 1983).

A. El Agraa (ed.), *Britain within the European Community: The Way Forward* (Macmillan, 1983).

European Political Data Newsletter, published by the European Consortium for Political Research and the Norwegian Social Science Data Services.

J. Fitzmaurice, *The European Parliament* (Saxon House, 1978).

E. Haas, *The Uniting of Europe* (Stevens and Sons, 1958).

Hansard Society for Parliamentary Government, *The British People: Their Voice in Europe* (Saxon House, 1977).

S. Henig, *Power and Decision in Europe* (Europotentials, 1980).

V. Herman and M. Hagger, *The Legislation of Direct Elections to the European Parliament* (Gower, 1980).

V. Herman and J. Lodge, *Direct Elections to the European Parliament. A community perspective* (Macmillan 1982).

V. Herman and R. Van Schendelen, *Changing Patterns of Relations between the National Parliaments and the European Parliament* (Saxon House, 1979).

M. Hodges (ed.), *European Integration* (Penguin, 1972).

J. Holloway, *Social Policy Harmonisation in the European Community* (Gower, 1981).

R. Jackson and J. Fitzmaurice, *The European Parliament* (Penguin, 1979).

R. Jones, *The Making of Contemporary Europe* (Hodder and Stoughton, 1980).

R. Jowell and G. Hoinville, *Britain into Europe* (Croom Helm, 1976).
E. Kirchner and K. Schwaiger, *The Role of Interest Groups in the European Community* (Gower, 1981).
L. Lindberg and S. Scheingold, *Europe's Would-Be Polity* (Prentice Hall, 1970).
Mangas Martin, 'La participation du COREPER au processus du decision communautaire', *Cahier de Droit Européen* (1980), p. 25.
R. Mayne, *The Institutions of the European Community* (PEP, 1968).
The Recovery of Europe (Weidenfeld and Nicolson, 1970).
Postwar: The Dawn of Today's Europe (Thames & Hudson, 1983).
M. McLaughlin, 'The work and aims of the ESC, the EEC and Euratom', *Journal of Common Market Studies* (1978), p. 9.
R. Morgan and S. Silvestri (eds.), *Moderates and Conservatives in Western Europe* (Heinemann Educational, 1982).
E. Noel, *The European Community: How It Works* (Office for Official Publications of the Community, European Perspective Series, 1979).
Working Together: The Institutions of the European Community (Office for Official Publications of the Community, 1978).
M. Palmer, *The European Parliament* (Pergamon Press, 1981).
M. Palmer and J. Lambert, *European Unity* (G. Allen and Unwin, 1968).
G. Parker, *A Dictionary of the European Communities* (Butterworth, 1981).
G. Pridham and P. Pridham, *Towards Transnational Parties in the EEC* (Policy Studies Institute, 1980).
A. Robertson, *The Council of Europe* (Stevens and Sons, 1956).
European Institutions (Stevens and Sons, 1973).
G. Rosenthal, *The Men behind the Decisions: Cases in European Policy-Making* (Heath, 1975).
A. Sarre et al., *Decision-Making in the EEC: A Reappraisal* (Praeger, 1977).
P. Scalingi, *The European Parliament, Three-Decade Search for a United Europe* (Aldwych Press, 1980).
R. Schuman, *Pour l'Europe* (Nagel, 1963).
D. Swann, *The Economics of the Common Market* (Penguin 1972).
The Times Guide to the European Parliament, ed. D. Wood (Times Books, 1979).
K. Twitchett (ed.), *European Co-operation Today* (European Publications Limited, 1980).
D. Urwin, *Western Europe Since 1945* (Longman, 1981).
H. Wallace et al. (eds.), *Policy Making in the European Community*, 2nd edn (John Wiley, 1977).
W. Wallace, *National Decision-Making in the EEC* (Chatham House, 1973).
V. Willis, *Britains in Brussels* (European Centre for Policy Studies (Studies in European Politics, 7), published jointly by ECPS and RIPA, 1983).

Index